T0315030

# Why Not Default?

# Why Not Default?

## THE POLITICAL ECONOMY OF SOVEREIGN DEBT

Jerome Roos

PRINCETON UNIVERSITY PRESS

PRINCETON AND OXFORD

Copyright © 2019 by Princeton University Press

Published by Princeton University Press
41 William Street, Princeton, New Jersey 08540
6 Oxford Street, Woodstock, Oxfordshire OX20 1TR

press.princeton.edu

All Rights Reserved

LCCN 2018960616
ISBN 978-0-691-18010-6
British Library Cataloging-in-Publication Data is available

Editorial: Sarah Caro and Hannah Paul
Production Editorial: Brigitte Pelner
Production: Jacqueline Poirier
Copyeditor: Jay Boggis

This book has been composed in Minion Pro

Printed on acid-free paper ∞

Printed in the United States of America

1 3 5 7 9 10 8 6 4 2

# CONTENTS

# TABLES, FIGURES, AND BOXES

## TABLES

## FIGURES

## Boxes

# ACKNOWLEDGMENTS

I incurred many debts in writing this book—most of which I will never be able to repay in full. Here I will limit myself to acknowledging the contributions of a few key people without whom this book would not have existed in its present form. First, I would like to thank Pepper Culpepper, my former PhD advisor at the European University Institute in Florence, under whose supervision this project first saw the light of day. I could not have imagined a sharper mind and a keener set of eyes to help guide me along the way. I also wish to thank the members of my PhD jury—Robert Wade, Daniel Mügge, and Laszlo Bruszt—as well as four anonymous reviewers for their close reading of and constructive comments on various iterations of the manuscript. To Robert Wade I actually owe the original inspiration for this project: it was his course on the political economy of development at the LSE, at the height of the global financial crisis in 2008–2009, that first gave me the idea to pursue further research on this topic. I feel honored to now call him a colleague.

I am very grateful to Thomas Jeffrey Miley for inviting me to the Department of Sociology at the University of Cambridge as a postdoctoral researcher in 2016–2017, which gave me the time and peace of mind to transform the thesis into this book. I am most profoundly indebted to my editor, Sarah Caro, and the staff at Princeton University Press for their faith in the project and for all their help in getting it out into the world—it has been a tremendous privilege to collaborate with such an exceptional publisher. Finally, at the beginning and at the end of it all, there was always Tamara, *mi compañera de vida*, whose boundless brilliance and support undergird every single line on the hundreds of pages that follow.

I dedicate this book to the people of Greece who, in their hour of greatest need, opened their arms and doors to those fleeing war, poverty, and persecution abroad. Over all the years that I spent working on this text, they have taught me more than any scholarly publication or university degree ever could about the true meaning of solidarity.

London, February 2018

And many a man whom law or fraud had sold
Far from his god-built land, an outcast slave,
I brought again to Athens; yea, and some,
Exiles from home through debt's oppressive load,
Speaking no more the dear Athenian tongue,
But wandering far and wide, I brought again;
And those that here in vilest slavery
Crouched 'neath a master's frown, I set them free.

—Solon (c. 638–558 B.C.)

# Why Not Default?

# INTRODUCTION

## The Sovereign Debt Puzzle

The European sovereign debt crisis of the past decade has rekindled a set of longstanding debates about the power of finance and the consequences of contemporary patterns in international crisis management for social justice and democracy. This book aims to make a contribution to these debates by revisiting a seemingly simple question whose answer has nonetheless eluded economists for decades: why do so many heavily indebted countries continue to service their external debts even in times of acute fiscal distress? While we generally take it for granted that borrowing governments will honor their foreign obligations under all circumstances, historical experience belies the notion that this is somehow a natural condition. Indeed, in the prewar and interwar periods, sovereign default was widespread and generally considered unavoidable in major crises. During the Great Depression of the 1930s, virtually all European and Latin American borrowers suspended payments on their external debts. Today, by contrast, the declaration of such unilateral moratoriums is exceedingly rare: even as the crisis in the Eurozone reached a dramatic climax between 2010 and 2015, the total share of world public debt in a state of default fell to a historic low of 0.2 percent.[1] How do we account for this extraordinary degree of debtor compliance in the wake of the Great Recession?

The question itself is by no means new. In fact, economists have long recognized a fundamental paradox at the heart of international lending. Since the payment of interest on foreign debt effectively constitutes a wealth transfer from the borrower to its lenders, a distressed debtor that spends more of its tax revenues on external debt servicing than it attracts in new loans has an inherent incentive to suspend payments. In the absence of a world government or imperialist power capable of dispatching gunboats to enforce compliance with cross-border debt contracts, we would therefore expect sovereign default to be a much more widespread phenomenon than it really is. Indeed, if we were to draw the assumptions of neoclassical economics to their logical conclusion, a self-interested government should try to pile up as many foreign obligations as possible before repudiating them in total. As rational lenders would in turn refuse to extend further credit to opportunistic borrowers, the result would be a collapse of global capital markets—meaning there should be no such thing as external debt to begin with.[2] Yet this is clearly not what happens. Despite the frequency and intensity of international financial crises in recent decades, the total amount of outstanding sovereign debt has actually skyrocketed to a record $60 trillion, or over 80 percent of global GDP (see figures 0.1 and 0.2). Although this increase has been more pronounced in some regions than in others, with many developing countries even reducing their debt-to-GDP ratios over the past two decades, the global upward trend still raises the question how national governments are able to sustain such enormous sovereign debt loads, and why they willingly continue to honor their foreign obligations in times of crisis.

The puzzle of sovereign debt repayment is further compounded if we consider its far-reaching redistributive implications. As a result of the rapid expansion of global finance and the widespread insistence on full repayment, recent decades have witnessed a vast and largely uninterrupted flow of capital "upstream": from public hands in the global periphery to private hands in the advanced capitalist core. In the years since 1982, developing countries have thus ended up transferring an estimated $4.2 trillion in interest payments to their creditors in Europe and North America, far outstripping the official-sector development aid these countries received during the same period.[3] Meanwhile, in an anxious bid to reassure investors that their growing debt loads will be honored in full, European governments have spent the greater part of the past decade pursuing deeply unpopular austerity measures and forcing distressed peripheral borrowers—most notably Greece—to push through painful structural adjustment programs reminiscent of those that had previously been imposed on the Global South. In both cases, the aggressive pursuit of austerity led to mounting social discontent and intensifying political instability. In light of the recent tumult in global financial markets and the antiestablishment revolts rocking the liberal world order, it would therefore not be an exaggeration to claim that the problem of sovereign debt repayment has become one of the defining and most contentious political issues of our time. Given this context, why do heavily indebted countries not simply suspend payments on their external debts more often? What moves them to assume the full burden of adjustment for recurring international crises, inflicting enormous damage on their own economies and untold suffering on their people, while letting their creditors off scot-free? Why not default?[4]

In this book, I aim to answer these questions through a wide-ranging comparative-historical investigation of the political economy of sovereign debt and international crisis management: from the rise of public borrowing in early-modern Europe through the era of high imperialism and the gunboat diplomacy of the late nineteenth century, on to the wave of sovereign defaults that caused international capital markets to collapse during the Great Depression, right up to the developing-country debt crises of the neoliberal era and the recent turmoil inside the Eurozone—culminating in the dramatic defeat of Syriza's short-lived antiausterity experiment in 2015. Delving into the *longue durée* of international government finance, and building on in-depth case stud-

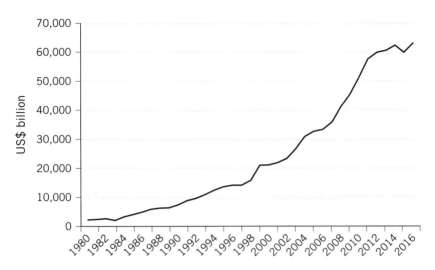

FIGURE 0.1. Gross world public debt, 1980–2016. *Source*: Bank of Canada (2017).

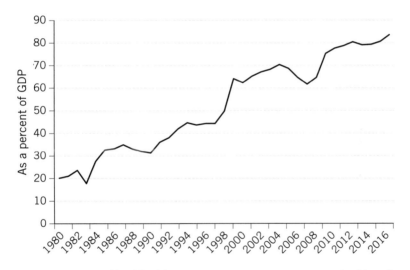

FIGURE 0.2. Gross world public debt/GDP ratio, 1980–2016. *Source*: Bank of Canada (2017).

ies of three of the most substantively important and theoretically interesting sovereign debt crises of the contemporary period (Mexico's lost decade of the 1980s, Argentina's record default of 2001, and the ongoing debt crisis in Greece), I aim to shed fresh light on the recent transformations of global capitalism and the often invisible enforcement mechanisms of debtor compliance that lie embedded deep within the global financial architecture. In the process, I hope to explain not only why heavily indebted countries generally honor their financial obligations, but also why they sometimes choose to defy their foreign lenders and default on their debts anyway.

My focus on the "hard times" of fiscal distress is deliberate. By noticeably intensifying distributional conflict over scarce public resources, sovereign debt crises tend to lay bare underlying power dynamics that, during normal times, are quietly at work beneath the surface. Identifying the exact nature of these power dynamics will allow us not only to find new answers to the intractable theoretical puzzle at the heart of this book, but also to engage with a number of long-standing debates in the social and political sciences on the fraught relationship between capitalism and democracy under conditions of globalization and financialization. As I will argue in the chapters that follow, it is the vast increase in the structural power of finance over the past four decades—revolving around the capacity of private and official lenders to withhold the short-term credit lines on which all states, firms, and households depend for their reproduction—that has driven the generalized trend away from unilateral default. Before I can further elaborate on the complex nature of these dynamics, however, we have to first dispense with a persistent misunderstanding that has long clouded our thinking about global finance and about sovereign lending in particular: the idea that all government debt is an essentially "risk-free" investment, and that heavily indebted countries always will (and always should) repay their foreign debts in full—or, as former Citibank chairman Walter Wriston infamously put it on the eve of the Latin American debt crisis of the 1980s, the notion that "countries don't go bust."

While Wriston's words may ring true in the context of the Eurozone today, where even Greece's nominally left-wing government has insisted on repaying an essentially unpayable debt, it does not necessarily hold up once we place matters in a more long-term perspective. In fact, the historical record of government borrowing is littered with examples of nonpayment, and the option to pursue a unilateral suspension of payments long featured prominently in the policy toolkit available to heavily indebted countries during times of crisis. The key question, then, is why this option is no longer being seriously considered in our contemporary era of neoliberalism (1980–present).

## A VERY BRIEF HISTORY OF SOVEREIGN DEFAULT

The starting point for this research project is the observation that things were not always the way they are today. Medieval kings and early-modern rulers regularly defaulted on their obligations to foreign bankers, as happened perhaps most famously in the case of Edward III of England, whose repudiation of a major war loan from the mighty Bardi and Peruzzi banks of Florence allegedly contributed to that city's banking crisis of the 1340s. Similarly, the serial defaults of Philip II of Spain are said to have nearly felled the illustrious Fugger and Welser banks of Augsburg, while investors on the Amsterdam capital market suffered the crippling consequences of mass sovereign default during and after the Napoleonic Wars. With the internationalization of finance under British hegemony in the nineteenth century, the suspension of payments by distressed peripheral borrowers became even more common, to a point where unilateral debt moratoriums came to be considered "normal and part of the rules of the game" during times of crisis.[5] As Max Winkler, one of the world's first sovereign debt scholars, wrote by the early 1930s, "fiscal history . . . is replete with instances of governmental defaults. Borrowing and default follow each other with almost perfect regularity. When payment is resumed, the past is easily forgotten and a new borrowing orgy ensues."[6] Figure 0.3 confirms this observation, showing how each of the three major international lending booms prior to World War II ended in a wave of sovereign defaults. The international debt crises of the 1820s, 1870s, and 1930s each stand out in sharp relief.

Take the first lending cycle of the 1820s, in which the independence struggles of a number of Latin American and Mediterranean countries coincided with a speculative craze on the London Stock Exchange. In the space of just three years, between 1822 and 1825, dozens of newly emerging states contracted multiyear loans on international capital markets to finance their costly independence wars. For the borrowers, the lending spree was a boon: it enabled them to raise armies, fight off their colonial masters, and establish themselves as sovereign nations in their own right. For investors, however, the experience ended in tears as virtually all these new states almost immediately suspended payments in the bust that followed. Peru was first to default, in April 1826, followed by Colombia. By 1829 all Latin American and southern European borrowers—with the exception of Brazil and the Kingdom of Naples—were in arrears, and there was remarkably little bondholders could do to recoup their investments.[7] The defaulting states mostly did not resume payments until after their economies had recovered, foreign-exchange reserves had been replenished, and the defaulted debt had been restructured on terms that were generally considered to be favorable to the borrowers. As a leading historian of the episode wrote, "during a quarter of a century most of [these new borrowers] maintained an effective moratorium on their external debts, which indicated an appreciable degree of economic autonomy from the great powers of the day."[8]

In the late 1860s and early 1870s, European capital began to flow back towards Latin America and the Mediterranean, but the expansion of international lending again turned out to be short-lived, with most borrowers suspending payments following the crisis of 1873. As in the previous wave, the defaults of the Long Depression (1873–1896) were unilateral and outright. An intermittent lending boom in the 1880s, centering mostly on foreign direct investments in railways, agriculture, and mining, culminated in the near-collapse of the

FIGURE 0.3. Share of countries in a state of default, 1800–1971. *Source*: Reinhart and Rogoff (2009).

*Note*: The data for this graph is based on a sample of 66 countries and does not include the defaults on U.S. war credits after World War I. The time series has been capped at 1971 (the year of the Nixon shock, which marked the collapse of the Bretton Woods regime) to indicate the prewar pattern in sovereign default and its steady decline in the immediate postwar years, when there was no significant cross-border lending. Reinhart and Rogoff's data series includes another major spike in the share of defaults in the 1980s, but as we will discuss in greater detail in the theoretical discussion in chapter 2 and in the Mexican case study, the defaults of the 1980s were qualitatively different from the prewar defaults, in that they merely involved a multilateral rescheduling of principal amortization (followed much later by the Brady deal) as opposed to the unilateral payment suspensions that characterized the default waves of the 1820s, 1870s, and 1930s.

mighty Barings Bank of London when a financial panic surrounding bad loans on several projects along the River Plate ended in the Argentine default of 1890. It was in this period—the classical gold standard era of 1870–1913—that the dominant creditor states began to assert themselves much more aggressively to defend bondholder interests and enforce cross-border debt contracts. With the rise of finance capital and growing intercapitalist rivalries feeding the expansionist ambitions of the European powers and the United States, the threat and use of force became an increasingly frequent fixture in the settlement of foreign debt disputes—a development that was famously analyzed and criticized by the classical theorists of imperialism.[9]

While scholars still disagree on how widespread military intervention really was in this period, one study has found that noncompliant borrowers risked a

30 percent chance of being subjected to foreign invasion, gunboat diplomacy, or the establishment of international financial control.[10] Often-cited examples include the imposition of European control over public finances in Egypt, the Ottoman Empire, and Greece; the naval blockade and shelling of Venezuelan harbors and coastal defenses; and the occupation of the customs houses of several Caribbean and Central American states by U.S. marines On the whole, however, it was generally the more subtle and indirect influence of *haute finance* itself—operating through the disciplinary mechanisms of the bond market, the structural constraints imposed by the international gold standard, and the monopoly power of major underwriting banks like the House of Rothschild—that enforced compliance. As Karl Polanyi poetically put it in *The Great Transformation*, "the Pax Britannica held its sway sometimes by the ominous poise of a heavy ship's cannon, but more frequently it prevailed by the timely pull of a thread in the international monetary network."[11]

After World War I brought the Pax Britannica and the hour of high finance to a violent end, the Roaring Twenties that followed gave rise to yet another major bout of speculative investment. As before, this third sovereign lending cycle quickly turned to widespread default in the international debt crisis of the 1930s. This time, however, the resort to military intervention had been all but ruled out in foreign debt disputes, leaving bondholders once again powerless in the face of a wave of unilateral payment suspensions. With the exception of Argentina and some of the smaller debtors, all Latin American countries suspended payments, as did the majority of European states. In his classic study of government insolvency, Winkler concluded that "defaults are inevitable when attempts are made by lenders to take advantage of temporarily embarrassed borrowers by exacting all sorts of concessions and imposing all sorts of impossibly harsh terms."[12] The lessons from history are therefore relatively unambiguous: not only was default common to the point of being considered "normal" or even "inevitable" in times of crisis, but in suspending payments the heavily indebted states of the prewar period also displayed a remarkable degree of economic autonomy, allowing them to shift at least part of the burden of adjustment onto foreign bondholders. While this certainly does not mean that the prewar period was more socially progressive than the contemporary period—in fact, it is widely understood that disenfranchised workers suffered the brunt of the adjustment costs during repeated crises under the classical gold standard—past research does seem to indicate that defaulting countries experienced faster recoveries than nondefaulters, while their debts were generally restructured on more favorable terms.[13]

Clearly, this historical experience contrasts sharply to the management of sovereign debt crises in the contemporary period. Even in the absence of a military enforcement regime, the repayment record of distressed borrowers appears to be better today than it has been at any other point in history following a major international crisis. By the early 1980s, a new rule seemed to have

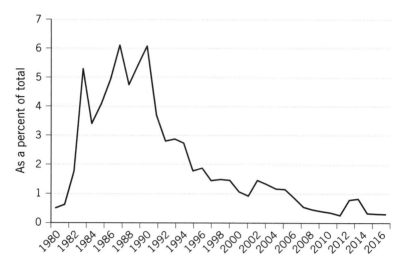

FIGURE 0.4. Share of world public debt in default, 1980–2016. *Source*: Bank of Canada (2017).

emerged: governments must repay their external debts and avoid a unilateral suspension of payments at all costs.[14] Of course, this is not to say that the problems of government insolvency or the risk of nonpayment have been eradicated altogether—in fact, given the rapidly rising public debt levels in some parts of the world, it is by no means inconceivable that we will witness further default waves in the future, with commodity exporters like Venezuela and some of the so-called frontier markets in sub-Saharan Africa possibly being first in line. But insofar as sovereign defaults still occur today, they generally take the form of orderly settlements undertaken at the initiative of private creditors, rather than the more confrontational unilateral payment suspensions that characterized the first three waves of default in the prewar and interwar periods. This observation is particularly puzzling if we consider the fact that the decades since the collapse of the Bretton Woods regime have been by far the most tumultuous in economic history, with financial crises twice as frequent after 1971 as they were during the first era of globalization before 1914.[15] Still, despite the intensification of market turmoil in recent years, the incidence of unilateral sovereign default today is remarkably low. While there was a brief uptick in negotiated debt restructurings in the 1980s, a point to which we will return later in the book, the phenomenon of sovereign default as such—in both its unilateral and negotiated forms—has been exceedingly rare since then. Even in the wake of the global financial crisis of 2008, during the worst economic downturn since the 1930s, the total share of world public debt in a state of default consistently remained well below 1 percent (see figure 0.4).[16]

The fact that sovereign borrowers usually repay their external debts, and that global capital markets have actually been thriving in spite of the frequency and intensity of sovereign debt crises in recent decades, is a clear indication of the fact that investors generally expect governments to honor their international obligations—even if they cannot. But how can these investors be so sure? Why are private creditors so confident that foreign governments will dutifully uphold their external debt service under all circumstances? That is the main question this book seeks to address.

## WHY DO GOVERNMENTS REPAY THEIR DEBTS?

The first to identify the so-called enforcement problem of cross-border debt contracts were economists Jonathan Eaton and Mark Gersovitz, who, in a seminal paper published in 1981, argued that policymakers ultimately repay their country's external debts because they are concerned about the government's future access to credit and want to safeguard their country's reputation as a "good borrower."[17] This reputational explanation caught on, but it was not without its critics. Soon a new body of literature emerged seeking to disprove the reputation hypothesis on theoretical and empirical grounds, with a different group of scholars proposing the role of sanctions, like lawsuits and trade embargoes, in enforcing compliance.[18] Others still proposed that the institutions of liberal democracy—especially a strong parliament, independent judiciary, and powerful central bank—compel the executive to respect creditor rights and credibly commit to its obligations.[19] Yet while economists have since published a raft of books and articles purporting to resolve the intractable paradox at the heart of the sovereign debt puzzle, they have failed so far to reach a conclusive answer on the matter. As three prominent scholars in the field noted on the eve of the European debt crisis:

> Almost three decades after Eaton and Gersovitz's path-breaking contribution, there is still no fully satisfactory answer to how sovereign debt can exist in the first place. None of the default punishments that the classic theory of sovereign debt has focused on appears to enjoy much empirical backing. . . . In sum, thirty years of literature on sovereign debt do not seem to have resolved some of the fundamental questions that motivated the field.[20]

In this book, I therefore propose to approach the problem from a somewhat different angle. Instead of looking at sovereign debt repayment as a purely *economic* question, I propose to build on the insights developed by a previous wave of political-economy scholarship—especially on the Latin American crisis of the 1980s—that highlighted the thoroughly *social* and *political* nature of these questions.[21] First of all, sovereign debt repayment is a *social* question insofar as the decision to honor or not to honor a foreign obligation has important redistributive implications—both between the debtor and the creditor, and within the debtor country itself. At the same time, it is also crucially a *political* question insofar as these distributional conflicts in turn feed into protracted power struggles between different social groups over who is to shoulder the burden of adjustment for the crisis.[22]

The basic questions thus become: who pays, and why? One of the main reasons why the traditional explanations of debtor compliance in the economics literature have had difficulties accounting for prevalent policy outcomes, I will argue, is precisely because much of this past work has tended to *depoliticize* the subject matter. In the real world, the decision to respect an international debt contract cannot be isolated from questions about who gets to call the shots and who gets to bear the burden of adjustment in the management of international debt crises or the repayment of sovereign debt more generally. Every time a government chooses to repay rather than suspend or repudiate its foreign obligations, it finds itself making a social and political as much as an economic calculation, and it does so within a context of domestic demands and international pressures that may structurally constrain the government's room for maneuver and systematically incentivize one set of policy choices over another. Understanding the role of such external constraints and internal motivations in enforcing compliance is therefore foundational to the effort of developing an adequate theory of sovereign debt and default. With this in mind, the theoretical discussion in Part I of this book will assess some of the shortcomings of past scholarly contributions in this area and propose the basic contours of a critical political economy approach that foregrounds the proliferation of distributional conflicts and political struggles in times of crisis.

As noted before, the central argument I aim to develop in these pages is that recent transformations in the global political economy have endowed private and official lenders with a peculiar form of power over their sovereign borrowers: what I will call *structural power*. In chapter 3, I review the extensive literature on this concept, before setting out to demonstrate how the structural power of finance ultimately revolves around a fairly straightforward capacity, namely the capacity to withhold the short-term credit lines on which all economic actors in the borrowing countries—states, firms, and households alike—depend for their reproduction. In a context of growing credit dependence, private and official lenders can inflict debilitating "spillover costs" onto a defaulting country simply by refusing to provide further loans, thereby unleashing a host of crippling knock-on effects that would threaten to undermine social harmony and the political legitimacy of the borrowing government. Crucially, these spillover costs have been greatly amplified as a result of the restructuring of the capitalist world economy since the 1970s, leading to a situation in which a unilateral suspension of payments has become all but inconceivable in most situations. As globalization and financialization have firmly entrenched the centrality of finance in the process of capital accumulation, the governments of territorially delimited

> BOX 0.1. THE THREE ENFORCEMENT MECHANISMS OF DEBTOR COMPLIANCE
>
> 1. The **market discipline** imposed by an **international creditors' cartel**, which can inflict debilitating spillover costs by withholding further credit in the event of noncompliance;
> 2. The **conditional loans** provided by the **international lender(s) of last resort**, which aim to keep the debtor solvent while simultaneously freeing up resources for foreign debt servicing, and which can also inflict debilitating spillover costs by withholding further credit;
> 3. The **bridging role** of fiscally orthodox **domestic elites**, whose hand is strengthened by their capacity to attract foreign credit at better terms than their more heterodox and democratically responsive counterparts, serving to internalize discipline into the debtor's state apparatus.

nation-states have grown increasingly subservient to international creditors for their own survival. This has in turn caused the international balance of power to shift decisively in favor of private financial interests, international financial institutions, and the dominant creditor states, while shifting the domestic balance of power decisively in favor of big firms and financial elites whose interests in repayment are broadly aligned with those of foreign creditors.

The idea that private firms enjoy a position of structural power in advanced capitalist democracies has a long-standing pedigree in the sociology and political science literature, going back to some of the foundational debates on business power and the capitalist state of the 1960s and 1970s.[23] After briefly falling out of vogue over the course of the subsequent decades—partly due to a broader shift in scholarly priorities, but also due to what was widely considered to be its rather unwieldy and deterministic original formulation—the structural power hypothesis has recently experienced somewhat of a revival in the comparative and international political economy scholarship on the global financial crisis.[24] This book aims to make a contribution to this (re-)emerging body of literature by developing a dynamic theory of the structural power of finance in sovereign debt crises that can account for debtor resistance and variation in social and political outcomes. My main objective in this respect is to uncover the *exact mechanisms* through which the power of private and official creditors operates in practice, and the *precise conditions* under which this power is effective and under which it breaks down. The argument outlined in the following chapters fundamentally revolves around what I will call *the three enforcement mechanisms of debtor compliance*, which are briefly summarized in box 0.1. Each of these mechanisms involves the capacity of a different group of lenders and intermediaries—foreign private creditors, foreign official creditors, and domestic elites, respectively—to withhold the short-term credit lines on which heavily indebted states depend for their reproduction, thereby inflicting debilitating spillover costs onto the borrowing country's wider economy, with unpredictable but far-reaching social and political consequences.

In the historical discussion and case studies presented in this book, I will trace the evolution of these three enforcement mechanisms over time and will show how their effectiveness has greatly increased in recent decades—even if it continues to vary from case to case, depending on the specific conditions prevailing in a given political-economic context. Moreover, I identify three specific developments of the neoliberal era that have significantly strengthened each of these mechanisms, namely (1) the growing concentration and centralization of international credit markets; (2) the effective integration of official-sector intervention and the IMF's lender-of-last-resort function into the global financial architecture; and (3) the growing dependence of the capitalist state—and the capitalist economy more generally—on private credit, which has tended to strengthen the position of financial elites in creditor and debtor countries alike. Taken together, these developments have conspired to gradually disempower those in favor of a more confrontational policy response and a more equitable distribution of adjustment costs, rendering debtors increasingly reluctant to suspend payments and contributing to a *generalized trend* away from unilateral default.

## The Three Enforcement Mechanisms
### of Debtor Compliance

To contextualize this argument about the structural power of finance in sovereign debt crises, we will first need to take a closer look at the structural background against which the three enforcement mechanisms of debtor compliance have evolved since the collapse of the Bretton Woods regime in the 1970s. In chapters 3 and 4, I will argue that the growing power of creditors is a direct consequence of the three interrelated processes outlined above. The first—the vast increase in the concentration and centralization of international credit markets—has led to a situation in which the liabilities of peripheral borrowers are now increasingly held by an ever-smaller circle of systemically important and politically powerful private banks and financial institutions in the advanced capitalist countries. As we will see in the contemporary case studies, it has made little difference whether sovereign lending took the form of bond finance or the form of bank loans: the point, I will argue, is that the international credit system as a whole—including the market for government bonds—has become much more concentrated and much more centralized in recent decades. Moreover, owing to the growing interdependence and increased fragility of the international financial system as a result of globalization, big banks and institutional investors tend to share a collective interest in repayment, making it easier for them to act as one and present a unified front against their sovereign borrowers in times of crisis. As we will see in the historical discussion, this situation contrasts sharply to the highly decentralized bond finance of the 1920s and 1930s, in which small and atomized retail investors were much more dispersed and found it much more difficult to maintain a unified creditor front, coordinate creditor action, and exert the requisite leverage over noncompliant borrowers.

Today, the highly concentrated and centralized structure of international lending has allowed private banks and institutional investors in the rich countries to successfully prevent opportunistic behavior by individual lenders, enabling them to form a relatively coherent international creditors' cartel capable of threatening an immediate withdrawal of further credit in the event of non-compliance.[25] At the same time, the fact that fewer lenders are involved—and the fact that these lenders' interests are now structurally interlocked at the level of a highly integrated global financial system—also makes it easier for them to coordinate a collective roll-over of maturing debts and keep providing further short-term credit lines to maintain the borrower's solvency and ensure maximum debt repayment. I will argue that, by facilitating this precarious balancing act between continued financing and the credible threat of a wholesale credit withdrawal, the concentration and centralization of international credit markets has greatly strengthened the first enforcement mechanism of *market discipline*. As an important side-effect, it has also helped ease private creditor coordination in international debt negotiations.

The second important structural change of the neoliberal era concerns the effective integration of official-sector intervention—both by the dominant creditor states and by international financial institutions—into the global financial architecture. This development is a corollary of the first, in the sense that the growing concentration and centralization of international credit markets has contributed to a situation in which many of the leading financial firms are now considered "too big to fail" by investors and policymakers alike. In a word, the accumulation of foreign government debt on the balance sheets of an ever-decreasing number of systemically important private financial institutions has meant that a disorderly default in the periphery now risks triggering a deep financial crisis in the creditor countries. As a result, a systemic need arises—from the perspective of global finance and the creditor states—for an international lender of last resort capable of "bailing out" distressed peripheral borrowers in order to prevent contagion towards the overexposed banks and institutional investors of the core countries. The provision of conditional emergency loans by creditor states, central banks, and international financial institutions thus presents an essential complement to the market mechanism, which, as we will see in the case studies, remains prone to failure in times of investor panic. Just like market discipline, this second enforcement mechanism revolves around a simple act of refusal, namely the lenders' capacity to stop providing credit to a noncompliant borrower that depends on it. Given the short-term economic consequences of a complete cutoff of foreign financing, the mere threat by official creditors to withhold future loan installments is generally enough to ensure compliance.

Over the past decades, different official-sector creditors have fulfilled the role of an international crisis manager or lender of last resort. The U.S. Federal Reserve and U.S. Treasury Department actively intervened in the developing country debt crises of the 1980s and 1990s, while the European Central Bank and EU creditor states—led by Germany and France—did the same during the more recent European sovereign debt crisis. In all cases, official-sector creditors disbursed sizable "bailout" loans that were made conditional on far-reaching budget cuts, tax hikes, privatizations, and market reforms aimed at maximizing foreign exchange earnings and freeing up public revenue for external debt servicing. From the early 1980s onwards, private lenders and creditor states have increasingly come to rely on the intervention of the International Monetary Fund, which, in addition to its conditional lending, has effectively assumed the role of a fiscal disciplinarian for distressed sovereign borrowers, monitoring their compliance with loan conditions to ensure full and timely repayment. Moreover, the stamp of approval provided by the IMF following the successful conclusion of a Stand-By Arrangement signals to private investors that a distressed debtor is pursuing "sound" policies and is committed to repaying its debts. Beside keeping the debtors solvent, the result of this growing reliance on IMF intervention has therefore been to endow the Fund with a gatekeeping function over market access that in turn helps the private creditors' cartel remain relatively unified as well. All in all, the IMF's growing centrality in international crisis management has ended up institutionalizing a set of financial surveillance, monitoring, and control functions that had hitherto been only partially, irregularly, and improvisationally fulfilled by private banks and creditor states themselves. In the process, it has served to entrench the second enforcement mechanism of *conditional lending*.

The third key change involves the thorough restructuring over the same period of state-finance relations and the domestic political economy of the borrowing countries themselves—a transformation that has been characterized by rising public debt levels and growing state dependence on private credit.[26] Ever since the 1980s, these developments have conspired with increased capital mobility and the far-reaching deregulation of financial markets to greatly intensify the competitive pressures on national governments, which now find themselves compelled to constantly reproduce the ideal conditions for foreign lending and private investment. Taken together, these developments have ended up strengthening the political position of those social groups whose material interests and ideological convictions are broadly aligned with those of foreign creditors, at the expense of those whose loyalties continue to lie with working people back home. Wealthy domestic elites and fiscally orthodox, business-friendly technocrats in particular tend to inspire the confidence of foreign creditors due to their shared interest in—and credible commitment to—continued debt servicing. This higher degree of "credibility" enables establishment forces inside the government and the financial bureaucracy to attract credit on better terms than their more democratically responsive counterparts, whose redistributive policy preferences tend to scare away investors. Over time, the result of this dynamic has been to internalize debtor discipline within the borrowing countries' state apparatus through a dramatic reconfiguration of domestic power relations, thus cementing the third enforcement mechanism: the *bridging role* of domestic elites with close ties to the international financial establishment.

These three structural changes have in turn gone hand in hand with a profound normative shift that has seen the firm entrenchment of neoliberal ideas about crisis management and the reaffirmation of a culturally embedded creditor morality that places the responsibility for adjustment squarely on the shoulders of the debtor. As Nietzsche pointed out long ago, this creditor morality is powerfully expressed in the German word *Schuld*, which means both debt and guilt, so that deep down a distressed debtor is always already considered to be responsible for their own predicament.[27] This shift in prevalent norms about debt repayment is clearly reflected in the stark contrast between the prewar concern with preventing moral hazard and the contemporary concern with defending creditor rights. The Palmerston doctrine of 1848, one of the cornerstones of the regime of laissez-faire liberalism, still held that the British government reserved the right *not* to intervene on bondholders' behalf in international debt disputes, so as to discourage "hazardous loans to foreign governments who may either be unable or unwilling to pay the stipulated interest thereupon."[28] Later, during the Great Depression, Franklin D. Roosevelt's good neighbor policy even propelled the U.S. president to personally apologize to his Latin American counterparts for Wall Street's "super-salesmanship" in the lead-up to the crisis, acknowledging that "of course" the debtor countries were "unable to pay either the interest or the principal" on their obligations to U.S. bankers.[29] Today, by contrast, the idea that nonpayment could be considered a permissible policy response or that unpayable debts could actually be written off is clearly anathema: all debts contracted by a sovereign state must and will be repaid on the stipulated due date, unless private creditors voluntarily agree to reschedule or restructure them. Ever since the early 1980s, the widely shared expectation is therefore that—irrespective of the social, political, and economic costs of continued repayment—the borrower will bear the full burden of adjustment even as the lenders are made whole.

## Consequences for International Crisis Management

Taken together, these structural changes and normative shifts in the global political economy have had far-reaching implications for the prevailing approach to international crisis management. By dramatically increasing the structural power of finance and greatly raising the spillover costs of default as well as the uncertainty surrounding more confrontational courses of action, the inter-related processes of globalization and financialization have ended up impos-ing considerable constraints on the economic sovereignty, policy autonomy, and fiscal room for maneuver available to the governments of heavily indebted peripheral states—undermining both the actual and the perceived viability of more equitable and more democratically responsive alternatives to austerity and full debt repayment.[30] After all, if a distressed sovereign borrower were to defy its creditors and default on its external debts today, it would not only be forced into fiscal balance right away, as lenders would refuse to extend fur-ther credit or roll over outstanding obligations; it would also have to contend with devastating and largely unpredictable collateral damage to its domestic economy.

The spillover costs of default would initially spread through the transmis-sion belt of the financial sector, with a default on foreign creditors likely to pro-voke capital flight, a stock market crash, and a collapse of domestic banks and pension funds. But given the centrality of finance to contemporary capitalism, the consequences would quickly ripple throughout the wider economy, risking massive social dislocation in the process. Exporters and importers would no longer be able to obtain trade credit, causing shortages of crucial consumables and industrial inputs; depositors would fear the safety and value of their savings and would likely instigate a bank run and mass capital flight, making the im-position of unpopular capital controls all but inevitable; producers would no longer be able to attract foreign or domestic investment and would start laying off workers in droves; households would see unemployment skyrocket while no longer being able to obtain credit for consumption, as a result of which aggre-gate demand would dry up—in sum, the bankruptcy of the state would risk pro-voking the bankruptcy of large parts of the domestic economy, with devastating social consequences (at least in the short term) and potentially grave implica-tions for the government's capacity to legitimize itself in the eyes of its citizens. Given the ability of foreign lenders to inflict such debilitating spillover costs sim-ply by withholding short-term credit lines, it is perhaps no surprise that many governments—including those of a leftist or even anticapitalist persuasion—are loath to defy their foreign lenders. Compliance becomes the rule.

As we will see in the contemporary case studies later in this book, the result of these dynamics has been to greatly reduce the room for maneuver avail-able to the governments of heavily indebted countries. As the spillover costs of default have been amplified by the financialization of the world economy, the policy response to major international debt crises has therefore increas-ingly come to be imposed from abroad by global financial markets, interna-tional financial institutions, and the dominant creditor powers, with the ac-tive collusion of domestic elites inside the borrowing countries. This in turn has had far-reaching implications for the democratic responsiveness of debtor country governments. Across the globe, parties of the left have begun to adopt the mantra of budgetary discipline and debt repayment that had long been the prerogative of the fiscally orthodox right. In the process, domestic party politics has effectively ceased to explain prevailing policy outcomes, rendering national elections increasingly meaningless. Germany's finance minister, Wolfgang Schäuble, infamously summarized the new status quo ahead of the 2012 parliamentary elections in Greece, when he noted that the Greeks "can vote however they want, but whatever election result we have will change nothing about the actual situation in the country."[31] While Schäuble's assessment may have been profoundly disturbing, he was not wrong. As political economists Klaus Armingeon and Lucio Baccaro observed early on in the Eurozone crisis:

> Governments of different political orientations, of different political strength, with different capacities for concertation with the social partners found themselves implementing essentially the same structural adjustment program centered on public sector cuts, pension reform, easing of employment protection legislation, weakening of unemployment insurance, and flexibilization of collective bargaining rules. The only type of choice left to governments was in the modalities used to mobilize popular consensus for, or at least blunt hostility against, austerity.[32]

Nevertheless, despite this generalized turn towards debtor compliance in recent years, it remains crucial to recognize that the power of finance is by no means absolute. Indeed, one of the key contributions of this book lies precisely in the attempt to explain why this power continues to vary from case to case, and why some distressed sovereign borrowers—most notably Argentina in 2001—still occasionally choose to defy their foreign lenders and suspend payments on their external debts. In the past, however, scholars working on the concept of structural power have often struggled to specify when this particular form of power is fully operative and when it is not, leading to a relatively deterministic account of political outcomes. In the theoretical section of this book, I will propose a two-pronged way out of this conundrum: first, by identifying the precise mechanisms through which the structural power of finance operates in practice, as well as the conditions and countervailing mechanisms under which these mechanisms are likely to fail or break down; and second, by taking social struggles seriously and allowing for the structural power of finance to be contested from below.

In subsequent chapters, I will show that—given the relatively open-ended nature of the distributional conflicts at the heart of international crisis management—borrowing governments never simply respond to external economic shocks in a coherent and completely predictable fashion. Different groups inside a country are likely to be affected differently by different policies, and some will stand to gain more from repayment than others. Moreover, since the spillover costs of default tend to be relatively short-lived, generally lasting no more than one or two years, those who expect to be negatively affected by austerity in the long run may come to favor a suspension of payments as a way out of their protracted immiserization. One common aspect of sovereign debt crises is therefore for social struggles to proliferate across the board, occasionally leading to intense popular contestation and demands for greater democratic representation that may undermine the perceived legitimacy of the borrowing government and destabilize the existing political equilibrium.

If those forces opposed to austerity and repayment manage to gain the upper hand in such struggles, or if they begin to threaten the political and economic privileges of the wealthy and powerful, the borrowing government may yet decide to pursue a more confrontational course of action, switching its policy preferences from compliance to default with an eye to alleviating domestic tensions by deflecting part of the burden of adjustment onto foreign lenders. Considering the instantaneous and destabilizing spillover costs of a credit cutoff, however, there is unlikely to be any meaningful confrontation with international creditors without a deep legitimation crisis and intense social mobilization leading to the rise to power of a prodefault coalition, or at least forcing the existing political and financial establishment to make far-reaching concessions to the domestic population in an attempt to restore the status quo and preserve its remaining privileges.

The Greek experience since 2010 has provided us with arguably one of the clearest contemporary manifestations of this fundamentally contested nature of international crisis management. The events surrounding the country's antiausterity referendum in 2015 plainly revealed how distributional conflict and asymmetries in the international and domestic balance of power are both key factors in sovereign debt repayment. Yet the conventional economistic approaches to the study of international government finance have generally dismissed such factors as irrelevant in their analytical frameworks, or have bypassed them as immeasurable in their formal mathematical models. In light of recent developments, it has become clear that future scholarship on sovereign debt—and on global finance more generally—can no longer bypass its social and political dimensions. The contentious politics of austerity and the rise of powerful antiestablishment forces across the globe unequivocally demonstrate that foreign debt servicing has important redistributive implications that economists and policymakers ignore at their peril. A critical investigation of the political economy of sovereign debt and default—one that looks specifically at the structural power of finance in shaping political outcomes to its advantage—is therefore in order. This book aims to provide just that.

# PART I

The Theory of Sovereign Debt

# ONE

## Why Do Countries Repay Their Debts?

The study of international government finance has long been plagued by a seemingly irreconcilable paradox. In theory, a sovereign debt contract is little more than an ownership title expressing a claim on part of the state's future tax revenues. But since the counterparty in question is by definition always a sovereign power—whose actions have legal force within a given territory and whose privileges include the ultimate authority to ordain and rescind laws—this immediately raises the question of how such contractual claims are enforced in practice. In the absence of a world government or a higher legal authority capable of enforcing cross-border debt contracts and compelling national governments to live up to the letter of their prior commitments, a country that is either unwilling or unable to meet its financial obligations should in theory be able to default on its external debts without repercussions. Seeing that the servicing of interest on international loans effectively constitutes a wealth transfer from the debtor to its foreign creditors, and assuming that government representatives always act rationally in defending the national interest, we would expect distressed borrowers in particular to suspend foreign debt servicing much more frequently than they actually do.

We have already seen how, at the extreme, the logic prescribed by the assumptions of neoclassical economics would therefore mean that a self-interested government should try to borrow as much as possible before repudiating its accumulated external debts in total. If all sovereign borrowers displayed such opportunistic behavior in face of their international obligations, rational lenders would assess the risks and simply refuse to disburse further credit, causing global capital markets to collapse and external debt to disappear altogether.[1] Yet this is clearly not what happens. If anything, the opposite is the case: global capital markets have been thriving ever since the 1970s, and heavily indebted peripheral countries generally do repay their debts, forking over hundreds of billions of dollars in interest payments to their rich-country creditors every year (see figure 1.1), even if they have to go through great pains to remain current on their foreign obligations. As the renowned sovereign debt lawyer Lee Buchheit puts it, "conventional wisdom is that sovereigns will rarely, if ever, default

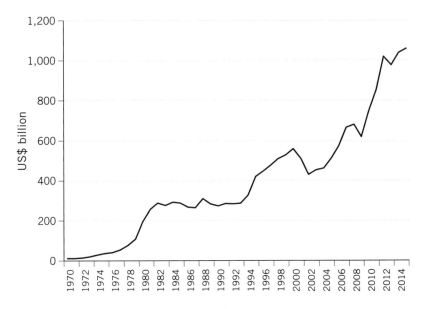

FIGURE 1.1. Low- and middle-income countries' interest payments on external debt, 1970–2015. *Source*: World Bank (2017).

on their external debts in circumstances where it is clear that they have the capacity to pay."[2] Economists at the IMF recognize that distressed borrowers appear to prefer avoiding default "even if that implies running down reserves, shortening the maturity of the debt, and ceding part of their economic policy sovereignty to multilateral institutions."[3] If, for whatever reason, a government finds itself unable to repay its debts in full or on time, it will generally prefer to negotiate an orderly settlement with its creditors over a unilateral suspension of payments. In practice, it therefore remains extremely rare for countries to simply stop paying, let alone to repudiate their obligations outright.

In the economics literature, this striking puzzle at the heart of international lending has long been known as the "enforcement problem" of cross-border debt contracts: clearly there is some kind of cross-border enforcement at work, but the precise mechanism through which it operates is not immediately observable, and economists still do not understand how exactly it works.[4] Apparently most governments do consider default to be costly, preferring to impose painful austerity measures on their own citizens instead. But why is this so? Over the past three decades, this question has inspired a number of hypotheses about the precise costs of default and the exact enforcement mechanisms of debtor compliance. In the resultant debates, four explanations emerged, centering on (1) the borrower's long-term reputation; (2) legal and trade sanctions; (3) democratic institutions; and (4) spillover costs, respectively. Yet despite the important advances that have been made by a new wave of sovereign debt scholarship in recent years, the economics literature is still at pains to answer the most basic question of all: how can external sovereign debt even exist in the first place?

In this chapter, I will briefly discuss the four conventional explanations of debtor compliance found in the economics literature and assess their validity in light of the available evidence. Since economists were the first to identify the puzzle at the heart of this book, it is important to take a closer look at why their abstract theoretical models have so far struggled to account for real-world outcomes. Given the somewhat specialist nature of these debates, the lay reader may want to skip this theoretical discussion and delve straight into the politics and history of sovereign debt in subsequent chapters.

## REPUTATION: THE THREAT OF LONG-TERM MARKET EXCLUSION

The sovereign debt puzzle outlined in the introduction really became an issue of interest for economists only in the late 1970s and early 1980s. The wave of sovereign debt defaults during the Great Depression had caused global capital markets to freeze up for the next forty years, and it was not until after the emergence of the Eurodollar markets in the 1960s and the eventual collapse of the Bretton Woods regime in 1973 that capital really began to flow across borders again. This in turn led to renewed scholarly interest in international lending. The first paper to systematically identify the fundamental paradox at the heart of the sovereign debt puzzle was the aforementioned theoretical contribution by Eaton and Gersovitz, who argued that countries ultimately honor their foreign obligations because they are concerned about their long-term reputation as borrowers.[5] In this reputational model, governments borrow in order to smooth out consumption in the event of unforeseen shocks on the economy, giving them an inherent incentive to repay in order to retain access to international capital markets. "Should the country refuse to repay," Eaton and Gersovitz write, "we assume that it faces an embargo on future loans by private lenders and that this embargo is permanent." In short, countries honor their debts because repudiating them would leave them "forever unable to use international borrowing to smooth absorption across periods of varying income."[6] In a somewhat less restrictive formulation, governments may still be able to access foreign credit following a default, but face significantly higher borrowing costs than their more compliant counterparts, as lenders assess the country's past repayment record and become more skeptical about its capacity to repay in the future, charging a higher risk premium to reflect these lingering fears of potential nonpayment.[7] Schematically, we can represent the causal mechanism at the heart of this account as follows:

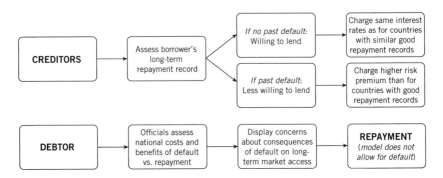

FIGURE 1.2. Reputation hypothesis.

From a quick glance at this visualization, it immediately becomes apparent that the reputation hypothesis hinges on two key assumptions: first, that lenders can and do act rationally and monolithically in their refusal to extend further credit in the event of a default; and second that they actively discriminate between sovereign borrowers on the basis of their past repayment records and demand a higher risk premium from borrowers with a history of default. When it comes to the three case studies undertaken as part of this research project, neither of these assumptions appears to hold up against the empirical evidence.

On the first point, it turns out that the countries that defaulted in the 1930s did not borrow systematically less in the 1970s, nor did they borrow on terms different from nondefaulters.[8] While Latin American borrowers faced severely restricted credit access in the decades following the defaults of the 1930s, the effect was just as strong for a compliant borrower like Argentina, which did not default, as it was for the other countries that did.[9] In fact, when international lending was resumed in the 1970s, there was no noticeable difference in borrowing costs between past defaulters and nondefaulters. Lenders were eager to let bygones be bygones; what mattered was not the historical repayment record of individual sovereign borrowers, but the immediate prospect of easy profits.[10] The evidence from the 1980s therefore points in the direction of a relatively myopic investor attitude towards risk assessment, which was perhaps most blatantly expressed in the statement by Citibank CEO Walter Wriston, just before the crisis broke out, that "countries don't go bust." Angel Gurría, the current secretary general of the OECD who served as Mexico's director of public credit during the 1980s, recounts that "the banks were hot to get in" ahead of the crisis of 1982. "They showed no foresight. They didn't do any credit analysis. It was wild. . . . We just issued promissory notes. We were selling them like hotcakes."[11] For foreign creditors, "the prospect of default seemed too extraordinary to consciously consider."[12]

This pattern of investor myopia was repeated in the lead-up to the Argentine default. If investors were really driven by past repayment records in their lending decisions, they should have remembered the country's reputation as a "debt-intolerant" serial defaulter.[13] Instead, by the mid-1990s, Wall Street had embraced Argentina—by far the most recalcitrant debtor of the 1980s—as an investor favorite and a poster child for the Washington Consensus. "Every time we finished a meeting, the orders would come," the country's deputy secretary of finance Miguel Kiguel recalled. "People were *desperate* to buy Argentina."[14] Subsequent research on the emerging market borrowing of the 1990s has confirmed that past defaulters again did not face higher risk premiums than those with an unblemished record.[15] As for the consequences of Argentina's default, the reputation hypothesis would lead us to expect a complete cutoff from all sources of foreign financing after December 2001. But while the government did lose access to international capital markets, it was still able to raise significant amounts of foreign credit through domestic bond auctions.[16] After the debt restructuring of 2005, demand for Argentine bonds was so strong that the *riesgo país*—the risk premium charged by investors compared to U.S. Treasury bills—converged with Brazil's, which did not default on its debts.[17] In fact, as soon as the restructuring was completed, the *riesgo país* that had plagued Argentina throughout its crisis returned to the levels previously experienced at the peak of the financial euphoria in 1997. More recently, in 2017, the right-wing Macri government re-entered international capital markets by issuing $2.75 billion worth in unprecedented 100-year bonds immediately after settling the country's long-standing legal dispute with U.S. vulture funds, raising widespread concerns that international investors might once again be overlooking Argentina's patchy repayment record.[18]

The story is no different for Greece. Instead of taking into account the country's long-standing reputation as a "serial defaulter," which suspended payments in every single prewar lending cycle and spent roughly half of its existence as an independent nation in a state of default, financial markets provided the Greek government with almost the exact same borrowing costs as Germany as late as 2008, its risk spread only rising above 1 percent following the collapse of Lehman Brothers and the bankruptcy of Dubai. It was not until the announcement by Prime Minister George Papandreou in late 2009 that the previous government had been cooking the books, and that Greece's real deficit and debt load were much higher than previously thought, that the Greek-German risk spread began to widen dramatically.[19] This appears to indicate that lenders were never really driven by Greece's long-term repayment record; rather, they based their investment decisions on short-term risk assessments. For years, until the global financial crisis of 2008–2009, investors appeared to reason that all debt in the Eurozone carried more or less the same default risk. As a result, Greece, with its perceived high growth potential, developed into an investor favorite, just as Mexico and Argentina had before it, and began to attract large amounts of credit in spite of its history of default—which is exactly the opposite of what the reputation hypothesis would lead us to expect.

It is perhaps not surprising, then, that subsequent research has cast significant doubt on the original reputation hypothesis. In a later study, published a decade and a half after his seminal contribution with Gersovitz, Jonathan Eaton was forced to acknowledge that the evidence to support his earlier theoretical paper was "ambiguous" at best.[20] While a number of scholars have since sought to resuscitate the reputational framework by relaxing some of its most stringent assumptions, even proponents of this line of argument now admit that empirical support for this explanation is mixed and that most research of the past three decades finds the default premiums in sovereign credit markets to be negligible.[21] To the extent that governments do pay higher interest rates after a default, most scholars would agree that these costs tend to be short-lived, ranging from a few months to about two years.[22]

Many of these subsequent empirical refutations were already foreshadowed in an influential theoretical paper by Jeremy Bulow and Kenneth Rogoff published at the end of the 1980s, in which the authors pointed out that countries actually have other ways of insuring themselves against adverse shocks on the economy.[23] Instead of repaying to retain access to international capital markets, a self-interested borrower could simply repudiate its obligations and invest the money it saves on interest payments in foreign capital markets, which—assuming sufficiently high returns—would provide a more profitable cushion for bad times. As a result, the reputational mechanism, hinging entirely on the debtors' need to retain credit access for future consumption smoothing, simply collapses. To have any effect at all, Reinhart and Rogoff conclude, "the reputation approach therefore requires some discipline."[24]

## SANCTIONS: ASSET SEIZURES, TRADE EMBARGOES, AND GUNBOAT DIPLOMACY

Building on Bulow and Rogoff's contribution, a second body of literature has proposed direct punishment as the main enforcement mechanism of debtor compliance. By imposing or threatening to impose sanctions, scholars in this tradition argue, private lenders and creditor states can directly coerce recalcitrant debtors to repay. Such creditor sanctions could take either of two forms: the seizure of a debtor's assets abroad, or the imposition of a trade embargo. Subsequent work has also highlighted the historical importance of so-called supersanctions, where external financial control, military coercion and the threat of outright occupation served as the principal enforcement mechanisms. What these different types of sanctions have in common is that they all seek, through

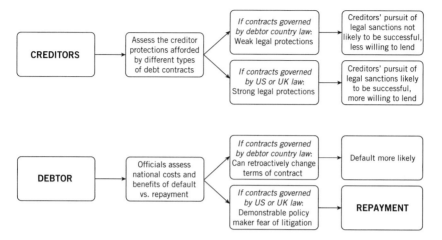

FIGURE 1.3. Legal sanctions hypothesis.

some form of direct creditor action, to "raise the cost of default sufficiently high to make repaying the foreign obligations in the self-interest of the sovereign debtor."[25] Like the reputation hypothesis, the sanctions approach therefore remains firmly within the boundaries of neoclassical cost-benefit analysis and rational choice theory. "In this sense," Reinhart and Rogoff note, "the reputation and legal approaches are not so different."[26]

In the legal approach, schematically represented in figure 1.3, sovereign borrowers will do almost anything to avoid default because of the danger of lawsuits inflicting further damage on an already strained national economy.[27] Since historically most emerging market and developing country debt has been denominated in foreign currencies and contracted in other legal jurisdictions, debtors have generally been liable to the laws of the country where the debt was issued (although this is now slowly changing, as emerging markets in particular have begun to issue more debt domestically and in their own currencies). The legal sanctions hypothesis holds that there is therefore no way for the borrower to protect itself from aggressive litigation pursued by creditors inside the issuing country. Selective default, discriminating between domestic and foreign creditors, is generally not an option either, especially in the case of securitized bond finance, where secondary markets add a veil of anonymity to bond holdings and where a suspension of payments is likely to trigger cross-default clauses. The notorious example of the U.S. vulture fund Elliot Associates buying up Peru's greatly depreciated postdefault bonds far below par, and then suing the government for its refusal to repay the face value, is often cited as an exemplary case of aggressive litigation bearing fruit for the persistent speculator.[28]

After Elliot succeeded in attaching some of Peru's foreign assets, including a Brady bonds payment that was to be channeled through a Brussels-based clearing house, Peru found itself forced to settle and repay part of its defaulted debt.

However, aside from anecdotal evidence like the Peruvian case, even legal scholars recognize that lawsuits alone could never constitute an effective enforcement mechanism at the global level. First of all, as the very nature of the sovereign debt puzzle already indicates, the central problem remains enforcement. Why would anyone worry about sovereign debt contracts if there is generally no way to enforce them in practice?[29] In the period prior to World War I, the legal doctrine of sovereign immunity, religiously adhered to by the courts of the two main issuing countries (the UK and later the United States), made it impossible for private creditors to sue foreign governments.[30] While this doctrine has since been greatly weakened in commercial dealings, the empirical evidence still appears to contradict the notion that legal sanctions are really taken seriously by debtor countries.

One of the first major studies of sovereign default, published in 1951, found that "judicial remedies of foreign bondholders are hardly effective."[31] During the crisis of the 1980s, a prominent *Financial Times* reporter observed that "bankers' hopes—and borrowers' fears—that crippling costs could be imposed on recalcitrant debtor countries through court action appear to be greatly exaggerated."[32] This investigation also did not find any demonstrable concerns among Mexican policymakers about possible creditor litigation. While it is impossible to confirm with certainty what would have transpired in the counterfactual case of a Mexican default, it is clear that the countries that did temporarily pursue a more confrontational line in the 1980s—most importantly Peru and Argentina—did not face any legal reprisals from their creditors afterwards. One leading scholar of the Latin American debt crisis observed that "the Peruvian experience has shown that after two years of unilateral action no legal response has come from the creditor banks to confiscate assets or other drastic measures; the only cost of the unilateral action, as regards creditor banks, has been their curtailment of short-term credit lines."[33] Argentina did not face any legal sanctions in the 1980s either, in spite of the country's brief period of noncompliance under its new democratically elected president in 1984.

As for the legal fallout of Argentina's later default of 2001, many observers have noted the aggressive litigation strategies pursued by the country's foreign creditors: just three years after the default, some 140 lawsuits had been filed against Argentina in several jurisdictions. But even though the creditors won most of these cases, their attempts to lay claim to Argentina's foreign assets over the next decade "turned out to be fruitless."[34] In 2005, a New York judge lamented that "not only have the [lawsuits] not yielded a hundred cents on the dollar, they have not even yielded one cent on the dollar."[35] A number of high-profile U.S. rulings later sought to force the defiant government of Cristina Fernández de Kirchner into compliance; one even allowed Paul Singer's hedge fund subsidiary, NML Capital, to briefly attach Argentina's flagship navy vessel *La Libertad* off the coast of Ghana. The ship, however, was quickly released after the UN Tribunal on the Law of the Sea unanimously upheld its sovereign immunity. Not long after, a highly controversial landmark ruling by Judge Griesa of the U.S. District Court of Southern New York barred Argentina from transferring funds to its exchange bondholders (the ones who did accept the 2005 and 2010 debt restructuring) if the country's government did not first reach an agreement with the holdouts (the ones who did not). Nevertheless, the ruling failed to exact any concessions from Fernández de Kirchner, who railed against the "senile" Griesa and derided the U.S. hedge funds as "vultures" preying off the country's defaulted debt. In July 2014, matters finally came to a head when Argentina tried to make a payment to its exchange bondholders, and its U.S. trustee, the Bank of New York Mellon, declared that it was unable to process the transfer as it would have been held in contempt of court, leaving the government with only two options: either to repay the holdouts in full or be forced to default a second time. Tellingly, Fernández de Kirchner chose the latter. This episode clearly confirms that, in the Argentine case at least, legal sanctions have not been an effective enforcement mechanism. While Griesa's contentious ruling has rocked the jurisprudence of sovereign debt with potentially far-reaching consequences for future restructuring deals, it was unable to reverse Argentina's original default. In fact, it merely triggered another. Argentina finally repaid its holdouts in 2016, but only after the investor-friendly multimillionaire businessman Mauricio Macri had come to power.

In a similar vein, legal considerations also did not prevent Ecuador from defaulting on part of its external debt in late 2008. In the wake of Ecuador's default, Lee Buchheit, who served as the country's contract lawyer in negotiations with foreign creditors, observed that "the breakdown of the [legal] line of defense is significant because this was the first time that the modern theory of supermajority creditor control of sovereign debt problems was tested in practice."[36] At the other end of the extreme, Greece has more recently *refused* to default even though, at the start of the crisis, the vast majority of its bonds—around 90 percent—were issued under Greek law.[37] This meant that if Greece had wanted to suspend payments or unilaterally write down its own obligations, legal sanctions would not have been able to stop it from doing so: the government always had the option of passing a bill through parliament to change the loan conditions on its domestic law bonds, forestalling legal reprisals by bondholders in the event of an imposed haircut. The law firm Allen & Overy pointed out that, from a legal point of view, Greece thus held "quite a good card" when the debt crisis first broke out.[38] If legal sanctions had truly been the decisive enforcement mechanism, the ability of the Greek government to disarm this mechanism simply by passing a statute through parliament and imposing a unilateral haircut on bondholders would lead us to expect a unilateral Greek default, which did not materialize. In sum, while legal considerations may play

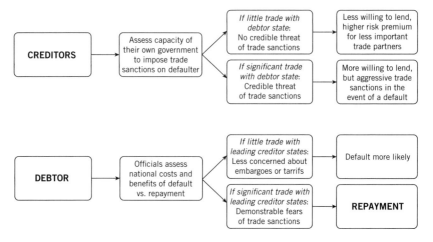

FIGURE 1.4. Trade sanctions hypothesis.

a limited role in deterring default, mostly in terms of preventing the hassle of having to deal with bothersome lawsuits, legal sanctions alone do not appear to make for a credible enforcement regime. Indeed, a recent study on the impact of lawsuits on bond yields found that there was no significant effect.[39]

What, then, about the second form of creditor punishment proposed by Bulow and Rogoff? Unlike legal sanctions, trade sanctions would be pursued not by the private lenders themselves but by their host government. Some scholars have claimed, for instance, that Argentina's decision to maintain payments in the 1930s, even though the rest of Latin America fell into arrears all around it, was due to fears that the British government would impose a particularly harmful embargo on Argentine beef imports.[40] The economic historian Carlos Díaz Alejandro argued that this would have had far-reaching repercussions domestically, as "tampering with the normal servicing of the Argentine debt would have involved not only a bruising commercial clash with the UK, but also probably a major restructuring of the Argentine political scene, at the expense of groups linked with Anglo-Argentine trade."[41] This argument does not appear to hold up to scrutiny, however, since Argentina still honored its obligations to U.S. banks, even if the United States was in no position to impose similarly harmful trade sanctions.[42]

The evidence from the three contemporary cases is even less convincing on this point. For one, there was certainly never any explicit threat of U.S. trade sanctions against Mexico during the 1980s; in fact, the relationship between the two neighbors remained extremely cooperative throughout the crisis, and it was clear to all actors involved that the United States only stood to harm itself by imposing import or export restrictions on its second-most important trading partner. Even more tellingly, when Argentina and Peru briefly defied their foreign lenders with unilateral action during the 1980s, the U.S. government never pursued or threatened to pursue trade sanctions against either of them. Similarly, in the case of Argentina's later default of 2001, there was never any risk of U.S. trade sanctions. Insofar as the Bush administration took an official stance at all, it actually pushed for default and later proactively sided with Kirchner in his wrestling matches with the private creditors and the IMF.[43] In the Eurozone, meanwhile, commercial restrictions are unlawful under EU treaties on the free movement of goods within the single market, so it is highly unlikely that the threat of trade sanctions functioned as a credible enforcement mechanism in the Greek case. Overall, while several studies have found that sovereign default is associated with a significant decline in bilateral trade between debtor and creditor countries, amounting to roughly 8 percent per year, it is unclear whether this negative effect is due to a "natural shrinkage" in trade credit, or due to a deliberate attempt by the government of the creditors' host country to deter default.[44] For commercial punishments to be an effective enforcement mechanism of debtor compliance, the fall in bilateral trade between the defaulting government and its creditor countries should be significantly larger than the fall in trade with noncreditor countries. There does not appear to be any evidence for this proposition.[45] Absent direct sanctions, in other words, "the channel linking default to trade remains a mystery."[46]

Finally, recent years have witnessed another heated debate about a third possible type of sanctions: so-called supersanctions. Some scholars have argued that the threat of military intervention and the imposition of international financial control served as the most important deterrents for sovereign debt repudiation in the classical gold standard era (1870–1914).[47] From European powers sending gunboats to Venezuela and taking over tax collection in the Ottoman Empire, Egypt, and Greece, to the occupation by U.S. marines of the customs offices of various Caribbean and Central American countries, there are plenty of examples of direct coercion by creditor states to restore repayment to private bondholders. Indeed, one study finds the likelihood of a defaulting government being subjected to supersanctions to have been almost 30 percent between 1870 and 1913, with "extreme debt sanctions" applied to over 40 percent of defaulted debt in that period.[48] Most importantly, after the defaulters were subjected to gunboat diplomacy or international financial control, their yield spreads fell by some 1,200 basis points—or almost 90 percent. Prior to these interventions, the countries in the sample spent nearly half of the gold standard era in a state of default, while the same set spent practically no time in default after being "supersanctioned."[49]

These findings, however, have been contested.[50] In his extensive study of three centuries of sovereign debt and default, Michael Tomz finds little evidence that creditors used—or threatened to use—gunboat diplomacy or military invasion to coerce debtors to repay, arguing that while sovereign default was often invoked as an excuse to undertake military action, the real motives had to do more with the underlying geopolitical interests of the respective imperialist powers.[51] Either way, while The Hague Peace Conference of 1907 ironically still recognized "the legitimacy of the use of force in settling debt disputes," the debate is a purely academic one in the postwar era, now that armed intervention has been fully ruled out as an acceptable enforcement mechanism.[52] We are therefore compelled to look beyond both reputational concerns and creditor sanctions to uncover the hidden dynamics of sovereign debt repayment today.

## INSTITUTIONS: CREDIBLE COMMITMENT AND DEMOCRATIC ADVANTAGE

One possible explanation that has been particularly influential among political scientists and developmental economists focuses on the role of liberal-democratic institutions in protecting creditor rights. Towards the end of the Cold War, at a time of great neoliberal triumphalism, Douglas North and Barry Weingast published an influential article emphasizing the connection between political and economic rights, or between the institutional underpinnings of free-market capitalism and liberal democracy: namely private property and limited government.[53] Extrapolating from a case study of England before and after the Glorious Revolution of 1688, North and Weingast argued that liberal-democratic institutions limiting the power of the executive greatly enhance a government's capacity to credibly commit to upholding property rights— including creditor rights—and hence honoring its debt contracts. In North and Weingast's own formulation, liberal-democratic institutions "do not substitute for reputation-building and associated punishment strategies," but "appropriately chosen institutions can improve the efficacy of the reputation mechanism by acting as a constraint in precisely those circumstances where reputation alone is insufficient to prevent reneging."[54]

More specifically, North and Weingast argued that the institutional innovations of an empowered parliament, an independent judiciary, a strong rule of law, and a central bank to safeguard "sound money" collectively served to "dramatically increase the control of wealth holders over the government," thereby constraining executive authority and reducing the likelihood of default.[55] Expanding on these ideas, later work by Schultz and Weingast posited the existence of a distinct "democratic advantage," enabling liberal regimes to borrow larger sums of money at lower interest rates than their less democratic or authoritarian counterparts.[56] "The institutions of limited government," Schultz and Weingast concluded, "can modify the incentives of the sovereign by increasing the ability of those with a stake in the repayment of debt to impose

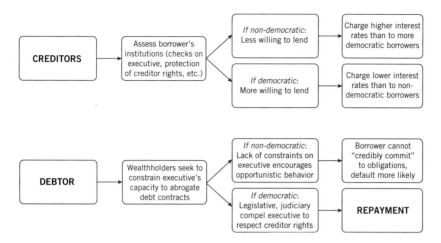

FIGURE 1.5. Democratic advantage hypothesis.

penalties on him."[57] The causal mechanism behind their democratic advantage hypothesis can be rendered as in figure 1.5.

The first problem with this argument is that its logic only holds when the state's private creditors are domestic constituents. While this may hold true for the advanced capitalist countries, which largely raise credit domestically and in their own currencies, it usually does not apply to developing or peripheral economies, which (until recently at least) have tended to depend on credit denominated in currencies and contracted under legal systems other than their own—a form of a foreign credit dependence that economists like to refer to as "original sin," and that is often considered an important determinant of default.[58] Since foreign creditors are not represented by the democratic institutions of these peripheral debtor countries (or at least are not supposed to be), the institutional explanation has still not resolved the enigma of *international* lending, in which foreign creditors may not always have legal or political recourse to the courts or parliaments of borrowing governments.

Aside from these theoretical challenges, there appears to be a further problem with the democratic advantage hypothesis: the empirical evidence simply does not stack up in its favor. First of all, pertaining to North and Weingast's case study, successive research has shown that the fall in interest rates following the Glorious Revolution was actually part of a much more long-term downward trend that went back to at least the late sixteenth century.[59] Furthermore, interest rates remained volatile even after the Glorious Revolution, and the establishment of democratic institutions ensuring credible commitment far from abrogated opportunistic behavior by the executive.[60] As a more general matter, David Stasavage has found that representative institutions in early-modern

Europe only really enforced compliance when merchant interests were dominantly represented; insofar as they were, the political regime in question tended to be *oligarchic* rather than democratic in nature—a point to which we will return in the historical section of this book.[61]

An innovative study by Flandreau and Flores on the development of global capital markets in the 1820s shows how the central role of financial intermediaries virtually dissolved the presumed democratic advantage: powerful merchant banks like the House of Rothschild actually displayed a distinct "bias in favor of arch-conservatives who had no remorse about implementing unpopular policies or even ruthless repression" to exact wealth and revenues from their respective populations for the servicing of foreign debts.[62] "This somewhat frightening conclusion," the authors note, "is antithetic to the 'democratic advantage' view, which neo-institutionalists have recently emphasized." In other words, while an authoritarian strongman may be willing and able to face down popular resistance to austerity measures and structural reform, democratic leaders may in fact "prefer protests from the financial markets to the protests from their own people."[63]

Research on contemporary international lending casts further doubt on the democratic advantage hypothesis. One study finds that the three big credit rating agencies also do not appear to favor democratic developing countries over comparable autocracies, while another has shown that, although democracies and nondemocracies paid similar interest rates between 1971 and 1997, democracies were actually *more* likely to reschedule their debts in that period.[64] Yet another study finds that "news about institutional reforms seldom had a rapid and significant impact" on bond yields, indicating that investors were often either unaware of (or otherwise unmoved by) the institutional specificities of their potential borrowers.[65] Finally, a recent study has found that "democratically-elected politicians respond with more aggressive policies towards foreign financial markets" than their autocratic counterparts, which makes sense if we consider that democratically accountable politicians are primed to be more concerned about the electoral repercussions of painful adjustment measures.[66]

The findings from the case studies presented in this book point in a similar direction. As it turns out, Mexico's authoritarian one-party regime, famously referred to by the Latin American author Vargas Llosa as "the perfect dictatorship," offered by far "the richest example of cooperation from a Latin American borrower."[67] The country had a powerful executive and virtually no democratic checks and balances, yet it was precisely these nondemocratic institutions that endowed it with the capacity to systematically shield financial policymaking from popular opposition to austerity and debt repayment.[68] Moreover, through a dual strategy of repression and co-optation, the subsequent governments of Miguel de la Madrid and Carlos Salinas actively prevented the emergence of an organized antiausterity coalition.[69] As a result, prodefault voices were effectively excluded from the public debate, and the ruling Partido Revolucionario Institucional managed to insulate itself from democratic pressures over the national debt. Argentina, by contrast, did exactly the opposite: after the fall of the military *junta* and the transition to democracy, the country briefly pursued a considerably more confrontational stance vis-à-vis foreign creditors. Upon assuming office in December 1983, President Alfolsín immediately declared a six-month moratorium on interest payments and began to openly call for the formation of a Latin American debtors' cartel to pressure foreign creditors into offering better terms.[70] Lamenting that "the debt of Argentina and of other Latin American nations is the product of perverse mechanisms that lend us money in order that we do not develop ourselves," Alfolsín declared that "we are not going to pay our debt by making our people hungry."[71] For the newly elected president, democratic responsibility meant that "the state cannot bow to international financial groups or privileged local groups." In a direct rebuttal of North and Weingast's theory, one observer noted that "the newly democratic government of Argentina . . . was by far the most defiant, [while] Mexico's party-based authoritarian regime has been most compliant."[72] For their part, U.S. investors did not appear to be very enthusiastic about the country's institutional checks and balances either. After meeting with Argentina's new democratically accountable negotiators, one senior banker complained that "we expected to get facts and figures, a detailed picture of the country's medium- to long-term economic plans. All we got were some platitudes about Argentina's new democracy."[73]

The evidence from Argentina's subsequent crisis of the late 1990s and early 2000s casts further doubt on the democratic advantage hypothesis. In fact, Argentina complied at a time when the democratic checks and balances that had been established in the mid-1980s were rapidly being eroded in response to international financial pressures. Insofar as political institutions can be said to have played a role in shaping the outcome of the crisis, it was precisely their relatively *un*democratic nature that shielded the executive from popular pressures and that ensured repayment throughout the 1990s. The origins of this development can be traced back to the resolution of the crisis of the 1980s, which had ended with the resignation of President Alfolsín following a bout of hyperinflation and intense riots. When Carlos Menem won the elections in 1989, he "soon realized that emergency management of the economy would demand concentration of power in the executive. So he tried and enlarged his authority by means of congressional delegation and by the use of NUDs [necessity and urgency decrees]."[74] Ever since the transition to democracy, lawmaking authority had been reserved to Congress, but after 1994, coinciding with his embrace of the Washington Consensus, Menem pushed through a constitutional reform that institutionalized the so-called *decretazo*, allowing the executive to bypass Congress and create laws by decree, endowing the president with great "agenda-setting power" and giving rise to a "hyper-presidentialist" regime in which the head of state effectively assumed the role of an "elected dictator."[75]

This expansion of executive power further intensified with the onset of the economic crisis after 1999. When the next president, Fernando De la Rúa, re-appointed Menem's old economy minister in a desperate bid to restore inves-tor confidence in 2001, "the technocratic Cavallo demanded vast discretionary powers over economic policy, just as he had done under Menem. This only . . . reinforced a policymaking process already heavily dependent on executive de-grees, marginalized Congress, and devalued the overall process of represen-tation."[76] Subsequent scholarship on Argentine democracy has stressed how "emergency powers, arising from poor economic conditions . . . have enhanced presidential power. Presidents seek to enhance their power by taking unilateral actions, especially in times of crisis."[77] The authors of the latter study conclude that in Argentina, "presidential power is difficult to control through formal in-stitutional checks." Yet it was precisely this erosion of democratic checks and balances that shielded financial policymaking from popular opposition. As we will see in the Argentine case study, the country only defaulted after intense popular pressure from below forced the political establishment to become less subservient to the creditor rights of foreign investors and more responsive to the social rights of its own citizens. For this reason, Michael Tomz categorizes Argentina's suspension of payments as a "democratic default." Noting that "vot-ers may favor noncompliance as the best way to promote the national interest or their personal welfare," Tomz argues that, insofar as the people who stand to benefit from a default strategy are represented politically, democratically re-sponsive institutions may actually *increase* the likelihood of noncompliance.[78]

We will see in the conclusion to this book how these dynamics played out in the more recent Greek case, but one thing is clear: it was only by making government *less* responsive to the concerns of the domestic population that investors could be convinced of Mexico's and Argentina's commitment to repay. Such observations have prompted scholars to ask a simple question: "where is the democratic advantage?"[79] Not only does the evidence seem to indicate that democratic institutions have little impact on bond yields, but it also points in a politically disturbing direction: when it comes to sovereign debt repayment, coldblooded autocrats may actually be more reliable partners for sophisticated Wall Street financiers than their more democratically accountable counter-parts.[80] Ceausescu's dogged insistence on full debt repayment in Romania is an infamous case in point. In one particularly telling study, Sebastian Saiegh even contends that, insofar as democracies can obtain credit on better terms than nondemocracies, this is only due to the intervention of multilateral lenders. Once the role of IMF policy conditionality is taken into account, Saiegh finds that "dictatorships are more likely to honor their debts than democracies," lead-ing to a provocative but not altogether far-fetched conclusion: "if multilateral agencies can condition democracies to behave as nondemocracies on debt matters, then the problem dissolves. Namely, if the decision-maker is no longer the median voter but the political leadership . . . repayment is assured." In other words: "we will bail you out but you promise to conduct yourself as if you were a dictatorship when it comes to repaying the debt."[81]

Paradoxically, then, the democratic advantage may consist of a mechanism whereby democratic governments are systematically conditioned by multilateral lenders to behave more like nondemocracies. The democratic advantage hypothesis, it seems, has the world standing on its head.

## SPILLOVER COSTS: BANK RUNS, PRIVATE BORROWING, AND OUTPUT LOSSES

The puzzle at the heart of this chapter—and at the heart of the academic literature on sovereign debt more generally—has therefore still not been resolved. "At some level," Reinhart and Rogoff acknowledge, none of the proposed models "seems quite adequate to explain the scale and size of international lending or the diversity of measures creditors bring to bear in real-life default situations."[82] Since democratic institutions, creditor sanctions, and the threat of long-term capital market exclusion do not appear to be sufficient reasons for governments to repay, and hence for private creditors to keep lending to foreign governments, a small but growing body of literature has recently focused on another set of factors: the so-called spillover costs of default. The groundbreaking research emerging in this area suggests that the main costs of default may be borne not so much by the government itself as by the private sector.

In short, scholars have in recent years become increasingly aware of the ways in which a sovereign default could directly affect the domestic economy, or indirectly harm the government's trust relationships with domestic businesses.[83] Because it is often difficult for a government to discriminate between domestic and foreign creditors, the costs of nonpayment could spill over into finance, trade, and production at home—not only harming bankers, traders, and industrialists, but also affecting overall economic performance, industrial output, and employment.[84] In various studies, sovereign credit ratings have been found to strongly impact the performance of bond and stock markets, while rising default risks tend to lead to a loss of confidence among investors and depositors, thereby feeding capital flight and bank runs and making it harder for domestic firms and households to obtain credit.[85] Most importantly, however, defaults tend to devastate the balance sheets of domestic banks and pension funds, especially in countries with more developed financial institutions in which banks and pension funds tend to be much more invested in their own government's debts.[86] The risk of a domestic financial collapse may therefore be one of the most

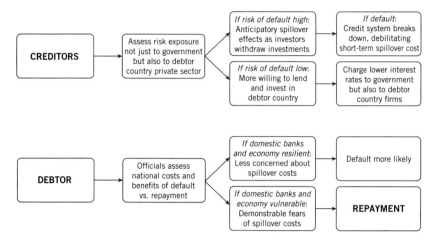

FIGURE 1.6. Spillover costs hypothesis.

important considerations of officials in determining whether or not to default, especially since such a collapse would have wide-ranging knock-on effects on credit allocation, private investment, and industrial production, causing the spillover costs of default to ripple throughout the economy, with far-reaching social and political consequences.[87]

In sum, the costs of nonpayment appear to include rising risk premiums on the stock market; reduced private sector access to credit; a fall in foreign direct investment; a loss of access to trade credit; and steep output drops that can tip an economy into recession or deepen an ongoing downturn, leading to higher unemployment rates that in turn tend to undermine the government's chances at reelection.[88] The causal mechanism behind the spillover costs hypothesis would therefore look something like figure 1.6.

As with capital market exclusion and credit embargoes, the evidence does seem to indicate that the spillover costs of default are generally short-lived. The impact of default on exports, for instance, tends to evaporate after one or two years.[89] Moreover, these short-term spillover effects have different impacts across different economic sectors, with default particularly costly for the domestic financial sector and exporting industries, which greatly depend on access to trade credit. Domestic import-competing industries, by contrast, may actually end up benefitting from a default, especially if it is accompanied by currency devaluation, which makes competing imports more expensive and thus less attractive to firms and consumers.[90] A recent Rabobank study therefore concludes that "the economic costs of sovereign default, as estimated by scholars, are found to be less drastic than most believe."[91] Yet these costs also appear to be relatively messy and unpredictable, and to disproportionately affect politically powerful banks and businesses, which will therefore tend to mobilize all their might to stop the government from defaulting. So what if it is not just the economics, but the *politics* of default that holds the key to the sovereign debt puzzle? Or, to be more precise, what if it is the complex and evolving relationship between the two that we should really be looking at?

# TWO

## A Critical Political Economy Approach

The spillover costs literature points in a very interesting direction. If default has strong negative effects on the domestic financial sector, as well as on domestic production, access to trade credit and the capacity of domestic firms to borrow, then one would expect banks and credit-dependent businesses—along with wealthy elites and businessmen who are invested in their own government bonds or dependent on the banks and stock market for their own income—to be strongly opposed to it. But such opposition to default does not necessarily hold for all social groups. In times of crisis, the alternative to default (full repayment) tends to require major sacrifices from workers in particular, often involving protracted austerity, deep wage, pension, and welfare cuts, steep tax hikes, and large-scale privatization of state assets. If these measures are sufficiently painful and broad-based, they may eventually push a growing segment of the domestic working class to oppose further austerity and favor a suspension of payments to deflect part of the adjustment costs onto foreign lenders.

Many scholars working within the spillover costs literature do not yet appear to fully grasp the theoretical implications of these observations: their findings risk undermining one of the unspoken assumptions in the economics literature, namely the conceptualization of sovereign debtors as "unitary agents" responding in utilitarian fashion to straightforward market signals—comparing the relative benefits of nonpayment versus its costs and only defaulting when the former are expected to outweigh the latter.[1] Once we accept that some social groups or classes inside the borrowing country derive greater utility from debt repayment than others, and that the precise costs and benefits of default are difficult to estimate with certainty, the unitary agent assumption begins to crumble and the decision whether to default or to repay can no longer be reduced to a straightforward pursuit of the "national interest" or maximization of utility. With the redistributive implications and uncertain consequences of default and repayment now exposed, the fundamentally *social* and *political* nature of sovereign debt repayment and international crisis management finally comes to the fore.[2]

If there is one thing that the competing explanations of debtor compliance in the economics literature have in common, it is that they have so far largely sidestepped such overtly social and political questions. Who benefits from default? Who benefits from repayment? How do different groups assess whether they are likely to lose or win out? And who ultimately decides upon the course of action to be taken? Political economists have long argued that the answers to these questions cannot be taken for granted; they must be subjected to critical theoretical analysis and thorough empirical investigation. In fact, the *depoliticization* of repayment appears to be one of the main reasons why the economics literature has so far struggled to account for the fact that sovereign debt can even exist in the first place. Only by taking a closer look at the redistributive implications of default and repayment, and the resultant political struggles between different social groups over the appropriate course of action to be taken, can we begin to craft a more nuanced understanding of the deeper dynamics behind the international regime of cross-border contract enforcement.

What I will propose, in this respect, is a sociologically informed critical political economy perspective that foregrounds these underlying power differentials and the related distributional conflicts over who gets to call the shots and who gets to bear the burden of adjustment in times of fiscal distress.[3] In this chapter, I will set out to provide some basic theoretical contours of such an approach, before developing it in greater detail in chapters 3 and 4.

## PROBLEMATIZING THE UNITARY AGENT ASSUMPTION

One of the principal blind spots of the conventional explanations of debtor compliance is that they generally tend to treat the borrowing country as a singular entity whose different social groups and classes are aggregated into an overarching national interest. Governments, then, are merely "representative agents" that negotiate with foreign creditors on behalf of their country as a whole. In the process of this aggregation, all conflicts of interest within the debtor country are quietly assumed away; different stratums of society are simply expected to share the same interest in compliance or noncompliance, repayment or default, and the country's government is presumed to apolitically represent this collective set of policy preferences.[4] Yet this approach clearly glosses over a stark social divide between those who stand to lose from the austerity measures required to repay the debt, and those who are more exposed to the financial fallout of a potential default.[5] Wealthy elites, in particular those who hold government bonds, own capital and/or run credit-dependent businesses, are likely to derive much greater utility from uninterrupted debt servicing than others, giving them a clear interest in compliance, even if this inflicts harm on the wider economy and on the population at large.[6] Insofar as borrowing governments can be said to represent the "national interest," future scholarship should therefore first try to establish how this national interest is determined and whose particular class or sectoral interests it truly reflects.[7]

The redistributive implications of repayment suggest that a government's decision to honor a specific obligation at a time of crisis is not just the outcome of a disinterested rational calculation taking place on an Excel spreadsheet somewhere in the country's debt management office, but is rather a product of a complex tug-of-war within the debtor country itself—and between the debtor country and its international creditors—over who will be made to pay for the crisis. As long as this struggle persists, domestic elites are likely to mobilize as much of their economic and political clout as possible in order to prevent nonpayment.[8] This is likely to be true even if these elites do not hold government bonds themselves, since the spillover costs of default tend to disproportionately affect the private sector and wealthy citizens, regardless of whether they own any government debt. As stock markets collapse, interbank lending freezes up, and firms can no longer obtain access to trade finance and foreign investment, many banks and businesses will find themselves facing serious losses.

By contrast, private-sector workers, civil servants, students, pensioners, the poor and unemployed—basically everyone who does not own government bonds and who relies on wage labor and/or state expenditure for their livelihoods—are much more likely, in relative terms, to be negatively affected by the austerity measures required to keep servicing the debt, possibly leading a growing share of working-class people to favor default over continued repayment, thus pitching them against both foreign creditors and domestic elites.[9] How these contradictory positions on fiscal policy are manifested in social conflicts, represented in political institutions, and eventually transformed into government policy—or not—is bound to be a matter of fierce power struggles between different social groups at both the domestic and the international level. In discussing the determinants of default, the inherently conflictual politics of repayment therefore cannot be ignored.

When it comes to the international dimension of these conflicts, the sovereign debt literature has also largely tended to bypass important political questions, like the asymmetric distribution of power within the global financial architecture.[10] Beside highlighting the redistributive implications of default and repayment, one of the most important contributions of a political economy approach to sovereign debt would therefore be to render visible the structure of international lending and the continually evolving distribution of interests and power within that structure, treating the resulting asymmetries and constraints as *endogenous* to the decision on whether or not to repay. This brings us right back to the question of cross-border contract enforcement. Crucially, the fact that there is no formal enforcement mechanism of debtor compliance does not preclude the fact that there may in fact be a set of *informal* mechanisms that surreptitiously produce the same outcome (or alternatively a set of formal mechanisms, like the IMF's policy conditionality, that unofficially serve a similar purpose).[11] In the next chapter we will see how such global power structures can become intermeshed with domestic power structures as foreign creditors, international financial institutions, and wealthy elites inside the borrowing countries come together in an international coalition of sorts in a concerted effort to discipline government and ensure full repayment.

## DISTINGUISHING BETWEEN WILLINGNESS AND ABILITY TO PAY

The assumptions of neoclassical economics also have important implications for our understanding of the determinants of default. As Wolfgang Streeck has noted, "the only politics [that standard economic] theory can envisage involves opportunistic or, at best, incompetent attempts to bend economic laws. Good economic policy is nonpolitical by definition."[12] Paraphrasing this observation with respect to sovereign debt, we could say that the only form of politics that standard economic theory can envisage is the "opportunistic" decision to default. Repayment, in contrast, is considered nonpolitical by definition. This presumption leads to a rather warped understanding of policy choices. On the one hand, the literature ends up *depoliticizing* repayment, simply considering it "good economic policy" and therefore not really a choice in the political sense of the term. On the other, it tends to lump together all forms of default and brand them, often without qualification, as universally political.[13] The result is somewhat paradoxical: while repayment is seen as apolitical compliance with the rule that governments should always repay their debts, nonpayment is stigmatized as an irrational and explicitly political choice, precisely because it goes against the established norm of sovereign debt repayment. For many economists, politics therefore comes in through the back door—only in the event of noncompliance—as something to be avoided. The fact that the norm of repayment is itself a pre-established political fact is conveniently overlooked. As Odette Lienau writes in *Rethinking Sovereign Debt*, "one of the most puzzling elements of the conventional narrative is the notion that the sovereign debt regime's repayment rule could be apolitical."[14] Indeed, it is hard to imagine how anything involving the word "sovereign" could be considered apolitical to begin with.

Moreover, while the decision to repay is necessarily always a political act with important redistributive implications, not all defaults are necessarily the result of the same political calculations. Often a government may simply be unable to service a debt in time or in full, even if it is politically committed to doing so. By depoliticizing repayment and universally politicizing all forms of default, much of the literature ends up collapsing the crucial distinction between ability and willingness to pay. Insofar as the distinction is still recognized, the former is often brushed away as irrelevant—all defaults are presumed to be a result of the lack of willingness to pay.[15] Ability to pay, by contrast, is often made out to be unimportant, since total national wealth will always be greater than the amount of outstanding obligations, meaning that a government could theoretically cut its discretionary spending to zero and sell off all its state assets in order to live up to its financial commitments.[16] In this line of reasoning, whether or not the debt is repaid is really just a question of how far a government is willing to go in slashing its expenditures and privatizing state property. At the extreme, this has led some economists to float the notion that there are no fiscal limits to repayment at all: "Greece, for instance, could theoretically sell the Parthenon or some of its sovereign territory."[17]

The distinction between a country's ability and its willingness to pay is, of course, a unique and crucial aspect of sovereign debt. While a country's ability to pay can largely be defined in economic terms of illiquidity and insolvency, its willingness to pay is indeed an inherently political question. A government may, for instance, be unwilling to push through painful austerity measures and structural reforms, preferring instead to renege on its foreign obligations.[18] Still, despite the repeated insistence that default is always the result of a political unwillingness to pay, there is overwhelming empirical evidence for the fact that external economic conditions play a crucial role in shaping default sequences. Indeed, it is now widely accepted that defaults tend to occur in clusters during "hard times," often involving a strong external shock to the regional economy and a marked deterioration in the terms of trade, governments' fiscal positions, and overall external debt burdens.[19] These findings strongly suggest that ability to pay—constrained not so much by national wealth but rather by an acute shortage of foreign-exchange reserves from which external debts are to be serviced—may be an important determinant of default after all. Prior to the mid-2000s, most developing country debt contracts (between 93 and 100 percent, depending on the measures) were denominated in foreign currencies—the "original sin" problem we encountered earlier.[20] This meant that an exchange-rate shock, a decline in the terms of trade, a serious bout of capital flight, or a sustained run on a borrower's currency could easily deplete a country's foreign-exchange reserves and lead to the failure of an otherwise compliant borrower to meet its contractual obligations in full and on time—which is precisely what happened in previous international debt crises like those of the 1930s and 1980s, confirming the observation that insufficient foreign-exchange reserves may well play a crucial part in circumscribing a government's ability to pay.[21]

Despite these well-known facts, the recognition of the size of currency reserves as a measure of liquidity, and of foreign-exchange depletion as an immediate constraint on the ability to pay, remains remarkably absent from much of the economics literature.[22] Insofar as ability to pay is discussed at all, economists focus almost entirely on national wealth as a measure of solvency. While it may be true that national wealth will, on paper, always tend to be greater than a country's total outstanding debt, making it difficult to objectively determine the long-term solvency of a sovereign borrower, such theoretical squabbles over the abstract notion of government solvency are ultimately beside the point. What matters in an acute fiscal crisis—like Greece's in 2010–2012 and again in 2015—is the government's ability to honor the obligations falling due tomorrow; not its ability to service a long-term debt five, ten, or twenty years from now, after the meager proceeds from the privatization of the Parthenon have finally been checked in. In many cases, the immediate factor inhibiting repayment is not unwillingness to pay, nor the insufficiency of national wealth, but simply the lack of available liquid resources.

## TOWARD A POLITICAL TYPOLOGY OF DEFAULT

This brings us to the final point, which is that a disorderly default arising from the inability to pay in the short term—due to a lack of foreign exchange, for example—is something very distinct from an outright denial of liability over a long-term government debt. Moreover, this qualitative difference has crucial political implications. As it turns out, much of the economics literature has not only depoliticized the borrowing country, the structure of international lending, the decision to repay, and the determinants of default; but by defining default in purely technical terms it has also ended up depoliticizing the concept of default itself.[23] What is needed, therefore, is an alternative typology of default that recognizes the different forms that nonpayment can take in practice, and that is capable of accounting for the political characteristics of each. So far, the past chapters have followed the literature in using default as a homogeneous catch-all term referring to the failure or refusal of a sovereign borrower to live up to its contractual obligations and repay its debts in full and on time. This standard definition, widely used in the sovereign debt literature, is due to the credit rating agency Standard & Poor's, which considers a country to be in default whenever it fails to make an interest or principal payment within the stipulated grace period following the contractually specified due date, *or* if its debts are ultimately repaid on terms less favorable than those specified in the original loan contract.[24] While it may be easy to operationalize and quantify, the trouble with this technical definition is that it is far too broad. By lumping all types of default together into a single overarching category, it ends up stretching the concept beyond its analytical usefulness, representing what political scientist Giovanni Sartori—who coined the methodological term "conceptual stretching"—might have referred to as "a deliberate attempt to make our conceptualizations value free."[25]

In the real world, defaults occur in many forms and guises. While few scholars make an explicit distinction between the different types of default, a small but growing body of literature has begun to recognize the underlying controversy over how sovereign default is to be defined in practice.[26] What especially concerns us in this book is the relative decline in the incidence of *unilateral*

TABLE 2.1.
A political typology of default

| Types of default | Delay of payments | Debt reduction |
| --- | --- | --- |
| Multilateral | Rescheduling | Restructuring |
| Unilateral | Moratorium | Repudiation |

*default* in the postwar era. Unilateral default can be understood as a form of nonpayment whereby a debtor singlehandedly imposes losses on its creditors. It can in turn be divided into two subtypes, taking the form of a *debt moratorium* (a temporary suspension of payments) or of a *debt repudiation* (a wholesale rejection of liability).[27] Historically, outright repudiations have been extremely rare, only occurring in the wake of destructive wars (as in the wake of World War I) or following the revolutionary overthrow of established regimes (like Mexico in 1914, Russia in 1918, China in 1949, and Cuba in 1960). Moratoriums, by contrast, once used to be relatively common, especially in times of crisis. The main question this book seeks to address is why this particular type of unilateral default—the moratorium—has become so rare in recent decades. As we will see, part of the answer lies in the fact that it has been replaced with another type of default, what we could call "negotiated" or "multilateral" default. Like unilateral defaults, these can be further divided into two subtypes: a *debt rescheduling* (a negotiated delay of payments) or a *debt restructuring* (a negotiated write-down of part of the debt).

Tables 2.1 and 2.2 outline and summarize this alternative typology of sovereign default, which breaks down and *repoliticizes* the concept by identifying four specific subtypes, organized along two different axes.[28] The distinctions between the different forms are heuristic but real: even if there exists a considerable grey zone between unilateral and negotiated types of action, with different gradations of coercion blurring the line between "voluntary" and "nonvoluntary" agreements, important conceptual gains are to be made by breaking down the literature's broad and technical definition of default into these four "ideal types"—as long as we keep in mind that even these conceptual distinctions can never be fully reflective of the immense heterogeneity of real-life default situations.

One thing that should be emphasized from the start is that default is never simply a black-and-white proposition. As we will see in the case studies later in this book, the outcomes of the negotiated debt restructurings in Mexico and Greece, for instance, were relatively lenient on the creditors, while the negotiated restructuring in Argentina was much more coercive. Nevertheless, the fact that there continues to be variation *within* these different "ideal types" of default

TABLE 2.2.
Definitions of the different types of default

| Types | Definitions |
|---|---|
| Rescheduling | A debt rescheduling is a negotiated agreement between a debtor and its creditors to delay payments on (part of) the outstanding obligations by extending maturities, interest payments, or amortization schedules on existing contracts with a view to repaying the principal in full at a later date. Reschedulings are agreed to by creditors primarily to bridge periods of illiquidity and do not involve any reduction in the face value of the debt. |
| Restructuring | A debt restructuring is a negotiated agreement between a debtor and its creditors to cancel (part of) the outstanding obligations by writing down or "forgiving" them with a view to securing full repayment on the remaining debt at a later date. Restructurings are pursued primarily to deal with insolvency in an orderly fashion and can take place through a reduction in the face value or a lowering of the contractually agreed interest rate. They are also referred to as "haircuts," "write-downs," "debt relief," or "orderly defaults." |
| Moratorium | A debt moratorium is a unilateral suspension of payments by the debtor on (part of) the contractually specified interest and/or principal payments with a view to resuming debt service at a later date. As such, moratoriums involve an attempt by the debtor (either explicitly declared or implicitly enacted) to bridge a period of illiquidity or fiscal distress. Moratoriums do not involve a formal denial of liability nor any reduction in the face value of the debt. |
| Repudiation | A debt repudiation is a unilateral refusal by the debtor to recognize the binding nature of (part of) its obligations with a view to never repaying them. As such, repudiations involve a formal declaration, publicly announced by an authorized official, in which the government explicitly denies liability over (part of) the sovereign's obligations, regardless of its capacity to honor these obligations or the creditors' willingness to accept the government's rejection of liability. |

does not take away the fact that there are important qualitative differences *between* them—qualitative differences that in turn have an important political dimension. Most sensible observers would agree, for instance, that the Bolsheviks' debt repudiation of 1918 was something qualitatively distinct from the Mexican Brady deal following the crisis of the 1980s, or the Greek debt restructuring of

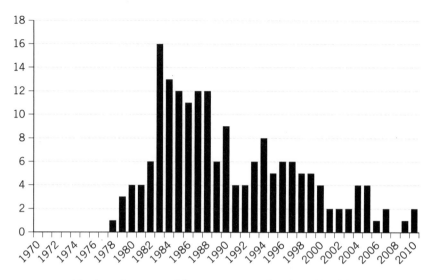

FIGURE 2.1. Number of sovereign debt restructurings (bonds and bank loans), 1970–2010. *Source*: Das, Papaioannou, and Trebesch (2011).

2012. What this alternative political typology does, therefore, is to remind us that sovereign default in the broad sense of the term is not always necessarily an aggressive or confrontational act imposed by a recalcitrant sovereign borrower on its poor and hapless lenders. As we already saw in the introduction, the unilateral payment suspensions that were once prevalent in the pre- and interwar period, and which were highly damaging to creditors' interests, have become extremely rare in recent decades. Often, sovereign default (in the broad sense of the term) will now tend to take the form of an orderly multilateral debt restructuring—although even those are now on the decline (see figure 2.1).

While nominally "negotiated" debt restructurings have, in some cases, turned out to be highly coercive and relatively advantageous to the debtor, the case studies in this book will demonstrate that they are often—though not always—pursued and designed at the initiative of the creditors themselves, with their own self-interest firmly in mind.[29] This observation leaves unilateral default strategies as the only types of nonpayment that seek to unambiguously prioritize the debtor's interests over those of its creditors, with the former deliberately shifting the costs of adjustment onto the latter. Even if real-life default situations are generally not as binary as this, and even though policy outcomes continue to display great diversity in practice, the conceptual differentiation matters. After all, only a government that refuses to honor its debts even if it is financially capable of doing so can be said to be "sufficiently powerful to translate resentment into effective resistance."[30] By contrast, in a world where governments keep honoring their debts even when they are widely considered financially incapable of doing so, that power may have already been so thoroughly eroded as to undermine the very basis of sovereign authority on which the prevailing understanding of democratic politics continues to rest. It is to this tension between sovereign authority and creditor power that we must turn next.

# THREE

## The Structural Power of Finance

We have now established that the question of power lies at the heart of the sovereign debt puzzle—and how could it be otherwise? Denoting supreme authority over a given polity, the very notion of sovereignty is inexorably tied up with the exercise of power. Europe's recent encounter with financial markets offers some useful insights in this respect, shedding fresh light on the dramatic political consequences that can ensue when the supreme authority of the state comes into direct conflict with the power of its creditors. During the darkest hours of the European sovereign debt crisis in late 2011, it even became somewhat of a fashion among financial commentators to highlight the political implications of these increasingly acute tensions. When democratically elected leaders in Greece and Italy were toppled and replaced by unelected technocrats amidst a loss of investor confidence and rising risk spreads on their government bonds, the *New York Times* wrote that "the power of financial markets has upended traditional democratic processes."[1] A later piece in the same paper noted that "the bond market has emerged as a mighty protagonist in Europe's economic crisis, representing a seminal shift in power from politicians to investors and a relatively obscure cohort of bankers."[2]

When the crisis intensified, some spoke of the return of the dreaded "bond vigilantes" that had stalked developing countries in the 1990s. Others complained that democracy itself was under attack by an algorithmically enhanced army of private speculators. Martin Wolf, arguably the world's leading financial commentator, noted that "in a big crisis, creditors rule,"[3] while investment banker Roger Altman penned an opinion piece for the *Financial Times* in which he dramatically declared that "financial markets [are] acting like a global supra-government":

> They oust entrenched regimes where normal political processes could not do so. They force austerity, banking bailouts and other major policy changes. Their influence dwarfs multilateral institutions such as the International Monetary Fund. Indeed, leaving aside unusable nuclear weapons, they have become the most powerful force on earth.[4]

Notwithstanding some of the inevitable journalistic hyperbole of the moment, the shared premise behind these observations—coming not from the far-left, as one might expect, but from within the financial establishment itself—appears to hint at an important shift in the international balance of power. If it is even remotely true that "creditors rule" in times of crisis, and that finance itself has been acting as a sort of "global supra-government" keeping democratically elected policymakers in check, the presumed enforcement problem at the heart of the sovereign debt puzzle suddenly begins to dissolve. As long as creditors are capable of limiting the sovereign authority of borrowing governments by imposing structural constraints on their policy autonomy and fiscal room for maneuver, the risk of noncompliance is greatly reduced. The key questions then become: What are the precise mechanisms through which finance exerts its power? Under what conditions are these mechanisms likely to be effective, and under what conditions are they likely to break down? How have these dynamics been impacted by the globalization and financialization of the capitalist economy in recent decades? And what, if anything, can still be done to counteract the power of finance from below?

## BUSINESS POWER AND THE MODERN STATE

These questions clearly do not arise in a theoretical vacuum. Political scientists and sociologists have long debated the role of corporate influence on political decision-making in capitalist democracies, and the study of financial power has a long-standing and distinguished pedigree in the Marxist literature in particular.[5] The main bones of contention in these debates have remained fairly constant over the years: Who really rules in a capitalist society? What is the nature of the modern state? And how do the economically powerful exert their influence over the political process? While there is unfortunately no space here to discuss the origins of this literature among the classical political economists and their critics, the publication of C. W. Mills's landmark study, *The Power Elite*, in 1956 may provide a useful starting point for our discussion. At a time when open criticism of capitalist democracy was considered especially circumspect in U.S. academic circles, Mills's radical indictment of the fundamentally undemocratic nature of the American political system clearly struck a nerve. "Not wishing to be disturbed over moral issues of the political economy," the Columbia University sociologist lamented, "Americans cling to the notion that the government is a sort of automatic machine, regulated by the balancing of competing interests." Aiming to disprove this received wisdom, Mills set out to show how political power is in fact concentrated among a small and interconnected "power elite" of well-connected businessmen, bankers, army chiefs, and party leaders, who together keep the levers of government tightly in their grip.[6]

The argument, potent and provocative as it was, immediately forced mainstream political science scholarship onto the defensive. Several years later, in

1961, Robert A. Dahl published his landmark study, *Who Governs?*, which he formulated as an explicit rebuttal to Mills and his followers.[7] In his in-depth case study of municipal politics in New Haven, Dahl argued that power elite theorists crucially ignored conflicts of interest *among elites*, rendering the entire concept of a dominant class problematic to begin with. Instead, Dahl found that different actors and groups pursued their own sectional interests, vying for political influence not only against other groups like trade unions or civil society organizations, but also among themselves. Coining the term "polyarchy," or the rule of the many, he thus portrayed the political institutions of capitalist democracy as a relatively balanced multipolar system in which contending interest groups compete for specific policy decisions and state power more generally, allowing no single group to ever become dominant over the others. For Dahl, there were "a number of loci for arriving at political decisions," meaning that "businessmen, trade unions, politicians, consumers, farmers, voters and many other aggregates all have an impact on policy outcomes."[8] The implicit value statement behind this argument was clear: while the ideal of a thoroughly democratic polity as envisioned by Mills and others might be fundamentally unattainable, polyarchy contains within its institutional design a sufficient set of checks and balances to guarantee at least an acceptable degree of democratic responsiveness. Americans, in other words, should rest assured: Mills and his followers had wildly overestimated the power wielded by elites—there would be no need for any radical changes to counter corporate control over political decision-making.

Dahl's pluralist model went on to become the dominant paradigm in Anglo-American political science. It took several years for critics to develop a convincing retort to his arguments, but when they did, the response made waves in social science departments around the English-speaking world. In 1969, the British political sociologist Ralph Miliband published *The State in Capitalist Society*, which he purposefully formulated as a Marxist retort to pluralism. Echoing the elite theory of C. W. Mills, Miliband set out to disprove Dahl's "plural elites" hypothesis by identifying, through careful empirical investigation, the predominance of corporate elites—united through their shared ideological, educational, and professional backgrounds—at the commanding heights of the political system. Far from being populated by the "many," as proponents of polyarchy had long argued, Miliband carefully showed how state institutions were in fact dominated by a small cabal of wealthy businessmen. He thus identified the existence of a distinct ruling class that "owns and controls the means of production and . . . is able, by virtue of the economic power thus conferred upon it, to use the state as its instrument for the domination of society."[9] As his key indicator of business power, Miliband pointed towards the extent to which members of the capitalist class controlled "interlocking positions in the governmental, administrative, coercive, and ideological apparatuses."[10] This observation in turn led Miliband and his "instrumentalist" followers to adopt a particular interest in—and a narrow focus on—the social composition of the administrative elite. Since Miliband considered power to be located *within* the state, the question of who controlled its various branches logically became the main subject of inquiry. That in turn justified an empiricist focus on the "colonization" of state institutions by members of the business establishment.

After an extended period of relative scholarly forgetfulness, Miliband's propositions have recently resurfaced with the emergence of new empirical evidence in their favor. In a breakthrough statistical study, Martin Gilens of Princeton University and Benjamin Page of Northwestern University now find that "economic elites and organized groups representing business interests have substantial independent impacts on U.S. government policy, while average citizens and mass-based interest groups have little or no independent influence."[11] The authors, whose research builds on multivariate analysis of 1,779 policy issues between 1982 and 2002, note that their findings "provide substantial support for theories of Economic Elite Domination and for theories of Biased Pluralism." Citing Miliband and the instrumental Marxists as early proponents of their argument, Gilens and Page conclude that the United States' political system—far from being a polyarchy, as neopluralists continue to claim—in fact constitutes an *oligarchy*: the rule of the few.

Miliband's instrumental approach to business power was never without its left-wing detractors, however. No sooner his book had been published, than a critique appeared in the *New Left Review* penned by the Greek political theorist Nicos Poulantzas, who took Miliband to task for ceding far too much methodological ground to the pluralists. For Poulantzas, the narrow focus on elites at the expense of a more theoretical investigation of class structures and the specifically capitalist nature of the state risked reproducing two unspoken assumptions in the pluralist literature, namely the idea that power is located *within* the state apparatus, and the notion that "social classes or 'groups' are in some way reducible to inter-personal relations."[12] Poulantzas praised Miliband for demystifying the myth of polyarchy, but at the same time accused him of confusing cause and effect: the direct participation of business leaders and wealthy elites in the state's administrative apparatus, he argued, is not the *reason* for their power but its logical *outcome*.[13] Businessmen are not powerful because they are in government; they are in government because they are powerful. Poulantzas, who came out of the Althusserian school of structural Marxism, saw the relationship between the dominant class and the state apparatus as an *objective relation* that cannot be reduced to interpersonal connections, the direct participation of business elites in politics, or "the *motivations of conduct* of individual actors."[14] Pointing to all the socialist parties that had conquered state power and had nevertheless failed to transform the dominant relations of production, he wanted to show that "far more must be at work in the operations of the state and social policy than mere occupation of the state apparatus by the personnel of a particular class."[15]

The central concept Poulantzas developed in this context was that of the state's "relative autonomy" from the capitalist class, which holds that the political system must retain a certain distance from the interests of particular capitalists in order to be able to reproduce the ideal conditions for the process of private capital accumulation and thus serve the collective interests of the capitalist class as a whole. Abandoning the somewhat deterministic overtones of his earlier work, Poulantzas eventually came to think of the state as "a relationship of forces, or more precisely the material condensation of such a relationship among classes and class fractions, such as this is expressed within the state in a necessarily specific form."[16] Considering specific state-forms to be historically contingent on the outcome of concrete conflicts between opposing social forces, Poulantzas argued that the state was in fact shot through with internal divisions, as various classes and class fractions engage in protracted power struggles within and between its different branches, thus making it impossible for any one group to gain complete control over the political apparatus. Workers' mobilizations and social movements therefore take on much greater importance in Poulantzas' later work, as the state becomes a site of struggle where power is continuously contested from below.

It was in this intellectual environment of burgeoning Marxist scholarship on business power and the capitalist state that Charles Lindblom, one of the founding scholars of the pluralist tradition in political science, slowly became aware of the limitations of his own approach. In his classic 1977 book, *Politics and Markets*, Lindblom famously distanced himself from his friend Robert Dahl by contending that business in fact occupies a "privileged position" in polyarchy.[17] Identifying a key puzzle left unresolved in the pluralist literature, Lindblom starts out by asking why, if no social group can truly be considered dominant in polyarchy, not a single democratic polity has ever voted to abolish private property and socialize its means of production (Allende's Chile might be considered an exception, although it paid dearly for this). Noting that a move towards democratic socialism might be favored by a majority of voters, who are workers, but that it would spell catastrophe for private business, Lindblom poses a simple but subversive question: could it actually be the businessmen, not the voters, who really call the shots in the advanced capitalist democracies? "We must at this point consider the possibility," he writes, "that existing polyarchies are not very democratic, that political debate in them is not very free, and that policymaking in them is actually in the hands of persons who want to protect the privileges of business and property."[18] This claim proved so controversial that it moved Mobil Corporation to take to the *New York Times*' op-ed pages to denounce Lindblom's book in public—thereby inadvertently propelling it onto the paper's Editors' Choice list.

In Lindblom's conceptualization of politics under polyarchy, the market becomes more or less like a prison, effectively "locking in" the political process by structurally constraining the amount of things policymakers can do without wreaking havoc on economic performance and thereby undermining their own approval ratings.[19] The most remarkable thing, Lindblom argued, is that this disciplinary mechanism largely works automatically, through the collective decisions of market actors to invest or not to invest. "Punishment is not dependent on conspiracy or intention to punish," he wrote. "Simply minding one's own business is the formula for an extraordinary system for repressing change."[20] Political leaders thus find themselves faced with the imperative to maintain a healthy investment climate under all conditions, and to immediately restore business confidence whenever key indicators start trending downwards. As sociologist Fred Block later summarized in a dual critique of both Miliband and Poulantzas, "it appears that even when the business community is not able to influence the state in the traditional ways," through lobbying, staffing government positions, drawing on personal contacts, and doling out campaign contributions, "policy outcomes [still] tend to be favorable to business concerns." This, he observed, would suggest that "there are 'structural' factors that operate at a different level from the exercise of personal influence." In other words, "even with a change in government personnel, the power of business would continue to have a large influence over governmental policies."[21]

Business, scholars like Block and Lindblom noted, is therefore fundamentally different from any other interest group. As the primary source of investment for the productive economy, wealth-holders and businessmen fulfill a crucial public function in capitalist society: they allocate scarce economic resources and thereby shape material outcomes. If the government were to pursue policies that run counter to business interests, the latter could simply withhold further investment or even stage an outright "capital strike," negatively impacting overall economic performance and employment opportunities. Since democratically elected leaders generally depend on a healthy economic environment for their re-election, they feel compelled to induce businesses to "keep firing on all cylinders" by continually reproducing the ideal conditions for private investment.[22] Crucially, this disciplinary market mechanism appears to be operative irrespective of the ideology or partisan affiliations of those in power; it is the mere threat of divestment that forces government officials to "anticipate and defer" to business interests. It was this insight that led Lindblom to argue that "businessmen cannot be left knocking at the doors of the political systems, they must be invited in."[23]

## THE STRUCTURAL DEPENDENCE OF THE STATE

These debates—between pluralists and elite theorists on the one hand, and between instrumental Marxists and structural Marxists on the other, with Lindblom and Block squeezed somewhere in the middle—dominated the academic study of business power and the capitalist state for much of the past half-century.

Yet, for all their obvious differences, there was one remarkable similarity between them that somehow managed to escape many thoughtful commentators at the time: none of these leading social and political thinkers ever really seemed to ask the crucial question how the modern state is *financed*. Yet it is precisely here, in the somewhat arcane realm of public finance, that the connections between politics and economics, and the intricacies of the state-finance relation in particular, most explicitly come to the fore.[24] Not coincidentally, it is also here that our discussion of business power and the state finally begins to converge with the question of government borrowing and sovereign debt. After all, what could be more foundational to business power and state-finance relations than the fact that public spending—which forms the bedrock of all state activity—can only be sustained in the long run by collecting taxes and borrowing funds from private hands?

A genuine theory of business power and the modern state must therefore start with an appreciation of the centrality of taxation and the public debt to the reproduction of capitalist power relations. A century ago, the Austrian sociologist Rudolf Goldscheid already remarked that the government budget can be considered "the skeleton of the state stripped of all misleading ideologies." His contemporary interlocutor Joseph Schumpeter concurred, famously noting that "the public finances are one of the best starting points for an investigation of society, especially though not exclusively of its political life."[25] One of the few postwar state theorists to pick up on this proposition was the American sociologist James O'Connor, who in his influential work on *The Fiscal Crisis of the State* observed an inherent contradiction between the state's two main functions: *legitimation* on the one hand, and *accumulation* on the other. If the state fails to establish legitimacy in the eyes of its people, O'Connor observed, it will end up undermining its basis of popular support; if it fails to recreate the conditions for capital accumulation, by contrast, it "risks drying up the source of its own power, the economy's surplus production capacity and the taxes from this surplus (and other forms of capital)."[26] State administrators therefore find themselves in a bind: on the one hand, the state's need to establish legitimacy compels them to respond to ever-growing social demands for new spending; on the other, its need to keep expanding the economy prevents them from raising taxes on business and the wealthy sufficiently high to finance this increase in public expenditure. The result of this contradiction, in O'Connor's view at the time, would be a fiscal crisis of the state, resulting in a stagnation of capital accumulation on the one hand and a deepening legitimation crisis on the other.

While the predicted fiscal crisis did not immediately materialize in the 1970s, mostly because O'Connor appeared to have underestimated the extent to which the state could still borrow its way out of trouble, his general theoretical framework did identify a number of elements in the state-finance relation that are of great relevance to the study of financial power and sovereign debt today. One of the most important relates to the sources of state revenue. O'Connor was one of the few Marxist state theorists to appreciate the significance of the seemingly banal observation that—barring inflationary money creation or the outright looting of colonial territories—the modern capitalist state can only sustainably finance itself in three ways: through the operation of state-owned enterprises, through taxation, and through public borrowing. All three of these sources of financing, O'Connor noted, directly position the state within the private process of capital accumulation.

As a result, to reproduce itself—in other words, to maintain its basic administrative functions and its various budget outlays over time—the state is compelled to continuously engage with the capitalist economy by producing its own surpluses through the operation of state-owned enterprises, by claiming part of the existing surplus through the levying of taxes on profits and wages, and by convincing private investors and wealthy citizens to recycle their untaxed surpluses by lending them back to the state against a pledge of future tax revenues. Since the latter source of financing—public borrowing—did not play a very important role at the time, O'Connor paid relatively little attention to it. Still, he rightly highlighted the contradictory nature of the public debt, which at once enables and constrains state authority; endowing the treasury with spending power that it would not otherwise have had, while at the same time rendering the state dependent on a narrow subgroup of wealthy financiers who command sufficient capital to advance the requisite funds.[27] Observing the same paradox, Ernest Mandel referred to the public debt as "the golden chains of capital," tying the state to big business and vice versa. As he explained:

> No government could last more than a month without having to knock on the door of the banks in order to pay its current expenses. If the banks were to refuse, the government would go bankrupt. The origins of this phenomenon are twofold. Taxes don't enter the coffers every day; receipts are concentrated in one period of the year while expenses are continuous. That is how the short-term public debt arises. . . . But there is another problem—a much more important one. All modern capitalist states spend more than they receive. That is the long-term public debt for which banks and other financial establishments can most easily advance money, at heavy interest. Therein lies a direct and immediate connection, a daily link, between the state and big business.[28]

The state, then, is structurally dependent on the provision of private credit to be able to reproduce itself and carry out its social, political, and economic functions over time. The effect of this dependence is to constrain the state's relative autonomy from finance and impose certain limits on the room for maneuver available to government.[29] Of course, this is not to say that the state has no autonomy at all, or that policymakers will always be subservient to the interests of private financiers. Rather, the connection between finance and the state should be conceptualized as a symbiotic and at times conflictive relationship characterized by mutual interdependence, in which neither side can do without the other.[30] The state may rely on finance for credit, but finance also relies on the state for a host of public goods, ranging from market-making and monetary stability to contract enforcement and the security of private property. That being said, however, the fact that the state cannot properly function without access to credit does mean that state administrators will be extra careful to keep their creditors happy and not to scare away potential investors, as this would cause borrowing costs to rise and force the government to cut back spending or raise taxes to reassure lenders that the budget is under control. It is the state's structural dependence on credit—and, indeed, the wider economy's structural dependence on credit—that ultimately endows finance with the unique form of power it wields under capitalism: *structural power*.

The concept of structural power, which will be central to the theoretical approach developed in this chapter and the next, can be contrasted to the instrumental power emphasized by both pluralists and elite theorists, who tend to conceive of political influence narrowly in Weberian or relational terms, as actor A intentionally mobilizing its resources in order to force actor B to do something it would not otherwise have done.[31] Lobbying, campaign financing, and the direct occupation of government offices can all be considered indicators of instrumental power in that respect. Structural power, by contrast, does not necessarily work through overt forms of coercion or established political channels, and may be operative even when its bearer cannot be seen to exert direct influence or control over the political process. The emphasis therefore shifts from the resources of specific actors and their individual behavior vis-à-vis one another within the political sphere, toward the broader social relations and economic systems in which these actors are embedded. Crucially, structural power theorists point out that different positions within a given social order do not endow equal privileges; rather, they distribute *asymmetric privileges*, in the form of structural inequalities and relations of dependence as a result of which some actors or social groups gain a systematic advantage over others.[32]

At its most elementary level, we can define structural power as the capacity to withhold something upon which another depends. This capacity bequeaths its bearer with a peculiar type of power: the power to punish by *not doing*; the power to discipline through refusal—the power, in other words, to shape the opportunity structure within which subjected actors and groups have to operate simply by providing or refusing to provide something that is essential to their performance, well-being, or survival. The British political economist Susan Strange once explained that structural power enables its bearer "to change the range of choices open to others, without apparently putting pressure directly on them to take one decision or to make one choice rather than others."[33] By subtly incentivizing a particular course of action and raising the costs of deviant forms of behavior sufficiently high, it can alter the cost/benefit calculation of subjected actors to the point where acting in their perceived self-interest becomes all but inconceivable. Structural power, then, can be said to impose "a bias on the freedom of choice."[34] Conceived in these terms, the outsize influence that finance wields over the political process is ultimately a product of its structural position in the capitalist economy and its systemic role as a lynchpin in the process of private capital accumulation.[35] The source of its power resides in the capacity to withhold something on which everyone else—states, firms, and households alike—depends for their reproduction, namely credit. As the principal creator of credit-money in a system that has grown increasingly dependent on it, finance acquires the capacity to make or break the fortunes of its borrowers simply by refusing to loan further funds in the event of noncompliance. It is precisely this capacity that distinguishes finance from other forms of capital, and that today places it at the very pinnacle of capitalist power relations.

Yet the structural power of finance is never simply a one-way street. Since the debtor-creditor relation is always characterized by a complex dynamic of mutual interdependence, debtors also wield a discrete form of counterpower over their creditors, which similarly hinges on a type of refusal: namely the threat to withhold further debt repayments. Just as states, firms, and households depend on private credit to reproduce themselves, so their private creditors depend on a steady stream of interest payments to thrive in a competitive marketplace.[36] If a big borrower or a large-enough group of small borrowers suddenly stop servicing their outstanding financial obligations, private creditors could be in serious trouble. As J. P. Getty's famous adage has it, "If you owe the bank $100 that's your problem. If you owe the bank $100 million, that's the bank's problem." Rather than presuming finance to be almighty, we should therefore understand the debtor-creditor relation as an unequal two-way power relation, marked by ongoing distributional conflict over payment versus nonpayment. While fundamentally asymmetric at heart, this power relation is nevertheless characterized by a degree of mutual interdependence, with either side relying on the other to reproduce its respective structural position within the given social order. During times of calm, these inherent distributional conflicts and power asymmetries may not always be immediately apparent, but in times of crisis, when resources become scarcer and internal tensions and contradictions are heightened, the two sides are bound to intensify their struggle over their respective shares of the social wealth and the distribution of adjustment costs. It is this inherently contentious nature of sovereign debt repayment that makes international debt crises such fascinating case studies for those interested in unearthing the underlying power relations between debtors and creditors, or between the state and its financiers.

The task of structural power analysis, then, is not to assume a predetermined outcome in these unfolding distributional struggles, but rather to uncover who has the upper hand in any given situation. The variegated capacities and complex power dynamics at the heart of the debtor-creditor and state-finance relation are never predetermined or written in stone; they will depend on a host of conditions and are ultimately a reflection of the prevailing balance of forces in

a particular place and time—all of which renders the power of finance historically contingent on the outcome of a continually unfolding process of social and
political struggle. Just as the position of the financial sector has evolved over the
course of capitalist development, and just as it has evolved in different ways in
different countries and contexts, so the structural power that flows from that
position has fluctuated over time and continues to vary between places. It is in
this light that we should consider the structural changes in the global political economy over the past four decades—changes that have had far-reaching
implications for the balance of power within capitalist democracies, and for
the nature of the relationship between territorially delimited nation-states and
their internationally mobile private creditors.

## THE FINANCIALIZATION OF THE WORLD ECONOMY

Ever since the 1970s, the interconnected processes of globalization and financialization have profoundly transformed the position of financial interests—
and of big banks in particular—in the advanced capitalist democracies. The
first thing to note in this respect is the transformative effect of international
capital mobility on state autonomy and financial market discipline. Starting
with the emergence of the Eurodollar markets in the 1960s and the breakdown
of the Bretton Woods regime in the early 1970s, and culminating in the widespread abolition of capital controls and the worldwide wave of financial deregulation in the 1980s and 1990s, recent decades have witnessed a vast increase in
cross-border capital flows—from $500 billion in 1980 to nearly $12 trillion on
the eve of the global financial crisis in 2007.[37] It is widely argued that the result
of this international capital mobility has been to endow private investors with
a credible exit threat against national governments. In this line of analysis, policies considered to be unfriendly to business are now much easier to punish by
redirecting investment towards another jurisdiction; a situation that is said to
have greatly increased the competitive pressures on policymakers.[38] According
to the "capital mobility hypothesis" formulated at the height of the globalization debate in the mid-1990s, "the degree of international capital mobility systematically constrains state behavior by rewarding some actions and punishing
others," as a result of which "the nature of the choice set available to states . . .
becomes more constricted."[39] By transforming the incentive structure and reducing the ability of individual states to effectively regulate, control, or tax internationally mobile capital, globalization not only contributes to the gradual
erosion of fiscal autonomy; it also strengthens the hand of multinational corpo-
rations vis-à-vis domestic constituents.[40]

One scholar who took a particularly keen interest in the growing tensions
between globalized financial markets and territorially delimited nation-states
was Susan Strange. Such was Strange's concern with the role of private firms and

big banks in international affairs that she ended up playing a leading role in the creation of a new academic subdiscipline to study its causes and consequences. Credited as one of the co-founders of the field of International Political Economy (IPE), Strange is also remembered as one of the most vocal proponents of the structural power hypothesis. Crucially, she argued that, while states and firms once used to rely on more overt and more coercive forms of state power like gunboat diplomacy and outright imperialism, the globalization of finance has given increased prominence to more indirect and less visible forms of power. "In the competitive games now being played out in the world system between states and between economic enterprises," she argued, "it is increasingly structural power that counts far more than relational power."[41]

Crucially, Strange reserved a special place in her analytical scheme for the global financial structure, which she considered to be "*the* prime issue of international politics and economics."[42] After all, whoever controls the creation and allocation of credit now controls the purchasing power and policy options available to states, firms, and households around the globe. If credit "is literally the lifeblood of a developed economy," as Strange never tired of pointing out, then the financial sector effectively constitutes its beating heart, constantly pumping liquidity into the wider world economy. But despite the growing centrality of international credit to the functioning of the world economy, relatively few scholars seemed to explicitly establish the intimate connection between the immense power this endowed private financiers with, and the relative decline in the incidence of sovereign default since the 1980s.[43] Yet it is precisely here, in the resurrection of global finance and the gradual turn toward increased debtor discipline, that the skewed impact of globalization most clearly comes to the fore. It is the quest for international credit, Strange argued, that ultimately compels all states to "dance to the fast or slow rhythms of financial markets," causing even the most powerful governments to eventually "run up against the limits set by international finance."[44]

The globalization literature therefore hinted at two very important dimensions of the structural power of finance: the vast increase in international capital mobility and the growing centrality of international credit. More recently, however, scholars have come to question the adequacy of the stark state-market dichotomy that underpinned much of the globalization debate of the 1990s and early 2000s. In the wake of the global financial crisis, in particular, it has become increasingly difficult to speak of a "retreat of the state," as Strange and many other IPE scholars did at the time.[45] In fact, the record bank bailouts after the collapse of Lehman Brothers in 2008 have clearly demonstrated just how central the state really remains within today's globalized economy. Many scholars now argue that, far from being on the retreat, state action—and the hegemonic role of the United States in particular—has been foundational both to the transformations of the global financial architecture since 1973, and to the survival of the world financial system in the wake of 2008.[46] Others, like Saskia

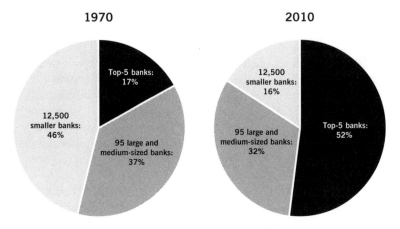

FIGURE 3.1. U.S. bank assets as a share of total industry assets, 1970 vs. 2010.
*Source*: Federal Reserve Bank of Dallas (2012).

Sassen, have long pointed out how these global transformations, far from lead-ing to the retreat of the nation-state, have actually transformed and empowered specific elements of the state apparatus, most notably the finance ministries and central banks, at the expense of others.[47]

Recognitions like these have gradually exposed the limits of the mainstream globalization discourse and in turn prompted a growing interest in the related concept of *financialization*, which its proponents argue allows for a more fine-grained understanding of the ultimate driving force and main beneficiary be-hind the global transformations of recent decades.[48]

Despite the lack of agreement on a precise definition, most scholars working in this area agree that financialization involves a vast increase in the influence of financial markets, financial institutions, financial elites, financial motives, and financial rationalities over economic policy and social and political outcomes.[49] The exact dynamics behind these developments are complex and multifaceted, but for our purposes here three key dimensions stand out. First, the finan-cialization of the world economy has gone hand in hand with a vast increase in the concentration of the financial sector and a spectacular centralization of international credit markets, with a growing share of loans made—and an increasing number of assets held—by a rapidly decreasing number of sys-temically important financial institutions (see figure 3.1). While there were 14,434 banks in the United States in 1980, roughly the same number as in 1934, this number had shrunk to 7,100 by 2009, or less than half. At the same time, the banking sector's contribution to overall corporate profits has radi-cally increased. In 1984, U.S. banks contributed 8.8 percent to total corporate output and 11.8 percent to total corporate profits; by 2011, their contribution

FIGURE 3.2. Concentration of U.S. banking system, 1933–2008. *Source*: Haldane (2010).

to corporate output had nearly doubled to 16.3 percent, while their share of corporate profits skyrocketed to 32.3 percent.[50] The size and concentration of the U.S. banking system, which had been relatively stable in the half-century between the 1930s and the 1980s, exploded as well, with the average size of U.S. banks relative to GDP increasing over threefold between 1990 and 2010 and the asset share of the three largest U.S. banks skyrocketing from 10 percent of total assets to 40 percent (figure 3.2).[51]

A very similar pattern has been underway internationally as well. Andrew Haldane of the Bank of England reports that the share of the world's five biggest banks in the total assets of the top-1,000 banks roughly doubled between 1998 and 2009.[52] The situation inside Europe is illustrative. Between 1997 and 2005 alone, the total number of monetary and financial institutions in the EU-25 declined from 4,228 to 2,683.[53] In terms of market concentration within nation-states, the average percentage of credit-sector assets controlled by the five largest banks for each country rose from 37.9 percent in 1980 to 57.1 percent in 1999.[54] The result of this growing market concentration has been to render most of the leading international banks at the heart of the global financial system "too big to fail" in the eyes of investors and policymakers, thus endowing these firms with a much more privileged position in economic policymaking—after all, their continued viability is now considered essential to the survival of the system as a whole. As Haldane puts it in his remarks to the Bank for International Settlements, "the too-big-to-fail problem has not just returned but flourished."[55] The UK is perhaps the most extreme example of this dynamic, with total banking assets shooting up from 50 percent of GDP to 550 percent of GDP over the past four decades, highlighting the thorough dependence of Britain's highly financialized economy on the City of London.[56]

The second aspect of financialization that deserves closer attention in this context is related to the first and concerns the growing importance of official-sector intervention in financial markets. Even if the dominant narrative in policymaking circles has been one of market liberalization and financial deregulation, the decades since the 1980s have in reality been characterized by a much more important role for state actors, central banks, and international financial institutions as market-makers and as lenders of last resort; a development that could be considered a direct consequence of the "too big to fail" problem described above. Far from hailing the retreat of the nation-state and the reign of free markets, then, the process of financialization seems to have involved the ongoing *restructuring* of the state apparatus and international organizations, with far-reaching implications for the distribution of power in the domestic and global political economy. David Harvey has referred to this development as the formation of a *state-finance nexus.*[57]

Even before the bank bailouts of 2008–2009 it had become clear that the "the state's role as lender of last resort, responsible for providing liquidity at short notice, [was] fully incorporated into the system."[58] As the "guardians of financialization," central banks in particular have seen their role transformed in recent decades.[59] Similarly, at the global level, the restructuring of the International Monetary Fund into a "fiscal disciplinarian" and a de facto lender of last resort for distressed peripheral borrowers has dramatically altered the global financial architecture and the structure of international lending to the advantage of private creditors. The Fund's aggressive interventions in the debt crises of the 1980s, 1990s, and 2010s, during which it provided massive international bailout loans under strict policy conditionality in order to prevent sovereign default (see figure 3.3), has served to insulate the balance sheets of the big commercial banks, which are now much better protected from the potential losses resulting from their own imprudent lending decisions. By the late 1990s, scholars like Jagdish Bhagwati and Robert Wade were already decrying the noxious role of a "Wall Street-Treasury-IMF complex" and its entrenchment of a strong pro-creditor bias in international crisis management.[60]

A third key aspect of financialization has been the growing state dependence on private credit, which has in turn further eroded the state's relative autonomy from finance and dramatically reconfigured domestic power relations inside the borrowing countries in favor of financial firms, financial elites, and financial officials. Reviving some of the insights from earlier work in Marxian state and crisis theory, Wolfgang Streeck has recently argued that the transformations of democratic capitalism over the past decades are ultimately a delayed manifestation of the fiscal crisis predicted by O'Connor in the early 1970s. At the heart of this development lies the rise of what Streeck calls the *debt state*, "or a state

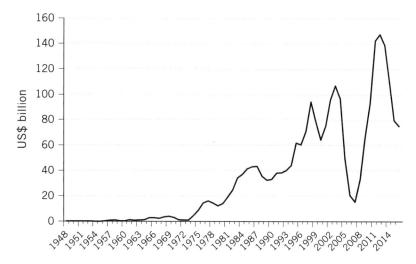

FIGURE 3.3. Total IMF credit and loans outstanding, 1948–2015. *Source*: International Monetary Fund (2017a).

which covers a large, possibly rising, part of its expenditure through borrowing rather than taxation," thus contributing to a growing "debt mountain that it has to finance with an ever greater share of its revenue."[61] Figure 3.4 shows how the weight of general government debt as a share of gross domestic product has indeed been rising steadily in the advanced capitalist countries since the 1970s, with a particularly rapid increase after the global financial crisis of 2008. Figure 3.5, meanwhile, shows how the developing world experienced a sharp increase in *external* indebtedness between the 1970s and the late-1990s, although these levels have declined significantly since 2000.

For Streeck, this transformation of the classical Schumpeterian "tax state" into a neoliberal "debt state" is not just a fiscal development; rather, it should be seen as "the rise of a new political formation with its own laws," whose defining feature is the emergence of private creditors as a second constituency alongside national citizens.[62] The state's growing dependence on credit since the 1970s increases the vulnerability of government officials to a withdrawal of further loans, which in turn implies a vast increase in creditor power.[63] Streeck even argues that "the emergence of finance capital as a second people ... marks a new stage in the relationship between capitalism and democracy, in which capital exercises its political influence not only indirectly (by investing or not investing in national economies) but also directly (by financing or not financing the state itself)." As a result, the debt state "must take care to gain and preserve its confidence, by conscientiously servicing the debt it owes them and making it appear credible

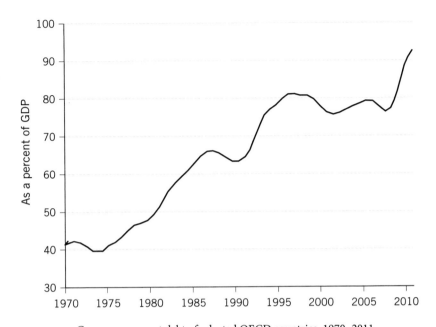

FIGURE 3.4. Gross government debt of selected OECD countries, 1970–2011.
*Source*: Streeck (2014); OECD Economic Outlook.
*Note*: Countries included in unweighted average: Austria, Belgium, Canada, France, Germany, Italy, Japan, Netherlands, Norway, Sweden, UK, USA.

FIGURE 3.5. External government debt of low- and middle-income countries, 1970–2015. *Source*: World Bank (2017).

that it can and will do so in the future as well."[64] Indeed, "the first priority of the international community of debt states is that all members, including the weakest, maintain the fullest possible servicing of their existing debt."[65]

At the same time, as a formal capitalist *democracy*, the "debt state" also retains an important legitimation function that it somehow needs to fulfill in a context of growing structural constraints on public spending, forcing officials to perform an increasingly precarious balancing act between maintaining the loyalty of their citizens while at the same time retaining the confidence of private investors. "Which of the two sides commands greater attention from a debt state's government," Streeck argues, "will depend on their relative strength. This in turn depends on how likely a threatened withdrawal of confidence or loyalty, respectively, appears to be, and on how much pain it would cause to the country and its government."[66] The conclusion is that a distressed sovereign borrower will only ever choose to renege on its financial obligations if the social costs of repayment have become unbearable and citizens threaten to withdraw their loyalty to the state. Only in the context of a destabilizing legitimation crisis and a citizens' revolt from below will the administrators of a contemporary "debt state" ever contemplate defying their private creditors by defaulting on their financial obligations.

# FOUR

## Three Enforcement Mechanisms

The insights derived from the theoretical discussion in the previous chapters allow us to begin piecing together a general framework for understanding the structural power of finance in sovereign debt crises. Briefly put, this power is a product of the financial sector's position as the principal creator of credit-money within the capitalist economy, and it revolves around its capacity to withhold the short-term credit lines on which all states—as well as firms and households—depend for their reproduction. Crucially, the structural power of private creditors has been greatly strengthened since the mid-1970s as a result of three interrelated developments: first, the globalization of finance and the financialization of the world economy, which have resulted in a much more concentrated financial sector and much more centralized international credit markets; second, the restructured and much more interventionist role for creditor states, central banks, and international financial institutions like the IMF; and third, the vast increase in the state's dependence on credit and the private lenders capable of providing it—as well as those domestic elites who can fulfill a bridging role to these foreign creditors. Taken together, these developments have not only raised the spillover costs of default and thereby tipped the balance of power between international creditors and sovereign borrowers decisively in favor of the former; they have also produced a major shift in the balance of power *within* the borrowing countries in favor of financial firms and wealthy elites with close ties to the international financial establishment.

However, we also noted that the power of finance is by no means absolute, and that its relative strength varies over time and between places. Unfortunately, it is precisely on this point that the original formulation of the structural power hypothesis—as formulated by scholars like Lindblom, Block, and Strange—generally fell short.[1] Culpepper notes how in recent years "theories of the structural power of business have been marginalized in the face of careful studies showing how often business organizations fail to get what they want."[2] Of course, the fact that business organizations do not always get their way does not mean that they therefore lack power; different business organizations may simply want different things, with some more successful than others at

---

Box 4.1. Conditions under which Enforcement Mechanisms Are Effective

1. **Market discipline** depends on:
   a. *The ability of private creditors to maintain a coherent creditors' cartel:* the cartel tends to be at its strongest when the debt is highly concentrated and creditor interests are structurally interlocked.
   b. *The debtor's dependence on the creditors' cartel:* this dependence tends to be at its greatest when the debtor does not have an outside option for external financing and when its financial and commercial self-sufficiency is low.
2. **Conditional lending** depends on:
   a. *The ability of official creditors to present a unified front:* official creditors tend to be most unified and determined to avoid default when the risk of contagion is high and the creditors' internal opposition to further emergency lending is low.
   b. *The debtor's dependence on the lender of last resort:* this dependence tends to be at its greatest when the debtor does not have an outside option for external financing and when its financial and commercial self-sufficiency is low (same as 1b).
3. **The bridging role** depends on:
   a. *The capacity of domestic elites to attract foreign credit:* this capacity tends to be high when elites' preferences are aligned with those of foreign creditors, and when the institutional capacity to carry out fiscally "responsible" policies is in place.
   b. *The ability of elites to retain control over financial policymaking:* this tends to be high when the domestic legitimation crisis can be contained and economic policymaking is effectively shielded from popular pressures.

---

obtaining their preferences. Nevertheless, it is now widely recognized that the early literature put far too much emphasis on the independent and automatic nature of market punishment, leaving it ill-equipped to account for variation in outcomes and causing it to suffer from deterministic overtones.[3] As a result, Helleiner observes with reference to Strange's work, "even the chief advocate of structural power analysis failed to grasp its full potential."[4] To salvage the important insights of the structural power hypothesis, what is needed today is a more dynamic theoretical framework and a more refined methodological approach that can explain why the structural power of finance varies over time and between places. As Benjamin Cohen has put it, the challenge for contemporary structural power theorists "would then be twofold: to identify the key conditions that determine, first, when [structural power] is or is not likely to be used . . . ; and second, when the use of power is or is not likely to be successful."[5]

---

BOX 4.2. CONDITIONS UNDER WHICH ENFORCEMENT MECHANISMS BREAK DOWN

1. **Market discipline** tends to break down when:
   a. *Private lenders fail to hold together a creditors' cartel:* the debt is highly dispersed, and the lending structure incentivizes freeriding by individual lenders;
      *Or when:*
   b. *The debtor no longer depends on the creditors' cartel:* the debtor has an outside option or is very self-sufficient in financial and commercial terms.
2. **Conditional lending** breaks down when:
   a. *Official creditors pull the plug on further financing:* more likely when the risk of contagion is low and domestic opposition to bailouts in creditor countries is high.
      *Or when:*
   b. *The debtor no longer depends on the lender of last resort:* the debtor has an outside option or is very self-sufficient in financial and commercial terms.
3. **The bridging role** breaks down when:
   a. *Domestic elites are no longer capable of attracting foreign credit:* creditors lose trust and cut the debtor loose, especially if there is an ideological misalignment and/or a failure to satisfy bailout conditions (this point is connected to point 2a).
      *Or when:*
   b. *Elites are ousted or forced to make concessions:* the state loses the loyalty of its citizens as they revolt against further austerity amidst a deep legitimation crisis.

**Central hypothesis:** a heavily indebted peripheral borrower will only pursue a unilateral payment suspension on its external obligations when *all three enforcement mechanisms have broken down* as a result of a combination of the conditions and/or countervailing mechanisms spelled out above.

---

Ever since the global financial crisis, a growing body of political economy scholarship has sought to do just that.[6] This book aims to make an original contribution to this (re-)emerging literature by proposing a two-pronged way forward: first, to shift the focus from the somewhat abstract notion of structural power itself, which remains a notoriously difficult concept to operationalize and measure in empirical research, toward the causal processes through which this power operates in practice; and second, to allow for the power of finance to be contested from below. In short, a theoretically and methodologically reflexive approach to structural power analysis should try to specify the *precise enforcement mechanisms* through which structural power is brought to bear on subjected actors, and to identify the *exact conditions* under which these mechanisms will tend to be effective, as well as the precise conditions or countervailing mechanisms under which they are likely to break down. With this dual objective in mind, the following section will introduce the three enforcement mechanisms of debtor compliance through which the structural power of finance is hypothesized to operate, specifying in each case the precise conditions and countervailing forces bearing on their overall strength and effectiveness. These are also summarized in boxes 4.1 and 4.2.

## THE MARKET DISCIPLINE IMPOSED BY THE CREDITORS' CARTEL

The first enforcement mechanism—*market discipline*—is a product of private creditors' capacity to inflict highly damaging spillover costs on a debtor's economy by withholding further credit and investment in the event of noncompliance. I use the term "market discipline" in a deliberately broad sense here, referring to any market-based form of pressure exerted on policymakers through the aggregate economic processes of buying and selling, investing and divesting, or lending and not-lending. As such, manifestations of market discipline on sovereign borrowers can include anything from international capital flight and the dumping of government bonds by foreign investors to the curtailment of commercial bank lending. The key point is that the market behavior of private investors, banks, and other financial institutions has the capacity to discipline the behavior of heavily indebted peripheral governments by raising the costs of noncompliance to a point where it begins to appear increasingly unattractive to domestic elites to default. One of the main reasons why heavily indebted states generally repay, I argue, is because government officials fear that suspending their debt service would immediately cause credit circulation to grind to a halt and lead to destabilizing international capital flight and crippling knock-on effects on the domestic economy, which would be especially harmful for domestic owners of capital.

Although this market mechanism shows some similarities to the reputational mechanism outlined in chapter 1, with both hinging on a market-imposed "credit embargo" of sorts, it differs in at least three key respects. First of all, in the market mechanism of the structural power hypothesis, policymakers are less concerned about the state's access to credit than they are about the *spillover effects* of higher borrowing costs or a potential credit cutoff on wider economic performance. The main cost of default, in the structural power hypothesis, is not just the state's future ability to borrow but the overall health and performance of the domestic private sector. More specifically, it is not just the government's long-term smoothing capacity but the immediate vulnerability of domestic banks and businesses that is at stake. In the market mechanism of the structural power hypothesis, then, it is ultimately the threat of debilitating economic spillover costs, and the associated political opposition of those social groups that expect to be harmed by these costs, that imposes an internal check on a government's willingness to default.

The second important difference from the reputational mechanism is that the credit embargo on which the structural power of finance hinges tends to be of a *temporary*—as opposed to a permanent or more long-term—nature. I argue that private lending decisions are not a matter of a debtor's prior credit history; as we saw in chapter 1, investors generally do not distinguish between past repayment records and display relatively little foresight in their risk assessment. Rather, even if they often fail to adequately discriminate between different borrowers, investors generally seek to punish or reward specific policies and politicians by charging higher or lower interest rates, or even refusing to extend any further credit at all. This means that policymakers do not need to be very concerned about future market access several years out; they will, however, tend to be very concerned about the *immediate* consequences of noncompliance on economic performance. Even if the short-term spillover costs of default tend to ease off in a matter of months or several years at most, they can still wreak short-term havoc on the domestic economy and undermine the government's capacity to legitimize itself in the eyes of its citizens. Unsurprisingly, it turns out that few elected officials are willing to countenance the political implications of a wholesale financial meltdown and economic depression on their watch—let alone the risk of social unrest this might imply.

Third, unlike the reputation mechanism, the power of private creditors is not necessarily limited to abstract, automatic, or apolitical market behavior. In fact, private lenders are capable of purposefully exploiting market dynamics and deliberately wielding the threat of a credit cutoff as a *political* weapon to force a noncompliant borrower back into line. In this respect, Culpepper and Reinke have made the useful theoretical clarification that the concept of structural power should not be reduced to those forms of power that are exercised impersonally and automatically. Structural power is not simply a "background condition against which politics plays out," but also "an active resource employed by business in the political arena." Instead of understanding structural power exclusively in terms of an "automatic punishing recoil" mechanism, then, we should also look out for its more overt manifestations. "Although structural power can certainly work automatically," Culpepper and Reinke write, "it can also be deployed deliberately, with strategic intent." What makes this form of power *structural*, then, is not the way in which it is exercised—whether strategically or automatically—but the *source* of the power as such, which always "flows from the economic position of the firm in an economy."[7] In our case, the structural power of finance flows from its position as the principal creator of credit-money in a globalized and financialized capitalist economy. It can work both *automatically*, through the selling of government bonds or the decision to stop lending to a particular borrower, as well as *strategically*, through the purposefully deployed threat to withhold further credit in the event of noncompliance.

Taken together, the effectiveness of this weapon—both in its automatic and in its strategic forms—depends on two crucial conditions: first, on the capacity of private lenders to maintain a relatively coherent international "creditors' cartel"; and second on the debtor's dependence on this creditors' cartel for further financing. On the first point, the threat to punish a noncompliant borrower by withholding further credit can only be credible and effective if all creditors stop lending at the same time, maintaining a full-fledged "credit strike" until the defaulted debt is renegotiated under conditions favorable to the creditors. If a sufficiently large group of lenders break ranks and offer a defaulting government new loans on better terms in the hope of outcompeting their rivals, the threat of a short-term credit cutoff loses its credibility, and the disciplinary mechanism will break down. It is therefore crucial that private lenders remain relatively unified in the pursuit of their collective interest as creditors, rather than in the pursuit of the narrow self-interest of individual lenders competing with one another for market share. The concept of a "creditors' cartel," developed in the literature on the Latin American debt crisis, aims to capture this capacity of private lenders to resist incentives for individual free-riding and to present a unified front in their dealings with sovereign borrowers.[8]

This observation in turn raises an important question: what are the conditions under which the creditors' cartel will manage to maintain its internal coherence, and what are the conditions under which it will break down? One of the key arguments of this book is that the *structure of lending* and the consequent *ownership structure* of the debt are two crucial factors conditioning the internal coherence of the creditors' cartel. To be more precise, what matters is *market concentration* and the resultant *debt concentration*, which impacts the number of lenders involved and the degree to which the lending structure aligns creditor interests, eases creditor coordination, and incentivizes collective action as opposed to opportunistic behavior by individual lenders.[9] When concentration is high and creditor interests are interlocked by the structure of international lending, the degree of creditor coherence will also tend to be high, and market discipline will be strengthened. If, by contrast, concentration is low and the lending structure incentivizes individual free-riding, creditor coherence will also be low, and market discipline will be weakened. In practice, this means that syndicated lending and highly concentrated bond finance will make default less likely, while decentralized bond finance will make it more likely.

The second factor determining the effectiveness of the threat to withhold further credit—the debtor's dependence on the creditors' cartel—in turn rests on two further conditions: the availability of an *outside option*, and the extent to which the debtor country is *self-sufficient* in financial and commercial terms. If the debtor country has an outside option, like a friendly foreign government or a regional multilateral lender willing and able to provide an alternative source of financing, or if it has enough of a financial buffer to absorb the economic shock of a foreign credit cutoff, the spillover costs of a short-term credit cutoff will be lower, and the strength of market discipline will be diminished. The debtor's capacity to individually cushion the impact of a short-term credit cutoff will tend to increase when the country is running a primary surplus (taking in more in revenues than it spends before interest); a trade surplus (exporting more than it imports); sizable foreign-exchange reserves (to defend the value of the currency against devaluation pressures and to pay for crucial imports); and the capacity to provide liquidity to its own financial system (requiring control over the central bank, a relatively healthy and well-capitalized banking system, and the ability to impose capital controls to stem capital flight after a default). When these conditions apply, the consequences of a short-term credit cutoff may appear somewhat less damaging to a distressed borrower, possibly making nonpayment a relatively more attractive option than continued foreign wealth transfers. While this obviously does not mean that a country will automatically suspend payments the moment it obtains a trade surplus, for instance, having such a surplus would endow it with an alternative source of foreign exchange, which may provide a noncompliant government with a cushion for bad times and somewhat greater room for maneuver in the event of a credit cutoff.

The conclusion is therefore that the disciplinary power of financial markets will be increased when the debt concentration is high, creditor interests are aligned, and the debtor depends on the creditors' cartel for external financing. Conversely, it will be weakened when concentration is low, creditor interests are not aligned, and the debtor has an outside option or is relatively self-sufficient in financial and commercial terms. This argument can be contrasted to claims made by scholars who hold that decentralized capital markets are more disciplinary than concentrated bank lending, since they offer a more credible exit threat to individual investors and therefore increase policymakers' fears of investor punishment.[10] While it is true that government debt is in principle easier to dump on a "perfect" and highly liquid bond market, it turns out that this investor exit option actually makes decentralized bond markets susceptible to panicky or opportunistic behavior by individual lenders, who may be tempted to break ranks and either continue lending to a noncompliant government to outcompete their rivals (thereby causing the threat of a short-term credit cutoff to break down), or refuse to participate in the collective effort of keeping a distressed but compliant borrower solvent (thereby making a default more likely). As we will see in the individual case studies, preventing default actually involves a complex balancing act in which lenders need to be able to credibly threaten noncompliant borrowers with a curtailing of short-term credit lines *while at the same time keeping distressed debtors solvent so they can continue to service their*

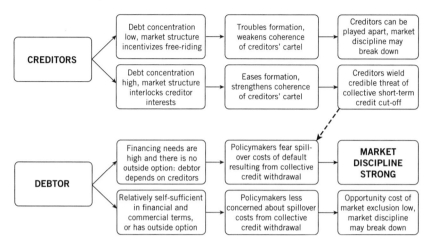

FIGURE 4.1. First enforcement mechanism of market discipline.

*debts.* This in turn requires a high degree of creditor cohesion and debtor monitoring that a diffuse body of small bondholders will find much more difficult to achieve than a handful of systemically important, politically powerful, and financially sophisticated repeat players—like big international banks—whose interests in repayment are structurally interlocked by the nature of international lending and who have an existential stake in systemic stability. When only a small number of highly interdependent financial institutions are involved in lending, it is much more likely that creditors will succeed in coordinating a balanced and unified response to liquidity problems or noncompliance.[11]

Still, even a relatively unified creditors' cartel will struggle to keep a big borrower afloat when the risk of default rises to the point of imminent bankruptcy. In those instances, the incentive to collectively withdraw credit to avoid crippling losses may simply become too great for individual lenders to countenance. The risk of a self-fulfilling prophecy, whereby investors rush for the exits and thereby produce the outcome they were hoping to prevent, combined with the fact that many of the biggest private lenders today are considered "too big to fail," gives rise to a systemic need—from the creditors' perspective, at least—for official-sector intervention to keep distressed sovereign borrowers afloat in the face of escalating market panic. As Susanne Soederberg has noted, "to recreate the power relations within the international credit system it is necessary to ensure that debtors are kept within the lending game."[12] The market mechanism, even when the lending structure is highly concentrated, remains prone to failure. Taken by itself, it is therefore a necessary but insufficient barrier to default. To be truly effective it requires some counterbalance.

## The Conditional Lending of Official Creditors

The second enforcement mechanism—the conditional emergency lending by creditor states and international financial institutions—serves to provide just that. By disbursing "bailout" loans to distressed debtors under strict policy conditionality, official creditors do not merely intervene to keep the debtor solvent, effectively assuming the role of an international lender of last resort, but also to enforce and monitor the type of policies and reforms that would free up the maximum amount of public revenue and foreign exchange for continued debt servicing. The main threat in the hands of official creditors is the same as the one that underpins the structural power of private creditors: the capacity to withhold credit in the event of noncompliance, which would leave a defaulting country without any access to external financing, thereby inflicting debilitating spillover costs on its domestic economy. In the hands of official creditors, however, this threat is enhanced by the fact that emergency loans are disbursed in tranches: a debtor will only receive its next loan installment if it remains current on its obligations to private creditors and carries out the demanded structural adjustments. At the same time—unlike the market mechanism, which will tend to break down in an investor panic—the disciplinary role of official creditors is theoretically without bounds, as the latter can maintain their conditional lending even in the absence of a perspective on profits. It is also more strategic in its exercise, in the sense that the structural power of official-sector creditors does not depend on any automatic recoil mechanisms but rather on a deliberate decision to disburse or not to disburse the next credit tranche.

As we will see in the historical chapters of this book, during the prewar period the role of fiscal disciplinarian and international lender of last resort was only partially, intermittently, and improvisationally fulfilled by underwriting banks and creditor states. In the global financial architecture of the postwar period, by contrast, all these functions—providing conditional loans, exacting structural adjustment, monitoring finances and policies, determining future market access, and so on—now rest with the International Monetary Fund, which has in recent decades been backed in its crisis management role by the U.S. Treasury Department and the U.S. Federal Reserve, and which has more recently worked together with EU member states, the European Commission, and the European Central Bank in managing the sovereign debt crisis in the Eurozone.[13] The IMF's structural role in this respect is not limited to the amount of money it lends or the fiscal discipline it enforces; by giving its stamp of approval for a debtor's policies and economic performance, the Fund also provides trusted nonprice signals to market actors to indicate the credibility and creditworthiness of specific borrowers, thereby acting as an official gatekeeper for market access and fulfilling a coordinating function for the private creditors' cartel.[14] The Fund thus acts as a "collective creditor" of sorts.

What, then, are the conditions under which the second enforcement mechanism breaks down and a distressed debtor can defy the lender of last resort? This book argues that once again the effectiveness of the disciplinary mechanism is a result of the debtor's dependence on foreign financing and of the capacity of official creditors to present a unified front vis-à-vis the debtor. The conditions for the debtor's dependence are the same as those described in the previous section, relating to the availability of an outside option and the debtor's financial and commercial self-sufficiency (whether it has a primary fiscal surplus, a trade surplus, currency reserves, and control over domestic liquidity). When a government has sufficient domestic buffers or alternative sources of financing, it may be significantly less inclined to abide by the unpopular austerity measures and structural reforms demanded by official lenders, and may be more inclined to forego future loan installments in exchange for a recovery of national sovereignty and the capacity to shift at least part of the adjustment costs onto foreign creditors.

The conditions for the coherence of the official creditor front, however, are a more complex and less predictable question revolving around domestic politics in the creditor countries, as well as the broader geopolitical context and the nature of the relationship between the creditor states and the IMF (or any other international organization involved in conditional emergency lending). While the domestic politics of the creditor states lie outside of the scope of this study, the cases presented in the following chapters do suggest at least two preliminary hypotheses. First, if the debt of a crisis-ridden country is highly concentrated among a set of systemically important financial institutions in the core countries, the governments of the leading creditor countries and the IMF will share a common interest in a bailout: the IMF because it would thereby fulfill its mission to ensure global financial stability, and the creditor countries because IMF intervention would allow them to use other people's money to avoid financial contagion and the need to recapitalize their own overexposed financial institutions following the losses incurred in a default. If the big banks and financial institutions of the dominant creditor countries hold very little exposure, by contrast, the risk of systemic contagion toward the core will be lower, and official creditors may be less inclined to continue providing public goods for private creditors in the form of international bailout loans for distressed sovereign borrowers.

The second preliminary hypothesis holds that, when the provision of further bailout loans to foreign governments encounters insurmountable domestic opposition and becomes politically unpalatable inside the dominant creditor countries, or if there are overriding geopolitical concerns that keep these creditor countries from imposing strict discipline on a distressed or noncompliant sovereign borrower, a split may emerge among official lenders that leads the creditor states to withdraw their consent for further bailouts altogether, leaving the IMF isolated. Alternatively, if a borrower consistently fails to meet the IMF's

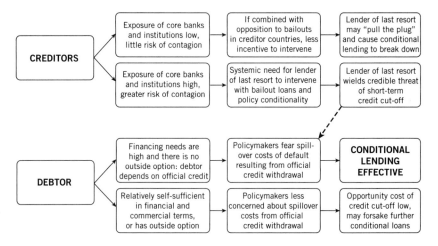

FIGURE 4.2. Second enforcement mechanism of conditional lending.

loan conditions, or if the latter concludes that its debt is unsustainable, thereby disqualifying it from making further loan disbursements, the Fund's management and staff may find themselves inclined to terminate their own Stand-By Arrangement. If any of these factors combine with limited exposure of financial institutions inside the creditor countries, reducing the risk of contagion toward the global capitalist heartland, official lenders may in fact decide to stop providing further emergency credit altogether, thereby provoking the default their original bailout was supposed to prevent.

In practice, the party most likely to pull the plug on an international bailout program will tend to be either a conservative and isolationist government inside the dominant creditor countries (when public opinion turns against sending taxpayer money abroad), or the IMF itself (when its own statutes prevent it from disbursing further loan installments due to noncompliance or insolvency). On the first point, Lawrence Broz has shown how conservative members of the U.S. Congress tend to be more opposed to further increases in IMF quotas, for instance.[15] On the second, the recent spat between the IMF and the European creditor states, especially Germany, has shown how—at the time of writing—the Fund may yet pull out of the Greek bailout program over its long-standing concerns about the country's long-term debt sustainability. It is crucial to remember in this context that the governments of creditor states have a domestic constituency to answer to, as well as broader foreign policy objectives to keep in mind, while the IMF has an international reputation to defend: continuing to lend to an insolvent or noncompliant government could harm the domestic approval ratings or broader foreign policy objectives of the former, just as it could undermine the latter's standing as an evidence-based multilateral lender in the eyes of its member states, thereby damaging its credibility and its ability to contain future crises. The possibility therefore exists that official lenders will eventually decide to cut the debtor loose from further international financing, thereby directly provoking the default that their original bailout was supposed to prevent.

## THE BRIDGING ROLE OF DOMESTIC ELITES

These two international enforcement mechanisms—the market discipline enforced by a creditors' cartel and the conditional lending of the international lender(s) of last resort—have in turn been complemented by the *internalization* of debtor discipline within the borrowing country's state apparatus. As we saw before, the growing dependence of the state on private credit has dramatically realigned established power relations in the global political economy over the past four decades, strengthening the hand of international creditors at the expense of domestic constituents. To this we must now add the intermediary role fulfilled by domestic political and financial elites inside the borrowing countries. In a context of high state dependence, we should expect those social groups considered to be most capable of attracting affordable credit to find their position strengthened relative to those who lack this capacity. In practice, this means that internationally mobile, financially integrated, and ideologically orthodox elites inside the borrowing country will obtain a privileged position in financial policymaking thanks to the "bridging role" they fulfill towards foreign creditors. As Sylvia Maxfield has argued in relation to Mexico, domestic elites—bankers and technocrats in particular—will grow considerably more powerful as the state's dependence on credit deepens: "the greater the need for good relations with international creditors, the more weight the creditors and those bankers with close ties to them have in the policy process."[16]

This third enforcement mechanism may involve interpersonal connections between foreign creditors and domestic elites, but it is by no means dependent on such direct ties—and it is certainly not the outcome of an international bankers' conspiracy intent on taking over the debtor's state apparatus. To the contrary, it mostly depends on a structural and normative alignment of the material interests and ideological convictions of domestic elites and foreign creditors, both of whom stand to lose from a unilateral default and both of whom will tend to benefit from and believe in the virtues of fiscal discipline, market liberalization, "sound money," and uninterrupted debt servicing. Like foreign lenders, domestic elites tend to oppose a unilateral default, not only because they tend to hold a disproportionate share of their own government's debt, but also because a default would cripple the financial sector and domestic businesses, thus undermining the basis of their own power: their bridging role towards the global financial establishment and their privileged position in domestic politics. As a result of their alignment with foreign creditors' preferences for repayment, domestic elites therefore tend to be much more willing to commit to the type of orthodox fiscal policies required for continued debt servicing, which creditors will in turn reward with better terms on future loans.[17]

The strengthening of domestic elites tends to sideline political actors whose loyalties continue to lie with working people back home, and who cannot or do not want to credibly commit to the austerity policies and structural reforms required to unlock further credit tranches or regain market access. This dynamic helps explain why, in times of fiscal constraint, left-leaning governments are generally pulled towards the center, while antiausterity radicals are either marginalized or subjected to intense domestic and international pressure to fall back in line with fiscal orthodoxy. What emerges is a powerful and relatively coherent international coalition between foreign creditors and domestic elites—an alliance of convenience and conviction, based mostly on shared interests and ideas, not necessarily the result of interpersonal connections—that strongly opposes a suspension of payments. Domestically, this coalition will generally try to insulate itself from popular pressures by precluding the political expression of social opposition to fiscal austerity and structural reform, for instance through constitutional checks on government spending, legally binding agreements with official creditors, and the sidelining of the legislative power at the expense of the executive. Over time, as domestic elites succeed in entrenching their privileged position, debtor discipline is gradually internalized into the state's financial bureaucracy, with far-reaching implications for the distribution of adjustment costs and the democratic responsiveness of national government.[18]

This indirect form of creditor control over the political process inside the debtor countries will often take on a technocratic veneer, with unelected central bankers and financial administrators assuming important positions of power to ensure full repayment and other investor-friendly policies. While such arrangements are usually presented in terms of economic necessity and expertise, they are really an attempt to shield financial elites from political opposition by depoliticizing fiscal policy and naturalizing austerity, making them appear as economic inevitabilities, when in reality they constitute political interventions aimed at shifting the burden of adjustment from private creditors and domestic elites onto less privileged and less powerful segments of society. In keeping with the insights developed in the previous chapter, however, it should be stressed that wealthy elites are powerful not because they personally control financial policymaking, but they control financial policymaking *because they are powerful*. As with the international creditors, the source of their power is structural in nature and ultimately a product of the state's dependence on credit. This means that, even with a change in government personnel, the privileged position of domestic elites will continue to constrain the readiness of a fiscally distressed government to defy its foreign lenders. In fact, recent research has shown that, the more developed and deeply integrated a country's financial markets, the more discipline the domestic financial sector will exert over its own government through precisely this mechanism.[19]

What, then, are the conditions under which the third enforcement mechanism is operative and the conditions under which it breaks down? Since domestic elites derive their privileged position at least in part from their bridging role towards foreign creditors, the mechanism appears to be conditional on three factors: first, on the government's dependence on foreign credit; second, on the ability of domestic elites to attract that credit; and third, on the ability of elites to fend off popular opposition from below and retain political and administrative control over the "commanding heights" of economic policymaking—especially the finance ministry and the central bank. On the first point, a growing state dependence on foreign credit will tend to strengthen the hand of domestic elites, while lower dependence will weaken it. When the government does not need any foreign credit at all, the bridging function becomes less important and may completely dissolve. On the second point, the ability of domestic elites to attract foreign credit depends on their capacity to convince international investors of the credibility of their commitment—a factor that is not the result of liberal-democratic institutions per se, as North and Weingast famously argued, but of the ability and willingness of policymakers to carry out fiscally "responsible" policies and to continue servicing their debts. This ability and willingness will be high when the material interests and ideological convictions of domestic elites are structurally and normatively aligned with those of foreign creditors. The willingness will be low when the material interests and ideological convictions of financial policymakers are *not* aligned, while the ability to commit will be low when the political or institutional capacity to carry out fiscally "responsible" policies is lacking. If domestic elites are unable and/or unwilling to carry out the type of creditor-friendly policies that allow them to attract further loans on decent terms, their bridging role (and hence the privileged position that flows from it) may crumble and fall apart. Finally, on the third point, the ability to fend off popular opposition to painful fiscal adjustment depends on the capacity of domestic elites to contain the legitimation crisis resulting from the unequal distribution of adjustment costs and to shield policymaking from popular pressures for default. When indignant citizens begin to withdraw their loyalty from the state and revolt against the political establishment, the option of a unilateral payment suspension may finally begin to look more attractive to policymakers. Such a moratorium could be pursued either as the explicit policy preference of a new prodefault coalition that has just come to power by ousting the creditor-friendly establishment, or it could be part of a strategic retreat by domestic elites to relieve social tensions and restore political stability through the deflection of part of the adjustment costs onto foreign lenders.

Whatever the case may be, it should be stressed that, while a successful debtors' revolt or electoral victory of a prodefault coalition may alter the policy

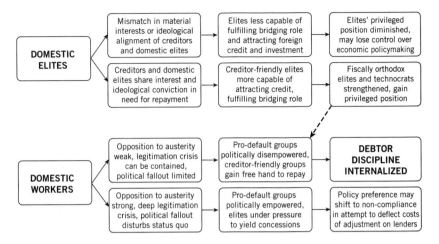

FIGURE 4.3. Third enforcement mechanism of internalized discipline.

preferences of a borrowing government, it cannot by itself overcome the state's dependence on credit or the structural power of finance. For policy preferences to be transformed into political outcomes requires a degree of autonomy on the part of the debtor state. In other words, for a country to be able to unilaterally suspend payments on its external debts without being forced back into compliance as a result of devastating short-term spillover costs, *all three enforcement mechanisms* will need to break down. This means that, even if a prodefault or antiausterity coalition takes power in the face of a deep legitimation crisis, it may still encounter the external constraints imposed by highly concentrated international credit markets and unforgiving official lenders. In other words, even a government that has resolved to end austerity and make its creditors pay may eventually be compelled to comply if the balance of power remains stacked against it.

# PART II

A Brief History of Sovereign Default

# FIVE

## The Making of the Indebted State

W ith the basic contours of our theoretical approach now in place, we can finally turn to the *longue durée* of international government finance—from its earliest manifestations in the Italian city-states to its spectacular collapse during the tumultuous interwar period. Tracing the history of sovereign debt and default back to its roots in early-modern Europe is a particularly useful exercise for the purposes of this research project because it will help us arrive at a better understanding of the ultimate sources of financial power and a better grasp of how this power evolved over the course of capitalist development. With over eight centuries of economic history condensed into three short chapters, it should be clear that any such discussion is bound to be cursory. The purpose of the following discussion is therefore not to provide an exhaustive overview, nor to engage in rigorous empirical hypothesis-testing, but rather to illustrate a number of basic points that will help contextualize the postwar decline in the incidence of sovereign default by setting this development against a broader historical canvas.

The following chapter will start out by locating the origins of financial power firmly within the state's structural dependence on credit, which has historically given rise to a powerful creditor class. After that, we will see how sovereign debt repayment has always been a highly contentious affair from the very beginning, regularly resulting in intense distributional conflicts between creditors and taxpayers, and protracted power struggles over fiscal policy and democratic representation. Finally, the last part of the chapter will draw on two early-modern examples—Genoese lending to King Philip II of Spain and the development of the Amsterdam capital market—to show how international lending was made possible in the early-modern period despite the regular recurrence of default and the contested nature of repayment. The main argument here is that key elements of the first enforcement mechanism—the market discipline imposed by a highly concentrated international creditors' cartel—were already present in embryonic form at an early stage of capitalist development, making international lending reliable and profitable enough, at least in case of a limited number of borrowers and lenders, to keep it up even in the face of regular sovereign defaults. After this brief outline of the early-modern history of sovereign debt, the next chapter will then illustrate the same point with reference to the internationalization of finance under the Pax Britannica in the nineteenth century, while chapter 7 provides a brief account of the wave of unilateral payment suspensions during the Great Depression.

## THE RISE OF PUBLIC BORROWING

Earl Hamilton, one of the founders of the discipline of economic history, once wrote that "a national debt is one of the few important economic phenomena without roots in the Ancient World."[1] While premodern rulers and medieval monarchs did occasionally borrow and default, the amounts involved were generally small, and the obligations widely understood to be of a personal nature—most kings and prices simply repudiated their predecessor's obligations upon assuming the throne. It is only with the birth of the first merchant republics in the Italian city-states during the late Middle Ages that sovereign borrowing became properly public in character. Genoa was probably the first independent republic to float a municipal debt in 1149, followed shortly thereafter by Venice in 1164 and Florence in 1166.[2]

In subsequent decades and centuries, cities like Siena, Arras, Bremen, Cologne, and Barcelona all developed their own systems of public credit— followed much later, from the sixteenth century onwards, by territorial states like Castile, Naples, France, the Netherlands and the Papal States.[3] The earliest public loans were generally compulsory, involving the forced concession of a fixed sum by wealthy citizens, mostly merchants and merchant bankers, against a pledge of specific public income streams derived from future tax revenues and other sources of income. Over time, these loans became voluntary and more long-term, and from the second half of the thirteenth century onwards outstanding public debts began to be consolidated into perpetual obligations that could be sold to interested counterparties or passed on to future generations, thus giving rise to the development of an active secondary trade in government debt and laying the foundations for the rise of modern financial markets.[4]

The emergence of the public debt thus signaled a historic shift from the social order of feudalism to a protocapitalist international state system. As Marx would later remark in *Capital*, the birth of the national debt "marked with its stamp the capitalistic era," giving rise to "joint-stock companies, to dealings in negotiable effects of all kinds, and to speculation, in a word to stock-exchange gambling and the modern bankocracy."[5] While feudal sovereigns had mostly relied on demesne income to sustain their military campaigns and court expenditures, only occasionally engaging in short-term borrowing on a personal title, the Italian merchant republics developed complex tax and credit systems to finance their struggles for independence and subsequent military campaigns.

The main driving force behind the emergence of public credit was therefore invariably the exigency of war.[6] To gain independence, conquer overseas territories, fend off envious princes, and prevail in internecine conflicts with rival city-states, the early-modern republics had little choice but to raise sizable navies and militaries. With their small and mostly urban populations, however, maintaining a standing army made little sense: permanently mobilizing citizens for war would put far too great a burden on the local economy, and the wealthier city-dwellers in particular had long since ceased to take to the battlefields. Moreover, a small homegrown army would be no match for the vast territorial empires that loomed large on the other side of the Mediterranean and the Alps. As a result, the Italian city-states increasingly came to rely on the costly war-making and empire-building services provided by mercenaries.[7] The resultant expenses in turn fed into the need to develop complex systems of taxation and public borrowing.

Over the centuries, this growing state dependence on private sources of financing generated lucrative opportunities for rent-seeking and speculation, spawning a class of wealthy financiers who became heavily invested in their own city-states' debts. As Luciano Pezzolo notes, a structural change took place in late-medieval and early-modern Italy: "As long as state finance was not under severe and extended pressure, the system represented a 'moneylender's paradise'. Principal was paid back in relatively short time and interest was also paid regularly."[8] This immediately raises the question why local rulers were so punctual about repaying their debts. Pezzolo argues that it was a result of the fact that the state's creditors and its governing elite were often the same people: "The key feature that underpinned the system," he writes, "laid [sic] in the close permeation between major bondholders and [the] power elite. As long as this identity subsisted it would have been unlikely the government defaulted."[9] Stasavage reaches a similar conclusion, finding that oligarchic regimes empowered the wealthy merchants who held government bonds and ensured the insulation of fiscal policy from popular pressures for default. As a result, city-states that "were more oligarchical in form tended to have better access to credit than did those with more open systems of political representation."[10]

The power of the emerging creditor class reached its first apogee in renaissance Florence—the city that give birth to modern banking. In 1427, the Tuscan city was drowning in what seemed like an unpayable debt. A protracted war with Milan had left the municipal government in dire fiscal straits, and citizens were growing increasingly restive about the heavy tax burden required to service the resultant financial obligations. A century later, the city's historian Francesco Giucciardini would look back on the crisis and reflect that "either the debt destroys Florence or Florence destroys the debt."[11] In an attempt to shore up the public finances, the Florentine city government decreed the most thorough and most innovative tax survey of the early-modern era, the *Catasto* of 1427, whose high level of detail has provided economic historians with an unprecedented insight into the nature of wealth distribution in one of early-modern Europe's most important cities. Interestingly, the *Catasto* reveals the extreme concentration of Florence's public debt in the hands of a small creditor oligarchy: almost 60 percent of the republic's bonds were held by only 2 percent of the population.[12] This high concentration of the public debt and the acute state dependence on private credit had far-reaching political implications, directly feeding into the rise of the Medici as the city's—and eventually the continent's—dominant banking family. As Pezzolo notes, "to be creditors to the government meant sharing the destiny of the regime and, consequently, supporting it. In Florence, the Medicean regime [thus] tied to itself an oligarchy that profited from the management of the government debt."[13]

It was in Genoa, however, that the private management of the public debt was first properly perfected. The founding in 1407 of the world's first chartered bank, the Casa di San Giorgio, proved to be a historic landmark in this respect. The Casa was essentially a consortium of private bondholders that established direct creditor control over the management of the public finances.[14] Machiavelli famously referred to San Giorgio as a "state within a state"—and Genoa's ruling elite needed it. The city was exceptionally fractious and regularly underwent popular revolts and shifts in the balance of power between competing merchant families. The Casa di San Giorgio served to effectively shield fiscal policy and public debt management from popular pressures and political instability, lowering the risk of default and enabling the commune to borrow at much lower rates than most of its rivals. As Michele Fratianni notes, the "top managers of San Giorgio were drawn from the same social groups from which sprang top decision-makers in government." Creditor control over public finances thus "ensured that San Giorgio's interests were aligned with the Republic's. This, in turn, reduced the risk that the Republic would repudiate its debt."[15] Low default risk meant greater access to credit, and the abundance of cheap credit in turn allowed Genoa to develop into a financial and maritime powerhouse over the course of the fifteenth and sixteenth centuries—a period Fernand Braudel famously referred to as the "great age of Genoese finance":

> For three-quarters of a century, "the Genoese experience" enabled the merchant-bankers of Genoa, through their handling of capital and credit, to call the tune of European payments and transactions. This is worth studying in itself, for it must surely have been the most extraordinary example of convergence and concentration the European world-economy had yet witnessed, as it re-oriented itself around an almost invisible focus. For the focal point of the whole system was not even the city of Genoa itself, but a handful of banker-financiers (today we would call them a multinational consortium). And this is only one of the paradoxes surrounding the strange city of Genoa which, though apparently so cursed by fate, tended both before and after its "age of glory" to gravitate towards the summit of world business. To me Genoa seems always to have been, in every age, the capitalist city par excellence.[16]

## THE CONTENTIOUS POLITICS OF REPAYMENT

It is therefore safe to say that the state's structural dependence on credit and the consequent entrenchment of a distinct creditor class were foundational to the emergence of modern finance, international commerce, and European capitalism more generally. But these same political-economic developments also had a number of far-reaching social implications. In fact, the emerging public credit system quickly revealed itself to be a powerful vehicle for the redistribution of wealth from the bottom of society to the top. Wherever debt ownership was highly concentrated and the general body of taxpayers did not hold a significant share of government bonds, the profits derived from the state's interest payments tended to flow straight into the pockets of the members of the politically powerful creditor class. By contrast, the taxes that had to be raised to repay these debts—which in the early days mostly took the form of highly regressive consumption and land taxes—generally imposed a much heavier burden on the *popolo minuto*: the little people.[17] The result was a steady stream of tax revenues from the laboring classes, especially peasants and artisans, towards a small ruling oligarchy of bondholding elites, turning the public debt into a major source of distributional conflict and a lightning rod for growing social discontent—especially in times of crisis. Marx noted how the public debt thus became "one of the most powerful levers of primitive accumulation," making possible the "improvised wealth of the financiers" and creating a formidable "aristocracy of finance" in the process.[18] Not coincidentally, given the fact that in many of the early merchant republics state creditors directly controlled government, distributional conflicts over taxation and debt repayments would often go hand in hand with popular struggles for greater political representation and public control over the state finances.[19] The politics of debt repayment, in short, were contentious from the very beginning, and have always been closely intertwined with demands for greater democracy.

One of the first and most spectacular manifestations of open conflict over the public debt and political representation was the revolt of the Florentine wool carders, the so-called *Ciompi*, between 1378 and 1382. In the wake of a devastating banking crisis—sparked in part by the default of Edward III—and still crippled by the economic after-effects of the Black Death, some of the city's poorest and most disenfranchised laborers rose up and briefly seized power. Unrepresented by the established artisans' guilds and fed up with the privileges of the patrician oligarchy, which continued to impose forced loans to wage war and raise taxes to service the resulting debts, the *Ciompi* set out to form what was arguably Europe's first workers' government. Tellingly, one of their first actions in power was to try to reduce the burden of the public debt by repudiating the most onerous loans. Although they were soon ousted from the *Signoria* by the old patrician elite, the resultant political tumult not only fundamentally altered the course of Florentine history but also foreshadowed later developments elsewhere in Europe—and, indeed, the world.[20] In his classic work on historical cycles of financialization, Giovanni Arrighi therefore refers to Florence as "the clearest of all antecedents," noting that "at no other time and place have the socially polarizing effects of 'financialization' been more in evidence. From this point of view, all subsequent financial expansions have been variations on a script first played out in the Tuscan city-state."[21]

Similar debt-and-tax revolts broke out elsewhere on the Italian peninsula. A century earlier, in 1259, a popular revolt motivated at least in part by widespread anger over deteriorating public finances had already rocked the city of Genoa. Lamenting that "Genoa's debt was held by the wealthy while the bulk of the tax burden was borne by popular groups," one of the first acts of the rebel leader Guglielmo Boccanegra upon seizing power was to consolidate the commune's debts. In 1339, another revolt brought Boccanegra's grandson Simone to power, whose government immediately went on to burn the city's official credit records—literally destroying the state's outstanding debts to rival merchant families in the process. In 1408, the same fate befell the records of the newly founded Casa di San Giorgio. And political contestation over the public finances was by no means limited to the Italian city-states; wherever a public debt arose, distributional struggles soon followed. Between 1456 and 1458, for instance, as Henry VI's monarchy languished in the throes of a deep fiscal crisis, riots broke out in London against Italian and Flemish merchants, leading to violent bouts of looting and arson and forcing the evacuation of the city's Italian community to Winchester. Cologne presents another striking example, undergoing a series of popular revolts in 1371, 1396, 1481, and 1513, with the public finances high on the list of grievances on each of these occasions. The uprising of 1513 even led to the overthrow of the established merchant elite and a partial repudiation of Cologne's public debt, confirming the importance of continued creditor control over political institutions for continued debt servicing.[22] Shortly thereafter, in 1520–1521, an uprising against Charles V of Spain rippled through Castile. The Revolt of the Comuneros, as it came to be known, was partly motivated by widespread popular outrage over the crown's attempt to impose further tax increases on local communities to keep servicing Charles V's ballooning debts to German bankers. Similar frustrations over rising national debt and tax burdens later contributed to the Dutch Revolt (1568–1648), the English Civil War (1642–1651), the French Revolution (1789) and the United States' Whiskey Rebellion (1794).[23]

These early conflicts over sovereign debt repayment were by and large domestic in nature. Even if public animosity towards moneylenders was often targeted at "outsiders" and expressed in religious, ethnic, or protonationalistic terms, as with the persecution of Italian merchants in London or the spread of anti-Semitism across Europe, most state creditors lived within the city walls and were part and parcel of the ruling merchant elite. In the early *quattrocento*, for instance, only around one-tenth of Florence's debt was in foreign hands, while some 92 percent of the principal of the Casa di San Giorgio was held by Genoese citizens and institutions during the first half of the seventeenth century.[24] Over time, however, the development of the system of public credit would give rise to powerful financial institutions, and eventually a complex continent-wide network of merchant banks arose on the back of the emerging creditor class. Before long, prominent banking families in the Italian city-states and the Holy Roman Empire began lending to sovereigns across the continent.

## THE EMERGENCE OF INTERNATIONAL LENDING

The rules involved in this type of international lending were radically different from those governing the management of the domestic debt. For one, foreign lenders did not have personal control over the political institutions of their sovereign borrowers, and thus they had no way to directly enforce their cross-border debt contracts. It should not come as a surprise, then, that Europe's early-modern sovereigns regularly reneged on their foreign obligations. As Winkler noted, it was "in the course of this period that defaults were beginning to become more popular (with the borrower). Suspension of payment, reduction of interest and principal were frequent occurrences."[25] The most famous examples are probably the default by Edward III of England on the Bardi and Peruzzi, which allegedly provoked the Florentine banking crisis of the 1340s, and the serial defaults by Charles V and Philip II of Spain on the Fugger and Welser of Augsburg.[26] According to Arrighi, the Medici drew important lessons from this historical experience, concluding that international lending to foreign sovereigns was risky business. While the Medici did develop a complex international credit system of their own, they chose their sovereign customers carefully and decided to specialize in the public finances of Florence and the papacy, over which they could at least exercise direct control.[27]

Just like the management of the domestic debt, the art of international banking was first perfected by the Genoese, who developed an ingenious system of syndicated bank lending to Philip II of Spain that financed his many wars and colonial conquests while bringing untold riches to the Ligurian coast. The system of international credit developed by the Genoese over the course of the sixteenth century was so sophisticated that the Spanish king—who depended on foreign loans to sustain his military campaigns in the Americas and the rebellious Netherlands—soon felt his room for maneuver significantly constrained by the structural power of his private bankers. As Richard Ehrenberg noted, "it was not the Potosí silver mines, but the Genoese fairs of exchange which made it possible for Philip II to conduct his world power policy decade after decade." Ironically, however, it was that very reliance on credit that, as the jurist Suárez de Figueroa lamented in 1617, would gradually reduce the Iberian peninsula to "the Indies of the Genoese."[28] Even though Philip II repeatedly suspended payments, Italian bankers were able to prevent the king from repudiating his obligations outright and kept forcing him back to the negotiating table by refusing to disburse further credit until the defaulted debt had been settled on favorable terms. So how did these foreign lenders manage to get their way against the most powerful monarch in the world?

The answer, Mauricio Drelichman and Hans-Joachim Voth suggest in a groundbreaking new study of Philip II's finances, lies in the structure of international lending and the market-based power of the Genoese bankers. Drelichman and Voth find that "the lending system functioned not least because the bankers acted as one in times of crisis, cutting the king off from fresh loans when he was not servicing old ones."[29] This creditor coordination was eased by the fact that lending was heavily concentrated, with the top-ten Genoese banking families accounting for over 70 percent of all loans. By lending in overlapping syndicates, which structurally interlocked creditor interests and prevented free-riding by individual lenders, the highly concentrated Genoese creditors' cartel managed to present a unified front to the Spanish king that could credibly threaten to withhold further credit in the event of noncompliance.[30] While Philip II still defaulted twice after the Genoese took over from the Fugger and Welser as his principal financiers, these defaults were of a relatively short duration and generally considered "excusable" by the lenders, most of whom managed to recoup their investments and avoid losses in subsequent negotiations.[31] Drelichman and Voth conclude that, given the lack of direct creditor control over the Spanish court, "market power—the ability of the Genoese network to extract favorable terms and conditions from a borrower heavily dependent on credit—must be an important part of our story."[32] While the authors interpret this finding as conditional evidence for the reputation hypothesis, their evidence of the king's dependence on credit and the highly concentrated and interlocked lending structure developed by the Genoese bankers also resonates in important ways with the structural power hypothesis developed in this book. Of course this early form of market discipline was still a relatively incomplete enforcement mechanism by contemporary standards—most importantly, it lacked the backstop of a lender of last resort that could prevent Philip II from running out of gold reserves in times of crisis—but it was sufficiently strong to make lending profitable even in the face of the king's repeated payment suspensions. Indeed, Drelichman and Voth find that, "despite the less than stellar repayment record of the Crown, almost no banking family lost money."[33]

Over the course of the seventeenth century, as the Spanish began to lose ground (and sea) to the Dutch, Genoa was gradually displaced as Europe's leading financial center—first by Antwerp and then by Amsterdam. As with the Italian city-states, Amsterdam's success in international finance was a product of the highly advanced public credit system that had previously been developed in the Dutch provinces under Habsburg rule. Ironically, it was the very attempt by Charles V of Spain to find alternative sources of tax revenue to repay his debts to German and Italian bankers that triggered the Dutch Revolt of 1568. As James Tracy has noted, the Spanish effort to increase tax income from the Netherlands meant that "control of tax revenue had to be relinquished into the hands of the very same urban oligarchs . . . who themselves had heavy investments in state debt."[34] In other words, as the United Provinces of the Netherlands rose up against Habsburg rule, private creditors once again established direct control over the public finances of a rising capitalist power, contributing to a dramatic fall in Dutch borrowing costs that would prove to be the republic's greatest weapon in its Eighty Years' War against the Spanish. "Equitable or not," Tracy concludes, "control of fiscal policy by men who themselves had heavy investments in state debt was the real genius of the Netherlands' system of public borrowing both in its Habsburg beginnings and in its seventeenth-century grandeur."[35] By 1740, Braudel tells us, the Dutch had firmly entrenched their position as bankers to the continent, and "by the 1760s all the states of Europe were queueing up in the offices of the Dutch money-lenders: the emperor, the elector of Saxony, the elector of Bavaria, the insistent king of Denmark, the king of Sweden, Catherine II of Russia, the king of France and even the city of Hamburg . . . and lastly, the American rebels."[36]

Once again, this raises the question how Dutch lenders managed to enforce these international loans. The puzzle is compounded because the credit structure developed by the Dutch in the eighteenth century was very different from the sixteenth-century system devised by the Genoese. Unlike the syndicated bank loans of the latter, Dutch lending rested on the foundation of the Amsterdam capital market, in which private investors bought up the debt instruments of foreign governments—mostly perpetual annuities and long-term bonds— through various financial intermediaries. As a result of this particular credit structure, debt ownership tended to be highly dispersed and individualized, with many different investors holding claims on distant foreign governments that they could not possibly be expected to enforce in a similarly coordinated manner as the highly concentrated Genoese bankers' cartel had. Dutch investors, in short, tended to be far too disorganized to avoid individual free-riding and collectively withhold further credit in the event of default.[37] How, then, was sovereign lending even possible under Dutch hegemony in international finance? Why did the Amsterdam capital market not collapse amid a wave of foreign debt repudiations?

The answer appears to lie at least in part with the intermediaries that underwrote the loans: the city's most powerful banking firms. The Amsterdam capital market actually formed a very hierarchical credit structure that, while broad and dispersed at the base, became increasingly concentrated and organized towards the top. Sitting at the very apex of that structure, a small group of private banks would mobilize their respective networks of private brokers and commission agents to float the government bonds of a total of ten European states, including the Dutch Republic itself, with each house tending to specialize in dealings with a specific country or region. Unlike the individual investors who ended up buying the bonds from local brokers, these intermediary banks were very few in number, with just a handful of leading firms "exercising nearly monopolistic control over advances to foreign governments."[38] By the late-eighteenth century, James Riley notes, "most foreign governments seeking credit had settled on the banker or bankers to whom they would customarily apply," rendering these governments increasingly dependent on good relations with their chosen banker to be able to keep tapping into the Netherlands' sizable capital surpluses.[39] Acting as gatekeepers to the Amsterdam capital market—the only market that was deep and liquid enough to raise the requisite funds for large sovereign loans—a small group of strategically positioned Dutch bankers thus ended up effectively controlling both the credit access of the major European powers and the foreign investment opportunities of Dutch retail investors.[40] This in turn endowed these bankers with a privileged position from which they could threaten to refuse to arrange further loans to defaulting governments, even if the investor base itself was highly atomized. It appears to have been the peculiar nature of this highly concentrated and geographically specialized underwriting business that ultimately compelled the European powers to honor their obligations to Dutch investors. Despite the very different shape of the Amsterdam capital market, Dutch government finance therefore did show an important similarity to Genoese lending: both fundamentally revolved around the monopoly power of a highly concentrated bankers' cartel that could credibly threaten to withhold further credit in the event of a default.

The key conclusion we can draw from this historical discussion is that the first enforcement mechanism of market discipline was already present in embryonic form at an early stage in capitalist development. At the same time, however, this mechanism was still prone to failure in times of crisis, especially when Dutch hegemony suddenly began to wane towards the end of the eighteenth century. A suspension of payments by prerevolutionary France in 1788 hailed the start of a continental debt crisis that would eventually culminate in sovereign defaults by Austria, Sweden, Denmark, Russia, and Spain and then again by France. The economic fallout of these cataclysmic events would "terminate once and for all Dutch centrality in European high finance."[41] By 1809, Riley writes, "Amsterdam had lost its influence over debtors" and "virtually dried up as a source of foreign loans," paving the way for its main rival on the other side of the Channel to take the development of modern banking and international finance to new heights.[42]

# SIX

## The Internationalization of Finance

From the ashes of the Revolutionary and Napoleonic Wars arose a powerful new force in world politics: the City of London. By the time of its ascent to global prominence, English finance had already been undergoing a quiet transformation for over a century. Following the Glorious Revolution of 1688, which had brought *stadtholder* William of Orange to the throne of England as William III, the City had adopted and perfected a number of financial practices and innovations that had previously been developed in Italy and the Netherlands—most importantly the creation of the Bank of England, largely inspired by the Dutch example of the Wisselbank and the Genoese example of the Casa di San Giorgio.[1] Over the course of the eighteenth century, the resultant financial revolution gradually turned London into a modern-day equivalent of the late-medieval moneylenders' paradise, with the City eventually displacing Amsterdam as Europe's leading financial center and banker to the world.[2] By the early nineteenth century, London had firmly established itself as the throbbing heart of a rapidly expanding capital market, and in 1818 the UK branch of the Rothschild bank underwrote the first international loan denominated in sterling, to the Kingdom of Prussia. Within the space of a decade, England became the main source of foreign financing not just for most continental European powers, but for the newly independent states of Latin America and the Mediterranean Basin as well.

The result of this spectacular internationalization of finance was to make sovereign default an increasingly widespread phenomenon.[3] As we already saw in the introductory chapter of this book, each of the three speculative lending cycles in the nineteenth and early-twentieth centuries ended in a wave of unilateral payment suspensions (see table 6.1). Time and again, British bondholders turned out to be both zealously overconfident in the lead-up to the crisis and strikingly powerless in the face of the resultant defaults. Once more, this raises the question we already tried to grapple with in the previous chapter: if sovereign default was so common and private investors so powerless in the face of their borrowers' moratoriums, then why did they continue to lend to unreliable foreign governments? How was international lending even possible in the

TABLE 6.1.
The three historical waves of sovereign default

|  | 1828 | 1877 | 1933 |
|---|---|---|---|
| *No. of defaulting countries* | 15 | 17 | 24 |
| *As % of independent states* | 29% | 37% | 39% |
| *Share of blocked credits** | 22% | 23% | 35% |

Source: Suter (1989).

*Note: Countries with a population of less than one million in 1980 have been excluded. Percentages in the bottom row ("share of blocked credits") are an estimation made on the basis of data from 1828, 1878, and 1935, respectively. These percentages were obtained by dividing the total amount of debt in default by the sum of accumulated foreign investment abroad of Great Britain and France (see Suter 1989, 37).

nineteenth century? The answer, this chapter proposes, is the same one we came across in relation to Genoa and Amsterdam, namely the fact that key elements of the first and this time also the second enforcement mechanism—market discipline and conditional lending—were already present in embryonic form at an early stage in capitalist development. Beside occasionally resorting to the instrumental power of gunboats, especially during the imperialist era, the partial effectiveness of these two mechanisms generally ensured compliance during the good times, thus laying the foundations for the internationalization of finance over the course of the nineteenth century, even as the relative weakness of the underlying enforcement mechanisms meant that periods of calm were still regularly punctuated by unilateral payment suspensions in times of crisis. In this chapter, we will take a closer look at the main lending cycles of the 1820s and 1870s, as well as the creditors' responses to the subsequent waves of default, before turning to the mass defaults of the Great Depression in the next chapter.

## THE INTERNATIONAL DEBT CRISIS OF THE 1820S

The London stock market bubble of 1822–1825 marked the first major episode of speculative lending to non-European governments. During these years, over two-thirds of international loans made in London went to the newly independent nations of Latin America, whose governments relied on foreign credit to finance their struggles for self-determination against the Spanish and Portuguese.[4] So exuberant were market expectations in these early years of international lending that one particularly notorious swindler, a Scottish fortune hunter and former privateer by the name of Gregor MacGregor, managed to convince hundreds of unsuspecting retail investors to gobble up some £200,000 worth in government bonds from the entirely fictitious Central American kingdom of Poyais. The collapse of MacGregor's brazen confidence trick was only a harbinger of the wider financial crisis that would finally engulf Europe in 1825. The spectacular crash of the London Stock Exchange that year caused international capital flows to come to a sudden stop, leaving most Latin American independence leaders incapable of refinancing their outstanding obligations. Simon Bolívar's assessment of the continent's financial predicament was stark: "God save us from the debt," he wrote, "and we shall be content." The first Latin American debt crisis had begun in earnest.[5]

Initially, the borrowers tried their best to repay. Bolívar even encouraged the Peruvian finance minister José de Larrea to "liquidate [Peru's] national debt by selling all its mines and common lands, which are immense." But the attempts at consolidation were mostly in vain. Across the continent, a collapse in the terms of trade caused the borrowers to rapidly run out of gold, silver, and foreign exchange. By April 1826, Peru was forced to suspend payments, followed shortly thereafter by Gran Colombia and the majority of Latin American borrowers. Carlos Marichal, who has written the definitive history of the continent's recurrent debt crises, concludes that "default was not only inevitable but also virtually irreversible. . . . Despite repeated efforts by envoys of European bondholders to recover their monies, all governments (with the exception of Brazil) systematically refused to resume payments."[6] The defaults generally lasted for fifteen to thirty years, and were only negotiated at the initiative of the borrowers once their respective economies had recovered and new financing opportunities beckoned. In the early nineteenth century, then, even the relatively weak countries of the global periphery still retained a significant degree of autonomy from international finance.

The situation in southern Europe was similar to the one in Latin America. Greece, which had contracted its first European loans in 1823 to finance its war of independence against the Ottoman Empire, almost immediately declared a unilateral debt moratorium in 1826, followed several years later by Portugal (1828), Spain (1831), and a number of Italian republics.[7] In a sign of the prevailing balance of power at the time, there was remarkably little that bondholders could do to recoup their investments. In 1845 and again in 1846, the British government even threatened Greece with military intervention if it failed to meet the terms of a guaranteed loan, but as Borchard and Wynne report in their classic history of government insolvency, "despite these warnings and subsequent British remonstrances, not a penny of the debt service was met from the Greek treasury." The dispute dragged on for years, eventually leading to an outright occupation of the port of Piraeus by French and British troops in 1854, "ostensibly on the ground that by supporting Russia in the Crimean war Greece was misapplying revenues pledged to the service of the guaranteed loan."[8] Nevertheless, apart from a small annuity paid in 1860, Greece continued to uphold its protracted moratorium for decades. In 1878, it finally agreed on a settlement with its creditors, having spent its first half-century as an independent nation in a near-continuous state of default.

While the creditor powers generally took a hands-off approach towards defaulting foreign governments in the first half of the nineteenth century, Greece was not the only country to be confronted with the threat of armed intervention during this period. Wherever debt disputes converged with broader geopolitical interests, the British and the French did occasionally decide to flex their military might, especially when it concerned strategically important smaller states in the Caribbean and the eastern Mediterranean. The British approach to the use of force was famously encapsulated in the Palmerston doctrine of 1848, according to which Her Majesty's government reserved the right to either intervene or not to intervene in foreign debt disputes, with military or diplomatic action considered "neither a right of the bondholders nor a duty of the government," but a sovereign decision for the latter to take as it saw fit.[9] At the time, Sir John Simon of the Foreign Office warned investors that, if they "choose to buy foreign bonds with a yield of 10 percent rather than British government bonds with a lower yield, they should not expect as a matter of right that the British government would intercede on their behalf in the event of a default." The Palmerston doctrine thus articulated a foreign policy of "constructive ambiguity" in financial affairs, standing in stark contrast to the lender of last resort theory that was to be developed by Bagehot in the 1870s, which instead rested upon the unambiguous state guarantee of limitless financial support in times of crisis.[10] As we will see in the case studies later in this book, the intervention of an international lender of last resort has become an increasingly prominent fixture in the management of sovereign debt crises in the contemporary era. Palmerston's approach, by contrast, while certainly not unfriendly to private investors in principle, generally prioritized the government's geopolitical interests and its concerns about moral hazard over bondholders' qualms about financial stability and creditor rights. As the noted American historian Herbert Feis explained:

> The doctrine which [Palmerston] enunciated created an expectation that dishonest governments could not count on too much forbearance, that on the other hand too imprudent investors could not count on aid. It was sufficiently broad to permit the British government to justify any course it chose to take, sufficiently flexible to permit the measurement of advantage in each situation. . . . Swayed between political and financial considerations, the government now resisted, now yielded to the pressure of the interested parties. The outlook of the ministry in power, the course of domestic politics, the allies that injured bondholders could find—all these might, and sometimes did, enter to turn events. Small wonder then that the record shows a fitful, hesitant policy, a tendency now to drift with events, now to act with sternness, now to evade.[11]

After its somewhat hesitant initial application in Greece, the potentially explosive consequences of the Palmerston doctrine first became painfully apparent in Mexico. Like most of its Latin American counterparts, the Mexican government had unilaterally suspended payments on its external obligations in the international debt crisis of the 1820s, and in subsequent decades the unwillingness of Mexican officials to reach a settlement with their creditors produced growing frustrations among European bondholders and their official representatives.[12] Mexico eventually reached an agreement with its creditors to repay parts of its defaulted debt, but in the spring of 1861 the republican forces of Benito Juárez took power and repudiated the renegotiated obligations outright. Several months later, in July 1861, Juárez's liberal government suspended payments on all of Mexico's outstanding debts, which finally prompted the European powers to respond in force. The following winter, the governments of Britain, France, and Spain dispatched a combined military expedition to invade Mexico and occupy the country's main ports and customs offices. While the British and Spanish soon withdrew their troops, a 30,000-strong contingent of French soldiers pushed on towards Mexico City, where they installed a short-lived colonial administration under the aegis of Archduke Maximilian of Austria, who with the blessing of Napoleon III crowned himself emperor of Mexico and set up a throne at the Capultepec Castle.[13] Maximilian was later overthrown in an uprising led by Juárez's republican forces, who ousted the French army and subsequently repudiated Maximilian's debts.

The spectacular failure of this colonial venture, and the humiliation it caused the French in particular, actually had the effect of making the European creditor powers more reluctant to engage in similar outlandish experiments in the future. When a comparable situation arose in Venezuela in 1866, for instance, the British government deliberately refused to intervene. While it did provide bondholders with diplomatic representation to demand the return of their confiscated assets, the fact that Britain abstained from military action was a clear manifestation of the deliberately ambiguous nature of the Palmerston doctrine.[14] In sum, with debtor states possessing a significant degree of autonomy from global capital markets and in the absence of an international lender of last resort or a reliable pattern of state intervention to back up their claims, bondholders were often left to guess about the security of their foreign investments.

## SOVEREIGN DEFAULT IN THE ERA OF HIGH IMPERIALISM

Nevertheless, by the late 1860s and early 1870s a new lending frenzy had gripped investors on the London capital market. As in the 1820s, the countries of Latin America and the Mediterranean benefited most from the inflows during the boom years and were hit hardest by the subsequent bust. Within the space of several years, the Ottoman Empire, Egypt, Tunisia, Greece, Spain, Bolivia, Costa Rica, Ecuador, Honduras, Mexico, Paraguay, Peru, Santo Domingo, Uruguay, and Venezuela had suspended debt servicing or reduced interest payments on their outstanding obligations, leaving 54 percent of bonds issued in London in arrears by 1883.[15] Of all these defaults, the ones by Turkey and Egypt would prove to be the most politically consequential. Led by the dominant creditor nations, Britain and France, the European powers established a regime of external control over the Ottoman and Egyptian finances and, after several decades of simmering conflict and crisis, eventually invaded the latter outright. The international debt crisis of the 1870s can therefore be held up as one of the starting shots of the Age of Imperialism, in which the ascendancy of high finance, the export of capital from the core countries to the periphery, and the escalating international competition between capitalist firms and imperialist states led to an increasingly interventionist approach on the part of the dominant creditor powers. These developments eventually prompted Rosa Luxemburg, the German-Polish theorist and revolutionary, to write that "though foreign loans are indispensable for the emancipation of the rising capitalist states, they are yet the surest ties by which the old capitalist states maintain their influence, exercise financial control and exert pressure on the customs, foreign and commercial policy of the young capitalist states."[16]

Despite the saber-rattling in Egypt and the imposition of external financial control in Turkey, however, the resort to military action remained a relatively exceptional phenomenon in the settlement of foreign debt disputes during this period. "On the whole," Feis tells us, "the resolution not to intervene was maintained during the decade of the seventies. . . . [I]n all cases except Turkey and Egypt, the government left the burden of negotiation with the debtors to the bondholders."[17] While the creditor regimes established at Constantinople and Cairo certainly helped enforce the Ottoman and Egyptian debts with remarkable efficiency, it is therefore unlikely that the same mechanism helped enforce other countries' debts as well. In Latin America, where the lending boom of the late 1860s and early 1870s led to a wave of unilateral defaults, "the official response was muted," leaving bondholders without recourse to military coercion to protect their claims.[18] The lenders did not find much sympathy in their own courts either: the doctrine of sovereign immunity generally overrode creditor rights, meaning that contracts between private investors and foreign states were by no means considered inviolable. Despite Peru's massive default of 1876, for instance, the English Court of Chancery in 1877 reached the conclusion that the country's "so-called bonds amount to nothing more than engagements of honor, binding, so far as engagements of honor can bind, the government which issues them, but are not contracts enforceable before the ordinary tribunals of any foreign government."[19] Peru, by far the largest Latin American debtor of the 1870s, thus did not face anything like the foreign intervention that its counterparts in the eastern Mediterranean had to endure during the same years.

How, then, had cross-border debt contracts been enforced in the good years before the crisis of 1873? In the absence of legal or military sanctions, it seems that foreign investors' main source of leverage was their capacity to sell the bonds of defaulting governments, thereby causing their stock valuations to tumble. The problem, however, was that the bondholders were generally dispersed and disorganized, making it difficult to effectively coordinate collective action to keep distressed debtors solvent or to fully exclude a noncompliant borrower from international capital markets after a default.[20] In 1868, investors founded the Corporation of Foreign Bondholders (CFB) in an attempt to counter this lack of creditor coordination by presenting a unified front in negotiations with foreign borrowers. Even more important than its function as a diplomatic pressure group, however, was the CFB's capacity to cut off defaulting governments from further credit by working together with the London Stock Exchange in refusing to list their bonds.[21]

The centralized institution of the stock exchange and the unified creditor front presented by the CFB thus allowed atomized bondholders to wield an early form of structural power—still premature and limited in many respects, but nevertheless sufficient to impose at least some market discipline on the borrowers in the absence of outright financial control.[22] As Polanyi noted in *The Great Transformation*, "debtor governments were well advised to watch their exchanges carefully and to avoid policies which might reflect upon the soundness of the budgetary position."[23] Borchard even concludes that, while "the judicial remedies of foreign bondholders are hardly effective" and "diplomatic remedies . . . are not reliable," stock market exclusion was possibly the bondholders' only "powerful and persuasive weapon to help bring a delinquent debtor to terms."[24] For the defaulting governments, after all, the lack of access to foreign credit had a negative impact not just in terms of future government borrowing, as the reputation hypothesis would lead us to expect, but especially in terms of the immediate economic spillover costs. As Borchard noted:

> [T]he most effective sanction for the service and payment of a foreign bond in the minds of bankers is the consequence of default on a nation's credit and the effect on all credit-seeking subdivisions and even private business. By making new loans unavailable, or obtainable only at a cost commensurate with the risk involved, prolonged default may exert a depressing if not disastrous effect on the economic life of a country.[25]

Although this market-based enforcement mechanism successfully prevented further borrowing by noncompliant sovereigns, it was not strong enough by itself to force the defaulting governments to repay. As a result, the Latin American debtor states retained a relative degree of autonomy throughout the crisis of the 1870s and managed to extend their unilateral moratoriums for up to a decade or more, thereby gaining much-needed fiscal breathing room until their economies had recovered and the debt could be settled on relatively favorable terms.[26] In this respect, the prevailing policy response to the international debt crisis of the 1870s generally resembled that of the 1820s.

Despite this widespread default during the 1870s, by the late 1880s yet another brief speculative craze was sweeping Europe's financial markets. Unlike previous lending cycles, this time the majority of funds flowed abroad in the form of foreign direct investments. The outcome, however, was a similar—although much smaller—succession of sovereign defaults. When the boundless optimism of this *Belle Époque* suddenly turned to investor panic, precipitating the economic depression of the 1890s, many foreign direct investments of the preceding decade turned sour, and a number of governments were forced to suspend foreign debt payments in the ensuing downturn. Argentina's suspension of payments in 1890 was probably the most prominent default of this period, as it nearly led to the collapse of the mighty Barings bank of London. Several smaller countries in Latin America and the Caribbean also halted their debt service. In Europe, Greece and Portugal reduced interest payments while Spain and Serbia both teetered on the brink of bankruptcy.[27] Greece's debt crisis of the 1890s is particularly interesting as it presents some striking historical resonances with contemporary experience. Ever since the country's partial default of 1893, its German bondholders—with Deutsche Bank in the lead—aggressively petitioned the Imperial Chancellor for the establishment of a European debt commission modeled on the Ottoman Public Debt Administration. "During this period," Wynne wrote in 1951, "the German press was extremely hostile to Greece and pressed more and more insistently for international financial control. By 1897 the Reich was ready to support the German bondholders to the full."[28] Following Greece's defeat in the Greco-Turkish war of 1897, the German government convinced the other European powers to subject Athens to an intrusive form of creditor control, resulting in the establishment in 1898 of the International Financial Commission, which was charged with the administration of Greece's foreign debt and the collection of specific revenue streams earmarked for the liquidation of its outstanding debts.[29]

Throughout this period, European creditors openly decried Greece's "laxity in tax collection, relative extravagance in expenditure, and, above all, large outlays for military purposes," issuing oft-repeated criticisms of the government's failure "to adopt necessary measures of reform."[30] The Greeks, in turn, bitterly complained of having lost their national sovereignty to foreign creditors and having effectively been reduced to a European debt colony, with key decisions about public spending and taxation being made in Berlin and elsewhere. The International Financial Commission was to remain in Athens until 1936, successfully enforcing compliance with Greece's foreign obligations until the Great Depression finally pushed the country into default anew. Historians generally agree that "the settlement of 1898 worked out very satisfactorily . . . for the holders of all the remaining Greek foreign loans," and that "certainly only the scheme of control enabled the investors in Greek loans to receive their full interest payment during the stormy years that both preceded and followed 1914."[31]

## THE TWENTIETH-CENTURY TURN TO GUNBOAT DIPLOMACY

Despite the extension of financial control in the eastern Mediterranean, it was only at the turn of the twentieth century that the resort to military action became an increasingly frequent—and, as a result, an increasingly contentious—fixture in the settlement of foreign debt disputes. The most paradigmatic episode of creditor intervention in this period was undoubtedly the aggressive European response to the default of Venezuela. In 1899, the liberal army commander Cipriano Castro had overthrown the country's sitting government and seized power following a brief period of violent revolutionary upheaval. Foreign investors did not emerge from the turmoil unscathed: among other violations of European property, Castro suspended payments on the previous government's obligations to British bondholders. In 1902, after three years of failed diplomatic efforts, the British, German and Italian governments responded by dispatching their gunboats, blockading Venezuela's main ports, shelling its naval defenses, and occupying its customs houses to exact compensation for damages done to European investors. After several months of mounting international pressure, Castro finally relented and agreed to settle with his foreign claimants at The Hague Tribunal, bringing the Venezuelan crisis to an end.[32]

A lively academic debate has since ensued on what to make of this particular historical episode. Early studies generally agreed that the turn towards gunboat diplomacy marked a major shift in British foreign policy away from the Palmerston doctrine and towards full-fledged military support for private investors. In 1906, John Latané claimed that it was "perfectly apparent" that the intervention in Venezuela was "undertaken in the interest of bondholders," and in 1930 Herbert Feis similarly opined that "the government had swung full circle; the whole force of the state had been put behind the foreign investor."[33] More recently, however, Michael Tomz has argued that "British bondholders were an afterthought, not an inspiration, for military intervention."[34] The real reason, according to Tomz, was bodily harm done to UK citizens and the violation of property and seizure of boats belonging to British subjects.

Whatever the case may be, it is clear that the European intervention in Venezuela proved to be an important turning point in the management of sovereign debt crises: not only did it precipitate an angry diplomatic response from other Latin American governments; it also provoked a major strategic realignment by the United States government, which henceforth resolved to take over the role of a regional debt collector in a bid to forestall future European military action in "its own backyard."[35]

The Latin American governments themselves responded to the Venezuelan crisis by overwhelmingly backing a proposal by Luis Drago, the foreign minister of Argentina, to add a corollary to the Monroe doctrine stipulating that "the public debt of an American State cannot occasion armed intervention, nor even the actual occupation of the territory of American nations by a European Power." Building on the principle of sovereign immunity, the Drago doctrine held that "the issuing state is the sole judge of its ability to pay. The investor, therefore, buys with full notice and assumption of the risks and has weighed the possibilities of large profits against the danger of loss."[36] At The Hague Peace Conference of 1907, the United States subsequently submitted an amended version of this proposal that became known as the Porter proposition, according to which "the Contracting Powers agree not to have recourse to armed force for the recovery of contract debts claimed from the government of one country by the government of another country as being due to its nationals." However, unlike the Drago doctrine proposed by the debtors, the Porter proposition included the crucial caveat that "this understanding is . . . not applicable when the debtor state refuses or neglects to reply to an offer of arbitration, or, after accepting the offer, prevents any *compromise* from being agreed on or, after arbitration, fails to submit to the award."[37] It was this caveat that would subsequently allow the U.S. government to take over the enforcement of international debt contracts in the region. In doing so, it directly built upon the corollary to the Monroe doctrine that Theodore Roosevelt had promulgated in response to the Venezuelan crisis three years earlier, in which he declared:

> If a nation shows that it knows how to act with reasonable efficiency and decency in social and political matters, if it keeps order and pays its obligations, it need fear no interference from the United States. Chronic wrongdoing, or an impotence which results in a general loosening of the ties of civilized society, may in America, as elsewhere, ultimately require intervention by some civilized nation, and in the Western Hemisphere the adherence of the United States to the Monroe Doctrine may force the United States, however reluctantly, in flagrant cases of such wrongdoing or impotence, to the exercise of an international police power.

The United States, in short, felt compelled to prevent Latin American borrowers from reneging on their obligations to European bondholders, since this was the main pretext the European powers had drawn upon to justify their military escapades in the region. The U.S. government seemed to believe that the best way to prevent future defaults would be to establish direct financial control over a number of Central American and Caribbean states. As a result, American and European bondholders alike increasingly came to rely on the deployment of U.S. marines to enforce their claims in the region. Between 1905 and 1929, the U.S. government took military action or established financial control in the Dominican Republic, Cuba, Haiti, Honduras, Mexico, Nicaragua, Costa Rica, and Panama. The intervention in the first three of these countries culminated in an outright military occupation, with U.S. officials assuming administrative authority over Cuba in 1906–1909, 1920, and 1917–1922; Haiti in 1915–1934; and the Dominican Republic in 1916–1924. The ostensible motivation behind this turn in U.S. foreign policy was growing concern within the U.S. establishment that further European interventions in the region might prioritize the interests of those countries' bondholders over those of the Wall Street bankers, who—with the rise of J. P. Morgan and Rockefeller—were becoming an increasingly powerful force in American politics.[38]

That said, the resort to gunboats and the establishment of international financial control remained limited to two regions: the Caribbean (the U.S. sphere of influence) and the eastern Mediterranean (the British sphere of influence). None of the bigger countries in Europe or mainland Latin America were subjected to a similar regime. On the whole, official intervention remained the exception rather than the rule. While Greece's and Serbia's government finances were placed under creditor control in the crisis of the 1890s, for instance, no such regime was established for Portugal and Spain, despite those countries' contemporaneous crises and defaults. Similarly, while Venezuela was subjected to gunboat diplomacy following its default in 1902, a decade earlier Argentina's bondholders had been left to fend for themselves following that country's default of 1890, while a decade later the UK foreign secretary Edward Gray responded to the Brazilian default of 1914 by telling Parliament that "British financiers have to make their own arrangements with the Brazilian government," confirming that official intervention remained patchy and unpredictable throughout this period.[39] Even where the creditor powers did move decisively to intervene, there were often prominent critical voices inside the legal and financial establishment decrying the government's infringement on the principle of sovereign immunity. Responding to the British decision to participate in the establishment of financial control over Greece, *The Economist* lamented that "it is no part of the business of our Foreign Office to audit the accounts of other nations and certify as to their solvency or insolvency."[40] This view, while it occasionally lost out, generally prevailed in the management of international debt crises.

Moreover, in the few cases where creditor states did pursue military action, the motivations behind their interventions were rarely limited to bondholder interests alone.[41] Sovereign default occasionally constituted a convenient pretext for an expansion of colonial control, but as Tomz has persuasively argued it was not necessarily the driving force behind Western aggression, which appears to have been principally motivated by the broader geopolitical ambitions of the creditor states themselves. Former U.S. president Ulysses S. Grant appeared to recognize as much when he warned the Japanese emperor of the looming threat of European imperialism, noting that "the purpose of lending money is to get political power for themselves."[42]

## THE STRUCTURAL POWER OF *HAUTE FINANCE*

The historical discussion in this chapter therefore leaves us with an important puzzle. If individual bondholders were dispersed, disorganized, and relatively powerless, and if creditor states could not always be relied upon to back up their claims in the event of default, then how did creditors enforce cross-border debt contracts in the nineteenth century? The resort to military action clearly did not constitute a fail-safe enforcement mechanism during the early decades of the Pax Britannica—at least not until the rise of imperialist finance at the turn of the twentieth century made foreign intervention a more frequent phenomenon in certain parts of the world. Some scholars have highlighted the role of bondholder organizations in countering the atomization and facilitating the coordination of dispersed investors, but the UK Council of Foreign Bondholders was not founded until 1868 and not properly instituted by Parliament until 1898, while the U.S. Corporation of Foreign Bondholders Act was not enacted until 1933.[43] How, then, was international lending made possible in the first half of the nineteenth century, and how did it continue to thrive in the second half? Clearly unilateral moratoriums were widespread in the major international debt crises of the 1820s and 1870s, but most sovereign borrowers nevertheless tried their best to repay during the good times, only suspending payments once their foreign-exchange reserves had been depleted, and rarely repudiating their foreign obligations outright. This tendency towards compliance outside of the "hard times" of acute fiscal distress, even in the absence of gunboats or external financial control, appears to signal the existence of a subtle underlying enforcement mechanism of debtor compliance. The main question is what this mechanism looked like and how exactly it operated.

Once again, the highly concentrated nature of the underwriting business and the centralized international credit structure appear to have been an important part of the story. While bondholders tended to be dispersed and disorganized, the large international banking houses that underwrote the biggest bond issues were not. Flandreau and Flores have found that total market share for the three leading intermediary banks never fell below 50 percent throughout the Pax Britannica. In the first major lending boom of the 1820s, the Rothschild and Barings banks alone initiated over half of all emerging market loans, with "the House of Rothschild surpass[ing] all other underwriters in terms of market share, capital stock, and performance."[44] As in Genoa and Amsterdam in previous centuries, a handful of elite bankers effectively ended up controlling sovereign access to international credit, allowing them to set the terms of borrowing even for some of the world's most powerful governments. To defend their enormous market share, prestigious underwriters like the Rothschilds and Barings had a strong incentive to maintain their unblemished record by only floating loans to reliable sovereigns, and by actively monitoring the fiscal policies of their customers to ensure full and timely repayment. Conversely, the borrowers themselves had a strong incentive not to upset their trust relationship with these prestigious underwriters, whose privileged access to the London capital market furnished them with reliable credit at the best possible terms.

The underwriting banks, then, carried both a carrot and a stick: whenever a borrowing government was at risk of default, they would first try to keep the debtor solvent by continuing to provide loans conditional on policies that maximized the likelihood of full repayment, while at the same time wielding the credible threat to withhold further credit in the event of noncompliance. If the latter transpired, the borrower would be forced to turn towards the less prestigious underwriters instead, which would inevitably confront it with a less reliable source of financing and higher borrowing costs. In the worst-case scenario, it would be excluded from international capital markets altogether, leaving it at a distinct disadvantage in the competitive games being played out in the imperialist arena. "The outcome," Flandreau and Flores observe, "was a highly hierarchical, highly concentrated, and highly persistent global bond market, which turned out to be sustained by its very monopolization."[45]

Sitting at the top of this international credit structure, the Rothschild bank in particular carved out for itself a position of unparalleled power in world politics. As Polanyi put it, "the Rothschilds were subject to no *one* government; as a family they embodied the abstract principle of internationalism; their loyalty was to a firm, the credit of which had become the only supranational link between political government and industrial effort in a swiftly growing world economy."[46] Another contemporary opined that "there is but one power in Europe and that is Rothschild." When it comes to the deeper sources of its power, however, the notoriously persistent anti-Semitic conspiracy theories surrounding this most prominent banking family in modern history entirely miss the point: the Rothschilds derived their influence in international affairs not from their cunning conspiracies, but from the structural position of their firm as the principal gatekeeper of credit access in an emerging capitalist world economy. Flandreau and Flores point out that the bank's monopolistic control over international government finance enabled it to engage in an early type of market-based conditional lending and exact a form of "structural adjustment" from its borrowers. To prevent default, it would regularly intervene in the early stages of potential crises to provide emergency liquidity under strict policy conditionality—effectively assuming the role of a crisis manager, to some extent combining the functions of an international lender of last resort and a fiscal disciplinarian, thereby blending the first and second enforcement mechanisms into one and turning the House of Rothschild, as one *New York Times* review put it, into the nineteenth-century equivalent of "Merrill Lynch, Morgan Stanley, J. P. Morgan, Goldman Sachs and the International Monetary Fund rolled into one."[47]

The resultant enforcement regime was spectacularly effective: at the height of the first international debt crisis in 1829, not a single Rothschild loan was in default. By contrast, all but three loans issued by less prestigious underwriters suffered payment suspensions in the 1820s.[48] The same enforcement mechanism ensured that, during the crisis of the 1890s, the Rothschilds' biggest Latin American borrower—Brazil—remained current on its obligations even as its neighbor Argentina defaulted on the Rothschilds' main rival, provoking the Barings crisis in the process. As Brazil's fiscal position deteriorated, the Rothschilds "strongly advised" its president-elect against a debt moratorium: "besides the complete loss of the country's credit," the bankers warned him, "the measure could greatly affect Brazil's sovereignty, provoking reactions that could arrive at the extreme of foreign invasion."[49] In other words, even if sovereign default remained a widespread phenomenon in the nineteenth century, the remarkable compliance of the Rothschilds' borrowers provides evidence that the combination of highly concentrated market discipline and an early form of conditional lending—backed up in exceptional cases with resort to gunboats or the establishment of external financial control—greatly strengthened the structural power of *haute finance* and reduced the likelihood of sovereign default on the loans it had underwritten. As Flandreau and Flores conclude, echoing Polanyi, "those looking for the sound and fury of 'gunboats' were at risk of overlooking the muffled noise of market-based conditionality."[50]

Bit by bit, finance was gaining the structural power needed to discipline foreign borrowers and enforce compliance with its own cross-border debt contracts. But before private creditors would learn to perfect that power in the last quarter of the twentieth century, they would first have to pass through the greatest financial cataclysm of all.

# SEVEN

## From Great Depression to Financial Repression

The early twentieth century witnessed another major shift in the international balance of power, this time from the Old World to the New. Just as the City of London had displaced Amsterdam as banker to Europe in the wake of the Napoleonic Wars, so the City of New York slowly began to displace London as the world's leading financial center in the wake of World War I.[1] With the Barings Bank still reeling from the crisis provoked by the Argentine default of 1890 and the Rothschilds gradually losing their position of unrivaled prominence in international affairs, powerful new Wall Street bankers like J. P. Morgan and Rockefeller emerged to take over the reins of international lending. During the Roaring Twenties, the United States firmly established itself as the world's main creditor country, initiating almost two-thirds of all foreign government loans between 1924 and 1931. By the end of the decade the dollar had supplanted sterling as the dominant global currency and U.S. hegemony in international finance was a fact.[2]

It quickly became clear that American investors had learned little from the nineteenth-century experience of their British counterparts. Just as in London in the 1820s, 1860s and 1880s, the New York Stock Exchange soon found itself in the grips of a major speculative craze, with billions of dollars gushing towards Latin America and Europe in search of attractive yields and sovereign lending accounting for a significant share of these vast international capital flows.[3] As the major loan originators on Wall Street aggressively peddled foreign securities to ordinary investors and unsuspecting small savers at home, the total number of Americans invested in foreign government bonds quintupled from roughly 200,000 at the start of World War I in 1914 to over a million by the time of the Great Crash in 1929.[4] As before, the boom inevitably turned to bust in the financial crisis that followed, leaving investors scrambling for the exits and causing global capital flows to come to a sudden stop. As credit dried up and commodity prices collapsed, dozens of sovereign borrowers saw their foreign exchange earnings drop and were eventually forced to suspend payments on their external debts, triggering what today still remains the largest sovereign default wave in history.

How are we to account for the widespread payment suspensions of the 1930s? Clearly the economic shock played a decisive role in depleting foreign-exchange reserves and circumscribing the debtors' ability to pay—but the economic shock was only part of the story. In fact, as we will see in this chapter, the nearly universal resort to unilateral debt moratoriums in the 1930s was made possible at least in part by the relative weakness of the three enforcement mechanisms of debtor compliance, which left dispersed bondholders without the necessary leverage and coordination capacity to keep the debtors solvent while simultaneously imposing discipline on them. In the following pages, we will first take a closer look at the moratoriums themselves before turning to the conditions that caused the three enforcement mechanisms to fail. The chapter's conclusion will then briefly summarize the consequences of the defaults, before we turn to the first international debt crisis of the contemporary period—the Latin American debt crisis of the 1980s—in the next section.

## THE UNILATERAL DEBT MORATORIUMS OF THE 1930S

Like their nineteenth-century antecedents, the defaults of the 1930s were the direct consequence of a systemic convulsion that originated in the financial center. The economic slowdown that began in late 1928 and culminated in the Wall Street crash of 1929—which in turn led to a protracted worldwide depression and the pursuit of aggressive protectionist measures by national governments—caused global demand to collapse and borrowing costs to rise, hitting the commodity-exporting countries of Latin America particularly hard. Export revenues fell by an average of 50 percent between 1928 and 1933, while short-term real interest rates shot up to over 15 percent.[5] Barry Eichengreen notes that "the developing countries had few options. They could use their remaining foreign-exchange earnings to keep current the service on their external obligations, or they could husband their central bank reserves and defend the convertibility of their currencies."[6] Hesitant to upset their foreign lenders or decouple from gold, the debtors initially tried to have it both ways, defending the convertibility of their currencies while repaying their debts. But after several years of falling export earnings and continued debt servicing, they had largely depleted their foreign-exchange reserves. Once again, the result was a cascading series of sovereign defaults.

In January 1931, Bolivia became the first Latin American borrower to suspend payments on its external debt, followed shortly thereafter by Peru, Chile and Brazil. Colombia, Uruguay, Costa Rica, Panama and the Dominican Republic all followed suit the next year, and by 1933 at least sixteen Latin American borrowers were in default. In Europe, the incidence of nonpayment was similarly widespread, with Germany, Turkey, Greece, Hungary, Romania, and Austria all suspending external debt service, while Belgium, Czechoslovakia,

Finland, France, Italy, Norway, and Spain all pursued various "softer" varieties of default, as did Japan, Canada, Australia, and New Zealand (see table 7.1).[7]

Even if these defaults greatly differed in terms of intensity and degree of coercion, ranging from partial reductions on interest service or sinking funds to outright debt moratoriums, the overall tendency strongly inclined towards unilateral debtor action. All in all, around one-third of foreign government bonds bought by U.S. investors went into arrears over the course of the Great Depression, rising to 76 percent of all loans made to Latin America. By one count, almost half of all borrowing countries worldwide defaulted during the 1930s.[8] "Never had the scale of defaults been so large and their incidence so widespread," writes Andrea Papadia of the London School of Economics. "Up to this day, such rampant insolvency is unique."[9] To be sure, not all countries suspended payments during the Great Depression. Those whose custom houses remained under U.S. financial control—like Haiti, Honduras, and Nicaragua— mostly honored their foreign obligations, as did a number of other small states in the region.[10] The most remarkable outlier, the only major Latin American debtor not to unilaterally suspend payments, was Argentina, which promptly repaid its foreign debts even as its neighbors fell into arrears all around it. "Yet even in the Argentine case," Marichal writes, "negotiations with the foreign bankers were necessary," and for the rest of the decade "all the Latin American governments were involved in complex readjustments of their debts with United States and European banks and bondholders."[11]

Perhaps the most striking aspect of the defaults of the 1930s is how widely accepted they appear to have been at the time. The defaulting governments themselves generally showed no remorse about pursuing unilateral action, and many contemporary observers saw the moratoriums as an unavoidable outcome of the collapse in the terms of trade, which "made suspension of payments on debts a logical defensive measure."[12] As Max Winkler put it in his classic 1933 book, *Foreign Bonds: An Autopsy*, "defaults are inevitable when attempts are made by lenders to take advantage of temporarily embarrassed borrowers by exacting all sorts of concessions and imposing all sorts of impossibly harsh terms."[13] It was widely recognized that, insofar as the borrowers had acted irresponsibly by accumulating far too much debt, the lenders were at least equally to blame for extending such excessive amounts of credit in the first place—and the debtors certainly could not be blamed for the external economic conditions that brought on the crisis and that had left their foreign-exchange reserves dangerously depleted.[14] Borchard insists that "although financial mismanagement in various forms helped engender the wave of insolvencies which disrupted the contractual relations between borrowing states and their foreign creditors during the early 1930s, that cataclysm was largely attributable to circumstances beyond the debtors' control."[15] If the debtor states were not to blame for the crisis, it logically followed that the creditors should be expected to assume their fair share of the burden of adjustment—making temporary unilateral payment

TABLE 7.1.
List of sovereign defaults during the Great Depression

| Europe | | Latin America | |
|---|---|---|---|
| Austria | 1938, 1940 | Bolivia | 1931 |
| Belgium* | 1930s | Brazil | 1931, 1937 |
| Bulgaria* | 1930s | Chile | 1931 |
| Czechoslovakia* | 1930s | Colombia | 1932, 1935 |
| Denmark* | 1930s | Costa Rica | 1932 |
| Finland* | 1930s | Dominican Republic | 1931 |
| France* | 1930s | Ecuador | 1929 |
| Germany | 1932, 1939 | El Salvador | 1932, 1938 |
| Greece | 1932 | Guatemala | 1933 |
| Hungary | 1932, 1941 | Mexico | 1928 (1914) |
| Italy* | 1930s | Nicaragua | 1932 |
| Norway* | 1930s | Panama | 1932 |
| Poland | 1936, 1940 | Paraguay | 1932 |
| Romania | 1933 | Peru | 1931 |
| Spain* | 1930s | Uruguay | 1933 |
| Turkey | 1931, 1940 | Venezuela* | 1930s |

*Source*: Reinhart and Rogoff (2009) for all countries for which specific years are provided. With the exception of Bulgaria, which is marked a "heavy defaulter," all the countries marked with asterisk (*) are listed as "light defaulters" by Eichengreen and Portes (1985), and are not included in Reinhart and Rogoff's list. No specific dates are provided for these defaults, so the years are simply marked "1930s." N.B.: Mexico repudiated its debts during its revolution (1914) and remained in default through the 1930s.

suspensions followed by coercive debt restructurings a relatively uncontroversial policy response on the part of the distressed borrowing governments, which had already gone through great pains to try to stay current on their obligations in the first years of the crisis. The defaults, in short, were considered to be excusable.[16]

President Franklin D. Roosevelt recognized as much when, receiving Bolivia's president at the White House in 1943, he personally apologized for Wall Street's "supersalesmanship" in the lead-up to the crisis. Referring to a high-interest loan made to the Bolivian government in 1926 or 1927, which Roosevelt considered to be an act of "financial exploitation" by the New York bankers, the U.S. president declared that "of course . . . Bolivia was unable to pay either the interest or the principal" on the obligation.[17] But while Roosevelt was widely understood to be relatively unsympathetic towards Wall Street, the president was far from the only one blaming the bankers for the debtors' financial predicament. As early as 1925, for instance, Moody's was already sending out warnings to American investors "who are primarily interested in reaping unreasonable profits in their dealing with foreign borrowers, taking advantage of the pressing needs of the latter and their perhaps temporary fiscal difficulty." In a clear expression of the prevailing attitude at the time, Moody's included that:

> If we ever expect to become international bankers who will command respect in the world's commerce and finance, we are treading on dangerous ground. If we feel that the credit of a nation is sound enough to justify our extending of credit to it, we ought to do it on decent terms. To demand the "last pound of flesh" is decidedly wrong economically as it is wrong on ethical and moral grounds. It is financing of the above character and the inevitable results which do infinite damage to the foreign securities markets, tending to bring into disrepute all foreign bonds irrespective of their investment merit.[18]

Even on Wall Street and in the White House, in short, the crisis of the 1930s was largely seen as the inevitable outcome of excessive and irresponsible lending by private investors, which in turn gave the debtors significant leeway to inflict losses on their creditors in response to the depletion of their foreign-exchange reserves. Indeed, as we already saw in the introduction to this book, the declaration of debt moratoriums was generally considered to be "normal and part of the rules of the game" in the interwar period.[19] The surprise with which investors met Argentina's exceptional insistence on full repayment clearly reveals the fact that default—not compliance—was the norm. One financial commentator remarked that "it is astonishing to many observers that the country has been able to maintain service on its national debt so faithfully. The efforts and sacrifice involved have, in fact, been tremendous."[20] In the 1930s, Argentina's "almost superhuman" efforts to repay were the exception that proved the rule.

## INEFFECTIVENESS OF THE THREE ENFORCEMENT MECHANISMS

How, then, can we account for the widespread resort to unilateral debt moratoriums in the 1930s? In line with the structural power hypothesis developed in this book, we would expect the default wave of the Great Depression to have been the result of the relative weakness of the three enforcement mechanisms of debtor compliance—and there is considerable evidence to corroborate that line of analysis. First, in the absence of a powerful monopolistic underwriting bank like the House of Rothschild to coordinate creditor action, the decentralized nature of prewar bond finance tended to greatly atomize and disorganize bondholders, making it impossible for them to sustain a unified creditors' cartel and thereby weakening the force of market discipline in ensuring debtor compliance. Second, in the absence of an international lender of last resort and active state intervention, the distressed debtors were left without access to emergency credit and without a fiscal disciplinarian to enforce compliance, thus making widespread government insolvency virtually inevitable. And third, the presence of powerful popular pressure from below pushed policymakers in many heavily indebted countries to pursue a more equitable distribution of adjustment costs, while the relatively low dependence on foreign credit endowed state administrators with a degree of autonomy from global finance, which in turn tended to empower those domestic groups that preferred a heterodox policy response—including a unilateral suspension of payments—over continued foreign debt servicing. The result of these dynamics was to bring about a breakdown of the enforcement mechanisms that had served to ensure at least partial debtor compliance during the good times before 1929, giving the sovereign borrowers of the 1930s considerably more freedom to pursue a unilateral course of action.

On the first point, economists and historians have long considered the anonymity of securitized lending and the atomization of private investors a particularly important feature of prewar and interwar bond finance.[21] All long-term government loans in the lead-up to the crisis came in the form of bond issues that were floated on the stock exchange, with the vast majority of securities finding their way into the hands of small savers who enjoyed nothing like the political and economic clout that the Wall Street banks commanded and who were generally scattered and disorganized—hundreds of thousands in number and spread out across various jurisdictions. Organizing this dispersed creditor base to pursue a coordinated response to the debt crisis proved difficult, if not impossible. In the United States, an estimated 800,000 individual bondholders were affected by the defaults of the 1930s, and efforts to rally them largely turned out to be in vain. As investors panicked and the stock market collapsed, credit dried up, and the borrowers were cut off from their financial lifelines. In short, there was no way for the creditors to coordinate collective action and keep the debtors in the lending game. In 1933, the U.S. government helped investors create a bondholders' organization in an attempt to counter this atomization, but, as Fishlow notes, "in the absence of the lure of future capital flows (and the threat of their blockage) the power of the US Bondholders Protective Council was nil."[22]

While successful government lending had historically been sustained by a degree of concentration and centralization in the international credit structure— which, as we have seen, tended at various points in time to be dominated by powerful creditors' cartels like the Genoese bank syndicates, the Amsterdam loan originators, or the Rothschild and Barings banks of London—in the 1930s the decentralized nature of international capital markets made it all but impossible for investors to establish and maintain a unified international creditors' cartel. In the absence of effective creditor coordination, it proved impossible to carry out the complex balancing act between disciplining distressed borrowers through market mechanisms while simultaneously keeping them solvent and servicing their debts by rolling over maturing obligations or continuing to provide further loans. There was therefore no way, within the structure of the international capital market, to counteract the "sudden stop" in credit provision to the peripheral countries. Moreover, once the debtor countries had suspended payments, the creditors turned out to be far too disorganized to present a unified front vis-à-vis the defaulting governments, endowing the latter with significant leverage in subsequent debt negotiations. As Jorgensen and Sachs note, "the difficulty in resolving interwar defaults was a reflection of the myriad of bondholders whose consent was required . . . it was this very same dispersion that allowed final settlements to include partial debt forgiveness."[23] In sum, decentralized bond finance made it next to impossible for atomized bondholders to maintain a unified front, leading to a wholesale breakdown of the first enforcement mechanism. Frieden points out how, as a result, "the threat to default was eminently credible, for the international financial system had collapsed and the threat of being frozen out of it was entirely empty. 'Exiting' from effectively nonexistent international financial markets was not very costly to debtors, while foregoing debt service payments was very costly to creditors. The debtors held virtually all the bargaining power."[24]

In terms of the second mechanism, the evidence points in the same direction. While in the nineteenth and early twentieth centuries the creditor states had occasionally intervened in foreign debt disputes to enforce bondholders' contractual claims, in the 1930s no such military action or international financial control was forthcoming. Britain and the other European powers had experienced significant imperial decline since World War I, leaving them incapable of mustering the military might they had previously wielded in countries like Mexico, Egypt, and Venezuela. Meanwhile, the U.S. government was just shifting its foreign policy stance from Theodore Roosevelt's corollary to the Monroe doctrine, which had guided the interventionist dollar diplomacy of the first quarter of the century, toward Franklin Roosevelt's "good neighbor" policy, which was much less subservient to Wall Street interests and considerably more accommodating to foreign debtors, as we already saw with respect to his apologies to regional leaders for the bankers' "supersalesmanship." When the U.S. government finally returned towards more active intervention during World War II, it actually joined the fray on the side of the debtors rather than the creditors, "subordinating the private economic interests of the bondholders to the political and military requirements of 'hemispheric cooperation.'" In the Mexican case, for instance, U.S. insistence on "good neighborliness" resulted in bondholder losses of up to 90 percent on the nominal value of their claims.[25]

Beside this waning state support for private bondholders, another crucial factor in the 1930s was the lack of an international lender of last resort and fiscal disciplinarian capable of disbursing emergency loans under strict policy conditionality to keep the debtors solvent and compliant with their international obligations. While the Rothschild bank had fulfilled a monitoring, surveillance, and crisis management function for a limited number of borrowers during the nineteenth century, regularly engaging in conditional lending to distressed debtors in order to prevent defaults on the loans it had originated, no such organization—private or official—was capable of fulfilling a similar role during the Great Depression. Contemporary observers considered it "obvious that much of the responsibility for the present chaotic state of the international money market must be laid to the lack of effective supervision of any kind."[26] As Charles Kindleberger famously noted, "there was no international lender of last resort" during the crisis of the 1930s: "Britain, weakened by the war, was unable to help; the United States and France were unwilling to."[27]

It was precisely the lessons learned from this experience that eventually moved the U.S. and UK governments to establish the International Monetary Fund at the Bretton Woods conference of 1944, which, as we will see in the following chapter, was to dramatically transform the dynamics of crisis management in the international debt crises of the 1980s, 1990s, and 2010s.[28] In contrast to the contemporary period, the absence of an international lender of last resort in the 1930s meant that there was no backstop to the breakdown of market discipline; no "collective creditor" or fiscal disciplinarian capable of acting in the bondholders' joint interest by keeping the debtors solvent while imposing rectitude on their public finances to free up domestic resources for foreign debt servicing. The absence of this second enforcement mechanism ultimately made a wave of sovereign defaults all but inevitable.

These dynamics were further compounded by the malfunctioning of the third enforcement mechanism: the privileged position of domestic elites fulfilling a bridging role towards foreign creditors and internalizing fiscal discipline into the debtors' state apparatus. Two factors conspired to keep this mechanism relatively weak in the 1930s. First, for many peripheral countries dependence on foreign credit tended to be lower in the 1930s than it is today. Since welfare spending in the poorer countries was still relatively anemic and domestic firms and households did not depend on private credit as much as they do today, the spillover costs of default and the economic consequences of a foreign credit cutoff were comparatively manageable. The result of this lower dependence on credit—especially in the wake of 1929, when the availability of foreign loans dried up altogether and borrowers had no real opportunities to obtain foreign private financing anyway—was to erode the bridging role of domestic financial elites, along with the privileged position they derived from it. The Mexican experience is a case in point. Sylvia Maxfield has convincingly shown how the country's autonomy from international capital markets following its postrevolutionary debt repudiation enabled the national-popular administration of Lázaro Cárdenas to pursue a considerably more heterodox policy current than that preferred by international investors and the orthodox bankers' elite centered on Mexico City.[29] This enabled the Mexican government to take an aggressive stance towards foreign bondholders, even proposing the imposition of a collective continent-wide debt moratorium to extract better terms.

The second reason why the third enforcement mechanism broke down in the 1930s had to do with the significant popular pressure exercised from below. Previous revolutionary episodes in Mexico (1914) and Russia (1917) had already demonstrated how powerful social mobilizations for a more equitable distribution of wealth and power in society could lead to outright sovereign debt repudiations. Neither the Mexican nor the Russian default, of course, had anything to do with the Great Depression, but the internal dynamics and external conditions giving rise to them did highlight the room for maneuver available to debtors in pursuing unilateral action in the prewar and interwar years. In both cases, strong popular pressure from below combined with decentralized bond markets and a lack of international organizations or imperial powers willing and able to discipline the bigger sovereign defaulters. While outright repudiations remained extremely rare even during this tumultuous period in international financial history, the favorable external conditions and strong internal pressures that ultimately led to the Mexican and Russian repudiations did hold up elsewhere in Europe and Latin America during the Great Depression, when the combination of relative state autonomy and powerful popular mobilizations from below for a more equitable distribution of adjustment costs made the declaration of unilateral debt moratoriums a much more likely outcome.

In Europe, for instance, Eichengreen notes that the expansion of the franchise in the wake of World War I and the associated rise of strong labor parties and trade unions imposed internal political constraints on the capacity of the debtor states to pursue the type of orthodox adjustment measures required to maintain external discipline.[30] In Latin America, meanwhile, powerful social movements arose against the consequences of the crisis and the tax hikes required to service foreign debts. Marichal notes that "during the initial stages of the Great Depression (1929–33) more than one Latin American government fell as a consequence of the mass demonstrations and strikes directed against the politicians who had contracted huge foreign debts and against the corruption those debts had engendered." As had already happened on so many previous occasions throughout history of sovereign debt, from the taxpayers' revolts in late-medieval and early-modern Europe to the nineteenth-century 'Urabi uprising in Egypt, "in numerous instances such protests led to outright default."[31] The lessons from the 1930s are therefore clear: it was the combination of the external economic shock (which led to a collapse of export earnings, rising borrowing costs, and a rapid depletion of foreign-exchange reserves) and the malfunctioning of the three enforcement mechanisms (which greatly reduced the creditors' capacity to keep their distressed borrowers solvent and impose discipline on their foreign debt servicing) that made a cascading series of defaults not only possible, but exceedingly unavoidable. The idiosyncrasies of individual borrowing countries in turn helped shape the specifics of debtors' respective policy responses and the intensity of their defaults.[32] It was the combination of these internal and external factors that, in a marked contrast to today, helped shape the outcome of the Great Depression to the advantage of the debtors and the disadvantage of the creditors.

## LESSONS FROM THE HISTORY OF SOVEREIGN DEBT AND DEFAULT

The historical discussion of the last three chapters allows us to draw a number of conclusions with important implications for the study of sovereign debt repayment and international crisis management in the contemporary period. First, as we saw in chapter 5, the politics of sovereign debt repayment have always been contentious and fraught with redistributive implications, regularly leading to intense social and political conflicts over the distribution of adjustment costs and to protracted power struggles over fiscal policy that have long been intertwined with broader demands for greater democratic representation. Wherever possible, private financiers have historically tended to respond to the resultant threat of repudiation by seeking to insulate fiscal policy from popular pressures and establishing direct creditor control over the administration of the state finances—a phenomenon that has been referred to as the "private management of the public debt."[33] At different points in history, the exigencies of war fed into the state's structural dependence on credit, which in turn contributed to the rise of a powerful creditor class with close ties to the existing political establishment.[34] Cross-border lending during this period was made possible by an early form of market discipline derived from the high concentration of credit markets, which eased the formation of powerful bankers' cartels that controlled the credit access of foreign sovereigns.

Second, as we saw in chapter 6, the internationalization of finance during the Pax Britannica of the nineteenth century made payment suspensions an increasingly widespread phenomenon, with global capital markets rocked by major default waves in the 1820s, 1870s, and to a lesser extent the 1890s. Since military intervention by creditor states remained a relatively unpredictable affair, international financiers came to rely on more subtle market-based forms of power to force foreign governments to comply with their cross-border debt contracts. This structural power of *haute finance*, revolving around the capacity of strategically positioned international banks to inflict damaging economic spillover costs by withholding further credit to noncompliant borrowers, tended to be at its greatest when the lending structure was highly concentrated, either because the creditors were organized into interlocked bank syndicates (as in Genoa in the sixteenth century) or because relatively few repeat players dominated the underwriting business (as in Amsterdam and London in the eighteenth and nineteenth centuries). Throughout the early history of sovereign debt, then, the embryonic forms of the first and second enforcement mechanisms—market discipline and conditional lending—were generally strong enough to make cross-border lending profitable and therefore possible, even if the partial and incomplete nature of these mechanisms meant that they could not prevent widespread unilateral payment suspensions in times of systemic crisis.

Finally, as we saw in this chapter, the prevailing policy response to the Great Depression highlights the relative weakness of the three enforcement mechanisms during the systemic financial crises of the prewar period. Coming on the heels of the third major international lending cycle, the combination of a destabilizing external shock and a wholesale breakdown of enforcement produced a groundswell of government insolvency that remains unparalleled in scope and intensity to this very day, and that presents a particularly stark contrast to the outcome of the more recent Great Recession. By declaring unilateral moratoriums on their external debt service, most of the sovereign debtors of the 1930s succeeded in deflecting part of the adjustment costs onto their foreign lenders, obtaining much-needed fiscal breathing room that allowed them to recover faster than their nondefaulting counterparts.[35] Jorgensen and Sachs conclude that "the defaults of the 1930s present lessons for contemporary experience because these countries actually ceased payment on their foreign debts and these defaults were acknowledged, accepted, and eventually negotiated on terms favorable to the debtors."[36]

The long-term consequences of these defaults were momentous. The combined effects of the Great Depression and World War II caused international capital markets to collapse altogether, with no significant cross-border lending taking place for the next four decades. At the end of the war, the U.S. and British governments moved swiftly to ensure that global finance could not resume the dominant position it had enjoyed in the lead-up to the calamities of the 1930s and 1940s. Under the "embedded liberalism" of the Bretton Woods regime, private investors and financial institutions were trapped within national borders through far-reaching capital controls and subjected to strict financial regulations and moderate inflation.[37] By forcing down real interest rates and demoting private investors to the status of a captive audience, national governments thus took a tentative first step towards Keynes's envisioned "euthanasia of the rentier," allowing state administrators to borrow more cheaply and extinguish much of their postwar debt overhang through inflationary means. At the same time, the treasuries and central banks of the advanced capitalist democracies

FIGURE 7.1. Share of marketable debt in central government debt, 1900–2011.
*Source*: Ali Abbas et al. (2014).

began to engage in widespread experimentation with various unconventional forms of state financing, devising innovative off-market techniques to fund rising rates of public expenditure. While in the prewar period practically all government debt had taken the form of marketable securities, the postwar period saw a precipitous decline in the share of marketable debt (see figure 7.1), greatly reducing the state's dependence on private credit and hence the structural power and privileged political position that finance derived from it.[38]

This postwar strategy of "financial repression" allowed states to briefly expand their relative autonomy from finance and significantly increase their room for maneuver. Real interest rates in the advanced economies fell into negative territory roughly half of the time between 1945 and 1980, allowing the U.S. and UK governments to liquidate their debts from the Great Depression and World War II at an average rate of 3–4 percent of GDP per year.[39] Buoyed by high growth rates, policymakers temporarily succeeded in turning the redistributive implications of public finance on its head, shifting the burden of adjustment for the postwar debt overhang from taxpayers to creditors. As Mark Blyth explains, financial repression effectively functioned like a tax on captive bondholders, bringing about a sustained welfare transfer from private investors to the beneficiaries of public spending, obviating the need for fiscal austerity or outright default in a context of high state indebtedness.[40] Meanwhile, as governments in the core countries kept their bankers on a tight leash, the countries of the periphery mostly turned to official-sector credit—in the form of bilateral loans from the West European and North American countries or multilateral loans from the Bretton Woods institutions—to fund domestic investment. Combined with the strict regulation of finance, the absence of private cross-border lending during this period removed the risk of speculative manias and caused the incidence of banking crises and sovereign debt crises to fall to a historic low, lending an unusual degree of financial stability to the postwar recovery (see figure 7.2).[41]

Nevertheless, the international regime devised at Bretton Woods in 1944 soon succumbed to its own internal contradictions, and by the late 1960s the strains on the system were already starting to become painfully apparent. The emergence of the offshore Eurodollar markets, the result of a regulatory loophole that allowed U.S. banks to maintain dollar-denominated deposits in overseas jurisdictions, mostly in the City of London, led to a resumption and expansion of cross-border capital flows that gradually began to hollow out the capacity of the United States government to uphold the international dollar-gold standard. These so-called Euromarkets, marginal at first but steadily expanding over the course of the 1960s, provided private investors with their much-coveted exit option, allowing the Wall Street banks to escape strict financial regulations and

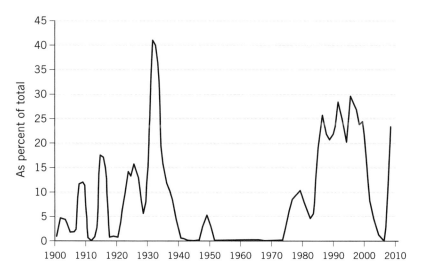

FIGURE 7.2. Share of countries with a banking crisis (weighted by share in world income), 1900–2008. *Source*: Reinhart and Rogoff (2008).

*Note reproduced from source:* "Sample size includes all 66 countries listed in Table A1 [of the source cited] that were independent states in the given year. Three sets of GDP weights are used, 1913 weights for the period 1800–1913, 1990 for the period 1914–1990, and finally 2003 weights for the period 1991–2006. The entries for 2007–2008 list crises in Austria, Belgium, Germany, Hungary, Japan, the Netherlands, Spain, the United Kingdom, and the United States. The figure shows a three-year moving average."

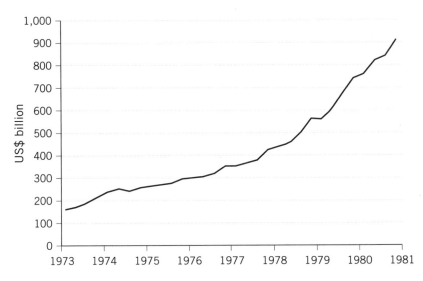

FIGURE 7.3. BIS banks' total cross-border liabilities in foreign currencies, 1973–1981. *Source*: Alvarez (2016); Bank of England's Quarterly Bulletin and Financial Accounts of the United States.

low interest rates at home, and slowly subvert the Bretton Woods regime from within. By 1971, the resultant pressures on U.S. bullion reserves moved the Nixon administration to suspend the convertibility of the dollar into gold—the infamous Nixon shock. Two years later, the Bretton Woods system collapsed, and Western governments began to lift their capital controls and financial regulations one by one, allowing for a rapid expansion of cross-border international bank lending (see figure 7.3).

No longer capable of keeping private investors captive within national borders and with the Federal Reserve dramatically raising interest rates in 1979 to break the back of the inflationary crisis that had crippled the U.S. economy for much of the previous decade, the short-lived era of financial repression came to a sudden end.[42] Governments in the core countries began to turn back towards public borrowing and marketable debt instruments to finance state spending, while governments in the periphery switched from official-sector loans to attracting credit and investment from private lenders. By the turn of the decade, finance found itself back at the heart of a brave new world of unrestricted global capital flows, and another major international lending boom was well underway—with Latin America once again attracting the lion's share of the resultant speculative investments. Soon the specter of widespread government insolvency would come back to haunt the creditors with a vengeance. This time, however, was to be different.[43]

# PART III

The Lost Decade:
Mexico (1982-1989)

# EIGHT

## Syndicated Lending and the Creditors' Cartel

On Friday, August 20, 1982, Mexico's finance minister Jesús Silva Herzog stunned the global financial community by announcing that his government had run out of foreign exchange and could no longer meet its obligations to international creditors. As Latin America's second-largest debtor at the time, the Mexican government owed $82 billion to as many as 1,400 commercial lenders. To avoid sparking a potentially catastrophic series of Latin American defaults that risked bringing down some of the world's biggest banks, the U.S. government and the International Monetary Fund orchestrated an emergency credit line for the Mexican government and helped negotiate a series of private sector roll-overs of its scheduled principal payments on nearly $20 billion worth of public debt. The dramatic episode, which sent shock waves through global financial markets and shivers up the spines of bankers and policymakers around the world, marked the beginning of what would eventually escalate into the worst economic downturn in Latin American history. Over the next months and years, as private investors rushed for the exits in a panic-stricken attempt to reduce their exposure, some thirty-five developing countries—including most Latin American borrowers—were pushed into arrears on their amortization schedules and eventually were forced to request IMF assistance and a rescheduling of their external debts. As Silva Herzog himself would later remark about his fateful announcement, "the world was different after that."[1]

It really was. The Latin American debt crisis that followed would become the first major international debt crisis since the 1930s, marking the end of postwar stability in the world economy and the start of four decades of global financial turmoil. But while the crisis of the 1980s displayed some striking similarities to its predecessor in terms of the underlying economic dynamics, with a strong external shock leading to rising borrowing costs and falling export earnings, rapidly depleting the debtors' foreign-exchange reserves in the process, the prevailing policy response could not have been more different.[2] Unlike the 1930s, when debt moratoriums were widespread, the debt crisis of the 1980s was marked by a striking absence of unilateral default.[3] Even Fidel Castro's Cuba dutifully honored its obligations to European banks, while the Sandinistas of

Nicaragua voluntarily assumed the debts of the Somoza regime they had just overthrown. With payment suspensions effectively ruled out as a permissible policy response, debtors and creditors now engaged in a concerted effort to reschedule the amortization of principal, refinance maturing obligations and prevent an interruption of interest service at all costs.

The result of this new approach to crisis management was a protracted economic downturn, far worse for most Latin American borrowers than the Great Depression, with severe social consequences. Poverty rates on the continent climbed sharply and hit nearly 50 percent by the end of the decade.[4] In 1989, Mexico's gross domestic product was still 11 percent lower than it had been at the start of the crisis, while some 15 million Mexicans had been born in the intervening period. As millions saw their jobs and life opportunities vanish, the 1980s became known as *la década perdida*—"the lost decade." By the 1980s, a new norm seemed to be firmly entrenched: come what may, the public debt must be repaid.[5] U.S. Treasury Secretary Donald Regan neatly summarized the rules of the game as follows: "I don't think we should let a country off the hook just because they are having difficulty. As debtors, I think they should be made to pay as much as they can bear without breaking them. You just can't let your heart rule your head in these situations."[6] Thus began a new era in the history of global capitalism, in which the resort to a unilateral debt moratorium to deal with an external economic shock was to become anathema. As David Harvey puts it, "the Mexico case demonstrated . . . a key difference between liberal and neoliberal practice: under the former, lenders take the losses that arise from bad investment decisions, while under the latter the borrowers are forced by state and international powers to take on board the cost of debt repayment no matter what the consequences for the livelihood and well-being of the local population."[7]

What explains the remarkable and unprecedented degree of debtor compliance with this shift in international policy priorities in the 1980s? As Susan George of the Transnational Institute put it in an influential book on the crisis, "why don't Third World countries simply refuse to pay . . . ? Such behavior has been a constant in international relations for about five hundred years, so why not today?"[8] A closer look at Mexico, which remained at the heart of the Latin American debt storm and at the forefront of the financial firefighting for most of the decade, can provide us with a unique perspective on that question. As we will see in the following chapters, the decade of the 1980s was to witness Wall Street's stunning ascent to the commanding heights of a rapidly changing global political economy; the active intervention of the U.S. government into the fiscal affairs of the borrowing countries; and the steady evolution of the IMF into a lender of last resort and fiscal disciplinarian at the head of a global creditors' cartel. Meanwhile, inside Mexico itself, the crisis would also reveal the growing dependence of the state and the national economy on foreign credit and investment, strengthening the position of political and financial elites who shared with their foreign creditors a strong interest in full debt repayment. In this sense, the year 1982 marked a watershed for the global political economy, not only because it demonstrated for the first time how successful international creditors had become in forestalling widespread sovereign default, but especially because it helped to cement the three enforcement mechanisms of debtor compliance that continue to undergird the structural power of finance today.

In the following chapters we will take a closer look at these three enforcement mechanisms as they gradually entrenched Mexico's status as a "model debtor" for the rest of the continent. First, in this chapter, we will see how the highly concentrated and interlocked nature of syndicated lending contributed to the emergence of a coherent international creditors' cartel that was capable of effectively coordinating collective action among the major Wall Street banks, keeping the debtors in the lending game by rolling over maturing obligations while simultaneously imposing strict market discipline on the borrowing governments through the credible threat of a refusal of further credit in the event of noncompliance. In the next chapter, we will then see how active intervention by the U.S. government combined with the emergence and subsequent transformation of the IMF into an international lender of last resort and fiscal disciplinarian to keep the debtors both solvent and servicing interest through a combination of emergency bailout loans and the imposition of strict policy conditions geared towards freeing up domestic resources for foreign debt servicing. Third, the chapter after that will detail how the growing dependence of the Mexican state on credit contributed to the rise of a domestic "bankers' alliance" made up of financial elites and orthodox technocrats who gradually found their position strengthened as the crisis deepened, allowing them to effectively sideline the national-popular wing of Mexico's one-party regime. Finally, the last chapter of this Mexican case study briefly turns towards the outcomes of the crisis—including its resolution through the Brady deal debt restructuring of 1989–1990—and draws some general conclusions from the comparison with the outcomes of the 1930s.

## A CONCENTRATED AND INTERLOCKED LENDING STRUCTURE

The first major difference between the Great Depression of the 1930s and the Latin American debt crisis of the 1980s lay in the structure of international lending and in the emergence of syndicated bank loans as the principal source of financing for developing country governments. Whereas the lenders of the 1920s had been a scattered multitude of individual bondholders who were notoriously vulnerable to collective action problems and who in the absence of coordination by powerful underwriters generally failed to sustain a coherent creditors' cartel, the lenders of the late 1970s were mostly commercial banks that were in turn organized into international lending syndicates revolving around a small circle of syndicate leaders. The latter were mostly systemically important and politically influential Wall Street banks, although European and Japanese lenders also played a part.[9]

From the early 1970s onwards, these banks began to engage in a highly lucrative trade that became known as petrodollar recycling, which saw them take the surpluses from large petroleum producers in the wake of the oil shocks and reinvest the accumulated deposits at a significant profit elsewhere. Since the crisis of stagflation reduced the profitability of domestic investments in the rich countries, their banks increasingly began to turn towards developing countries to absorb the surplus. The result was a steady increase in the external debt of Latin America (figures 8.1 and 8.2) and other developing regions in the Global South, as well as the concentration of a large share of the resultant obligations on the balance sheets of some of the largest private lenders in the United States, the so-called money-center banks. All in all, the largest nine U.S. banks ended up accumulating some $53 billion in Mexican debt alone.[10]

Given the easy and seemingly safe rewards of petrodollar recycling, investors piled in on the trade without taking into account the risks involved. For some time in the 1970s, over half of the total profits of Citibank—the leading financial institution in the United States at the time—came from loans made to various Latin American governments. Even Fidel Castro's regime, which had repudiated Batista's debts to foreign bankers following the Cuban Revolution two decades earlier, was able to accumulate an external debt of $3.2 billion to European banks.[11] Yet the tide was always bound to go out again. On October 6, 1979, Federal Reserve Chairman Paul Volcker gave what some commentators later referred to as "the final tug" that pulled the rug from underneath Latin America's feet.[12] In an attempt to deal once and for all with the crippling crisis of stagflation that had beset the U.S. economy, Volcker suddenly hiked the prime rate from 9 percent in October 1979 to 20 percent in May 1980—or "the highest interest rate since the birth of Jesus Christ," as West-German chancellor Helmut Schmidt put it at the time. Since most syndicated bank loans had been contracted on the basis of variable interest rates, the Volcker shock sent the interest payments of developing countries through the roof (see figure 8.3).

In Mexico, fears of an impending debt crisis and currency devaluation led wealthy citizens and companies to move vast amounts of capital out of the country, rapidly depleting the central bank's foreign-exchange reserves in the process. Between 1973 and 1982, the external debt shot up at an average of 30 percent a year, from $4 billion to over $80 billion, while capital flight after the Volcker shock forced the Bank of Mexico to borrow ever-greater sums just to be able to replenish its reserves.[13] The Mexican state was now effectively borrowing abroad just to repay its old foreign debts—a vicious cycle that could only go on as long as the Wall Street banks remained willing to keep rolling over the

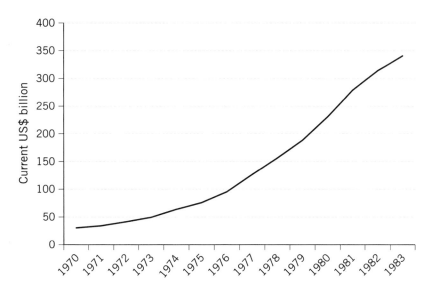

FIGURE 8.1. External debt stocks of Latin America and the Caribbean (excluding high income), 1970–1983. *Source*: World Bank (2017).

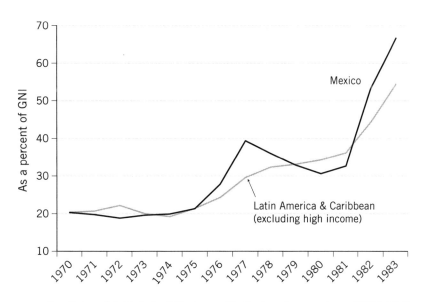

FIGURE 8.2. External debt stock of Mexico and Latin America as a share of GNI, 1970–1983. *Source:* World Bank (2017).

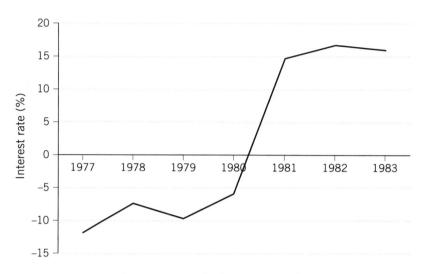

FIGURE 8.3. Average real interest rate on developing country floating debt, 1977–1983.
*Source*: Maddison (1985, 47).

government's maturing obligations. Moreover, in a sign of investors' growing concerns about the sustainability of Mexico's debts, the maturities on these new loans began to shorten dramatically. As Wall Street belatedly recognized the risks, almost all the new money came in the form of six-month loans or less.[14] This credit crunch extended far beyond Mexico: whereas the 1.5 years prior to mid-1982 had seen $42 billion in new loans flowing into Latin America, that amount dropped to $9 billion in the 1.5 years following mid-1982.[15] The banks were rapidly closing the tab.

By early 1982, it was already clear to financial officials in Mexico that if the government wanted to stay current on its foreign obligations, it desperately needed an IMF loan. As Finance Minister Silva Herzog noted in April, "signals of the impending crisis became more and more evident."[16] According to World Bank estimates and official calculations by the Bank of Mexico, capital flight reached $27 billion between 1978 and 1982, while independent economists made estimates ranging from $40 billion to $55 billion.[17] Combined with a huge disequilibrium in the external balance, a growing government deficit, and increasing inflationary pressures, it seemed that the country was now destined for an international bailout. But President López Portillo, who represented the left-leaning national-popular wing of the ruling Partido Revolucionario Insti- tucional (PRI) and who had come into office in 1976 under an IMF program, had no intention of leaving office under similarly humiliating circumstances. As he put it, "I came in under the IMF yoke, and I'm not going to go out under it."[18] Nevertheless, market discipline eventually caught up with the president's personal pride, and López Portillo was forced by rising interest rates and capital flight to cut back spending and pursue structural reforms to avoid defaulting on Mexico's towering debt load. As one observer of the crisis noted, "economic pressures were so strong in early 1982 that Mexico initiated its own adjustment *sans* IMF," producing a 17-point austerity and reform program in April to reassure investors that its budget was under control.[19]

## THE CREDIBLE THREAT OF THE CREDITORS' CARTEL

It was not enough. Borrowing costs continued to rise (see figure 8.4), maturities on the outstanding debt had shortened significantly (figure 8.5), and the Bank of Mexico kept hemorrhaging foreign exchange (figure 8.6). By June 1982, Silva Herzog recounts, officials were confronted with a "dramatic and recurrent reality" in which crucial decisions on how to obtain and spend critical resources were made on a day-to-day basis: "Tomorrow we have to pay $40 million to cover maturities due to banks X and Y; and we have only half of that amount. We need to borrow $20 million at twenty-four or forty-eight-hour terms from bank Z to cover our financial obligations. We will see, afterwards, how we solve the problem for the day after tomorrow." At the end of July, the Bank of Mexico was losing up to $200–$300 million in foreign exchange a day, and total reserves had dropped to a level where they only covered two weeks' worth of imports.[20] Silva Herzog remarks that "what entered the country one day went out the following day." Mexico was now rapidly careening towards a disorderly default. Faced with this reality, why did Mexican officials not simply suspend the country's external debt service, as previous Mexican governments had done on so many occasions?

The country's financial policymakers themselves claimed to be most concerned about the immediate consequences a default would have had on the government's access to short-term credit, on private sector confidence, and on international trade. In his written account of the crisis, Finance Minister Silva Herzog observed that "a suspension of payments is always an attractive alternative for debtors; but for Mexico, in those months, that alternative had some serious risks."[21] Citing the fact that the country imported 30 percent of its domestic consumption of corn—the country's main food staple—from the United States, and that his government feared losing access to trade credit, and citing furthermore the facts that Mexican industry remained "highly dependent on imports"; that a payment suspension would "run counter" to Mexico's dependence on foreign resources; that such a moratorium would likely trigger greater private sector uncertainty; and that "a condition of autarky" produced by a failure to service the country's towering debts "would have gone against the growing interdependence among nations," the finance minister seemed to firmly underline the fact that Mexico's financial and commercial integration

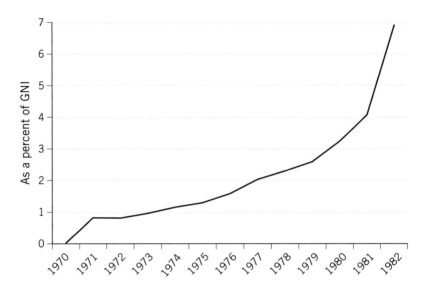

FIGURE 8.4. Mexico's interest payments on external debt as a share of GNI, 1970–1982.
*Source*: World Bank (2017).

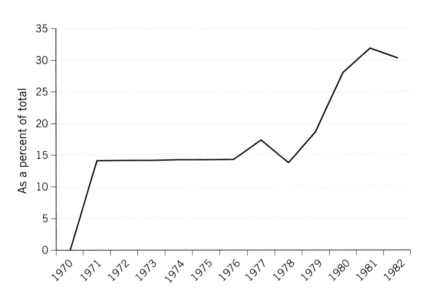

FIGURE 8.5. Mexico's short-term debt as a share of total external debt stock, 1970–1982.
*Source*: World Bank (2017).

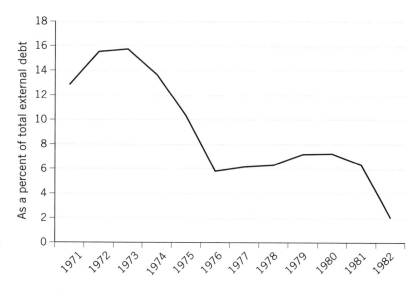

FIGURE 8.6. Mexico's foreign exchange and gold reserves as a share of total external debt, 1971–1982. *Source*: World Bank (2017).

into world markets—and especially its dependence on trade with the United States—had greatly raised the economic spillover costs of default.[22] The fear was that a unilateral suspension of payments would lead creditors to refuse further loans not only to the government but to the private sector as well, causing widespread social dislocation with unpredictable political consequences for the PRI.

Angel Gurría, the finance ministry's director of public credit, highlighted similar concerns in an interview, citing as the first and foremost consideration "the loss of access to short-term credit," along with the danger that a default would cut off investment flows to the private sector and threaten the steady supply of corn from the United States.[23] After all, Gurría emphasized, access to credit is the "bread and butter of trade," and there was a serious risk that "the banks would stop all loans" in the event of a default.[24] The small crisis team saddled with the responsibility of assessing the government's policy options at the start of the crisis in mid-1982 did discuss the possibility of a suspension of payments, which the deputy director of the Bank of Mexico, Alfredo Phillips, referred to as "the atom bomb, the ultimate weapon." But for Finance Minister Silva Herzog, this confrontational course of action "was not an option." Instead, he pledged that "Mexico would behave as a responsible debtor."[25] Whence this concern with being "responsible"? When pressed on the question, Angel Gurría once again mentioned the fear that the government and private sector would be cut off from foreign credit and investment, and that this would inflict debilitating spillover costs on both the Mexican and the world economy: "if we defaulted, everybody would be bankrupt—but it would also stop capital inflows to Mexico."[26] Silva Herzog remembers that "we asked ourselves the question what happens if we say, 'No dice. We just won't pay,'" and he notes that "there were some partisans of that" inside the government. In the end, however, he decided that defaulting "didn't make any sense."[27] As he later explained, "certainly a moratorium was discussed, but it was rejected. We decided to negotiate and avoid confrontation."[28] Angel Gurría confirms this, noting that "our logic was simple: there can be no default."[29]

These explicitly stated government fears about the spillover costs of a short-term credit cutoff did not occur in a vacuum; they have to be seen against the background of the international credit structure that emerged with the rise of the Eurodollar markets and petrodollar recycling in the 1970s. As we already saw, the syndicated lending of the time involved groups of commercial banks and institutional investors pooling funds to make large loans to foreign governments under the leadership of the big Wall Street money-center banks. As in Genoa in the sixteenth century, this syndicated form of financing resulted in a very high debt concentration and an interlocked lending structure that greatly eased the ability of the big commercial banks not only to establish common positions amongst themselves, but also to enlist the support and allegiance of smaller banks and nonbank investors.[30] Having already begun to perceive themselves as *international* players with close ties to financial institutions in other countries and a shared interest in global financial stability and full debt repayment, the institutional lenders of the 1980s found it much easier to coordinate collective action amongst themselves than the dispersed bondholders of the 1930s had.[31] By managing to hold together a coherent international creditors' cartel, the banks were able to prevent opportunistic behavior by individual lenders, which in turn made the threat of a credit cutoff—and the spillover costs this would imply—much more credible and considerably more damaging, as it would be next to impossible to secure alternative sources of financing in the event of default.[32] The debtors' dependence on a highly concentrated and structurally interlocked creditors' cartel thus served to strengthen the force of market discipline and constrain the policy options available to the debtor countries.[33] As a Citibank vice-president explained, the debtors "don't have a weak committee of individuals across the table, but a powerful group made up of the biggest banks in the world. Any default and the whole banking system would be against them. They would get no credit at all, not even short-term."[34]

The creditors' market-based power was further cemented by their collective approach to crisis management and their divide-and-rule strategy with respect to the debtors. As one Latin American country after another fell into arrears on their amortization schedules from 1982 onwards, creditors embarked on a complex set of negotiations with debtor country governments to reschedule principal payments, refinance outstanding debts, and ensure the continued servicing of interest. Again, the highly concentrated and interlocked nature of lending eased coordination among the creditors, allowing them work together in rolling over maturing obligations and providing fresh credit where necessary, thereby preventing an immediate default, all the while presenting a unified front in negotiations with the debtors. The central tenet in these negotiations was that each country was responsible for its own fiscal problems and each crisis should therefore be dealt with on an individual, case-by-case basis.[35] While considered a logical and inconsequential self-evidence by the creditors themselves, academic observers have pointed out that the "case-by-case approach wasn't innocent at all."[36] In reality, it served to isolate the borrowing countries and diminish their capacity to organize collective action, thereby precluding the formation of an opposing debtors' cartel and frustrating collective efforts to play the private creditors off against one another.[37] The result, as Barbara Stallings has noted, was the informal institutionalization of a fundamentally unequal power relation that made it "much more difficult to call a moratorium in the 1980s" than in had been in the 1930s; indeed, "unilateral defaults cannot occur on any large scale because of the differences in lenders as well as the new international political-economic context."[38] By 1982, "creditor clubs ha[d] successfully replaced unilateral default with multilateral debt consolidation."[39]

Together with the active intervention of the IMF, whose role we will discuss in greater detail in the next chapter, the emergence of a coherent international creditors' cartel thus allowed the banks to keep their borrowers within the lending game while simultaneously disciplining them through the credible threat of a credit cutoff, which would in turn produce devastating spillover costs on the borrowers' domestic economies. In this respect, the syndicated lending of the late 1970s and early 1980s endowed private creditors with much greater structural power than they had enjoyed in the prewar period. Carlos Marichal, for one, notes how "the combined power of the commercial banks and multilateral agencies is much greater than the power previously wielded by the foreign bankers involved in Latin American loans":

> Prior to World War II, the investment banks of England, France, Germany, or the United States could usually obtain some diplomatic support from their respective chancelleries to pressure the debtor states to pay instead of declare bankruptcy. But when confronted with a severe international crisis, Latin American governments frequently did default, and in the short run there was little the bankers could do about this. In contrast, in recent years few Latin American states have gone so far as to threaten default.[40]

In sum, the nature of syndicated lending meant that the first enforcement mechanism of market discipline had been greatly strengthened by the time the 1980s debt crisis broke out, producing a historic shift in the international balance of power between the Latin American debtors and the international banks, which made it much more costly for the distressed sovereign borrowers of the

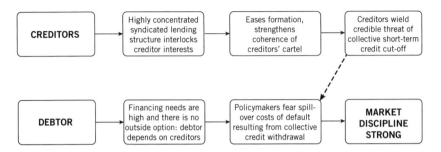

FIGURE 8.7. The first enforcement mechanism in Mexico.

1980s to unilaterally suspend their external debt service (figure 8.7 presents a basic visualization of this mechanism). As the crisis deepened, these dynamics led to a growing sense of despair among the region's heads of state. The Brazilian president José Sarney later described the powerlessness he experienced during the crisis in stark terms: "we cannot destroy the system," he said. "We can scratch it, but it can destroy us."[41] In Mexico, this sense of powerlessness was compounded by the country's growing dependence on international credit, by its depleted foreign-exchange reserves, by its exceptionally strong reliance on food imports from the United States, and—as we will see in chapter 10—on the international integration of its own financial elite and the vulnerability of its own banking system to a government default. As the crisis deepened and a turn to the IMF seemed increasingly inevitable, President López Portillo lamented that "my hand is on the helm of the ship, but I cannot direct the storm."[42]

# NINE

## The IMF's "Triumphant Return" in the 1980s

The second major contrast between the prewar and postwar periods lay in the role of official-sector intervention. While such intervention had been relatively patchy and unpredictable prior to World War II, from 1982 onwards it was to become a stable and consistent feature of the emerging regime of international crisis management.[1] Jorgensen and Sachs note that "the existence of the International Monetary Fund as a referee for the extension of new credit is especially important in creating a cooperative environment for avoiding outright default."[2] By disbursing emergency loans to distressed debtors under strict policy conditionality, the Fund was able to step in where no private lenders dared, keeping distressed borrowers solvent while at the same time imposing strict discipline on their domestic budgets and external debt service. In the process, it provided a crucial backstop to the first enforcement mechanism of market discipline, which remained prone to failure in the event of investor panic. According to Lindert, the 1980s thus "stand out as the era in which official intervention became global—and, so far, less concessionary." Not only did the debtor countries overwhelmingly shift their policy response from unilateral action to multilateral debt negotiations, with at least forty-nine countries engaging in over a hundred voluntary rescheduling agreements between 1980 and 1986, but the terms of these rescheduling deals also became considerably more creditor-friendly than they had been in the 1930s.[3]

This chapter will discuss how the second enforcement mechanism of official-sector intervention operated in practice. It will show how the large exposures of the big Wall Street banks to Mexico's highly concentrated debt greatly increased the risk of financial contagion, thus moving the U.S. government to intervene on its own banks' behalf and push for active IMF involvement. By coordinating the lending decisions of the private banks and disbursing emergency loans under strict policy conditionality, the Fund thus assumed a leading role as an international crisis manager and lender of last resort, serving both as a fiscal disciplinarian of the debtor governments and as the informal head of the private creditors' cartel. In this way, the creditors managed to keep the Mexican government in the lending game while at the same time freeing up domestic resources for foreign debt servicing, thereby not only preventing a disorderly default but also maximizing the likelihood of full repayment. As we will see, the lessons learned in Mexico were subsequently to be applied across Latin America and the developing world.

## The Situation Spins Out of Control

In the previous chapter we already saw how the force of market discipline had compelled the Mexican government to repay even as the crisis deepened over the course of 1982. By August, however, it was clear that the situation had spun out of control. The creditors' main source of leverage over the Mexican government's policy decisions—rising borrowing costs and capital flight—now threatened to undermine itself. As creditors became increasingly hesitant to lend to the Mexican government over fears of a potential default, the country was at risk of being cut off from affordable short-term credit and thereby rendered incapable of refinancing its outstanding obligations. This in turn sparked fears in U.S. policymaking circles of an impending global financial crisis that might lead to the collapse of some of the biggest Wall Street banks. The flipside of Latin America's highly concentrated debt, after all, was the dangerous over-exposure of U.S.—and to a lesser extent European and Japanese—commercial banks to developing country governments. Mexico's debt alone stood at $82 billion and amounted to 48 percent of the capital of the six largest U.S. banks, with some institutions holding a sum of Mexican debt equivalent to or in excess of their capital base (see figures 9.1 and 9.2 and table 9.1).[4]

And Mexico was far from the only concern. The total exposure of the nine largest banks to the seventeen largest developing countries stood at 194 percent of their combined capital.[5] According to a White House official, U.S. Federal Reserve Chairman Paul Volcker was convinced that "the banking system was about to collapse," and so he began to press both President Ronald Reagan and Treasury Secretary Donald Regan to take decisive action, increasing the U.S. contribution to the IMF and dispatching the Fund as both a financial firefighter and a fiscal policeman in the wider region.[6] Although the Reagan administration initially responded to these calls with typical *laissez-faire* bluster, refusing to underwrite the external debts of foreign governments with the money of U.S. taxpayers, Volcker eventually managed to impress the seriousness of the situation on Treasury Secretary Regan, who then convinced the president to build up the United States' defenses against a looming Mexican default.

On the weekend of August 12, Silva Herzog flew to Washington and, in the words of a U.S. Treasury official, "showed up on our doorstep and turned his pockets inside out."[7] The Bank of Mexico now had only $200 million left in its foreign-exchange reserves, and at the $100 million per day rate at which it was currently losing its last-remaining liquid resources, Mexico would be

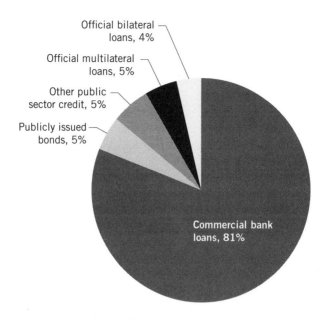

FIGURE 9.1. Composition of Mexico's external debt in 1983. *Source*: Alvarez (2016).

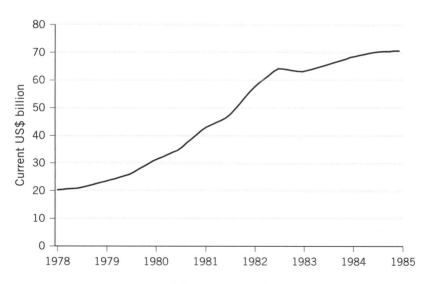

FIGURE 9.2. G10+ commercial banks' exposure to Mexico, 1978–1985. *Source*: Clement and Maes 2013, 16.

*Note*: Includes exposure of commercial banks in G10 countries plus Switzerland, Austria, Denmark, Ireland.

TABLE 9.1.
Exposure of top-6 U.S. banks to Mexico

|  | Loans to Mexico | Total capital | Share of capital |
|---|---|---|---|
| *Citicorp* | $2.72bn | $5.49bn | 49.59% |
| *Bank of America* | $2.5bn | $5.25bn | 47.65% |
| *Chase Manhattan* | $1.69bn | $3.84bn | 43.89% |
| *J. P. Morgan & Co* | $1.08bn | $3.31bn | 32.73% |
| *Manufacturers Hanover* | $1.73bn | $2.94bn | 58.74% |
| *Chemical Bank* | $1.5bn | $2.41bn | 62.16% |
| **Total (top-6)** | **$11.22bn** | **$23.25bn** | **48.28%** |

*Source*: Alvarez (2018); Salomon Brothers, CNBS, Call Report FFIEC 002, and Bank of England.

technically bankrupt by the time the banks reopened their doors on Monday. Sweder van Wijnbergen, the World Bank's chief economist for Mexico, recalls Angel Gurría's despair in a phone call: "he couldn't get a dime."[8] Finance Minister Silva Herzog himself states that "it seemed possible that all options had been exhausted and that the only possible action was a unilateral moratorium."

With private creditors refusing to extend further credit, the only way to avoid a disorderly default would be for an international lender of last resort to step in and provide a set of emergency loans to help Mexico meet its upcoming payments. And since the only ones capable of fulfilling such a role were the United States government and the International Monetary Fund, Silva Herzog had come to Washington "hoping to find alternatives." He met with IMF Managing Director Jacques de Larosière, who expressed his willingness to help but also insisted, in the words of official IMF historian James Boughton, that "Mexico would have to find a way to avoid defaulting on its debts."[9] Indeed, in an early sign that preventing default was to become the Fund's overarching policy objective from 1982 onwards, de Larosière informed Silva Herzog that the IMF could provide him with financial assistance only "if the government stayed current on its interest payments and reached agreement with its creditors regarding the rescheduling of principal payments." At the same time, the Mexican government would have to adopt painful austerity measures "to convince the outside world, particularly the banks, that the Mexican economy would indeed soon be set on the path of return to order and stability."[10] De Larosière's parting words to Silva Herzog clearly illustrated the striking contrast to the policy response of the 1930s: "don't do anything unilaterally."[11]

The next Friday, August 20, Silva Herzog flew back to the United States once more, first to meet the chairmen of the fourteen major international banks that were to form the "bank advisory group"—a steering committee that would come to represent all of Mexico's commercial creditors—and later to address a gathering of some two hundred hastily summoned representatives from banks all over the world. In the first meeting, after briefly outlining the severity of the payment problems his government was facing, Silva Herzog promised the assembled bankers that Mexico would do everything in its power to stay current on its interest payments, but announced that it now urgently needed the banks to roll over the principal, $1 billion of which was falling due in the next week alone. But when Silva Herzog floated the idea of a one- or two-year extension of maturities, "the bankers balked."[12] Walter Wriston of Citibank, in particular, objected that such a long delay would make Mexico's debt problems look much more serious than the short-term liquidity issues Silva Herzog claimed to be dealing with. Eventually, Wriston and the other bankers got their way and Mexico was granted a mere 90-day roll-over of principal payments on a pledge to maintain its interest payments—a temporary fix that was to be repeated several times over in the coming months and years. Two days later, an infamous 9-foot-long telex was sent to all of Mexico's creditor banks formally requesting a 90-day extension on the amortization schedules of its external debt.

Many economists today list this negotiated rescheduling of Mexico's principal payments as a sovereign default like any other.[13] But, as previous chapters have already highlighted, there are important qualitative differences between the unilateral payment suspensions of the prewar period and the voluntary renegotiations of the 1980s. Angel Gurría, Mexico's director of public credit, insists that in legal terms there was never a Mexican default during the 1980s since "interest on outstanding debt continued to be paid punctually."[14] Moreover, Gurría explains his government's avoidance of unilateral action as "a sense of responsibility on our part, not just because we were nice guys, but also because it was in Mexico's best interest not to default." He adds that "there were not too many options anyway."[15] At any rate, the dramatic events of the so-called Mexican weekend marked the proper start of the Latin American debt crisis, which was now on the verge of spilling over into a U.S. banking crisis of potentially catastrophic proportions. In a later study, the Federal Reserve Bank of New York wrote that "bankers and policymakers faced a threat of financial disorder on a global scale not seen since the Great Depression" if Mexico or another major Latin American debtor were to default on its obligations.[16] To prevent that from happening, the Reagan administration convinced Congress to raise the U.S. contribution to the Fund and at the same time insisted that further loans to Latin American borrowers be made conditional on strict austerity measures and far-reaching structural reforms to increase export earnings and ensure the uninterrupted flow of interest payments back to the commercial banks. The continued servicing of interest was crucial because under U.S. financial regulations the banks were required to write down any loans with 90-day arrears on interest payments as nonperforming, which in turn would compel them to make loan-loss provisions, cutting into their overall profit rates. Since Wall Street was particularly exposed to Mexico, and since Mexico was in the deepest trouble of all foreign borrowers, the U.S. government made the prevention of a Mexican default the pivot around which its international crisis management strategy was to revolve for the remainder of the decade.[17]

## THE FUND AS "COLLECTIVE CREDITOR" AND FISCAL DISCIPLINARIAN

As the crisis unfolded, most Latin American borrowers were eventually forced to turn to the IMF for official-sector financing (see figure 9.3), while the U.S. government began to insist ever more adamantly on transforming the Fund into both a "collective creditor" at the head of the international bankers' cartel and a fiscal disciplinarian of the debtor countries. This development marked another striking contrast to the 1930s, when there was no IMF and no dominant creditor power willing or able to act as a lender of last resort and an enforcer of bondholder interests.[18] Still, it should be emphasized that the importance of the IMF was not just a product of the scale of its emergency lending, which at any rate remained relatively modest compared to the later crises of the 1990s and 2010s, but rather of the fact that both creditor governments and private lenders almost always insisted on an IMF Stand-By Arrangement before opening rescheduling negotiations with the debtors.[19] By making the Fund's stamp of approval a prerequisite for an agreement with the banks, private sector creditors effectively catapulted the IMF into the position of an official-sector gatekeeper of market access, allowing it to threaten the debtors with an immediate and complete exclusion from all foreign sources of credit in the event of noncompliance.[20] This is how the IMF came to fulfill an increasingly central role in the management of the 1980s debt crisis, despite its relatively modest financial contributions: by assuming the monitoring and surveillance functions that had previously been only partially and intermittently fulfilled by creditor states and private underwriting banks.[21] This structural transformation in turn went hand-in-hand with a "purge" of Keynesian economists from the Fund's key departments, signaling a stark shift in its ideological alignment and its internal policy priorities. In short, from 1982 onwards, the IMF was to become much a more creditor-friendly institution.[22]

But the course of true love never did run smooth. A major turning point in the relationship between Wall Street and the Fund came during the annual IMF meeting on November 16, 1982, when Managing Director Jacques de Larosière told an assembled group of bankers that the IMF was no longer capable of shouldering the burden of keeping Mexico afloat by itself, and informed them that if they did not raise another $5 billion in new loans to the country the Fund would refuse to sign a crucial stabilization agreement with

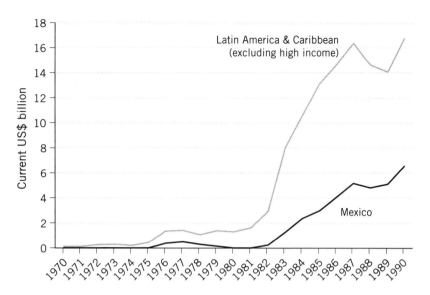

FIGURE 9.3. Total use of IMF credit, 1970–1990. *Source*: World Bank (2017).

the Mexican government. Since this would immediately force the country into default and thereby possibly tip dozens—if not hundreds—of international banks into bankruptcy, the seemingly casual announcement really amounted to an unprecedented order: lend or die.[23] Although the bankers were initially shocked and outraged by the IMF's sudden and unexpected shift towards concerted lending, they quickly realized that they had little choice in the matter. While it was in the narrow self-interest of each individual bank to withhold further loans and reduce its exposure, the sum of these seemingly rational risk-averse investor decisions risked tipping Mexico into insolvency—an outcome that would end up harming all creditors. As Stephany Griffith-Jones observes, "'involuntary lending' was in the interest of the *collective of creditors*, because it avoided default."[24] The banks in effect needed the IMF to help them counteract the logic of the free market, which, left to its own devices, would have inevitably resulted in a Mexican payment suspension and a major global banking crisis. The Fund's insistence on concerted lending enabled the creditors' cartel to keep the Mexican government solvent and servicing interest on its external debts.

Perhaps the most important contribution of the IMF, however, was its function as a financial watchdog capable of imposing strict policy conditionality on the debtors. As Citibank chairman Walter Wriston confirmed, "the fundamental contribution of the Fund is the discipline imposed on debtor countries, not the amount it lends."[25] Former IMF Managing Director Johannes Witteveen agreed, calling the Fund a "disciplinary mechanism" for indebted states that had lost their creditworthiness.[26] By disbursing its emergency loans in tranches, always making the next tranche conditional on compliance with its demands for fiscal stabilization and structural reform, the IMF was able to effectively enforce the type of policies that maximized the borrowers' capacity to repay their debts. After all, the mere threat to withhold future credit tranches risked cutting a noncompliant borrower off from all sources of foreign financing and thus raised the specter of debilitating spillover costs; which, for reasons we saw before, Mexican policymakers were adamant to avoid. Despite the inconvenience of concerted lending, then, the banks were generally quite happy to go along with a greatly empowered IMF, as its role in international crisis management would effectively provide private creditors with free public goods in the form of official-sector emergency loans, the coordination of the bankers' lending behavior, and the surveillance and monitoring of debtor policies.

Past experience also played a role in convincing Wall Street of the Fund's value as an international crisis manager: a failed attempt to exert direct control over Peru's government finances in 1978 had sensitized creditors to the fact that they needed the IMF "as a watchdog with real teeth to monitor Third World economies."[27] During the Peruvian crisis, a number of U.S. banks had tried to organize a rescheduling of the country's debts without IMF involvement, in a deal they made conditional on far-reaching austerity measures that were to be designed and monitored by the banks themselves. It was a dramatic failure. Peru's economy collapsed, budget targets were flouted, the debt spiraled out of control, and the banks were widely accused of "Wall Street imperialism." Having burnt their fingers once, private creditors "drew the lesson that commercial banks could not impose conditionality, only the IMF could."[28] And so the banks, content to let others do the dirty work for them, decided to retreat to the wings and leave the IMF to face the blame for imposing unpopular austerity measures and structural reforms.[29] Financial officials generally seemed to agree with this approach. Karl Otto Pöhl, West Germany's governor to the IMF, explained that "the IMF is our only hope. It is the only institution that can lend money and impose conditions for doing so. No government can do this, nor any bank."[30] The vice-president of the Bank of Canada similarly argued that "there certainly is a need for them to be in there, as a lender and as a disciplinarian and that's the thing all of us like about the IMF. They, perhaps like no one else, can make conditions on loans, which ensures some tightening of the belt."[31]

Given its central role in preventing default by disbursing emergency loans and imposing strict policy conditionality, it is no surprise that private creditors generally hailed what one banker referred to as "the IMF's triumphant return" in the 1980s.[32] The Fund's increasingly central role constituted a remarkable reversal in its fortunes compared to the capital-abundant conditions of the preceding decade: where in the late 1970s world financial markets had been awash with cheap credit, leaving the IMF increasingly incapable of demanding strict conditions from its borrowers, who could simply bypass the Fund and turn to the markets to refinance their outstanding obligations on more lenient terms, by the 1980s the severe global credit contraction put the IMF in a position of unparalleled power. As a result, the Fund's officials could demand much stricter conditions on their loans, and the proportion of upper credit tranche IMF lending under policy conditionality correspondingly increased from under one-third in 1973 to 96 percent ten years later.[33] By 1984, a total of 66 developing countries—over half the IMF's member countries in the Global South and 3 out of 4 Latin American countries—were under an IMF Stand-By Arrangement.[34] Even if the associated policy conditions were not always implemented as faithfully as the Fund would have liked, these numbers do point towards the emergence of a concerted international effort to reorient the borrowing countries' spending priorities—as well as the organization of their wider economies—in line with the prerogatives of external debt servicing. As de Larosière himself put it, "adjustment is now virtually universal. . . . Never before has there been such an extensive yet convergent adjustment effort."[35]

At the same time, the World Bank stepped up the conditionality of its loans as well, mostly through the expansion of structural adjustment lending and the creation of the Special Action Program, providing rapid disbursements of credit in return for far-reaching structural reforms. For some, the World Bank's conditionality was "arguably more demanding than the Fund's."[36] The aim, however, was the same: to increase exports and free up domestic revenue for foreign debt servicing, thereby maximizing the likelihood of full and timely repayment. As Lindert concluded by the end of the decade, "the 1980s have rewritten the official rules of international debt":

> Officials in creditor countries and international agencies have now intervened globally, apparently out of concern over the unprecedented exposure of major banks, especially in the United States. . . . To the extent that the new regime of the 1980s has prevented outright default, it has helped insure creditors against massively negative rates of return.[37]

In sum, the relative vulnerability of the first enforcement mechanism, which threatened to undermine itself over the course of 1982 as investors panicked and rushed for the exits, leaving the Mexican government incapable of refinancing its outstanding obligations, was adequately compensated for by the strength of the second enforcement mechanism of official-sector intervention. The IMF, in particular, intervened aggressively in the 1980s and assumed a position of unprecedented structural power, drawing on its capacity to withhold the disbursement of further conditional emergency loans in the event of noncompliance. Karin Lissakers, a U.S. Treasury official and later IMF executive director, openly lamented this development, accusing the Fund of acting as an "enforcer of the banks' loan contracts," imposing austerity on Mexico with the narrow objective of "free[ing] foreign exchange in order to service debts."[38] What even gunboat diplomacy and outright military invasion could never fully accomplish in the

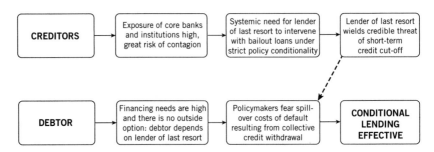

FIGURE 9.4. The second enforcement mechanism in Mexico.

nineteenth century, the IMF now seemingly managed to do—systematically and on a global scale—without any of the associated saber-rattling. Its bailout loans and strict policy conditionality became the backbone of the emerging regime of international crisis management, keeping the debtors both solvent and actively servicing interest on their foreign debts. From now on, having earned its stripes in the Mexican debt crisis, the Fund was to become a financial policeman for the developing world at large. Mexico's IMF adjustment program, de Larosière later reflected, "was the anchor of everything else."[39]

# TEN

## The Rise of the Bankers' Alliance

B eside the strong market discipline enforced by a highly concentrated and internally coherent creditors' cartel, and the emergency loans provided and strict policy conditionality imposed by the IMF, there was a third key difference between the crises of the 1930s and the 1980s—this one having to do more specifically with domestic factors. In fact, the compliance of the Mexican government was never purely imposed from abroad; from the very start of the crisis, there were powerful forces inside the country—especially within the state's financial bureaucracy—that firmly shared their creditors' interest in and ideological convictions about the desirability of fiscal austerity, structural reform, and full debt repayment. As the crisis intensified, these creditor-friendly domestic elites steadily gained the upper hand in long-standing political disagreements with their left-leaning counterparts inside the governing Partido Revolucionario Institucional (PRI), who tended to favor a more heterodox policy response and a more confrontational stance towards foreign lenders. Over the course of the 1980s, the orthodox technocrats representing the former group came to play an increasingly dominant role in financial policymaking, gradually transforming Mexico into what Wall Street bankers and IMF officials would eventually refer to as a "model debtor."

To understand the dynamics behind the Mexican government's staunch refusal to embrace a unilateral default strategy, we therefore need to carefully consider the contentious politics of sovereign debt repayment inside the debtor country itself. This chapter briefly recounts the story of the escalating conflict between the two competing factions within the ruling PRI—from the growing despair of the initially dominant radicals to the eventual triumph of technocratic orthodoxy. As we will see, it was the growing dependence of the Mexican state on credit that endowed those groups considered to be most capable of fulfilling a bridging role to foreign lenders and attracting credit on the best possible terms with a privileged position in economic policymaking, sidelining the PRI's more heterodox national-popular wing in the process. As the crisis deepened throughout 1982, the strengthened position of the former groups led to the steady internalization of fiscal discipline into the Mexican state apparatus, ensuring continued debt servicing and a cooperative stance vis-à-vis foreign creditors even in the absence of outright external impositions. This turn toward compliance was eased by the fact that popular opposition to continued debt servicing remained relatively muted due to the cooptation of the main labor and peasant organizations and the absence of powerful popular mobilizations against austerity.

## CONFLICTING POSITIONS ON THE EXTERNAL DEBT

To appreciate the importance of the third enforcement mechanism in the Mexican case, we have to briefly consider the main cleavages in its domestic political economy, which emerged from the long shadow cast by the Mexican Revolution of the 1910s. Out of the political reordering of that tumultuous decade emerged a relatively stable one-party regime that was famously referred to by the Peruvian author Mario Vargas Llosa as "the perfect dictatorship." Despite the political hegemony of the ruling PRI, however, this regime was internally divided along ideological and class lines. On the one hand stood the liberal metropolitan elites who had replaced the landowners as the dominant force in postrevolutionary Mexico. On the other stood the more radical workers' and peasants' movements that had carried much of original insurrectionary impulse but that gained relatively little in the subsequent postrevolutionary settlement. In her classic study on the evolution of Mexican capitalism, Sylvia Maxfield refers to these rivaling groups as the *bankers' alliance* and the *Cárdenas coalition*, respectively.[1] The former, Maxfield shows, has historically revolved around the politically influential circle of Mexico City bankers and the big industrial exporters of Monterrey who depend on them for credit, along with their technocratic allies in the state's financial bureaucracy. The latter, named after former president Lázaro Cárdenas (1934–1940), whose left-leaning government had sided with workers and peasants and who had set out to pursue some of the original goals of the Mexican Revolution, like the nationalization of oil and some of Zapata's envisioned land reforms, was made up of the PRI's national-popular wing.[2]

When the crisis broke out in 1982, the national-popular coalition held the presidency and the powerful ministries of labor and national patrimony, while the bankers' alliance controlled the finance ministry and the central bank. As the government's fiscal position deteriorated, an intense internal power struggle broke out between the two wings of the PRI over the appropriate course of action to be taken. As Finance Minister Silva Herzog put it, "inside the government there were conflicting positions" on how to respond to the external shock and the rapid depletion of foreign exchange, with the bankers' alliance favoring austerity and repayment while the national-popular coalition favored expansionary fiscal policy and debt repudiation.[3] In sharp contrast to their orthodox counterparts inside the central bank and finance ministry, the left-leaning officials inside López Portillo's administration emphasized the systemic causes of the crisis and insisted that Mexican citizens should not be made to pay for an investor stampede that had essentially been caused by the monetarist orthodoxy of the U.S. Federal Reserve. In Silva Herzog's view, these so-called radicals—who had dominated economic policymaking for most of the postwar period—believed "that it was possible to maintain the economic expansion and resist the pressure of the financial constraints."[4] But as the rapid loss of investor confidence highlighted Mexico's acute dependence on foreign credit, the next months were to reveal the growing capacity of the bankers' alliance to set the economic agenda, and the dramatic extremes to which López Portillo was willing to go in an attempt to counter them.[5]

After the fateful Mexican weekend late in August 1982, these conflicting positions exploded into the open, bringing to the fore deep-seated fault lines in Mexico's postrevolutionary political settlement. The bankers' alliance became increasingly central to the government's efforts to restore investor confidence, stem capital flight, and revive economic growth. Moreover, as the government pressed ahead with capital account liberalization as a condition for future IMF loans, big firms and wealthy individuals inside Mexico could much more easily move their money to the United States, where they would hold it in bank accounts, real estate investments, or stock exchange portfolios—safe and immune from steep inflation and the seemingly endless devaluations of the peso. The option of relocation and the credible exit threat that these domestic businesses and elites thereby obtained gave them considerably more leverage over economic policymaking. It was also precisely this deep integration of the domestic elite into the U.S. banking system that made it very unlikely that wealthy Mexicans would ever support a suspension of payments to begin with; after all, a government default now risked toppling the very U.S. banks that held their savings.

It was not just U.S. banks that were vulnerable to a Mexican default, however. Mexico's own banking system had already become highly leveraged (see figure 10.1) and deeply integrated into global financial markets by the early 1980s, making domestic banks—as well as the firms that depended on them for credit—particularly vulnerable to the spillover costs of a sovereign default.[6] Mexican banks had played an especially important role in intermediating the syndicated loans to their own government and lending back to Mexico from their foreign branches and agencies (see table 10.1), all of which made it exceedingly difficult for the government to discriminate between domestic and foreign creditors. As Sebastian Alvarez has shown in a recent study, "the imbalances which Mexican banks incurred in running their international operations eventually brought them to the brink of bankruptcy once the crisis began. Given that the banks that were at risk represented a large share of the domestic markets, . . . the whole Mexican banking system was threatened with collapse."[7] Alvarez presents archival evidence showing that "the fragility of the commercial banks and their overseas branches was a major worry for the Mexican financial authorities."[8] Since a moratorium on interest payments was clearly not in the

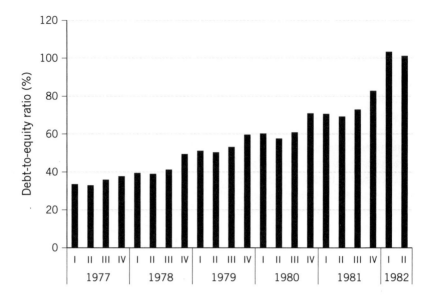

FIGURE 10.1. Leverage of Mexican banks, 1977–1982. *Source:* Alvarez (2017); Banco de Mexico's annual reports.

<small>TABLE 10.1.</small>
Exposure of Mexican banks to Mexico

|  | Loans to Mexico* | Total capital | Share of capital |
|---|---|---|---|
| *Banamex* | $1,135m | $280m | 405,36% |
| *Bancomer* | $1,200m | $260m | 461,54% |
| *Serfin* | $428m | $114m | 375,44% |
| *Comermex* | $624m | $52m | 1200,00% |
| *Banco Internacional* | $266m | $42m | 633,33% |
| *Somex* | $621m | $73m | 850,68% |
| **Total (top-6)** | **$4,274m** | **$821m** | **520,58%** |

*Source*: Alvarez (2018).
*\*Note*: Loans granted by Mexican banks' foreign agencies and branches to Mexican borrowers.

interest of the Mexican financial elite, which would be hit just as badly by the fallout as foreign creditors would be, this shared interest imposed an extra set of constraints on the national-popular wing of the PRI. Not only would a unilateral default ravage the domestic financial system; it also risked an internecine revolt of the PRI's technocrats inside the finance ministry and central bank, who were firmly opposed to any policies that would harm Mexican banks. And so President López Portillo felt compelled by a combination of external and internal pressures to follow the orthodox policy recommendations of the crisis team that had previously been convened by Finance Minister Silva Herzog and avoid a unilateral payment suspension at all costs.

Continuing to service interest, however, required painful austerity measures and structural reforms to free up domestic resources and preserve foreign exchange. As a result, Mexican workers found themselves bearing a heavy burden of adjustment. Between 1981 and 1983, imports and real wages fell by two-thirds, even as the country's total debt rose by over a third—dynamics that increasingly angered López Portillo and the radicals inside his administration.[9] The president was reportedly infuriated by regular reports of banks, businesses, and wealthy Mexicans sending billions of dollars to the United States while his government was forced to cut public spending and raise taxes on the poor, negatively affecting its approval ratings in the process. For some time now, López Portillo had found himself under growing pressure from his allies on the left of the PRI, whose intellectual figureheads had long been very critical of the domestic bankers' alliance, with some even describing the Mexican Bankers' Association as the "owner of the country."[10] In August 1982, López Portillo gave in to these demands from the left and decided that it was time for action. He summoned the country's leading radical economists, José Oteyza and Carlos Tello, and set up a secret advisory committee in Paris to study Mitterand's bank nationalization of 1981, aiming to replicate it at home.[11]

The appointment of Carlos Tello was particularly telling. Having studied under the heterodox economist Joan Robinson at the University of Cambridge, Tello was known for his socialist views and his perception of Mexican "finance capital as the dominant faction of capital in the 1970s."[12] Blaming the banks for undermining the state's room for maneuver and its prioritization of social objectives, Tello and his fellow radicals were strongly opposed to Mexico's deepening integration into the global financial system and repeatedly warned of the growing concentration of the country's banking sector, with 225 banks having merged into 87 over the preceding decade, leaving "powerful domestic financial groups . . . able to boost their market power via the centralization and concentration of finance capital."[13] One observer noted that "if, in the past, the president and the government were increasingly helpless in the face of bankers and businessmen in general, with the internationalization of banking . . . the possibilities of action were further limited."[14] Two banks in particular stood out: Banco Nacional de Mexico (Banamex) and Banco de Comercio (Bancomer). Between

**Bank assets, US$ billion (% of total)**

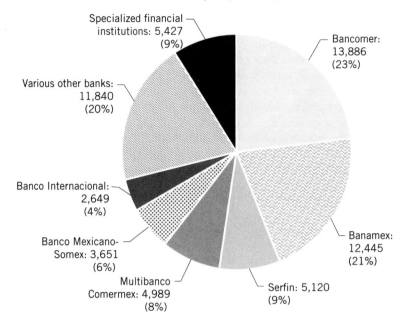

FIGURE 10.2. Composition of the Mexican banking market in December 1980.
*Source*: Alvarez (2017); Bulletin of the CNBS; and Banco de Mexico's
annual reports.

them, these two behemoths controlled nearly half of all total bank assets in Mexico in the early 1980s (see figure 10.2). There was therefore an acute awareness among the PRI's national-popular wing of the immense power wielded by the banks through their monopolistic control over credit access, and especially their role in financing and refinancing the state's *internal* debt.[15] To López Portillo and his advisors, it seemed self-evident that "nationalizing the banks would break the political and economic power of Mexican bankers and of the large-scale industrialists with whom they were associated," thus restoring a much-needed degree of policy autonomy to the fiscally squeezed state apparatus.[16]

And so, on Wednesday, September 1, 1982, just a week and a half after reaching a preliminary agreement with his foreign creditors on a rescheduling of Mexico's debt, President López Portillo—who was due to leave office on December 1—addressed the nation for his last annual *Informe*. There, from the balcony of the presidential palace, the head of state stunned the financial community by announcing the nationalization of the banking system and the imposition of capital controls to stem further capital flight. Looking out onto the roaring crowd of half a million PRI supporters in the Zócalo below, he declared that "in the last few years it has been a group of Mexicans, led and advised and supported by the private banks, who have taken more money out of the country than the empires that exploited us since the beginning of time."[17] "They have robbed us," López Portillo thundered from the lectern, "but they will not rob us again. . . . The revolution will speed up; the state will no longer be intimidated by pressure groups!"[18] The president cried. A banker fainted. Miguel Mancera, the central bank director who was known for his monetary orthodoxy and staunch opposition to capital controls, was ignominiously dumped and replaced by Carlos Tello. As officials arrived at the central bank headquarters later that day, they found the building surrounded by army troops.[19] Silva Herzog, who had been kept uninformed about the president's decision until the last moment, immediately tendered his resignation, but, in a sign of the crucial bridging role he had come to fulfill towards Mexico's foreign creditors, the president rejected it. Silva Herzog was needed for negotiations with the IMF, which were to resume at the critical Toronto summit just two days later. As Maxfield puts it, "Mexico's economic future depended on successful negotiation of the debt. Silva Herzog's key role in the negotiations left López Portillo no choice but to keep him in the cabinet."[20]

Still, Mexico's foreign creditors were horrified by the bank nationalization, which many feared to be the prelude to a unilateral moratorium or even a wholesale repudiation of Mexico's foreign debt.[21] But for all the radical rhetoric in which it was ensconced, the president's poorly planned decision ended up backfiring disastrously, producing a set of profoundly antisocial consequences. While the imposition of capital controls had been intended to stem the outflow of capital, the bank nationalization actually ended up feeding the investor panic and intensifying capital flight. Moreover, by taking over the banks, the government also assumed the bankers' debts, thus forcing them onto the shoulders of ordinary taxpayers. As Maxfield notes, "to some extent the nationalization served to bail out financially threatened banks and their industrial partners."[22] This in turn led some to remark that, although the language of the Mexican bank nationalization was very different from the 1983 bank bailouts in neoliberal Chile, "the substance of the intervention was quite similar."[23] In an attempt to fight the bankers, López Portillo had ended up nationalizing not their wealth and power but their *liabilities*, as a result of which the state now held almost the entire foreign debt of the private sector.[24] For his part, Angel Gurría admitted that "even though it could have been managed differently and the decision to nationalize might have been taken for the wrong reasons, the nationalization was a way of solving the financial difficulties of banks that would otherwise have had to declare themselves insolvent."[25]

## THE BANKERS' ALLIANCE STRIKES BACK

In the end, the nationalization did little to weaken the privileged position of the bankers' alliance in fiscal and monetary policymaking. Like a game of

Whack-a-Mole, the same bank owners almost instantly reemerged on the stock exchange, setting up a parallel banking system that allowed them to continue their lending and speculative activities in a new form, most notably through the operation of *casas de cambio*, the exchange houses that dealt in the majority of foreign currency transactions. Given the wild exchange rate gyrations of the 1980s—the peso was to lose more than 2,000 percent of its value against the dollar over the next six years—operating these exchange houses provided the bankers with ample opportunities for arbitrage. Moreover, with the nationalized banks heavily overexposed to the government, the administration was forced to turn to the stock exchange to refinance its internal debt, leading it straight back to the same bankers that López Portillo had tried to outsmart through the bank nationalization. The rapid resurgence of the bankers' alliance was therefore a direct consequence of the deepening debt crisis and the growing dependence of the Mexican state on private credit. Whereas the Bank of Mexico had funded over three-quarters of interest payments on the government's internal debt before 1983, basically moving the debt from one part of the state to another, after 1983 some 57 percent of the internal debt was being funded by the private sector, with local elites becoming the state's main source of new credit.[26] Since total interest payments on internal debt amounted to more than double the interest on external debt, the bankers not only gained control over "an extremely lucrative underwriting business" in internal debt, clawing back most of their losses from the nationalization, but also greatly boosted their privileged position in economic policymaking and their structural power over the government in the process.[27]

As the bankers' alliance grew more powerful in spite of the bank nationalization, hopes of a progressive exit from the crisis rapidly waned. In the months following the announcement of the bank nationalization, the technocratic representatives of the bankers' alliance set out to limit its impact by undermining its implementation. Maxfield highlights the fact that "Mexico's extreme international financial vulnerability in 1982 placed [Silva Herzog] in a very powerful position within the Mexican government."[28] The finance minister's close ties to foreign creditors, both private and official, enabled him to almost singlehandedly set the government's borrowing strategy and its spending priorities. Because he enjoyed the trust of the international banks, U.S. Treasury officials, and the IMF, Silva Herzog was considered to be most capable of extracting concessions and attracting credit on good terms, which in turn endowed him with significant leverage over López Portillo and Tello. This, combined with the systematic isolation of Tello by the close alliance that had already been forged between Silva Herzog, Volcker, and de Larosière, meant that Mexico's foreign debt policy remained shielded from López Portillo's resurgent radicalism. Despite complaining bitterly about the financial bureaucracy's alignment with the IMF and the banks, Tello never managed to outflank Silva Herzog or force foreign creditors to concede better terms. Carlos Salinas, the minister of budget and planning and future president, later confessed that he "had the feeling that de Larosière came away knowing he could be tough on Tello." One finance ministry official later referred to Tello's meeting with de Larosière, in which the heterodox central bank director vainly petitioned for leniency, as "Tello's last stand."[29] With the radicals isolated and Mexico's dependence on foreign credit growing stronger by the day, the lofty goals of the bank nationalization never materialized.

The definitive turnaround came on December 1 with the inauguration of Miguel de la Madrid as the 52nd president of Mexico. A Harvard-trained economist, De la Madrid was described as "an extremely cautious technocrat who had great admiration and respect for the international banking community."[30] In a sign that the bankers' triumph over the national-popular coalition was now complete, the first thing De la Madrid did upon assuming power was to partly reprivatize the banks. Although the new president could not fully reverse the nationalization, he "did whatever possible to ensure that the state administered to the needs and caprices of the old financial barons."[31] De la Madrid reinstated Miguel Mancera as head of the Bank of Mexico, kept Silva Herzog as his finance minister, and brought with him into government what was at the time considered to be "the most technocratic and homogeneous team ever to rule Mexico."[32]

This dramatic turn to orthodoxy raises the question why López Portillo, as leader of the national-popular wing of the PRI, ever handpicked De la Madrid as his successor in the first place. The worldwide ideological shift from Keynesianism to neoliberalism undoubtedly played an important role. But there was a more practical reason for the PRI's sudden embrace of its relatively unpopular technocratic wing: the state urgently needed financial resources to keep itself afloat in the face of rising borrowing costs and intensifying capital flight. To remain in power, the PRI had to attract foreign credit and investment on the most affordable terms. But for that to happen, it had to first establish *credibility* with international investors—and López Portillo himself was acutely aware that the national-popular wing of the party hardly inspired creditor confidence. According to Sarah Babb, who studied the rise to power of a small group of U.S.-trained Mexican economists, the decision by López Portillo to appoint De la Madrid as his successor "almost surely was a measure designed to inspire the confidence of bankers and investors."[33] Earlier, the president had appointed Silva Herzog to the finance ministry for the exact same reason. Just as Silva Herzog was considered by *The Economist* to be "more popular with the New York bankers than . . . with some of the folks back home," De la Madrid enjoyed a reputation among investors as "a technocrat, adept at modern economics but out of touch with Mexico's revolutionary traditions."[34] Both Silva Herzog and De la Madrid strongly backed IMF-led structural adjustment and "made a priority of keeping good relations with the international financial community by servicing [the] debt."[35] It is therefore safe to say that the growing fortunes of the bankers' alliance were a direct outcome of the state's growing dependence on credit, and the crucial bridging role that domestic elites fulfilled towards foreign lenders.

The final victory of the bankers' alliance over the national-popular coalition cemented the third enforcement mechanism of debtor compliance by internalizing fiscal discipline into the Mexican state apparatus. For the rest of the decade, aside from some heightened tensions following the disastrous earthquakes of 1985, Mexico remained by far the most compliant debtor on the continent. This turn to orthodoxy was further eased by the subdued popular response to structural adjustment and debt repayment. In fact, one particularly striking aspect of the Mexican case—in particular when contrasted to the country's own revolutionary history—was the relative absence of militant anti-austerity protest during the 1980s. An influential study of IMF riots across the continent notes that "austerity protest in Mexico has been muted by organized labor's preference for maneuvering within the theater of official institutions, by a defensive left, and by industrialists' exploitation of the crisis as an occasion to increase productivity."[36] While IMF riots contributed to the downfall of governments in Peru in 1980 and 1984, Brazil in 1983, Panama in 1985, and Haiti in 1986, the absence of similar mass mobilizations in Mexico gave the bankers' alliance free rein to pursue its orthodox policies, thereby largely deflecting the costs of the crisis onto less privileged segments of society. In the only extensive English-language study on the role of labor in the Mexican debt crisis, aptly titled "The Sounds of Silence," Kevin Middlebrook finds that "the economic reverses suffered by the urban working class do not distinguish the Mexican case from labor's situation in other Latin American countries." What does differentiate it, however, is the "generally restrained character of Mexican organized labor's response to these challenges."[37] Since the trade unions and peasant organizations were completely controlled by the PRI's party-state, a key channel for the expression of popular concerns and the defense of workers' and peasants' interests remained blocked.[38]

These developments constitute yet another important contrast to the 1930s, when powerful popular mobilizations and strong pressure from below moved Mexico's postrevolutionary political establishment to take a much more confrontational stance toward foreign lenders. At the International American Conference in Montevideo in 1933, the Mexican delegation had even proposed a resolution to challenge what they called "the international superbankers," whom they accused of having defrauded the continent during the lending boom of the 1920s. The Mexican initiative included a call for "the declaration of a continent-wide moratorium," contrasting sharply to the country's transformation into a model debtor half a century later, when the Mexican government actively undermined Argentina's short-lived calls for a similar continent-wide moratorium.[39] From 1983 onwards, close ties developed between the technocrats in the subsequent De la Madrid and Salinas administrations and the very "superbankers" their predecessors had agitated against in the 1930s. As a result, the austerity measures and structural reforms demanded by foreign creditors no longer needed to be strictly imposed from abroad; they were now to

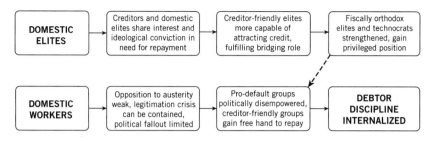

FIGURE 10.3. The third enforcement mechanism in Mexico.

be formulated and monitored in a collaborative effort between IMF staff and Mexican financial authorities. As one senior official at the Fund exulted in reference to the close and cooperative relations with Mexico's new technocratic administration: "we are all the same."[40]

To conclude, the third enforcement mechanism—the privileged position domestic elites derived from their bridging role to foreign creditors—served to effectively internalize debtor discipline into the Mexican state apparatus. Local bankers and orthodox financial officials would henceforth do everything in their power to keep the country compliant with its external obligations. Meanwhile, the creditors kept voluntarily rolling over principal payments to keep Mexico in the lending game. While the resultant amortization extensions have been considered a "default" under Standard & Poor's technical criteria, this was a very creditor-friendly form of default indeed. In fact, Wall Street traders openly rejoiced at the endless sequence of debt reschedulings—after all, every new roll-over implied hefty intermediation fees and the guaranteed accumulation of interest payments, as long as the principal was not retired. One U.S. banker even publicly exclaimed that Mexico "is a cash cow for us. We hope they never repay!"[41] This in turn prompted Karin Lissakers of the U.S. Treasury Department to lament that "the current solution to the international debt problem is disturbingly similar to the policies and processes that created the crisis in the first place."[42]

# ELEVEN

## "The Rich Got the Loans, the Poor Got the Debts"

Throughout the crisis of the 1980s, the three enforcement mechanisms of debtor compliance—the market discipline imposed by a highly concentrated international creditors' cartel, the conditional emergency lending and disciplinary role of the U.S. government and the IMF, and the internalization of discipline through the strengthened position of the domestic bankers' alliance and the marginalization of national-popular opposition to further austerity and debt repayment—combined to keep Mexico both solvent and punctually servicing the interest on its external debts, despite the high social and economic costs of protracted austerity and full debt repayment. The result of the sheer strength of the three enforcement mechanisms was to greatly reduce the room for maneuver of the Mexican government to pursue a more confrontational course of action.

This final chapter of the Mexican case study takes a closer look at the outcomes of the crisis and the consequences of the reduced state autonomy at the heart of the crisis of the 1980s. The first section considers the only brief period of tension between Mexican policymakers and their foreign lenders and briefly discusses Argentina as a counterfactual case in which a democratically elected government came to power that was strongly opposed to debt repayment. We will see how the first two enforcement mechanisms effectively kept both Mexico and Argentina in line, eventually compelling them to repay. The second part of the chapter then considers the final resolution of the Mexican debt crisis through the Brady debt restructuring deal of 1989–1990, which, far from constituting a coercive default, was actually undertaken at the initiative of the Wall Street banks with their own interests firmly in mind. Finally, we will take a quick look at the unequal distribution of adjustment costs inside Mexico as a direct consequence of the creditors' power to shape the outcome of the crisis in their favor.

### GREATLY REDUCED ROOM FOR MANEUVER

One of the key contentions of this book is that the vast increase in the structural power of finance and the intervention of official creditors since the late

1970s has significantly reduced the room for maneuver available to national governments.[1] For Mexico, this reduced state autonomy was especially evident in 1985–1986, when the country was suddenly struck by two further external shocks: a catastrophic earthquake that left over 10,000 people dead and much of Mexico City in ruins, and a 60 percent fall in the price of oil that caused the government to lose roughly 20 percent of its annual revenues over the space of several months.[2] With $1 billion in principal falling due shortly after the earthquake, Angel Gurría—fearing "that he and his colleagues in government would be lynched if they proposed such a use of scarce resources in the midst of this calamity"—saw himself forced to negotiate yet another voluntary rescheduling with the U.S. banks.[3] As a result, investor confidence collapsed. Gurría recalls that "the mood in Mexico was ominous. Rumors about tens of billions being requested were widespread, together with the fear of unilateral default by the world's second largest debtor. The drop in oil prices generated a wave of demand for immediately halting payments which included all sectors of society." He added that "even within the government, where such decisions were usually left to the minister of finance, a veritable chorus in favor of a moratorium arose."[4] The threat of default suddenly resurfaced with a vengeance.

Given the adverse circumstances and the obstinate posturing of the creditors, even the most orthodox technocrats inside the Mexican government were now openly starting to question if Mexico's compliant approach still made sense. Gurría wrote that "this 'dialogue of the deaf' caused increasing frustration within Mexico, and made even the most reasonable and sophisticated observers advocate a harder line of negotiation."[5] As a result, "the Mexican negotiating team . . . clearly started drifting towards a stronger response to the international financial community's apparent lack of understanding and support." It was clear to Gurría and his colleagues that "the year 1986 marked the climax of Mexico's worst economic crisis in the postwar period."[6] For the first time, the option of a unilateral default was seriously considered at the highest echelons of the Mexican government. President De la Madrid, the technocrat favored by Wall Street, openly accused the creditors of "choking Mexico to death" and threatened "an indefinite suspension of all debt service payments to commercial banks."[7]

In response to these growing concerns and to De la Madrid's explicit threat of a debt moratorium, U.S. Federal Reserve Chairman Paul Volcker flew down to Mexico City for a top-secret emergency visit, where he impressed the awareness upon the president that there would be "an immediate suspension of all bank credits the moment Mexico took unilateral action."[8] It was this explicit reminder of Wall Street's structural power over its borrowers that made De la Madrid climb down—but not before dumping his finance minister for having become too close to foreign creditors.[9] According to one Mexican official, Silva Herzog had become "a defender of the IMF without considering the internal repercussions."[10] In hindsight, the IMF's official historian James Boughton writes, Silva Herzog "wrestled with the idea of default throughout his term but always rejected it."[11] This rejection of unilateral action was to endure even after his departure from office, as Mexico remained compliant with its international debt contracts and its creditors' demands until the very end. Despite the havoc wrought by the earthquake and the fiscal squeeze caused by the collapse of oil prices, Gurría emphasizes that "we never used the threat of default. We stuck to the thesis that the country will lose its access to credit; it will lose its credit rating. . . . We never confronted the bankers. . . . There was a commitment to being responsible, being cooperative."[12]

Would a more radical or more democratically responsive administration have acted differently in the face of this convergence of crises? The answer is difficult to determine with certainty, but it is unlikely. In fact, even if the Mexican bankers' alliance had been ousted from government or forced by sustained pressure from below to promote national-popular interests at the expense of U.S. bankers, Mexico's room for maneuver was greatly constrained by the state's dependence on foreign credit and the vulnerability of the domestic economy. Regardless of who was in power, a default would have destroyed the national banking system, with potentially devastating consequences for overall economic performance and the government's capacity to legitimize itself in the eyes of the people. It is therefore doubtful that a more left-leaning administration would have behaved very differently—and even if it had, its attempt at defiance would likely have been defeated before long, as López Portillo's bank nationalization appears to indicate. In this respect, Argentina's short-lived defiance of its creditors in 1984 provides a useful counterfactual to test this book's hypothesis.

In December 1983, Raúl Alfolsín had taken office as Argentina's first democratically elected head of state since the fall of the military junta. In an attempt to protect popular living standards and ensure the new government's democratic legitimacy, his administration—led by the Radical Civic Union party— almost immediately declared a six-month moratorium on interest payments in the hope of obtaining better terms from international creditors.[13] Lamenting that "the debt of Argentina and of other Latin American nations is the product of perverse mechanisms that lend us money in order that we do not develop ourselves," Alfolsín defiantly declared that "we are not going to pay our debt by making our people hungry."[14] This, he recognized, "means that the state cannot bow to international financial groups or to privileged local groups." It was the first time since the start of the crisis that a Latin American debtor had taken such a confrontational stance towards its creditors, and Alfolsín's calls on his fellow Latin American leaders to join him in this rebellion had not gone unnoticed by the bankers themselves.[15] The French daily *Le Monde* called Alfolsín's defiance of the IMF and the banks a "revolutionary move," and scholars identified Argentina as "the single most resistant debtor in international finance."[16]

In June the next year, eleven Latin American countries gathered in Colombia to set up the Cartagena Group, where Argentina presented its plans for a common debtor-led response to the crisis. Among the creditors, there was widespread concern that the meeting would be the first step in the formation of a Latin American debtors' cartel to counter their own creditors' cartel. Such a debtors' cartel, they feared, would be able to credibly threaten a collective default and thereby extract better terms. And so the banks moved quickly to reassert their tested case-by-case approach, making concessions to Mexico's pliant technocrats in the hope that this model debtor would help them defuse the bombshell of a united debtor front from within. As one U.S. banker put it, "we still think [a cartel is] a danger, and we ought to be ready to do something. Those countries that comply with the terms of [IMF programs] should be rewarded with better terms."[17] One advisor confirmed that the U.S. government and the banks "are dissuading the Latin nations from collaborating by promising more rapid treatment if they act alone."[18]

Following the announcement of Argentina's moratorium, the Mexican government—in a clear display of what Cline has called "credit-rating self-preservation"—immediately moved to isolate Alfolsín, organizing a $500 million emergency loan by fellow Latin American debtor countries to cover Argentina's interest payments to its commercial creditors before the expiration of the 90-day legal limit on which the U.S. banks would have had to write down their loans as nonperforming.[19] As one observer put it, "the message was clear: Argentina would be totally isolated in any attempt to call the banks' or the U.S. government's bluff."[20] Far from leading to the formation of a defiant debtors' cartel and playing the creditors off against one another, Alfolsín's democratic brinkmanship united lenders and borrowers alike in their resolve to avoid an Argentine default. The banks insisted that that an IMF agreement was a prerequisite for any renegotiation of Argentina's debt and then waited, in the words of one Wall Street banker, "until the economy went into such a tail-spin that the recalcitrant debtor must come crawling back to the table."[21] To remind the Argentine government of the spillover costs of default, the U.S. Treasury Department sent out a list of crucial imports that would become unavailable in the event of a suspension of payments due to the withdrawal of trade credit. U.S. Deputy Treasury Secretary MacNamara even asked Alfolsín: "have you ever contemplated what would happen to the president of a country if the government couldn't get insulin for its diabetics?"[22] The message was clear: Argentina stood alone, and continued defiance would cost the country dearly.

By early 1985, rising borrowing costs and the resultant economic spillover effects had forced Alfolsín into an embarrassing U-turn, with the president finding himself in the humiliating position of having to sign an IMF stabilization program while pleading to honor the odious debts of the military dictatorship that had gone before him. "The only solution," he now told the Argentine people in a remarkable turnaround, "is a policy of austerity that will be very hard and will require great efforts by everyone; it's called, my dear compatriots, an economy of war."[23] In hindsight, for all the fear it stoked among creditors at the time, most observers now agree that the Cartagena conference is to be remembered chiefly for what it did *not* do: none of the attending countries followed Argentina in forming a debtors' cartel, none ever threatened unilateral action, and none of them suspended interest payments.[24] One Argentine scholar who studied the Cartagena group even referred to the gathering as a "phantom" that did "nothing revolutionary at all."[25] The debtors were simply too concerned about preserving their own credit rating: continued compliance seemed less costly in the short term than a collective act of defiance. Far from laying the foundations of a debtors' cartel, article 8 of the Cartagena declaration thus reaffirmed the debtors' willingness to honor their debts and to continue with the adjustment efforts, as well as their unwavering commitment to the case-by-case approach. As Silva Herzog aptly described it, Cartagena was "a debtors' cartel to pay, not not to pay"—or, as he put it elsewhere, "a payers' club."[26]

## The Brady Deal and the Resolution of the Debt Crisis

Given this limited room for maneuver, it was practically impossible for the Latin American borrowers to pursue unilateral action in the 1980s. But what is perhaps even more remarkable is that for seven to eight years there was no serious attempt on the part of the creditors to multilaterally resolve the international debt crisis either. It was not until the Brady deal of 1989–1990 that the external debts of developing country governments from Argentina to Zaire were restructured, one by one, starting with Mexico, slowly allowing cash-strapped governments to regain access to international credit markets. Up to that point, the international financial community had muddled through with one rescheduling after another, consistently refusing to force losses onto private creditors or to find a more lasting resolution to the crisis. By 1987, it was clear that this approach, while successful in allowing the commercial banks to escape losses, had dramatically failed to restore the creditworthiness of the borrowers. On November 30, 1987, the *New York Times* neatly captured the contradiction at the heart of the international approach to crisis management: "There is a consensus on two things. One is that the debt has to be paid, and the other is that the debt cannot be paid."[27]

A few months earlier, however, in May 1987, the crisis had already reached a subtle but important turning point when Citibank took the initiative to raise its loan-loss reserves by 150 percent with an additional $3 billion, boosting its overall capital ratio to a quarter of its Third World debt. In the second quarter of 1987, Wall Street as a whole added a total of $21 billion to its loan-loss reserves, as a result of which "the banks no longer had to live in terror of a Mexican default."[28] At least equally important was the proposal made by J. P. Morgan in December 1987 to exchange its discounted Mexican loans for securitized government bonds, which the bank could in turn sell on secondary markets, thus providing Mexico with a modest degree of debt relief while providing J. P. Morgan with an opportunity to reduce its exposure.[29] The Mexico-Morgan deal, concluded in 1989, was hailed as "a watershed for the debt strategy" and has been credited with "influenc[ing] later multilateral efforts to further alleviate Mexico's debt crisis [and leading] the way for the more sophisticated menu-driven deals of the Brady plan."[30] The build-up of loan-loss provisions and the reduction of outstanding loans greatly reduced the banks' vulnerability to an eventual debt restructuring. U.S. bank exposure to the 17 largest debtors, which had stood at 130 percent of capital reserves in 1982, fell to 27 percent by the end of the decade. The result, William Cline notes, "was to disarm the threat of the debt bomb to the international financial system."[31]

At the same time, some members of U.S. Congress were becoming increasingly vocal in their criticism of the administration's international bailouts and its approach to crisis management more generally, which they saw as "defending the interests of the banks to the detriment of U.S. manufacturing firms and their workers."[32] In January 1989, three bank regulators testified to Congress that Wall Street could now withstand a large default, indicating that the Latin American debt crisis no longer posed an existential risk to the U.S. financial system.[33] As a result, the bankers themselves began to change their attitude towards the idea of a debt restructuring. As one broker told the *New York Times*, the banks "have diminished vulnerability to Mexico. . . . The talk in 1982 was that the Mexican debt crisis meant the collapse of the financial system. [But] we have come a long way from that point."[34] While still vehemently opposed to involuntary losses, some degree of debt cancellation was increasingly starting to look attractive to private creditors as a way to keep Mexico and the rest of Latin America in the lending game. Finally, after the bloody repression of a major IMF riot in Venezuela—the infamous *Caracazo* of 1989, which by some counts left more than 3,000 people dead—U.S. officials, wary of stoking the flames of radicalism in the region, began to openly discuss the possibility of a multilateral debt restructuring. The result was Mexico's Brady deal of 1989, which paved the way for voluntary debt renegotiations across the developing world.

The full extent of debt relief obtained under the Brady plan has been a source of considerable debate among economists. In a letter to the IMF, Mexico's finance minister Pedro Aspe claimed that the Brady deal would save the country $4 billion a year until 1994, while the chairmen of Lloyds Bank and Midland Bank estimated that the plan would "save the country less than $1 billion in interest payments each year."[35] Sweder van Wijnbergen, the World Bank's chief negotiator in the Brady restructuring, has argued that the deal managed to avoid a bailout of the creditors.[36] Others, however, have contested this assertion. One account of the restructuring concludes that "the amount of debt reduction was quite limited, especially when new official debt was added to the calculation of net debt reduction," while net reduction for Latin America as a whole only amounted to 15 percent of the total debt.[37] Another influential study found that the banks made significant financial gains in the restructuring while the debtors suffered major losses.[38] Yet another found that "the amount of debt relief granted to Mexico was rather low, particularly when one compares it to historical standards."[39] While in the 1930s debt crisis Latin American debtors had managed to secure "substantial" debt relief, with Jorgensen and Sachs finding that "the terms of the final agreements settling the defaults of the 1930s were highly favorable to debtors,"[40] in the 1980s the creditors clearly had the upper hand in the negotiations—and the stance of the U.S. government and IMF was exceptionally favorable to Wall Street interests. Cline notes that "despite the high public profile of the IMF in calling for deep forgiveness, in the actual negotiations the institution did not press the banks."[41]

World Bank economists have since recognized some of these criticisms. Claessens, Oks, and Van Wijnbergen show that Mexico received a total cash flow relief of around $4 billion per year, $2 billion of which would have occurred anyway as amortization would have been rolled over in the absence of debt restructuring. Noting that "in a $200 billion economy, 2 or even 4 billion seems like a small tail to wag a large dog," the authors conclude that "the main benefit of debt relief was not to lower expected payments but to reduce uncertainty."[42] The Brady deal, as it turns out, was more effective at restoring investor confidence by reducing bank exposures and marking the remaining debt to market—thereby allowing the banks to more realistically estimate the true value of their assets—than it was in reducing the actual debt burden. By restoring confidence, however, the Brady deal instantly caused interest rates to drop over 20 percentage points, enabling Mexico to return to the markets and start borrowing from private lenders again.[43] The much-lauded Brady deal, in short, never really hurt the lenders: it was much more important for its psychological role in reducing uncertainty than it was in achieving a more equitable distribution of the burden of adjustment.[44]

## "THE RICH GOT THE LOANS AND THE POOR GOT THE DEBTS"

Given all the above, it should not come as a surprise that the costs for the crisis were largely borne by those who were least responsible for causing it. Indeed, Mexico's poor suffered a dramatic reduction in living standards while international lenders—having successfully prevented both a unilateral default and an early multilateral debt restructuring—emerged from the 1980s largely unscathed, even making big gains.[45] There is a broad consensus that, rather than serving the interests of working people in Latin America, the international response to the debt crisis primarily served the interests of the creditors, and of the major Wall Street money-center banks above all.[46] Indeed, over the course of the 1980s the Global South as a whole steadily became a net exporter of capital to the Global North, with developing countries sending abroad $52 billion more in debt servicing costs than they received in return in new foreign loans

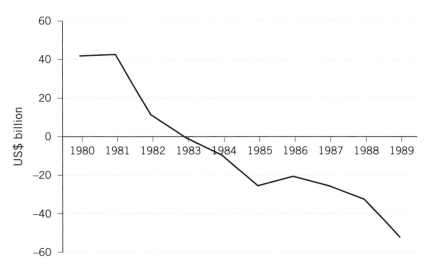

FIGURE 11.1. Net financial transfers from Global North to South, 1980–1989.
    *Source*: New Internationalist (1990).

and investments (see figure 11.1). Meanwhile, total external debt ratios and debt servicing costs in Latin America had actually *risen* for most of the 1980s (see figure 11.2), although the combination of dutiful debt servicing and the impact of the Brady deal would finally cause them to decline after 1987.[47]

Beyond the highly asymmetric international dimension, the distribution of adjustment costs *within* the debtor countries was also very uneven, as domestic elites and wealthy citizens successfully shifted the burden of debt repayment onto the weaker and less privileged segments of society.[48] In Mexico, workers, peasants and the urban poor paid a particularly heavy price under successive structural adjustment programs, even as wealthy domestic elites managed to largely escape the costs of inflation, successive devaluations, and higher taxation by moving their money out of the country.[49] With inflation averaging 93.1 percent a year between 1983 and 1987 and reaching 177 percent in 1988, the government enforced strict wage controls and dramatic cuts in public spending that saw the average standard of living drop dramatically over the course of the decade. Overall, per capita income fell at an average rate of 5 percent annually between 1983 and 1988, while real wages fell between 40 and 50 percent.[50] As a result, the labor share of income declined from 35.9 percent in 1982 to 26.6 percent in 1987.[51]

This erosion of poor people's livelihoods fits a broader pattern of bias in IMF and World Bank structural adjustment programs. Manuel Pastor, for one, finds evidence for a "strong and consistent pattern of reduction in labor share of income," both in absolute and relative terms, over the course of IMF

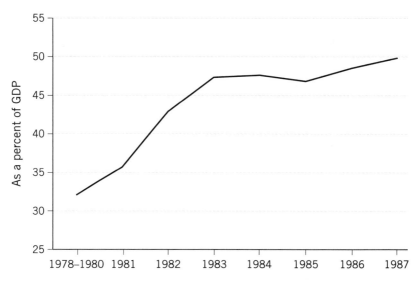

FIGURE 11.2. Latin America's external debt as a share of GDP, 1978–1987.
*Source*: Pastor (1987:97).

Stand-By Arrangements and Extended Fund Facilities; findings that have been confirmed by later studies on the redistributive implications of IMF policy conditionality.[52] While over half of Mexico's population already lived in poverty before the start of the crisis, the purchasing power of the minimum wage fell 66 percent over the course of the crisis.[53] By the mid-1980s it took 4.8 minimum wages for a family of four to meet essential needs, but 80 percent of households now had to get by on an income of 2.5 minimum wages or less. As a result, a wave of malnutrition spread among the poor. Official creditors eventually recognized the inequitable outcome of the crisis: World Bank chief economist Stanley Fischer, for instance, acknowledged that "most of the burden has been borne by wage earners in the debtor countries."[54] An internal study assessing the World Bank's stated objective of poverty reduction concluded that "poverty issues have seldom featured significantly in such dialogues, and the analysis of structural adjustment programs rarely considered who will carry the heaviest burdens of adjustment."[55]

At the same time, the crisis—costly as it was for Mexico's poor—turned out to be a boon for the rich. The failed bank nationalization of 1982 had effectively socialized the bankers' liabilities, while the top 10 percent of income earners managed to move between $64 and $80 billion (or more) out of the country by 1988, much of it returning a healthy profit in foreign investments, like stocks, bonds, and interest on deposits. This allowed wealthy Mexicans to "utilize income from these assets to advantage by transferring funds back into pesos whenever frequent devaluations allowed the elite to maximize its buying power."[56] According to one estimate, the interest on capital flight returned to wealthy local elites amounted to roughly 40 percent of total debt payments—private profits that could not be taxed by the Mexican government.[57] Far from helping to stem capital flight, the IMF actually made matters worse by insisting on capital account liberalization as a precondition for its loans. With wages down, private profits shot up across the board, while control over the foreign exchange houses and the anomalous mid-crisis stock market boom provided elites with ample opportunity for speculation. In the end, as the head of UNICEF concluded, "it is hardly too brutal an oversimplification to say that the rich got the loans but the poor got the debts."[58]

The outcomes of the Mexican debt crisis therefore present a stark contrast to the crisis of the 1930s. First, the low debt concentration and dispersed lending structure of prewar bond finance, which had made creditor coordination difficult and weakened the force of market discipline, gave way to the high debt concentration and the interlocked credit structure of syndicated bank lending, which eased creditor coordination and made the threat of a credit cutoff much more credible and much more damaging. The result was to facilitate the formation of a coherent international creditors' cartel and greatly increase the force of market discipline. Second, the absence of an international lender of last resort and active state intervention in the interwar period gave way to the aggressive intervention of the U.S. government and the IMF in the 1980s, with the Fund fulfilling the combined function of an international lender of last resort, a fiscal disciplinarian, and a coordinator of the creditors' cartel, keeping the debtors solvent while simultaneously compelling them to pursue the type of policies that maximized debt servicing. Third, the pressure from below and relative economic self-sufficiency of the Great Depression, which had emboldened national-popular forces and sidelined the metropolitan banking elite, gave way to a growing state dependence on credit and the relatively muted antiausterity opposition of the 1980s, strengthening the hand of the bankers' alliance and their technocratic allies, who were seen to fulfill an important bridging role to foreign lenders and were thereby able to attract credit at better terms—thus gaining a privileged position in economic policymaking, internalizing discipline into the state apparatus.

Table 11.1 summarizes these contrasts, showing how the prevailing conditions of the 1930s tended to increase the debtor's autonomy from global finance and eventually led to a unilateral default followed by an aggressive debtor-led restructuring, while the conditions of the 1980s reduced the debtor's room for maneuver and led to a soft creditor-led restructuring—resulting in a much more unequal distribution of adjustment costs. The outcome of the Mexican debt crisis of the 1980s therefore hints at a dramatic shift in the international balance of power between debtors and creditors (empowering the money-center banks, international financial institutions, and dominant creditor states vis-à-vis the peripheral borrowing countries), as well as in the domestic balance of power between financial elites and working people (empowering those social groups in the debtor countries that were seen to fulfill a bridging role towards foreign lenders). It was this shift in the underlying power relations that accounts for the striking absence of unilateral default in the 1980s, as opposed to its widespread incidence in the 1930s. As Manuel Pastor concluded at the end of Latin America's lost decade, "none of the more radical proposals—full or partial repudiation, debt service limits, or mobilizing the foreign wealth of local elites—will be adopted without a redistribution of political power." It is for this reason that we now turn to a case in which such a redistribution of power apparently did take place, with far-reaching consequences for that country's willingness to service its debts to foreign bondholders and international financial institutions.

Table 11.1.
Comparison between the crises of the 1930s and 1980s

## Mexico in the 1930s

**Securitized bond finance:**
Debt concentration low
Dispersed lending structure
Creditor coordination difficult
No credible threat of credit cut-off
*Market discipline weak*

**No lender of last resort:**
No international bailout loans
No creditor coordination to keep debtors solvent
No monitoring/supervision of debtor policies
No way to enforce debtor discipline
*No conditional lending*

**Relative debtor autonomy:**
Relative self-sufficiency in economic terms
Sidelining of domestic elites and technocrats
Powerful popular pressure from below
Strengthened national-popular coalition
***Breakdown of debtor discipline***

**OUTCOME:**
*Unilateral default*
Greater room for maneuver
Mexico calls for continent-wide moratorium
Mexico only restructures debt after recovery
Creditors and debtors share burden of adjustment

## Mexico in the 1980s

**Syndicated bank lending:**
Debt concentration high
Interlocked lending structure
Creditor coordination easy
Credible threat of credit cut-off
*Market discipline strong*

**Active U.S./IMF intervention:**
Sizable international bailout loans
Coordinated rollovers to keep debtors solvent
IMF monitoring/supervision of debtor policies
Policy conditionality enforces discipline
*Effective conditional lending*

**Limited debtor autonomy:**
Growing dependence on foreign credit and capital
Bridging role for domestic elites and technocrats
Popular opposition forestalled through cooptation
Strengthened bankers' alliance
*Internalization of debtor discipline*

**OUTCOME:**
*No unilateral default*
Room for maneuver constrained
Mexico develops into "model debtor"
Creditors only restructure debt after divesting
Highly unequal distribution of adjustment costs

# PART IV

---

# The Great Default:
# Argentina (1999–2005)

# TWELVE

## The Exception That Proves the Rule

On December 23, 2001, Argentina declared a unilateral suspension of payments on $82 billion in public debt, triggering the largest sovereign default in history. The sheer scale of the episode was staggering: as Latin America's biggest debtor, Argentina's bonds made up nearly a quarter of all emerging market debt traded globally.[1] The dramatic outcome of its crisis constitutes a remarkable contrast to the widespread debtor compliance of the 1980s and 1990s, and thus poses an interesting new research puzzle: if the trend after 1982 was for countries *not* to default on their external debts, then why did Argentina go against this historical dynamic by declaring a moratorium on its debt service? The observation seems all the more puzzling since, at the time, many observers were just beginning to argue that globalization had greatly increased the power of multinational corporations—and of global finance in particular.[2] Argentina's unilateral default, followed by its coercive debt restructuring and President Kirchner's scathing rhetoric against foreign creditors and the IMF, seemed to challenge some of these presumptions. Suddenly the dreaded and supposedly all-powerful "bond vigilantes" did not appear to be so omnipotent after all; apparently even a crisis-ridden peripheral debtor like Argentina was capable of challenging its foreign creditors and reneging on its external obligations. Noting this apparent discrepancy, some scholars have even explicitly posited the Argentine case as a challenge to the structural power hypothesis.[3]

Such narratives, however, largely pass over a crucial observation: Argentina's striking *over*-compliance in the months and years leading up to the default. In fact, right up until mid-2001, Argentina was widely considered to be a model debtor, resembling Mexico in terms of its commitment to repay. During the 1990s the country even became known as an IMF "poster child" and a darling of global capital markets. Presidents Menem (1989–1999) and De la Rúa (1999–2001) firmly insisted on full repayment and adherence to the Washington Consensus throughout their terms, also when the economy entered into stormy waters following the Mexican peso crisis of 1995, the East-Asian financial crisis of 1997–1998, the Russian default of 1998 and the Brazilian devaluation of 1999. Despite the fact that Argentina experienced a deep economic depression that saw unemployment rates climb sharply from 14 percent to over 25 percent between 1999 and 2001, De la Rúa steadfastly refused to pursue a unilateral default strategy even as his opponents openly called for it, his approval rates fell to historic lows, and Wall Street, the IMF and the U.S. government all pressed him to face up to the inevitable and simply suspend payments and renegotiate the outstanding obligations.

Finally, in December 2001, there was a historic rupture. After De la Rúa was forced from office following a massive popular uprising and a wave of deadly riots, his interim successor immediately declared a moratorium on all public debt payments.[4] What explains this sudden switch from compliance to defiance? Clearly, a convincing explanation of the Argentine financial crisis should be able to account not only for the default itself but also the earlier *refusal* to default; in other words, it should account for both the country's over-compliance in the first three years of the crisis and for the ways in which this over-compliance finally gave way to noncompliance at the end of 2001. This chapter demonstrates how the process leading up to the largest default in history, far from challenging the structural power hypothesis developed in this book, actually confirms it. Argentina, in short, is the exception that proves the rule. To understand why, we have to take a closer look at what happened to the three enforcement mechanisms of debtor compliance over the course of the crisis. Initially fully effective, we will see in the next three chapters how each of them gradually broke down over the course of 2001, making a disorderly Argentine default not only possible but increasingly unavoidable. The fourth and final chapter of the case study then considers the consequences of these exceptional dynamics for the outcomes of the crisis, leading up to the highly coercive debt restructuring that was concluded by President Néstor Kirchner in 2005.

## INTERNATIONAL LENDING IN THE LEAD-UP TO THE CRISIS

The first crucial difference between the Argentine case and the Mexican case discussed in the previous section has to do with the structure of international lending. The resolution of the Latin American debt crisis of the 1980s by means of the Brady deal had allowed the commercial banks to swap their outstanding loans for bonds, which could subsequently be sold on secondary markets. The Brady restructurings thus contributed to the demise of syndicated bank lending and the return of securitized bond finance as the principal form of cross-border lending from the early 1990s onwards (see figure 12.1). Governments in Latin America and across the Global South still mostly interacted with the major Wall Street banks, but these banks no longer served as the principal creditors themselves. Instead, they acted as loan underwriters and financial intermediaries between the borrowing governments and international investors—often major financial institutions in the rich countries like hedge funds, pension funds,

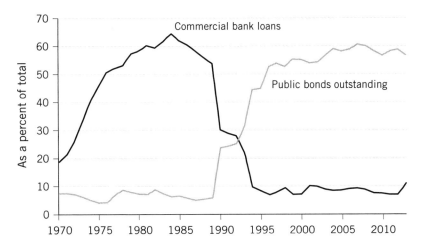

FIGURE 12.1. Bond issuance supplants bank lending, 1970–2013. *Source*: Kaplan and
Thomsson (2017).

*Note*: Aggregate data for sixteen Latin American countries.

and mutual funds, but sometimes also retail investors, small savers, and individual pensioners.

The return to bond finance did not stop the steady growth in external indebtedness of developing countries (see figure 12.2). Argentina, in particular, began
to attract large amounts of foreign credit and investment over the course of the
1990s (see figure 12.3). Even though the country had defaulted many times in
the past and had been by far the most defiant debtor under Alfolsín in the 1980s,
briefly suspending payments following the transition to democracy, it still
managed to rapidly establish itself as an investor favorite under Alfolsín's successor Carlos Menem in the 1990s, attracting more international loans than any
other developing country. As always, however, the boom was bound to turn to
bust. Just like in the 1980s, Mexico was the first domino to fall, with a sudden
fall in the value in the peso in 1994 rendering the country's external debts unsustainable, once more reviving the specter of a Mexican default. U.S. treasury
secretary and former Goldman Sachs executive Robert Rubin responded to the
Mexican peso crisis of 1994–1995 by orchestrating a record international bailout under strict policy conditionality.[5] Barely five years after the Brady deal had
brought the last great developing country debt crisis to an end, the next one was
already rearing its ugly head.

The repercussions of Mexico's debt troubles immediately threatened to spill
over to other developing countries in Latin America and East Asia. Between
1995 and 1998, Argentina's financing needs doubled to $20 billion.[6] "With hind-
sight," economists Dominguez and Tesar would later note, "it is easy to see that

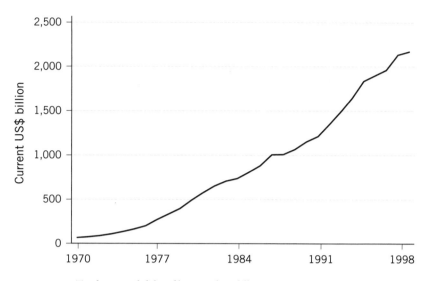

FIGURE 12.2. Total external debt of low- and middle-income countries, 1970–1999. *Source*: World Bank (2017).

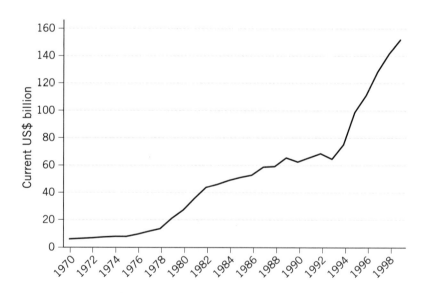

FIGURE 12.3. Argentina's total external debt, 1970–1999. *Source*: World Bank (2017).

Argentina's boom in the early 1990s . . . was in fact on precarious footing."[7] By 1998, the peso—whose value was tied to the dollar through the so-called Convertibility Plan, established by Menem's economy minister Domingo Cavallo in 1991—had become dangerously overvalued in real terms, undermining the competitive position of Argentine exporters, reducing export earnings, and depleting the foreign-exchange reserves that the country needed to service its dollar-denominated debts. These internal problems were further compounded by a sharp rise in interest rates as international investors panicked and lost their appetite for emerging market bonds in the wake of the East-Asian crisis of 1997–1998 and the subsequent Russian default. Meanwhile Argentina's total national debt, which had stood at $60 billion in 1989 when President Menem first came to power at the tail end of the previous crisis, reached $145 billion by the end of his second term in 1999. As a result, interest payments came to take up an ever-larger share of total public expenditure, reaching over a third by the time of the default (see figure 12.4). Unsurprisingly, this burden was starting to look increasingly unsustainable to the country's foreign lenders.[8]

After the presidential elections of 1999, Argentina's new president, Fernando De la Rúa, rose to power inside a monetary and fiscal straitjacket. Not unlike Greece's position inside the Eurozone today, the nature of the dollar-peso convertibility regime meant that Argentina was unable to adjust its exchange rate or print pesos to stimulate the economy or inflate away its debts. As a result, the growing interest rate spreads forced the government to choose between

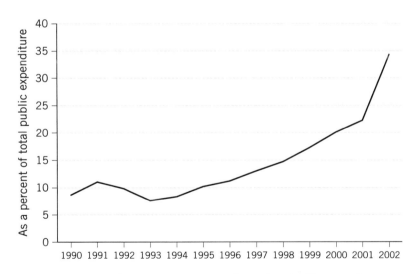

FIGURE 12.4. Argentina's interest payments as a share of total public expenditures, 1990–2002. *Source*: World Bank (2017); IMF, Government Finance Statistics Yearbook and data files.

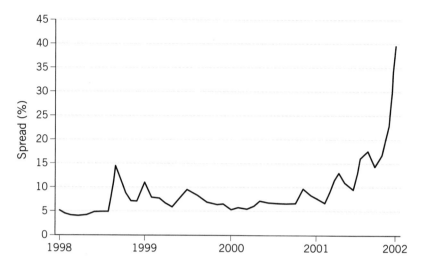

FIGURE 12.5. Argentine bonds' risk-spread (*riesgo país*) over U.S. Treasuries, 1998–2002. *Source*: Economist (2005); derived from Thomson Datastream, J.P. Morgan EMBI+ Argentina index.

Scylla and Charybdis: either it responded to the emerging fiscal crisis by halting payments on its external debt and suspending convertibility, or it pursued an internal devaluation to avoid a disorderly default and external devaluation of the peso, requiring a severe fiscal contraction and sharp wage reductions that in turn risked undermining aggregate demand and domestic welfare, further deepening the social and economic crisis in the process.

As investor confidence sapped and the so-called *riesgo país*—the risk premium Argentina had to pay on its bonds—rose sharply in the wake of the Russian default and Brazilian devaluation (see figure 12.5), De la Rúa found himself pushed towards the latter option, imposing ever more stringent austerity measures to reassure investors that the Argentine budget was under control.[9] As in the 1980s, market discipline effectively compelled the government to comply with investor demands for austerity and debt repayment even in the absence of a formal IMF program. Like their Mexican counterparts before, Argentine policymakers feared that noncompliance would cause foreign creditors to stop all loans, with crippling short-term consequences for the domestic economy.[10] Cavallo explicitly expressed a concern that "seeking meaningful debt relief meant losing access to domestic and external credit and immediately moving into fiscal and external balance."[11]

But in the context of the return to bond finance, this observation does raise an important question: why did the Argentine government express similar fears of a credit cutoff as the Mexican government, if the dominant form of international lending in the 1990s occurred through bond finance? If bondholders are really so much more difficult to organize than international bank syndicates—which was, after all, one of the key lessons from the comparison between the 1930s and the 1980s—then why did the bond market turmoil of the late 1990s not lead to more widespread sovereign default? During the Mexican peso crisis of 1995 and the East-Asian financial crisis of 1997–1998, developing countries and international financial institutions largely pursued the same orthodox policy response as they had in the 1980s; indeed, in many respects the austerity measures and structural reforms imposed in the 1990s were even harsher.[12] Like most developing countries, Argentina itself was—at least in the first years of its crisis—extremely subservient to the expectations of foreign investors and the prescriptions of the Washington Consensus. What explains this initial compliance in a context of bond finance? Why did Argentina and other emerging market borrowers not simply defy foreign bondholders as they had in the 1930s?

Again, a big part of the answer appears to lie with the key players dominating the international lending game in the 1990s, especially the big U.S. investment banks managing emerging market bond sales, and the institutional investors—like pension and mutual funds in the United States and Europe—that ended up buying these securities. In fact, contrary to widespread perceptions about the decentralized nature of bond finance, global capital markets in the 1990s still retained an important degree of hierarchy and centralization, with Wall Street giants like Goldman Sachs, Morgan Stanley, and Crédit Suisse–First Boston playing a key intermediary role in the marketing of emerging market bonds. In his authoritative account of the crisis, investigative journalist Paul Blustein notes that a small number of brokerage firms

> competed fiercely for "mandates" to be lead managers of government bond sales, especially in Argentina. . . . They found plenty of customers for the bonds in the United States and other wealthy countries among professional investors managing the hundreds of billions of dollars held in mutual funds, pension funds, insurance companies, foundations, and other large institutions.[13]

As long as emerging market borrowers continued to depend on a handful of U.S. investment banks to furnish them with access to institutional buyers of their government bonds, this hierarchical and centralized nature of international bond finance tended to ease creditor coordination and served to impose a degree of discipline on the debtors. After all, in the event of noncompliance, not only would institutional investors have had an incentive to divest from their high-risk bonds, but most importantly the powerful Wall Street investment banks would also have refused to continue marketing new bonds as a safe and lucrative investment, causing government borrowing costs to shoot up and robbing the country of its primary source of foreign financing. In this respect, at least, the centralized and investment-bank-dominated bond finance of the

1990s resembled the syndicated bank lending of the 1970s and early 1980s; the key difference being that sovereign bonds can easily be sold on secondary markets, providing institutional investors with an exit option and the ability to reduce their exposure in anticipation of a potential sovereign default.

This exit option proved to be particularly important in Argentina, once it became increasingly clear over the course of 2001 that the country would never be able to honor its towering debt load in full. As the government's creditworthiness began to be called into question, foreign pension and mutual funds grew increasingly wary of holding Argentine bonds as part of their portfolios. The result, Anna Gelpern notes, was that "the identity of Argentina's creditors . . . changed over time. . . . In the mid-1990s, Argentina borrowed chiefly from foreign institutional investors. As the recession wore on and institutional interest wore thin, Argentina tapped unprecedented numbers of European, and to a lesser extent Asian, retail investors."[14] The result was a stark change in the ownership structure of Argentina's external debt, the importance of which—as we will see in greater detail later—is difficult to overstate.

## THE RETURN OF THE COLLECTIVE ACTION PROBLEM

By mid-2001, it was clear to most Wall Street financiers that Argentina would soon have to declare itself incapable of servicing its towering foreign debt load. As this realization finally dawned, the U.S. investment banks moved in to orchestrate an obscure debt rescheduling deal aimed at buying the country's government and its big bondholders some much-needed time before the inevitable default. In May that year, Crédit Suisse–First Boston and seven other international banks joined together in a consortium that took the initiative to present Economy Minister Domingo Cavallo with a notorious refinancing scheme that became known as the *megacanje*, or "megaswap"—a deal that would exchange Argentina's maturing bonds with new ones carrying longer maturities but also much higher interest rates.[15] The megaswap thus postponed $15 billion in bond payments falling due in 2001, buying the De la Rúa administration some much-needed fiscal breathing room and pushing the moment of reckoning back until after the next presidential elections.

But in the process, the same deal also loaded the country with much higher interest payments and a growing debt burden in the long run. According to Blustein, the swap "ranks among the most infamous deals that Wall Street has ever peddled to a government—and with good reason: for [Crédit Suisse] and a half dozen other Wall Street firms, the megaswap would be a bonanza. . . . For Argentina, it would be a bust, rendering the country's solvency even more questionable than it was already."[16] The successful conclusion of the megaswap, however, raises a crucial question. In the words of political scientist Paul Lewis, "Why would the big international bankers agree to such a deal, knowing in advance that Argentina would never pay up?" The answer, he suggests, has to do with the ongoing shift in the ownership structure of Argentina's debt:

The composition of Argentina's creditors had changed. Back in the early 1990s, when Cavallo first became economics minister, he had had to deal with only a handful of powerful financiers to get what he wanted . . . , while big mutual fund and pension fund managers in the United States were eager to buy. By the end of the Menem period, however, those fund managers were becoming leery of Argentina's prospects, so the big brokerage houses turned to Europe, where regulations protecting small investors were less strict. There, most individual investors bought stocks and bonds through their local banks. . . . Thus, the big international brokerage houses succeeded in "atomizing" the risk of default by spreading it among literally hundreds of thousands of small investors in Italy, Germany, and the rest of Europe (and Japan), who bought into high-interest-bearing "emerging market" mutual funds through their pension plans. "That's what kept Argentina going," said an emerging market bond manager at Metropolitan Life Insurance Company. "Those poor suckers didn't have a clue as to what they were buying."[17]

By atomizing Argentina's creditor base, the megaswap had far-reaching consequences for the ability of the new bondholders to organize collective action among themselves. While the syndicated bank lending of the 1980s and Argentina's hierarchical and centralized bond finance of the 1990s had interlocked creditor interests by concentrating foreign government debt in the hands of a few systemically important repeat players, thereby easing the internal coordination of a coherent creditors' cartel, the dispersion of Argentina's bondholders over the course of 2001 brought back painful memories of the 1930s, when disorganized and geographically scattered small investors failed to walk the fine line between disciplining sovereign borrowers through the credible threat of a credit cutoff while simultaneously keeping them in the lending game through coordinated debt roll-overs. Anne Krueger, who served as the IMF's deputy managing director during the Argentine crisis, observed a stark contrast between the "generally orderly" crisis management of the 1980s, and the chaotic and unpredictable crises at the turn of the century, in which investors "were increasingly numerous, anonymous, and difficult to coordinate," just as they had been in the interwar period.[18] Miguel Teubal, an economist at the University of Buenos Aires, confirms this observation:

Through this mechanism [of selling government bonds on the secondary market] the foreign banks were divested of their exposure to Argentina's foreign debt, [which] was now transferred to individual bondholders, thus atomizing the foreign (and local) creditor universe. For this reason when default of foreign private debt was declared in early 2002, the main creditors affected were the retired and pensioners mostly of Europe and Japan that had been (ill-)advised by the banks to purchase Argentine government bonds due to their very high profitability.[19]

The breakdown of the international creditors' cartel—or rather, the existing cartel's success in passing on the risks and losses of a future Argentine default to an unorganized body of scattered retail investors—in turn helped to disarm the first enforcement mechanism of market discipline that had been so effective in the 1980s and that had, up to that point, served to enforce the compliance of the De la Rúa government. After the megaswap, however, Argentina was for all practical purposes excluded from international capital markets, and was now sending abroad more money in interest service than it was receiving back in further private financing (see figures 12.6 and 12.7). The Wall Street banks did not want to burn their fingers on further loans to a country that now seemed destined to default, and so they refused to float Argentine bonds until the government faced up to the necessity of a debt restructuring to render the country's enormous debt load sustainable. Meanwhile Wall Street started hedging its bets. By September 2001, it was clear to most of the international financial community that the Argentine government was on "the brink of default."[20] Anticipating a major credit event, the U.S. investment banks doubled down on their bets, not only embracing the inevitability of default but starting to aggressively push for a major debt restructuring. This is also the point at which the banks' hedge fund departments began swooping in on secondary markets to buy up the country's depreciated debt at mere cents on the dollar, hoping to land handsome profits from a widely anticipated future settlement—a point to which we will return in chapter 15 on the outcomes of the crisis.

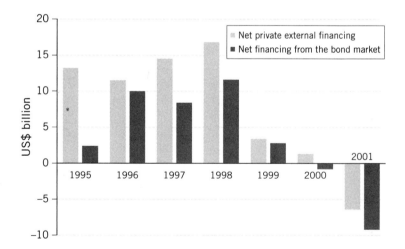

FIGURE 12.6. Argentina's access to private sources of financing, 1995–2001. *Source*: Setser and Gelpern (2006); Government of Argentina (external debt statistics); and BCRA.

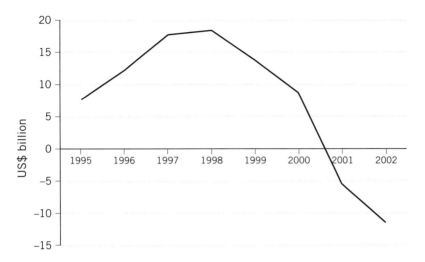

FIGURE 12.7. Argentina's net capital flows, 1995–2002. *Source*: Baer, Margot, and Montes-Rojas (2010).

In October 2001, a key meeting took place between IMF Managing Director Horst Köhler and the senior executives from some of the leading investment banks and institutional investors, including J. P. Morgan, Goldman Sachs, Citigroup, Crédit Suisse–First Boston, and AIG. According to one observer, the private financiers assembled at the meeting concluded that "Argentina was going to collapse and that nothing could be done to save it. A default was inevitable, and the best that the creditors could do would be to approve a restructuring under which they would voluntarily accept less than the face value of their claims."[21] As Paul Blustein emphasizes, "this was a remarkable moment. The major creditors of a country were effectively saying that the government should pay them less than they were owed, on involuntary terms."[22] But while the bankers' position may seem puzzling at first sight, their insistence on the necessity of an Argentine default had little to do with altruism: the lenders were simply hoping to restore Argentina's long-term creditworthiness, keep the country in the lending game and thus allow its government to come crawling back to the banks for further high interest loans after the anticipated debt restructuring. The losses from a haircut on the outstanding bonds, even in the form of a record-breaking and involuntary sovereign default, would be acceptable. After all, the principal institutional investors had already written down the remaining securities they still held on to; as long as Argentina could be prevented from repudiating its debts outright, they were unlikely to incur significant losses in any post-default debt restructuring. Indeed, their hedge fund departments might profit

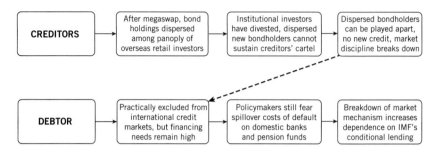

FIGURE 12.8. The first enforcement mechanism in Argentina.

handsomely from such a renegotiation, since they were now buying up the country's debts on secondary markets at sizable discounts.

By October 2001, Wall Street had not just reconciled itself with the impending default; it was actively pushing for it. The first enforcement mechanism of market discipline had broken down.

# THIRTEEN

## From IMF Poster Child to Wayward Student

The shift in Argentina's creditor composition over the course of 2001 was reflected in a comparable shift in the international financial community's stance towards Argentina. The role of the IMF was particularly important in this respect, and presents a second major contrast to the management of the Mexican debt crisis. As we saw in previous chapters, the Fund had played a crucial role in cementing the creditors' cartel and preventing a series of sovereign defaults in the 1980s debt crisis by disbursing credit facilities of last resort under strict policy conditionality. Together with the U.S. Treasury Department and the U.S. Federal Reserve, the IMF played an even more important role in the crises of the late 1990s, disbursing ever-larger international bailout loans and demanding even-stricter structural adjustments and austerity measures than before. Echoing the lessons from the 1980s, economists at the Center for Economic and Policy Research pointed out that "the role of the IMF is important, not so much because of its own resources or expertise, but because of its power—together with the U.S. Treasury Department—as head of a creditors' cartel that can deny Argentina access to sources of credit."[1] But if the International Monetary Fund had previously been so successful in wielding this threat of a credit withdrawal, then why did it not prevent Argentina's record default of 2001? Was it unable to stop it? Or did it not want to?

The answer, we will see in this chapter, was a combination of both. While the second enforcement mechanism of conditional IMF lending was initially fully operative, helping to enforce Argentina's compliance in the first years of the crisis, the outcome of the megaswap greatly reduced the risk of an Argentine default to the international financial system. Combined with mounting domestic opposition in the United States to further international bailout loans, this greatly weakened the IMF's capacity to impose fiscal discipline on Argentina, eventually leading the Fund to pull the plug on its own bailout program, causing the second enforcement mechanism to break down altogether. The following pages will recount the process through which this breakdown occurred.

## The IMF's Evolving Role in the Crisis

The first thing to note about the IMF's role in Argentina is the fact that the Fund was severely weakened by the time the crisis came around at the turn of the century. Having greatly overextended itself during the developing country debt crises of the 1990s (see figure 13.1), the IMF not only faced scathing criticism and growing opposition from across the political spectrum—especially in the United States, the Fund's main contributor and its most powerful board member—but also carried sizable exposures to Argentina and several other emerging markets. The second thing to note is that, after the inauguration of George W. Bush in 2001, the U.S. government grew increasingly preoccupied with the War on Terror and increasingly hostile to the massive bailouts that had been pursued by the Clinton administration, leading to an isolationist stance with respect to international crisis management that was enabled by the convenient fact that U.S. financial institutions no longer had a dog in the fight. As we will see, the first development led to a growing *inability* of the IMF in the period leading up to mid-2001 to compel De la Rúa to stick to his fiscal targets, while the second led to a growing *unwillingness* among the IMF's main sponsors in Congress and the White House to keep Argentina afloat in the face of a default that was now widely considered to be unavoidable. The two dynamics conspired in November 2001 to lead to the withholding of a critical IMF credit

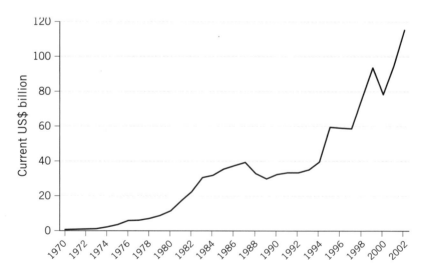

FIGURE 13.1. Low- and middle-income countries' use of IMF credit, 1970–2002.
*Source*: World Bank (2017).

tranche on the grounds that Argentina had failed to live up to the conditions of its IMF Stand-By Arrangement. The severing of the Fund's official credit line set in motion a sequence of events that three weeks later finally ended in default.

The IMF's approach to Argentina thus underwent a change at least as dramatic as—and very much in line with—the simultaneous change in debt concentration and creditor composition. We can identify three distinct phases in this trajectory. The first, which covered Menem's presidency from 1989 until 1999, was marked by very close and cooperative relations between Argentina and the Fund. Throughout the 1990s, the international financial community enthusiastically sponsored the neoliberal agenda pursued by Menem and Cavallo, which "matched perfectly with the reigning economic ideology" of the IMF, World Bank, and U.S. Treasury.[2] As late as 1998, Menem was invited to address the IMF annual meeting in Washington, D.C., to share his views on responsible fiscal and monetary policy—a particularly ironic twist, since Menem's policies and Cavallo's convertibility regime largely laid the foundations for the subsequent debt crisis.[3] At this point, the representatives of Argentina's financial establishment resembled the technocratic allies of Mexico's bankers' alliance, working closely with U.S. and IMF officials to establish "a high degree of agreement on the economic policies to be implemented."[4] The IMF's managing director Michel Camdessus exclaimed that "in many respects the experience of Argentina in recent years has been exemplary . . . clearly, Argentina has a story to tell the world: a story which is about the importance of fiscal discipline, of structural change, and of monetary policy rigorously maintained."[5] As late as May 1999, when the contours of the impending crisis had already begun to emerge, the IMF Board of Directors declared that "Argentina is to be commended for its continued prudent policies," noting that "the sound macroeconomic management, the strengthening of the banking system and the other structural reforms carried out in recent years in the context of the currency board arrangement, have had beneficial effects on confidence."[6] Argentina, in short, was celebrated as an IMF poster child.

The second phase, which covered the first part of De la Rúa's presidency from 1999 onwards and the lame duck phase of the Clinton administration, was marked by a deepening of the recession, the escalation of fiscal pressures, and increasingly forceful attempts to stave off an Argentine default. At the same time, however, this phase was also marked by the waning influence of the IMF and its growing inability to enforce its loan conditionality on the Argentine government. In the United States, Republican opposition to the unprecedented U.S.-led rescue operations in Mexico, East Asia, Russia, Turkey, and Brazil (see figure 13.2) had begun to gather steam. From 1998 onwards, influential voices inside the U.S. political establishment began to call for the wholesale abolition of the Fund, and the Clinton administration struggled to convince Congress to increase the IMF quota.[7] As a result, the Fund became severely overexposed to emerging market debt, with Turkey, Brazil, and Argentina accounting for

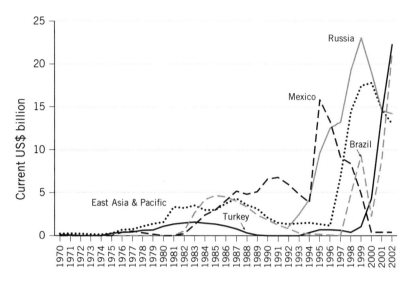

FIGURE 13.2. Use of IMF credit by selected countries, 1990–2002. *Source*: World Bank (2017).

73 percent of its outstanding liabilities at the end of the decade, and the IMF's reserves of $8.7 billion paling in comparison to the $16 billion in exposure it carried to Argentina alone.[8] All of this gave the Fund considerably less leverage over the Argentine government than it had enjoyed over the other developing country borrowers of the 1980s and 1990s.

Throughout this phase, however, the IMF nevertheless remained determined to avoid an Argentine default, working closely with the increasingly embattled economy minister Domingo Cavallo to keep the country in the lending game. Brad Setser and Anna Gelpern write that "Cavallo's core accomplishment was to draw on his considerable reputation [as a friend of the international financial establishment] to secure a series of additional injections of IMF liquidity to finance what turned out to be a classic gamble for resurrection."[9] In 2000 and 2001, the IMF disbursed several of the largest credit augmentations in its history (see figure 13.3), but even this failed to bring a halt to the investor stampede. Meanwhile, the IMF's top officials, who had not received advance notice of Cavallo's momentous megaswap, grew increasingly frustrated with the De la Rúa administration. Cooper and Momani note that the relationship "soured during this time as the Fund watched Argentina continue to announce policies that the IMF deemed 'misguided,' although these initiatives were overtly approved out of fear of a systemic collapse."[10] In September 2001, the IMF came to the rescue once again by adding another $8 billion lifeline to its Stand-By Arrangement from 2000; the third such augmentation in less than a year, bringing

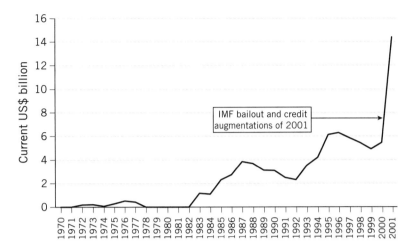

FIGURE 13.3. Argentina's use of IMF credit, 1970–2001. *Source*: World Bank (2017).

the total of extra credit to $22 billion. There now appears to be a broad consensus, including among the IMF's top economists, that these loan extensions constituted "the most contentious decisions regarding the IMF's involvement in the Argentine crisis."[11] Not only did the augmentations triple the Fund's exposure to Argentina and turn the IMF into the country's single biggest creditor; the Fund's own economists also held them responsible for "delaying the inevitable, postponing the default and amplifying the dislocation caused by the crisis."[12]

This period of muddling through finally gave way to the third phase, which covered the first years of the Bush administration and the final months of De la Rúa's presidency. At this point, the Fund's pent-up frustrations with Argentina turned to outright, full-blown hostility. First, as the economic performance of its former poster child grew from bad to worse, the IMF notably shifted its narrative. Whereas it had previously praised the fiscal discipline of the profligate Menem, it now began to blame the relatively compliant and technocratic De la Rúa for his fiscal ineptitude. This in turn reflected a change at the helm of the IMF and the U.S. Treasury. When the Mexican, East-Asian, Russian, and Brazilian crises struck during the Clinton administration in the 1990s, the Treasury and the IMF had prioritized firefighting over all other priorities— disbursing record international bailout loans under strict policy conditionality to keep the debtors solvent and servicing their debts. However, from Clinton's last treasury secretary Larry Summers on, the United States' interventionist role in international financial crises was gradually undermined from within by isolationist forces in U.S. Congress. In 1998, Republicans lawmakers had put up stiff resistance to a proposed $18 billion increase in IMF reserves to protest Clinton's East Asian bailouts. The increase eventually passed—but only on the condition that Congress establish a commission to review the IMF's role in international crisis management. This gave rise to the Meltzer commission, chaired by the right-wing libertarian economist Allan Meltzer, an influential advocate for the abolition of the Fund.[13] In its final report, the commission urged a radical downsizing of the IMF. Given this context, it is perhaps no surprise that Bush's response to the Argentine crisis amounted to little more than "a placeholder with relatively modest upfront financial commitments that deferred hard decisions."[14]

## EMBRACING THE INEVITABILITY OF DEFAULT

After a new management took over at the Treasury and the IMF following the inauguration of George W. Bush, the international stance towards the Argentine government hardened. The new treasury secretary, Paul O'Neill, expressed his opposition to further bailouts while his undersecretary for international affairs, John Taylor, even argued for doing away with the IMF altogether.[15] Bush's chief economic advisor, Lawrence Lindsey, was also on record for his staunch free-market convictions; views that weighed heavily on the administration's response to the Argentine crisis, which on the one hand became ever more *laissez-faire* in its approach to emergency lending and on the other much tougher in terms of the conditionality it imposed on the debtor.[16] Javier Corrales writes that "the first sign of hard-line posturing came when Secretary of the Treasury O'Neill, shortly after taking office in 2001, chided Argentina publicly for getting in trouble because it never did its homework, essentially ignoring Argentina's reform record of the past decade and the role of external crises."[17]

Moreover, after the megaswap of mid-2001, the Fund decided that "the fire in Argentina would not spread, mostly because bondholders had protected themselves (more specifically, most U.S. bondholders had already sold much of their Argentine debt)."[18] Indeed, figure 13.4 shows how the holdings of U.S. investors accounted for only around 9 percent of Argentina's total outstanding privately held bonds at the time of the default in December 2001, much of which had already been written down or sold on to Wall Street hedge funds. Carmen Reinhart, the Fund's deputy chief economist at the time, tried to ease the contagion fears of her colleagues by reassuring them that an Argentine default would probably have only limited repercussions for other developing countries or the world economy more generally. As she co-wrote in a staff memo of the IMF research department on August 15, "a 'credit event' in Argentina is widely anticipated and has been (partly) discounted by the markets for some time. The possibility that a default by Argentina triggers a sharp reversal of capital flows to other countries in South America is therefore relatively small."[19] Another internal IMF report showed that, while a few Spanish banks might take a hit, the

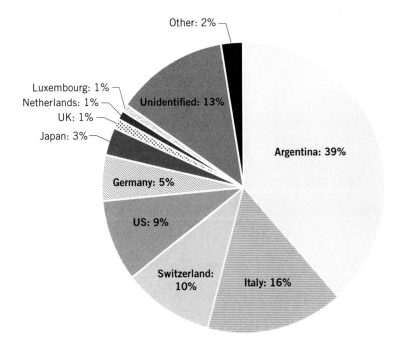

FIGURE 13.4. Ownership of Argentina's $82 billion privately held debt at time of default in late 2001. *Source*: Shapiro and Pham (2006).

risk of contagion and the threat to the international financial system were low.[20] At the same time, drawing on its past experience with currency devaluations in East Asia, the IMF had become convinced that Argentina's inflexible exchange rate had to go, which would in turn necessitate a sizable restructuring of the country's dollar-denominated external debt. None of this meant that Argentina would be granted any leeway, however; as the stance of the U.S. government and the IMF hardened, loan conditionality was only further ramped up.[21]

By now, influential economic commentators and leading figures in the U.S. financial establishment had already been openly expressing the inevitability and necessity of a default for quite some time. Back in March 2001, Columbia University economist Charles Calomiris and a group of Wall Street bankers had proposed that "Argentina declare itself bankrupt, request debt forgiveness, and start over with new policies intended to reward creditors only if its economy improved."[22] Calomiris was by no means a leftwing populist or Jubilee campaigner. Well-known in policymaking circles as a long-time champion of financial deregulation who kept the interests of Wall Street close at heart, Calomiris was convinced that there was only one way to keep Argentina in the lending game: by writing off a significant chunk of the debt. At this stage, "devaluation and default were openly discussed (particularly in financial and academic settings in the United States) and there was a widespread opinion that the debt and the convertibility regime were not sustainable."[23] With the IMF itself heavily overexposed to Argentine debt, Horst Köhler, the Fund's new managing director, began to investigate the possibility of private sector involvement in the burden sharing. Paul Blustein reports that Köhler "raised the possibility that the IMF and the Argentine authorities should consider something like Calomiris's 'haircut' proposal for forcing creditors to accept reduced payment of their claims."[24] And so the IMF's economists began to prepare various default scenarios—"Plan Gamma"—as a possible resolution to the crisis.

In April 2001, Calomiris went public with his default proposal in a *Wall Street Journal* article entitled "Argentina Can't Pay What It Owes." In the piece, he specifically argued that most U.S. institutional investors had already sold off their Argentine bonds and therefore U.S. policymakers did not need to fear the consequences of even a disorderly Argentine default. Highlighting the fact that "US institutions are already 'underweight' on Argentine debt," Calomiris pointed out that, while Argentina accounted for some 25 percent of emerging market bonds in circulation worldwide, it only made up 10–15 percent of the portfolios of the large U.S.-based mutual funds and pension funds (note that this was before the megaswap; these ratios were even further reduced as institutional investors offloaded their Argentine bonds in the swap). The opinion piece elicited a strong rebuke from Economy Minister Domingo Cavallo, who shot back that "I have thought a lot as to why honest people may dare to write a recommendation as to how Argentina may default. Who could conceive such a destructive idea for a country, and be bold enough to propose it? . . . There is a complete misunderstanding (almost omission) of the costs that a compulsory restructuring of our debt would have."[25]

By October 2001, Héctor Schamis writes, "it was obvious to most analysts that Argentina would have to default on its debt, but Cavallo—some said with an eye on his ties to Wall Street—stubbornly refused to admit it."[26] The perceived inevitability of a default, however, was already turning into a self-fulfilling prophecy. On December 5, the IMF announced that it would be withholding its next $1.24 billion loan installment out of frustration with the government's failure to keep its budget under control. With the lender of last resort pulling the plug on Argentina's financial lifeline, there was little the government could do to prevent the downward spiral that, three weeks later, would force the country to declare the largest unilateral default in world history. In a final act of desperation, Cavallo seized the country's pension funds and transferred the proceeds to the national treasury, allowing the government to keep paying its bills and to once more extend the moment of reckoning. In a meeting with IMF officials on December 7, when it was clear to everyone in the room that Argentina had no other option but to suspend payments and exit the convertibility regime, Cavallo refused to even discuss the option with Fund officials.[27] And so

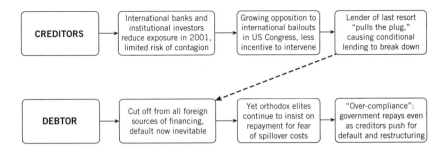

FIGURE 13.5. The second enforcement mechanism in Argentina.

the United States simply kept pushing Argentina further towards the abyss. "As if the message was not clear enough," Cavallo later fumed in indignation, "Allan Meltzer visited Buenos Aires to tell [opposition leader] Eduardo Duhalde and most of the senators that the debt restructuring process which the Argentinian government was engaged in would not generate enough of a haircut and Argentina should simply default on all its debt."[28] But Cavallo and De la Rúa would have none of it. In one of the most remarkable cases of overcompliance in recent financial history, the two men continued to defy the global financial community precisely by *not* defaulting. Both the first and second enforcement mechanisms had now broken down—but debtor discipline was so firmly internalized that the Argentine government continued to try everything in its power to repay a debt that everyone else now agreed was unpayable.

# FOURTEEN

## The Rise and Fall of the *Patria Financiera*

B y the end of 2001, Argentina's external debt compliance had become a case
of *incredible commitment*, in both senses of the term: in the sense that creditors no longer considered the government's commitment to honor its financial
obligations credible, and in the sense that the government nevertheless continued to display an extraordinary commitment to continued debt servicing.
After the dispersal of Argentina's bondholders in the megaswap and the IMF's
decision to pull the plug on its own financial lifeline, the first two enforcement
mechanisms had effectively broken down—yet De la Rúa and Cavallo continued to insist on full repayment. If Wall Street, the U.S. government, and the
IMF were now all actively pushing for Argentina to suspend its debt service,
why did the country's leaders not just get it over with and default? What drove
De la Rúa and Cavallo to repay? And what was it that eventually produced the
shift from overcompliance to default—and from there to Kirchner's outright
defiance of foreign lenders? So far, we have merely explored the gradual breakdown of the *international* enforcement mechanisms of market discipline and
policy conditionality; to answer the above questions, we will now need to take
a closer look at the redistributive implications and the contentious politics of
sovereign debt repayment inside Argentina itself.

This chapter traces the rise and fall of Argentina's version of the "bankers'
alliance" over the course of the crisis. It shows how the state's growing dependence on credit over the course of the 1990s initially strengthened the position of those considered to be most capable of attracting foreign credit and
investment, and fulfilling a bridging role to foreign lenders. As the crisis began
to bite, however, the social costs of austerity and structural adjustment gradually eroded the legitimacy of the political establishment and the country's
democratic institutions more generally, leading to mass demonstrations and
a demonstrable shift in popular preferences from repayment to default. It was
not until the end of December, however, that a citizens' revolt finally forced
De la Rúa and Cavallo from office, causing the third enforcement mechanism of
internalized discipline to break down. At that point, the interim government
declared a unilateral suspension of payments in a desperate attempt to restore

a degree of legitimacy to the state apparatus by deflecting part of the costs of adjustment onto foreign bondholders. The popular uprising was therefore the final push that eventually made the inevitable unstoppable.

## THE PRIVILEGED POSITION OF THE *PATRIA FINANCIERA*

Like most other countries, Argentina's political economy underwent a profound transformation in the last three decades of the twentieth century. In the early 1970s, the most important political faultline—apart from the divide between the authoritarian military and prodemocratic forces—had been the split between the leftwing and rightwing factions of the Peronist movement. The former advocated a *patria socialista*, a socialist homeland, while the latter advocated a nationalist and corporatist *patria Peronista*. The military coup of 1976 dramatically changed this situation. As in neighboring Chile, the left suffered bloody persecution at the hands of the *junta*, which killed, tortured, and imprisoned thousands while beginning to liberalize the economy.[1] But the end of import substitution and financial repression went hand in hand with the state's growing dependence on private credit and the rising indebtedness of the government to an increasingly concentrated domestic financial system. Schamis writes that "Argentines came up with the term *patria financiera* to refer to the main beneficiary of the liberalization process": the major banks and financial institutions of Buenos Aires.[2]

As in Mexico and other Latin American countries, financial elites grew increasingly influential during the debt crisis of the 1980s, as the state's dependence on credit increased. Their power arguably reached its peak under Menem and Cavallo in the 1990s. When the crisis of 1999 struck and the state's dependence on credit grew even more acute, the political advocates of the *patria financiera*—who shared foreign investors' interests and belief in fiscal stabilization, financial deregulation, the privatization of state assets, trade and capital account liberalization, deep economic integration into the world market, and the "soundness of money" guaranteed by the convertibility of the peso into the U.S. dollar—effectively monopolized economic policymaking, especially in the wake of the reappointment of Domingo Cavallo as economy minister. In this respect, Argentina's political trajectory in the first years of its crisis strongly resembled that of Mexico. Unlike in Mexico, however, the rise of the *patria financiera* and Cavallo's controversial policy response to the deepening financial crisis did not go uncontested by the general citizenry.

While the labor unions had been largely co-opted by the Peronist establishment and did not put up a very strong resistance to painful reforms and austerity measures, there was significant social mobilization and popular pressure from below to reverse Menem's neoliberal reforms and fight skyrocketing poverty and unemployment levels. The rise of the *patria financiera* in the 1990s

TABLE 14.1.
Consolidation and internationalization of banking system

|  | Dec. 1994 | Dec. 1998 | Dec. 2000 |
|---|---|---|---|
| *Total no. banks* | 166 | 104 | 89 |
| *No. foreign banks* | 31 | 39 | 39 |
| *No. foreign bank branches* | 391 | 1,535 | 1,863 |
| *Foreign share of total assets* | 15% | 55% | 73% |
| *No. public banks* | 32 | 16 | 15 |

*Source*: Perry and Servén (2003); Central Bank of Argentina.

thus closely corresponded to the growing dependence of the Argentine state and economy on increasingly concentrated, centralized, and internationalized credit markets (see table 14.1), while its eventual demise was a direct outcome of both the severing of the IMF's financial lifeline and the deepening legitimation crisis that grabbed hold of Argentine society as the social costs of the crisis made themselves felt. As we will see, the economic depression that began in 1999 led to a complete loss of public trust in the political establishment and the post-1983 democratic order more generally, culminating into a dramatic popular uprising that finally forced out the *patria financiera* and paved the way for Argentina's historic default.

Just as in Mexico, the crisis started out with two conflicting positions on the debt question. Unlike under Mexico's one-party regime, however, these conflicting positions could be openly expressed in competitive democratic elections, with the Peronist candidate Eduardo Duhalde of the Justicialist Party calling for default in his 1999 campaign and Fernando De la Rúa, who led a coalition between his centrist Radical Civic Union and the center-left Frepaso, pledging "to pay the debt under all circumstances."[3] But as international financial pressures grew stronger in the wake of the elections, the victorious De la Rúa found himself stuck between a rock and a hard place. On the one hand, the markets and the IMF demanded far-reaching fiscal stabilization efforts, while on the other popular opposition to such austerity measures was growing stronger by the day. As the country entered into a vicious cycle of rising risk premiums, deeper budget cuts, a worsening economic downturn, and widening social unrest, there seemed to be little the president could do to rectify the situation: pleasing investors angered voters, and pleasing voters scared away investors. Still, investors clearly had the upper hand, compelling the government to pursue painful austerity measures that gradually eroded De la Rúa's standing at home. By 2000, even fellow party members began to openly air their opposition to the president's policies. De la Rúa's predecessor and party leader

Raúl Alfolsín, for one, lambasted the government for its fiscal orthodoxy and called for a unilateral moratorium, just as he had done following the transition to democracy in 1983.

Increasingly incapable of sticking to the IMF's fiscal targets and desperate to strengthen his weakening grip on power in the wake of a corruption scandal that had led to the resignation of the vice-president and left him politically isolated, De la Rúa decided in March 2001 to replace his economy minister with Ricardo López Murphy, a fiscal hawk and former IMF economist who, he hoped, could help restore private sector confidence. But when the $4.45 billion austerity package López Murphy announced upon taking office triggered a wave of student protests, the Bulldog, as the press liked to call him, was forced to retreat with his tail between his legs. As a result, research staff at the IMF began to lose faith in Argentina's ability to repay its debt.[4] Chief economist Michael Mussa believed López Murphy was the only person who could have credibly reined in government spending—and he had just been mowed down by popular protest.[5] Meanwhile, as wealthy citizens started withdrawing and expatriating their savings and a slow-motion bank run quietly gained pace, it began to dawn on people that "default was only a matter of time."[6] But De la Rúa, determined to avoid that outcome, pledged once more that he would honor Argentina's obligations in full. To add force to that commitment, the president did something remarkable: he turned to his political opponent Domingo Cavallo, against whom he had squared off in the presidential elections of 1999, and reappointed the controversial former economy minister to the position he had previously held under De la Rúa's rival and predecessor Carlos Menem.

The economic motivations behind Cavallo's appointment were clear. With his close relationship to domestic and international finance as well as the U.S. government and the IMF, the Wizard, as Cavallo was known, was the man deemed most capable of providing a bridging role towards foreign creditors. In fact, Cavallo was so beloved by investors that when President Menem had announced on January 29, 1991, that he would be appointing him as economy minister the first time around, the Buenos Aires stock exchange instantly shot up 30 percent in a single day.[7] As one commentator noted, the main reason why De la Rúa now reinstated his one-time rival was because "he was hoping thereby to gather political support from economic and financial elites, as well as to put in place a man whom he could trust to attack the deficit aggressively, foster growth, and service the debt."[8] As had been the case with Silva Herzog in Mexico before, the combination of Cavallo's reputation as a financial savior and his bridging role to foreign creditors provided the economy minister with immense political leverage, which he wielded to near-autocratic effect.[9] As Cavallo himself put it, with remarkable frankness about the purpose behind his second coming, "it was perfectly clear that President De la Rúa intended to appoint me as his economy minister in order to avert a default on the debt and to preserve the convertibility regime."[10]

Why, then, were De la Rúa and Cavallo so adamant to avoid default? One important reason is that, since a significant share of the country's massive debt load was in the hands of domestic investors and financial institutions, a default "would reduce the financial wealth of those Argentines who had invested in the debt—banks and pension funds as well as wealthy Argentines with offshore accounts."[11] It would also have led to the collapse of the country's financial system and would have forced the government to come to the rescue of the country's banks and large pension and insurance funds. The vast capital injections this would have required were impossible to undertake in the fiscal and monetary straitjacket of the convertibility regime. A default would therefore have forced the government to abandon the convertibility regime—a situation not unlike Greece's precarious footing inside the Eurozone today. This in turn risked reviving the specter of devaluation and inflation that so haunted not only the lower and middle classes—who always bore the brunt of price increases—but also the investor class, since inflation cancels out real interest. Moreover, the convertibility regime cemented Argentina's integration into the world economy and into the U.S. financial system in particular, enabling wealthy Argentines to invest and safely deposit their savings abroad. A default was therefore clearly not in the interest of the Argentine elite—and De la Rúa and Cavallo, as solemn representatives of the embattled *patria financiera*, were determined to avoid harming this key constituency at all costs.

As the crisis deepened, the health of the domestic financial system became a particularly important concern for De la Rúa's government.[12] Cavallo's chief economic advisor, Guillermo Mondino, points out that "the population was very much aware of the exposure the banks had to government securities," and hence even the slightest hint of a default would risk triggering a bank run.[13] Cavallo himself stated that he was deeply concerned about the adverse consequences a default would have had on the domestic economy: "I made it clear that I would by no means join the government to devalue the peso and to declare default on the debt because I considered that such measures would create chaos."[14] Specifying the kind of chaos he expected, Cavallo explicitly identified the spillover costs that would have rippled out through the transmission channel of the country's fragile and overleveraged financial system:

> Defaulting on loan repayments would temporarily ease the burden of public debt interests on budgets; however, it would automatically bring about the collapse of the financial system, cause the destruction of pension funds, and adversely affect savers and workers, because over 50 percent of the bonds issued by the national state and the provincial governments represented the assets of those institutions.[15]

In sum, the growing dependence of the state on foreign loans and investment, combined with policymakers' fears of the domestic spillover costs of default, tended to strengthen the hand of orthodox and creditor-friendly elites who were seen to be capable of attracting sufficiently affordable credit, endowing them with a privileged position in economic policymaking and contributing to a gradual internalization of debtor discipline. The reason for Argentina's continued compliance, then, even after the first and second enforcement mechanisms had broken down, must be sought in its domestic political economy—in particular in the attempt by financial policymakers to shield domestic companies and wealthy elites from the consequences of a government default.

## LEGITIMATION CRISIS AND ANTIAUSTERITY PROTEST

The problem for the government, however, was that three years of economic crisis and over a decade of relentless austerity and neoliberal restructuring had left an indelible mark on the already fraught relationship between the government and its own electoral base, and between the political establishment and the citizenry more generally. De la Rúa's failure to do anything about the economic collapse, combined with his embarrassing corruption scandals and his seeming indifference to the suffering of the Argentine people, caused presidential approval ratings to drop to unprecedented lows. While the president's popularity had stood at 70 percent when he had taken office in 1999, by October 2000 it had dropped to 32 percent and by June 2001 it had was down to 15 percent, easily making De la Rúa the country's most widely despised democratically elected president ever.[16] In fact, a Gallup poll in November 2000 found that only 11 percent of voters believed that the government was doing a good job economically, while nearly half saw no difference between the policies of De la Rúa and those of the thoroughly corrupt and deeply unpopular *caudillo* Carlos Menem, from whom the president had so desperately tried to distance himself all these years.[17]

But it was no longer just the government that people despised. The anger ran deeper: citizens had begun to question the very legitimacy of the post-*junta* democratic order as a whole. As one observer put it, "there was a widespread feeling, if an ill-defined one, that the people had been let down by the entire political class."[18] As the government grew ever more committed to its obligations towards foreign bondholders and ever less responsive to its own citizenry, a deep crisis of representation took hold that saw public trust in the political establishment and in democratic institutions whither and eventually collapse. Several Graciela Römer polls during Menem's presidency had already indicated a slide in public confidence in political parties: while only 24 percent of those questioned expressed some or much confidence in 1993, this fell to a mere 10 percent in 1999, while confidence in Congress as an institution fell from 31 percent to 13 percent.[19] These dynamics were further aggravated by the economic crisis, and in particular by Domingo Cavallo's often erratic and increasingly autocratic approach to crisis management.

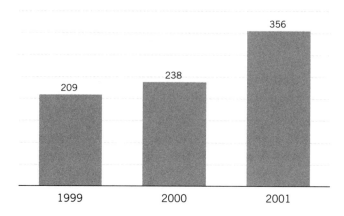

FIGURE 14.1. Frequency of strikes in Argentina, 1999–2001. *Source*: Tomz (2002).

Put simply, the majority of Argentinians simply lost faith in the established democratic process. Protests, strikes, and occupations took off across the country (see figure 14.1), and incensed citizens spontaneously began to attack government officials spotted in public. Social tensions reached a point where most politicians were too afraid to even go out for dinner or cross the street on foot. Senator Eduardo Menem, the former president's brother, was assaulted on an airplane; others were yelled and spat at in restaurants. According to another Graciela Römer poll taken around the congressional elections of October 2001, 70 percent of respondents were dissatisfied with political institutions.[20] The elections themselves were widely seen as a referendum on the government's economic policies. As Tomz points out, "all major parties addressed the default in their manifestoes, with some clinging to the status quo policy of payment and others seeking an immediate suspension of payments."[21] Eduardo Duhalde, representing the national-popular wing of the Peronist movement, restated the same default pledge he had made in the 1999 elections, and members of De la Rúa's Radical Party—including ex-president Raúl Alfolsín and De la Rúa's former cabinet chief, Rodolfo Terragno—publicly distanced themselves from the president by pledging a default on the external debt. Terragno even claimed to have made default "the leitmotif of my campaign."[22]

The outcome of the midterm elections (see table 14.2) was the clearest manifestation of the deepening legitimation crisis to date. Despite the fact that voting was obligatory, nearly a quarter of the electorate did not show up at the polls. Of those who did, an unprecedented 18 percent cast blank or spoiled ballots (the so-called *voto bronca*) in protest against the entire political class. Popular anger had now reached boiling point. One observer noted that "the cumulative social disillusionment with the [Radical Party] of Alfolsín, the [Justicialist Party] of Menem and the Alliance of De la Rúa gave rise to the idea that

Table 14.2
Outcome of 2001 midterm elections compared to 1997

|  | 1997 | 2001 | Change |
|---|---|---|---|
| *Positive vote* | 72.51% | 57.37% | -15.14% |
| *Abstention* | 21.53% | 24.54% | +3.01% |
| *Blank vote* | 4.65% | 8.11% | +3.46% |
| *Spoiled vote* | 1.31% | 9.98% | +8.67% |

*Source*: Epstein and Pion-Berlin (2006).

there was no place within the structure of the Argentine political system for the representation of broad and diverse social demands."[23] The leading newspaper *La Nación* simply headlined that "the people do not feel represented." In addition to the widespread abstention and the large *voto bronca*, Tomz shows that those who did cast a positive vote "overwhelmingly favored candidates who did not want to repay the foreign debt."[24] Thus the prodefault Peronists (the Justicialist Party) became the biggest grouping in the Lower House, while retaining their control over the Senate. Federico Storani, a leading figure in the ruling antidefault Radical Civic Union, admitted defeat and called it a "plebiscite against the government's economic policy."[25]

Meanwhile, polls revealed that public opinion had largely turned in favor of a unilateral suspension of payments. According to one poll in the city and greater metropolitan area of Buenos Aires, only 28 percent of Argentines wanted their government to stay current on its debt obligations, while 63 preferred to declare a unilateral moratorium. Another found that only 5 percent considered repayment to be a priority, while support for a total repudiation of the debt more than doubled from 11 to 27 percent compared to the last elections of 1999.[26] But De la Rúa still refused to give in. In fact, he decided to swim right against the current of public opinion by insisting on even more austerity to prevent what he considered to be a "catastrophic" default. The president declared, "I am going to give over my life to this struggle. We discard the idea of a devaluation or default." Despite losing his Congressional majority and witnessing his party disintegrate before his eyes, De la Rúa stood firm in his insistence on the full and timely repayment of the national debt. In a televised address, he euphemistically stated, "I know that many are not content with the government or with the form of my management and style, [but] it is time to face reality. . . . Argentina will not fall into a cessation of payments."[27]

The president's obstinacy, and the complete disqualification of the political class as a whole, left many Argentines hungry for political change. Strikes and protests became not only more frequent but also more militant. In the period between July and December 2001, the number of strikes per month tripled compared to the same months of the previous year. Tomz remarks that "the jump, sparked by a major new round of budget cuts and a 'zero deficit' plan . . . confirms that workers were becoming less tolerant of the austerity needed to continue servicing the debt."[28] Meanwhile, protesters blocked highways and major intersections, attacked government buildings, and on a number of occasions temporarily took officials "hostage" to demand public-sector jobs or unemployment benefits. As the government continued to lay off civil servants and cut salaries, pensions, and social security benefits, powerful social movements emerged across the country. Harvard economists Hausman and Velasco recount that "the new poor realized that their social collapse was unstoppable. They were going to carry on falling. It was at that point that new political actors appeared." Notably, these were "not the historical leaders of the working class because, when the labor market collapsed, the unions, as the political representatives of the working class, went with it."[29] Instead, the "new forms of political construction [were] built from within society rather than the political system, [and] emerged on the Argentine scene with unusual force."[30]

Emphasizing radical democratic principles and stressing their horizontal nature and their autonomy from political parties, trade unions, and the state apparatus more generally, these "new social protagonists" began to craft alternative forms of popular self-organization that touched upon the lives of millions. Given their widespread appeal and innovative grassroots practices—which included neighborhood assemblies, road blocks and the recuperation of closed factories and other workplaces—the traditional political actors largely failed to connect to these burgeoning social movements, let alone come up with a convincing political response.[31]

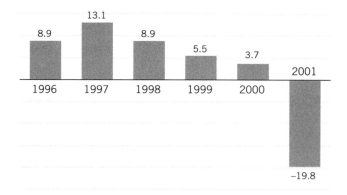

FIGURE 14.2. Change in bank deposits (%) in Argentina, 1996–2001. *Source*: Setser and Gelpern (2006).

At the end of November 2001, these dramatic social mobilizations from below coincided with equally dramatic political and economic developments from above: the *riesgo país* shot up to 5,000 basis points, leaving Argentina without any affordable external sources of financing. Worried that the impending default would lead to a collapse of the banking system and that a breakdown of the convertibility regime and a subsequent currency devaluation would eat up their peso-denominated savings, depositors began to withdraw over $1 billion per day.[32] This came on top of the $10 billion that had already fled the country in the wake of an earlier debt rescheduling in June that year, rapidly depleting the banks' reserves in the process (see figure 14.2). On December 1, Cavallo announced a set of draconian measures to halt the full-blown bank run: he shut down the country's private banks and declared his fateful *corralito*, or "ring fence"—freezing bank deposits, outlawing deposit transfers abroad, and imposing a withdrawal limit of 1,000 pesos per week. As one banker put it, "the *corralito* trapped the *perejiles*," the little guys. "The big players already knew what was going to happen and got out ahead of time."[33]

As was to be expected in the highly combustible social context of late 2001, the *corralito* failed spectacularly in its stated objective of restoring calm, prompting mass protests and setting in motion a series of events that would eventually culminate in Cavallo's political demise. A few days later, on December 5, against the backdrop of intensifying opposition in the streets, the IMF announced its equally fateful decision to withhold the next installment of its bailout program in response to the government's inability to stick to the loan conditions. From there on out, Argentina was on a one-way street to default, and the government found itself under immense pressure from all sides to simply get it over with and formalize what was by now widely considered a *fait accompli*.

## *"¡QUE SE VAYAN TODOS!"*

On December 19, after weeks of simmering tensions, the popular anger that had been building up all throughout the crisis finally came to a head when the streets exploded in furious anger. Food riots and looting first broke out in the central city of Rosario and rapidly spread to Santa Fe, Córdoba, La Plata, and Mendoza, and from there via the suburbs of Buenos Aires to the heart of the capital.[34] Within hours, violent clashes between protesters and police had erupted across the country. In a poorly calculated attempt to quell the uprising, De la Rúa went on national television to announce a suspension of constitutional rights and declare a 30-day state of emergency, deploying the federal police, the border guard, and the naval prefecture to restore order. Given the severity of the social unrest and the speed at which the riots spread across the country, the president briefly entertained the idea of shutting down all private radio and TV stations and mobilizing the army to put down the rebellion—but both options were roundly rejected by his cabinet. With the experience of the military *junta* still fresh in the country's mind, even the army leadership turned out to be unwilling to leave the barracks without express approval from Congress and so long as there remained a chance, however slim, that conventional political solutions might save the day.

Like Cavallo's *corralito*, the president's televised address backfired in the worst way imaginable. It was widely noted that "De la Rúa looked distant and insensitive to what was taking place. Some of his aides even qualified his speech as 'autistic.'"[35] Citizens felt that their legitimate expressions of indignation were not being taken seriously, and so they defied the curfew and descended from their homes in the hundreds of thousands. As protesters marched on the Plaza de Mayo, clashes broke out, and police violently cracked down on the impromptu demonstrations, killing seventeen people nationwide, five of them right in front of the presidential palace.[36] That night, De la Rúa, looking for a scapegoat, forced a publicly humiliated Cavallo to resign. Under judicial orders not to leave the country, in fear of being lynched by the multitude outside, and with his wife reportedly on the verge of a nervous breakdown, Cavallo holed himself up inside his apartment on the Avenida Libertador while a private security detail fended off angry protesters down below.[37] The curtain, it seemed, had finally fallen on the Wizard.

The rage, however, could no longer be contained so easily. On the morning of the next day, December 20, renewed protests broke out as thousands returned to the Plaza de Mayo to defy the curfew once more. Again, at least a dozen protesters were killed in the resultant clashes—but the demonstrations continued. When it finally dawned on the president that violent repression would not break the people's resolve, he again went on national television to invite the Peronists to join him in a "government of national salvation" and help restore "peace and order" to the country. The Peronist leadership roundly refused. Even De la Rúa's own cabinet members later declared that, watching the president's performance on TV, they could not escape the feeling that he was on another planet, far removed from what was truly going on "out there."[38] As his ministers and senators began to abandon him and the protesters only seemed to grow stronger in numbers and resolve, the politically isolated De la Rúa finally tendered his resignation. But security forces considered it too dangerous to evacuate the now ex-president from the *Casa Rosada* by car, so—in an image that would come to define Argentina's deepest political crisis since the return to democracy—De la Rúa was forced to escape the palace by helicopter. As he was airlifted from the rooftop of the building, the crowds below roared: *¡que se vayan todos!*—"all of them must go!" As Tomz puts it, the people "had just removed from power the most significant obstacle to default."[39] The third enforcement mechanism of debtor compliance had finally broken down.

Since the vacant position of vice-president had never been filled following an earlier corruption scandal that had forced De la Rúa's coalition partner to

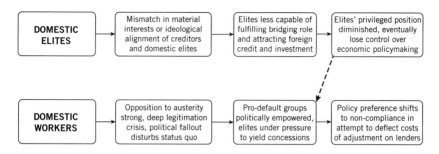

FIGURE 14.3. The third enforcement mechanism in Argentina.

step down, the role of interim-president fell to Ramón Puerta, the Peronist leader of the Senate, until Congress elected Adolfo Rodríguez Saá as the new head of state. The first thing Rodríquez Saá did upon taking office was to declare a unilateral moratorium on the service of Argentina's entire outstanding debt. In his inaugural address on December 24, he declared that "I believe in an Argentina without unemployment, without misery. I will govern for the most humble and for those who suffer. I call for the suspension of payments on the foreign debt until all Argentines have jobs." The interim-president lamented that "the gravest thing that has happened here is that priority has been given to foreign debt while the state has an internal obligation with its own people."[40]

But while Argentina thus entered into default on over $82 billion in privately held public debt, roughly two-thirds of which was in the hands of foreign investors, the new president almost immediately fell afoul of all his other pledges. As fresh protests took off, the most powerful Peronist governors came together and decided that Rodríguez Saá had to go. On December 30, Congress voted to replace him with Ramón Puerta, who resigned immediately. From there, the hot potato of the presidency passed to Eduardo Oscar Camaño, chairman of the Chamber of Deputies, who was a known supporter of Eduardo Duhalde, the former vice-president under Menem who had been De la Rúa's main opponent in the 1999 elections. On January 1, 2002, the power vacuum was finally filled when Camaño arranged for Duhalde to take over and complete the remainder of De la Rúa's term, with new elections set for December 2003. Duhalde, who had been the sole presidential candidate calling for a suspension of payments in 1999, would become the country's fifth head of state in just ten days' time. Now he was to preside over the dramatic fallout of the largest sovereign default in world history.

# FIFTEEN

## "Even in a Default There Is Money to Be Made"

The economic consequences of Argentina's default were immediate and traumatic. Foreign investors and international financial institutions immediately withheld all further loans and refused to deal with the new government unless it agreed to negotiate "in good faith" with its private creditors for an orderly restructuring of the defaulted debt—something that was politically unpalatable in the social environment that had given rise to the default. Beside the wholesale credit cutoff, international capital flight also accelerated dramatically, rapidly depleting the central bank's dollar reserves and leading to a breakdown of the convertibility regime at the start of January 2002, followed by an official devaluation of 30 percent and a government-decreed "pesification" of domestic bank deposits. After the abandonment of its fixed exchange rate with the dollar, the peso began to slide and would eventually lose 300 percent of its value.[1] Locked out of international capital markets and with the IMF refusing to provide any further emergency loans, Argentina effectively found itself in a state of financial autarky.[2] Credit markets froze up, and the economy fell into a deep depression.

As the interbank payment system ground to a halt (see figure 15.1), firms could no longer access the financing they needed to sustain their everyday activities. Sales dropped by 40 percent, and over 100,000 companies went bankrupt, leading to at least 280,000 layoffs.[3] In the first quarter of 2002, Argentina's GDP contracted by 16 percent and manufacturing output by 20 percent, while an investor strike undermined any hopes of an immediate recovery. The rate of investment to GDP, which had stood at 19.1 percent in 1999, fell to 11.3 percent.[4] Meanwhile, firms struggled to obtain export credits—a development about which the foreign ministry and Argentina's chamber of exports, as well as leading economists at the World Bank, repeatedly expressed their concern.[5] The ongoing bank run also intensified after the despised *corralito* was lifted. Total bank deposits collapsed from $70 billion at the start of 2002 to a mere $2.9 billion by October. Their capital base depleted, the banks closed 210 branches and fired 9,500 workers.[6] The social consequences of all this were devastating. Unemployment hit nearly one-quarter of the country's economically active pop-

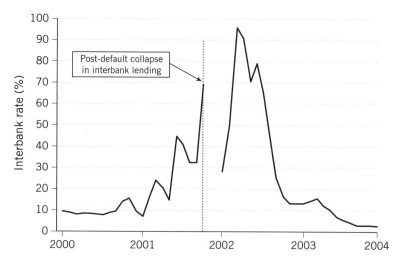

FIGURE 15.1. Interbank rate in Argentina, 2000–2004. *Source*: Miller, Garcia Fronti, and Zhang (2006).

ulation, the percentage of people living in poverty reached 57.5 percent, and extreme poverty doubled to 27 percent.[7] Observers noted that, when he took power in early 2002, "the Argentine economy threatened to disintegrate before Duhalde's eyes."[8] The collapse in output and the sharp increase in poverty and unemployment were the worst to hit a capitalist economy since World War II; in a country that less than a century ago had ranked among the ten richest in the world, one in four now "could no longer afford sufficient food."[9]

Nevertheless, despite their intensity, these spillover costs of default turned out to be relatively short-lived, and the trauma quickly began to subside once Argentina returned to very high levels of growth from late 2002 onwards. Figure 15.1 shows how the interbank rate spiked dramatically following the default (indeed, interbank lending collapsed altogether for some time), but quickly fell back to below its crisis levels. Figure 15.2 shows Argentina's postdefault return to growth, while figures 15.3 and 15.4 clearly demonstrate how poverty and unemployment rates steadily declined after the initial economic shock of the default, devaluation and depression. These observations are fully in line with the structural power hypothesis, which stresses the *immediate* consequences of a default on domestic credit circulation and its painful knock-on effects on economic performance, but which also emphasizes the *short-lived* nature of these spillover effects.

This chapter presents the main outcomes of the Argentine crisis—from the realignment of the domestic balance of forces in the wake of the default, to the aggressive debt restructuring concluded by President Kirchner in 2005. It seeks to

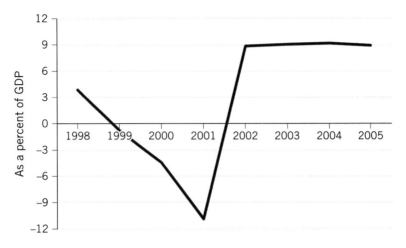

FIGURE 15.2. Argentina's GDP growth, 1998–2005. *Source*: Baer, Margot, and Montes-Rojas (2006).

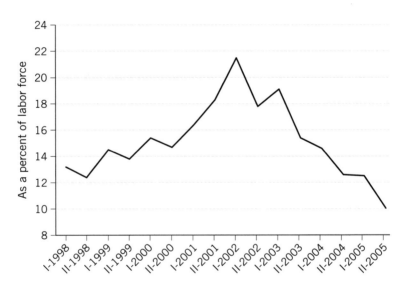

FIGURE 15.3. Argentina's unemployment rate, 1998–2005. *Source*: Mercado (2007); INDEC–Ministry of Economy.

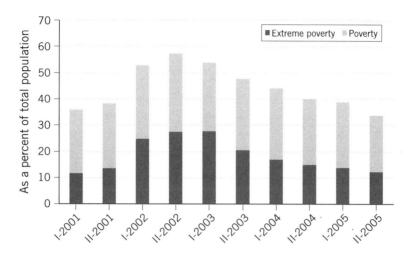

FIGURE 15.4. Poverty levels in Argentina, 2001–2005. *Source*: Mercado (2007); INDEC–Ministry of Economy.

explain why Kirchner was both willing and able to pursue such a confrontational stance towards the IMF and foreign bondholders, and presents the counterintuitive conclusion that—far from being harmed by the Argentine default—Wall Street actually managed to find innovative ways to turn it to its own advantage.

## OPENING AN UNIMAGINED SPACE FOR POLITICS

The first important outcome to note was a profound realignment in the domestic balance of forces in the wake of the popular uprising. As the economy briefly went into free fall in the first half of 2002, the widespread social dislocation wrought by the spillover effects of the default fed into further protests and strikes. The sheer power of popular mobilization eventually forced the political establishment to make a number of concessions to the domestic population, including a new set of redistributive social policies and antipoverty measures.[10] As the Argentine historian Ezequiel Adamovsky puts it, "it was the constant threat of looting, targeting of politicians, of rebellion, of occupations, of roadblocks, and assemblies that disciplined both management and local and international financial sectors, opening an unimagined space for politics."[11]

In the immediate wake of the December uprising, President Duhalde struggled to restore a degree of political stability and was constantly forced onto the defensive by the powerful social mobilizations and an increasingly restive population. Upon taking office, the president's approval rating stood at a mere

10 percent, and the initial wave of protests had "grown into a massive civic rebellion against the entire political elite."[12] A Gallup poll showed that 84 percent of respondents did not feel represented, while 87 percent rejected all parties outright.[13] Duhalde was therefore acutely aware of the need for some kind of shift in policy and rhetoric to outmaneuver the country's burgeoning social movements and restore at least a semblance of democratic legitimacy to the political system. He embarked upon a populist campaign to shore up support for the government and the wider state apparatus by pursuing a somewhat more equitable distribution of adjustment costs. Publicly railing against "the destructive alliance of 'political power and financial might' that had sold the nation out to foreign creditors and international financial institutions at the expense of internal production and consumption," the president tried to portray himself as a real man of the people.[14] He restored the yearly extra month's pay for public sector workers and earmarked $350 million for soup kitchens. In an address to Congress in March 2002, he for the first time publicly recognized the "formidable crisis of representation" that had undermined the public's trust in democratic institutions. Despite the acute fiscal crisis, he announced the implementation of the *Plan Jefes y Jefas de Hogar Desocupados*, a $1 billion household support program targeted at the unemployed, in a move that was widely seen as an attempt "to combat militant opposition by the *piquetero* movement."[15]

But these relatively superficial moves failed to subdue the rage people felt towards the authorities. The government remained trapped between the popular pressure for a redistribution of wealth and power from below and the total absence of foreign credit and investment from abroad. Duhalde, in a word, struggled to bridge the contradiction between the state's structural dependence on capital on the one hand, and its need to restore democratic legitimacy on the other. One observer identified the president's approach as profoundly "schizophrenic": while he embraced the radical rhetoric of the movements, Duhalde "began (gradually and almost secretly) to do as the IMF advised, not only devaluing the currency, but also securing an agreement with the provinces to cut spending, unifying the exchange rate, and changing a bankruptcy law to match international standards."[16] While at home he complained endlessly about the crimes and betrayals of the *patria financiera*, he simultaneously sought to placate his other audience—international investors—by exuding a market-friendly pragmatism abroad. As he failed to reconcile the two, street protests resumed and Duhalde was forced by intensifying social unrest to call early elections for April 2003.

These were the conditions that Néstor Kirchner inherited when he assumed the presidency in May 2003, having won the elections with just 22 percent of the vote in the first round, after his leading contender—the widely despised former president Carlos Menem, of all people—withdrew from the race when it became clear that he would suffer a humiliating defeat in the second round. To boost his standing, Kirchner, then known as a moderate and pragmatic center-left Peronist, immediately announced an economic program that prioritized growth and job creation and refused to resume payment of the external debt at the expense of social and economic recovery. In a return to the classical populist blend of left-Peronism, Kirchner praised the virtues of "national capitalism" as an alternative to the Washington Consensus that had led to the country's economic collapse. "It's not that we want not to comply, not to pay," he declared, echoing the words of his predecessor Raúl Alfolsín in the 1980s, "but neither can we pay at the expense of seeing more and more Argentines postponing their access to proper housing, a safe job, education for the children, and health services."[17]

In an attempt to restore the legitimacy of the political system and the dominant position of the traditional Peronist establishment, Kirchner set out to build a corporatist coalition consisting of an alliance between large-scale farmers, oil exporters, industrial capitalists, and leaders of the labor unions and the unemployed workers' movement. In a meeting with a group of Buenos Aires bankers on September 29, 2003, Kirchner declared that "it is crucial that national capital partakes in the process of the reconstruction of society. It is impossible to build a national project if we do not consolidate a national bourgeoisie." This followed an earlier statement by Alberto Alvarez Gaiani, head of the Industrial Union, who had argued that—with Argentina now cut off from foreign credit—the only way to see to the state's dependence on capital would be to resume domestic investment by strengthening the government's ties to Argentine firms. "There is a need for a national bourgeoisie," he declared. "A country is stronger when you have the owners of the most important companies in the country sitting around the decision-making table. Nobody is going to invest a single penny in this country for a long time."[18]

At the same time as opening up the government to domestic business, Kirchner pursued a classical Peronist strategy of co-optation with regard to labor and the popular sector. Now that the trade unions had practically imploded, the most militant opposition to the political establishment came from the various factions of the *piquetero* movement of unemployed workers. By incorporating the leaders of some of its more traditional and hierarchically organized groups into his government, Kirchner hoped to isolate the more radical autonomous wing of the movement, demobilize the grassroots resistance and at the same time obtain a strong ally in his political maneuvers against opponents.[19] Luis D'Elia, leader of the Federación Tierra y Vivienda, one of the more visible *piquetero* groups, was appointed undersecretary for land and housing. His followers, called *piqueteros-K*, became a crucial support base for Kirchner and a powerful weapon in the government's public confrontations with foreign companies.[20]

This rearrangement of the dominant class coalition—away from Menem's neoliberal alliance between national capital and the *patria financiera* and toward a classical Peronist alliance between national capital and elements of the popular sector—went hand in hand with the embrace of an alternative economic model that has often been referred to as "neodevelopmentalist" or "neo-extractivist." This transition was made possible by the advantageous external conditions in the postdefault period, including ample liquidity and the Chinese-driven commodity boom of the 2000s, which conspired to bring about a major transformation of Argentina's economy and agricultural sector, with commodity exports surging and a soy boom changing the face of the countryside. The dramatic events of 2001–2002 were therefore about much more than a just change in government; they marked a political-economic rupture in the development of Argentine capitalism and a transformation, however partial and contradictory, in the relationship between business and the state. The reduced state dependence on credit weakened the *patria financiera* and allowed for the emergence of a new balance of power that subordinated financial interests to the interests of extractive and exporting industries on the one hand, and of co-opted elements of the popular sector on the other. Kirchner's confrontational stance in the subsequent debt negotiations with foreign bondholders should be considered in light of this new political reality on the ground.

## NÉSTOR KIRCHNER AND THE 2005 DEBT RESTRUCTURING

Under the first Kirchner government, the realignment of social and political forces at home combined with a crucial transformation in the political and economic opportunity structure internationally, providing Kirchner with exceptional room for maneuver. While Eduardo Duhalde had struggled throughout his term to balance the contradictory needs to restart economic activity on the one hand and restore popular legitimacy on the other, Néstor Kirchner upon assuming office in 2003 found himself presented with ample space for much more confrontational action, creating the preconditions for the unusually aggressive postdefault debt restructuring. In early 2005, after a long and arduous negotiation process, Argentina reached a deal with its creditors that saw 76 percent of bondholders accept new bonds worth 25 percent of the original defaulted ones. The claims of the remaining 24 percent, a Baptist-Bootlegger coalition of European pensioners and U.S. hedge funds, were repudiated.[21] When Argentina briefly reopened the restructuring deal in 2010, more bondholders subscribed, reducing the remaining share of "holdout" creditors to a mere 9 percent (who were finally compensated for their losses by President Macri in 2016).

Ninety-one percent is a remarkably high degree of participation given the size of the haircut and the defiant posturing of the Argentine government. How was Kirchner able to get his way? As it turns out, there were a number of factors that played to Argentina's advantage. First, as we saw before, the country's bondholders were greatly atomized after the creditor-led megaswap of mid-2001, and mostly made up of so-called financially illiterate small savers and pensioners.

This had important consequences for creditors' bargaining power vis-à-vis the Argentine government. As Paul Lewis puts it, "most of the bondholders were 'small fry' and scattered geographically, making it difficult for them to coordinate any strategy."[22] The collective action problem of 1930s bond finance returned with a vengeance. "True to atomistic stereotype," Anna Gelpern observes, "bondholders could not hold a coalition. Each acted in its own self-interest." Moreover, "these [small] investors generally were not repeat players and knew little about emerging-market debt."[23] Others who have studied Argentina's debt negotiations confirm that "the lack of cohesion among the different organizations representing the creditors worked to the advantage of the government."[24] Kirchner made strategic use of these factors to play his creditors apart. When the representatives of the small lenders set up the Global Committee of Argentina Bondholders in an attempt to present a united front at the debt negotiations, he simply refused to talk to the group or even to recognize its existence.[25] Kirchner was able to do this because he did not depend on these dispersed bondholders for future credit; even if he restructured the debt on extraordinarily good terms for the creditors, most of the small bondholders had made a one-off investment and were unlikely to ever lend to Argentina again, so there was little incentive to cut them a break.

Argentina's unilateral suspension of payments also contributed to reversing the debtor-creditor power dynamic, just as it had done in the wake of the defaults of the 1930s.[26] Before Argentina's moratorium, bondholders had been receiving 100 cents on the dollar, and any reduction in the face value of these claims would have undoubtedly been considered an unacceptable loss. Now, some two years after the default, creditors were receiving 0 cents on the dollar, and—barring moral concerns over the violation of creditor rights—some form of debt restructuring, even an unusually harsh one, would at least allow them to mark their holdings to market and recover some profit from the restructured bonds. The moratorium, in other words, restored the initiative to the debtor and allowed it to wield the prospect of a restructuring as a carrot instead of a stick, creating an incentive structure for bondholders to sign up to a deal that they would otherwise never have agreed to. As Giselle Datz succinctly put it, "investors were not looking at losses taken in 2001, but at a scenario of gains in 2005."[27] Economy Minister Roberto Lavagna seemed to be under a similar impression when, just a month before the conclusion of the deal, he rhetorically asked why, despite the destruction of numerous debt contracts in 2001, investors were still so eager to buy Argentine bonds. His simple answer: "because today clearly they can get a very good rate of return."[28]

The benefits of Argentina's debt restructuring accrued especially to the financially literate repeat players: the Wall Street investment banks and the U.S.-based institutional investors that had a direct interest in keeping Argentina in the lending game. But these same benefits were not immediately clear to the small

European retail investors, who were unlikely to lend to Argentina again and who would have preferred a higher payout on their one-off investment. Kirchner was acutely aware of these conflicting interests among different groups of investors and exploited the fissure within the creditor base to full effect. By insisting on separate negotiations with the big international banks, while at the same time denying the very existence of the small bondholders and their formal representatives, he successfully drove a wedge in the (nonexistent) creditors' cartel—to the detriment of the pensioners and other small investors in Europe.

The second factor playing to Argentina's advantage was that its dispersed lenders received little or no support from their own governments, the IMF or the United States.[29] In its negotiations with private bondholders, Eric Helleiner notes, "the USA was . . . quite sympathetic to the position taken by the Argentine government."[30] When Bush met Kirchner at the Summit of the Americas on January 13, 2004, Bush "quite significantly did not echo Koehler's request that he consider paying more than just 25 percent to holders of bonds." As Assistant Treasury Secretary Randal Quarles put it: "it's not the IMF's role to impose any particular terms of the deal. . . . How much can Argentina repay? . . . I think that's something that the IMF and the U.S., as a shareholder in the IMF, should not have a view on." Treasury Secretary Taylor echoed the same sentiment: "the idea here is to allow negotiations but not to be in the middle, or choose sides. That's for the creditors and Argentina to work out."[31] The IMF's decision not to intervene and the lack of a unified creditor front clearly benefited the Argentine government.[32] It also greatly frustrated the small bondholders. As an Italian lawyer representing a group of pensioners who lost their life's savings in the default put it: "Argentina doesn't want to pay its debt, and Washington doesn't want to force it to pay. So the easiest thing is to send the bill to the bondholders in Europe, little people no one will ever see."[33] Another Italian lawyer pointed out to the *Wall Street Journal* that "with what's happening in Iraq and Afghanistan, you can be sure that Mr. Bush didn't want to start a battle with Argentina, just to defend some retirees in Europe."[34]

But the role of the U.S. government was not just characterized by lack of interest; the administration took an active stance in favor of Argentina's aggressive approach to private bondholders and the IMF. When Kirchner missed a $2.9 billion payment to the IMF on September 9, 2003, President Bush personally supported the move, further reducing the IMF's ability to defend bondholder interests in the debt negotiations.[35] A group of Argentine economists has noted that, "because there was a real risk of Argentina defaulting on its large obligations to international financial institutions, the Fund's leverage to influence the outcome of the private debt restructuring was much weakened all through the post-default phase of the crisis."[36] When Kirchner finally reached an agreement with the IMF that was uncharacteristically beneficial to the debtor country, the U.S. president personally called up his Argentine counterpart to congratulate him and express his satisfaction with the deal. Assistant Treasury

Secretary Quarles claimed that the administration had "deliberately pushed for the budget surplus targets [in the IMF Stand-By Arrangement] to be left undefined in the second and third years—over IMF objections—because it wanted the IMF not to take a stance in the debt negotiations with private creditors," stating that "it's not the IMF's role to take a stance to impose any particular terms of a deal."[37]

This active support from the Bush administration in turn allowed Argentina to segment not just its small bondholders and large institutional investors, but also its official and private creditors. By negotiating on two different tables at once, Kirchner effectively removed IMF conditionality from the equation when it came to his government's arm-twisting with private bondholders. And, indeed, when Kirchner finally offered his "take it or leave it" deal to foreign bondholders, the U.S. government "raised no objections to the Argentine offer."[38] In fact, the day after the final offer was made, Bush briefly met Kirchner at the sidelines of the UN General Assembly where the U.S. President "seemed to endorse" the deal. According to Kirchner's spokesperson, Bush told him the following words: "congratulations again for the agreement with the IMF; now you must keep negotiating firmly with private creditors." When Kirchner approached him later that day, Bush even had the wit to crack a joke about the deal to a group of assembled world leaders: "here comes the conqueror of the IMF!"[39]

The third factor playing to Argentina's advantage were the "extraordinarily good international conditions" it found itself faced with postdefault, most importantly the global commodity boom generated by rapid Chinese growth and the wave of liquidity sloshing through international financial markets thanks to the Fed's low interest rates in the wake of 9/11 and the collapse of the dotcom bubble.[40] These beneficial external conditions then combined with Argentina's own relative resilience in financial and economic terms. A study by the Center for Economic and Policy Research noted that "one of the great advantages that Argentina has over other countries confronting the creditors' cartel . . . in terms of recovering on its own is that the country is running large surpluses on both its trade and current accounts" (see figures 15.5, 15.6, and 15.7).[41] Between 1999 and 2002, the government managed to maintain a sizable primary budget surplus, leaving it much less dependent on external financing than most other peripheral countries facing balance-of-payments crises.[42] Unlike Mexico, Argentina was also self-sufficient in food production and a net exporter of commodities, while its large current account surplus greatly reduced its dependence on hard currency for the import of basic necessities. As a result, Argentina's foreign-exchange reserves never fell below four months' worth of imports, compared to two weeks' in Mexico in 1982 (see figure 15.8).[43]

Meanwhile, Argentina could count on the support of an important regional ally, Hugo Chávez, who came to Kirchner's aid by reinvesting part of Venezuela's oil revenues in special Argentine bonds. In 2005, the Venezuelan government lent a total of $3.1 billion, and the two countries even set up a special

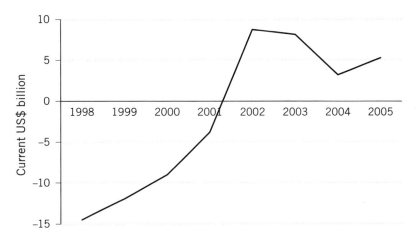

FIGURE 15.5. Argentina's current account balance, 1998–2005. *Source*: World Bank (2017).

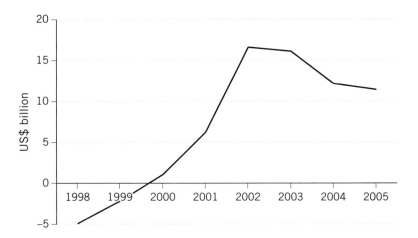

FIGURE 15.6. Argentina's trade balance, 1998–2005. *Source*: Baer, Margot, and Montes-Rojas (2006).

investment fund, the Fund for the South, whose official mission "was to free South America from dependence on the United States and the IMF."[44] The following year, Chávez purchased another $3.6 billion in bonds in 2006, adding a further $1 billion in 2007. Venezuela's loans thus provided Argentina with a helpful "outside option" for external financing that contributed to the country's relative autonomy from international finance and its insulation from the two

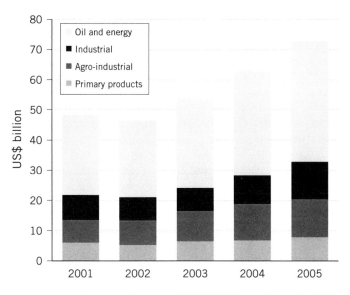

FIGURE 15.7. Argentina's exports by sector, 2001–2005. *Source*: Grugel and Riggirozzi (2007).

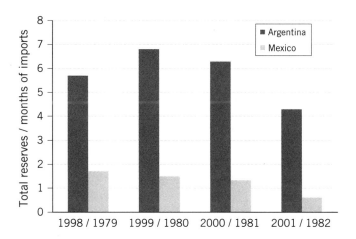

FIGURE 15.8. Total reserves in months of imports, Argentina (1998–2001) vs. Mexico (1979–1982). *Source*: World Bank (2017).

enforcement mechanisms of market discipline and conditional IMF lending.[45] All of these factors combined to boost Kirchner's standing at home and his self-confidence abroad, feeding his fiery anticreditor rhetoric. As Mortimore and Stanley emphasize, "the short-term cost [of Kirchner's defiance] to the country was minimal, since Argentina clearly had no possibility of obtaining external financing in the international financial markets anyway."[46]

With the prospect of continued high growth and the option to raise funds through domestic bond auctions, confrontation with powerless small bondholders overseas and the extremely unpopular IMF in Washington seemed like a sensible path to pursue—especially in light of the need to deflect attention away from the profound legitimation crisis at home. All of this goes to show how the prevailing international conditions endowed the government with considerably more room for maneuver after 2002 than it had enjoyed under Alfolsín in the 1980s. At the same time, the constant threat of a resumption of mass protests continued to exert pressure on the government from below, precluding any overt strategy of reconciliation with foreign creditors.

Still, it would be overly simplistic to conclude on the basis of Argentina's defiant stance that the structural power hypothesis somehow does not hold up in practice. Argentina's international opportunity structure in the wake of the December revolt and the subsequent default was highly idiosyncratic—a fact that is clearly confirmed by the observation that the country's unilateral moratorium and aggressive debt restructuring remain isolated and extremely rare occurrences. As Nouriel Roubini has pointed out, "the lesson of Argentina is that crisis and default are very costly and painful, not that they are costless. Otherwise, if default is so costless, how come we do not see dozens of highly indebted countries following Argentina and defaulting?"[47]

The Brazilian experience presents an interesting counterfactual in this respect. In 2002, as Argentina's northern neighbor prepared for presidential elections, it found itself facing similar pressures as Argentina itself had since 1999; pressures that were exacerbated by the prospect of a victory for Lula's Workers' Party. During the 1980s debt crisis, Lula, then still a devout leftwing activist and outspoken labor leader, had gained a degree of notoriety among investors for his vocal advocacy of a unilateral debt moratorium and an outright repudiation of the foreign obligations incurred by the military dictatorship. In its December 2001 electoral program, the Workers' Party still "spoke of denouncing the existing agreement with the IMF and auditing and renegotiating the external debt," pledging "a complete revision of the policy of giving priority to the payment of the debt service."[48] Unlike Argentina, Wall Street still carried significant exposure to Brazil in 2002, so when Lula began to advance in the polls, investors unsurprisingly took fright. Every time a new poll indicated a Lula lead, the "Brazil risk" shot up.[49] As the banks withheld further loans in fear of a default, Brazil's spreads skyrocketed, widening from 7 percent in March 2002 to 20 percent in September, as Lula rose from 30 to 40 percent.[50]

In response to this market pressure, and in an attempt to calm both foreign investors and potential voters at home, Lula decided to tone down his rhetoric over the course of the campaign. By January 2003, *The Economist* reported that, "since the final weeks of the election campaign, Lula has worked hard to turn investor panic into mere wariness. He has stressed that Brazil means to pay its debt and has chosen ministers who seem ready to carry that promise through."[51] After Lula's victory, economist Arminio Fraga, who had served as central bank director under the previous conservative government, noted that "the biggest event when Lula came to office in 2003 is that nothing happened."[52] Roubini writes that "Lula, as soon as he was elected, looked across the border and saw what default—even an unavoidable one like Argentina's—causes as its by-product, i.e., massive crisis and pain."[53] And so he eventually decided to appoint an orthodox finance minister and avoid default.

## "Even in a Default There Is Money to Be Made"

Argentina's payment suspension, then, should by no means be construed as a challenge to the structural power hypothesis. Not only does its moratorium remain an exceptional event in international finance, but its social and economic costs even became a cautionary tale for left-leaning leaders elsewhere. The remarkable developments in Argentina between 1999 and 2005 therefore show how the structural power of finance was fully operative throughout the crisis, initially leading to a case of unprecedented overcompliance and eventually producing devastating short-term spillover costs in the wake of the default—even if these spillover costs turned out to be relatively short-lived. Crucially, as we have seen in this chapter, the country only suspended payments *after* the three enforcement mechanisms had broken down: after the structurally powerful institutional investors had dumped their Argentine bonds on a dispersed body of small bondholders overseas and refused to loan further money; after the IMF had withheld its crucial financial lifeline, leaving the country without any sources of foreign financing; and after the *patria financiera* had been ousted following a mass antiausterity revolt.

Despite the breakdown of these three enforcement mechanisms, however, the substantive outcome of the Argentine default was not all that different from the outcome of the Mexican debt crisis of the 1980s. For one thing, as in Mexico, the burden of adjustment in Argentina was initially largely borne by workers and the poor. The imposition of the *corralito* in December 2001 was perhaps the clearest expression of this inherent pro-elite bias in the government's policy response. When he found himself compelled to shut down the banks, Cavallo had deliberately left a loophole in his deposit withdrawal scheme that allowed wealthy Argentines to pull billions of pesos out of the banking system anyway. Through a mechanism very similar the one used by Mexicans elites in the wake of López Portillo's bank nationalization, wealthy depositors were able to move their savings and investments to the stock exchange. Economists Kathryn Dominguez and Linda Tesar explain that "restrictions in the *corralito* . . . allowed investors to use their frozen bank deposits to purchase Argentine stocks, and, in so doing, provided a legal mechanism for transferring funds abroad."[54] The few lucky Argentines who still had real savings in the bank could simply buy stocks that were cross-listed in the United States to legally convert their Argentine shares (purchased with pesos) into American Depository Receipts (ADR), which could subsequently be sold for dollars and deposited in a U.S. bank account. Only this loophole in the *corralito* can explain the idiosyncratic 50 percent rise in Argentine stock exchange valuations in December 2001, at a time when the national economy was effectively in a state of meltdown: the local elite was simply pouring its money into shares to get it out of the country ahead of a default and devaluation. While the wealthy upper class had to contend with a very different political-economic environment after the inauguration of Néstor Kirchner in 2003, the latter's insistence on giving the "national bourgeoisie" a seat at the table ensured that the privileged position of domestic elites would never be fully eroded.

In the end, however, the main beneficiaries of the crisis were not Argentine elites but the speculative foreign investors who managed to find fresh profit opportunities in the country's debt troubles. While Argentina's policy choices may have been diametrically opposed to those of the debtors of the 1980s, the outcome was more or less the same from Wall Street's perspective; if not more favorable. As we saw before, by the time of the default in 2001, U.S. institutional investors had already dumped most of their bonds on a scattered group of European retail investors, meaning they largely emerged from the initial payment suspension unscathed. But by the time of the 2005 restructuring, some of these same dispersed retail investors—including many Italian pensioners who were terrified at the prospect of losing their life savings—despaired at Argentina's refusal to recognize their representatives in the debt negotiations and began to sell back their bonds, for mere cents on the dollar, to an eager army of traders at the Wall Street hedge funds. The opposition to the eventual deal came mostly from European pensioners who were understandably less than enthusiastic about taking such a big hit on their retirement schemes. The leading hedge funds, by contrast, hardly put up a fight and signed up to the restructuring deal by an overwhelming 90 percent—the remaining 10 percent being made up of so-called vulture funds that successfully held out for full repayment.[55]

This raises an important question: why would the hedge funds be so eager to jump on Kirchner's offer if they thought they were receiving such a bad deal? The answer is that they were, in fact, not receiving a bad deal at all. As Giselle Datz has shown, "some hedge funds bought these bonds at 17 cents [on the dollar] in 2002 and were happy to swap them for nearly double that amount in 2005." This, in turn, greatly eased the restructuring process for the government, "because instead of dealing with private international creditors who bought the bonds at 90 cents on the dollar, the government was dealing with those who paid around 20 cents."[56] In short, when the debt restructuring finally came around, the structurally powerful financial players had already won the battle by dumping most of their worthless bonds on powerless European pensioners and then *buying them back up* at greatly discounted prices to subsequently restructure them at a profit. Although the opaque nature of bond finance means that exact numbers are hard to come by, the *Wall Street Journal* reported that by the time of the 2005 debt restructuring, about half a million European and Japanese retail investors (including 450,000 Italians, 35,000 Japanese and 15,000 Germans and Central Europeans) held around 44 percent of Argentina's defaulted debt, with Argentine citizens, companies and financial institutions like banks and pension funds holding another 38 percent.[57] Small bondholders in Europe and Argentina thus ended up as the main losers in this game of financial arbitrage, while Wall Street emerged as the big winner.

Moreover, it turns out that the eventual debt reduction for Argentina was nowhere near as large as the 75 percent nominal haircut would seem to suggest. The reason is that the government added an obscure and rare "sweetener bonus" to the deal—a so-called GDP warrant—which paid bondholders an annual dividend in case Argentina's growth rates were to exceed a certain threshold. Since its GDP had contracted by almost 20 percent between 1998 and 2002, and since the country encountered such a favorable external environment after its default, it was to be expected that the Argentine economy would rebound rapidly and that investors stood to gain extensively from the GDP warrant. Because Argentina's average annual growth rates shot up to 9 percent after the default, the government actually found itself confronted with greater debt servicing costs as it emerged from the crisis. At the same time, the banks made significant profits from the intermediation fees they could charge for the restructuring itself. In fact, it was reported that "almost all the investment arms of leading Wall Street firms made lucrative deals" with the Argentine government.[58] In the end, it is therefore clear that Kirchner's scathing rhetoric against global finance was just that: rhetoric. His restructuring managed to impose severe losses on hapless foreign pensioners, but allowed Wall Street to continue to prosper. As the *Economist* dryly noted after the conclusion of the restructuring deal: "even in a default, there is money to be made."[59]

TABLE 15.1.
Comparison between the Mexican and Argentine crises

| Mexico in 1980s | Argentina in 2001 |
|---|---|
| **Syndicated bank lending:** | **Decentralized bond finance:** |
| Debt concentration high | Debt concentration low |
| Interlocked lending structure | Bondholders atomized/dispersed |
| Creditor coordination easy | Creditor coordination difficult |
| Credible threat of credit cut-off | No new credit forthcoming |
| *Market discipline strong* | *Market discipline weak* |
| **Active US/IMF intervention:** | **No US/IMF intervention:** |
| Sizeable international bailout loans | IMF pulls plug on Argentina's bailout program |
| Coordinated roll-overs to keep debtors solvent | No official coordination of small bondholders |
| IMF monitoring/supervision of debtor policies | U.S. isolationists push for reduced IMF role abroad |
| Policy conditionality enforces discipline | Policy conditionality breaks down |
| *Effective conditional lending* | *No more conditional lending* |
| **Limited debtor autonomy:** | **Relative debtor autonomy:** |
| Growing dependence on foreign credit and capital | Lenient int'l conditions, relative self-sufficiency |
| Bridging role for domestic elites and technocrats | Sidelining of domestic elites and technocrats |
| Popular opposition forestalled through cooptation | Legitimation crisis leads to antiausterity revolt |
| Strengthened bankers' alliance | Strengthened national-popular coalition |
| *Internalization of debtor discipline* | *Breakdown of debtor discipline* |
| **OUTCOME:** | **OUTCOME:** |
| *No unilateral default* | *Unilateral default* |
| Room for maneuver constrained | Exceptional room for maneuver postdefault |
| Mexico develops into "model debtor" | Argentina becomes most defiant debtor by far |
| Creditors only restructure debt after divesting | Debtor initiates aggressive debt restructuring |
| Highly unequal distribution of adjustment costs | Move towards more equitable redistribution |

PART V

The Specter of Solon:
Greece (2010–2015)

# SIXTEEN

## The Power of Finance in the Eurozone

The Greek debt crisis that began in late 2009 was the first major sovereign debt crisis to rock world markets since Argentina's record default of 2001. Coming barely a year after the collapse of Lehman Brothers and the start of the global financial crisis, the announcement by the incoming government of George Papandreou that its predecessors had been cooking the books and that the new administration faced a momentous €31 billion shortfall in annual public revenue (see figure 16.1) struck like a bombshell.[1] With the European banking system still reeling and the global economy in the throngs of its steepest downturn since the Great Depression, investors reacted to the news by taking flight. Although Greece only made up about 2 percent of the total economic output of the European Union, its government owed about €300 billion to various private lenders at home and abroad (see figure 16.2), raising fears that a disorderly Greek default might undermine the stability of the wider European banking system, lead to financial contagion across the periphery of the heavily indebted Eurozone (see figure 16.3), and call into question not just Greece's place within the single currency but the very survival of the monetary union.

Adamant to avoid such a scenario, the other EU member states banded together with the European Central Bank (ECB) and the IMF to organize the largest international emergency loans in history to prevent Greece from reneging on its foreign obligations. The onerous conditions attached to the three successive bailout programs sent the Greek economy into a nosedive, with the country entering a deep depression from which it has yet to recover. Losing almost a third of its total economic output and with a quarter of its population out of work, the country experienced one of the most severe contractions of any advanced capitalist economy during peacetime—with all the attendant social and political consequences. Yet despite the high costs of continued debt servicing, successive Greek governments of radically different political orientations consistently rejected unilateral action on the debt, preferring instead to pursue deeply unpopular fiscal adjustments and structural reforms. Even the formation of an antiausterity coalition under the leadership of the radical

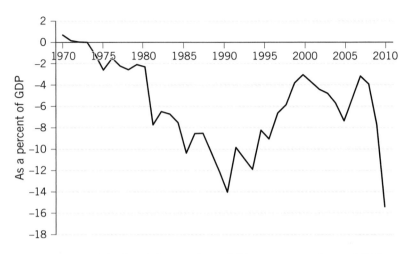

FIGURE 16.1. Greece's budget deficit as a share of GDP, 1970–2009. *Source*: OECD (2017).

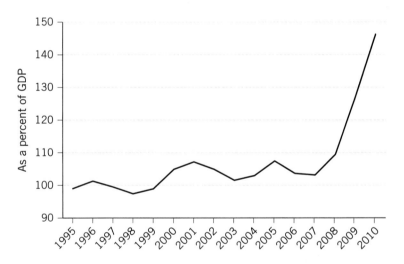

FIGURE 16.2. Greece's gross government debt as a share of GDP, 1995–2010. *Source*: Eurostat (2017).

left Syriza party in January 2015 and the resounding rejection of the creditors' bailout terms in a dramatic referendum that summer did nothing to change policy outcomes. Following a six-month standoff with its European lenders, the Syriza-led government was eventually forced to capitulate and sign up to a third bailout agreement whose terms and conditions were widely considered to be

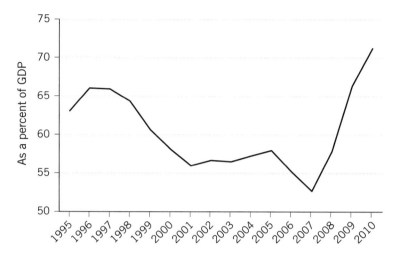

FIGURE 16.3.  EU countries' central government debt as a share of GDP, 1995–2010. *Source*: World Bank (2017); IMF Government Finance Statistics Yearbook, OECD GDP estimates.

even worse than those the leftists had so vehemently opposed while in opposition. How are we to account for this remarkable degree of debtor compliance in the Greek case, especially in light of the country's long-standing reputation as a "debt-intolerant serial defaulter" that spent nearly half of its history since independence in a state of default?[2]

The following chapters seek to answer this question through the prism of the three enforcement mechanisms of debtor discipline that we previously identified in the Mexican and Argentine cases. While much of the debate on Greece's policy response has centered on the question of the country's Eurozone membership, which has undoubtedly been a crucial factor shaping the response to the crisis, we will be digging a little deeper to uncover many of the same power dynamics that had been at play in the Global South in the 1980s and 1990s. Indeed, far from setting the country's debt troubles apart from past international debt crises, Greece's membership of the currency union—or, more specifically, its structural dependence on a "foreign" central bank for monetary policy and liquidity provision to its own banking system—served to both entrench and amplify existing structural power relations between the borrower and its lenders. Despite some of its distinctive features, then, the management of the Greek debt crisis does fit within the broader pattern of international crisis management that was first established in Mexico in 1982, with private and official creditors mustering all their collective might to ensure full repayment and prevent a unilateral payment suspension at all costs.

## FINANCIAL MARKETS AS A "GLOBAL SUPRA-GOVERNMENT"?

The first point to note, in this respect, is the central role played by the European sovereign bond market throughout the crisis. As we already saw in chapter 3 on the structural power of finance, the intensification of investor panic in late 2011 raised widespread concerns that financial markets had begun to act "like a global supra-government," imposing austerity and undermining established democratic processes in the debtor countries.[3] Yet this basic observation raises more questions than it answers. Who are these abstract and supposedly omnipotent "financial markets," and how did they come to be so powerful as to threaten the very foundations of the largest currency union in the world? On closer inspection, a familiar pattern emerges. Far from being characterized by decentralized or impersonal market dynamics, sovereign lending in the Eurozone actually revolved around a highly concentrated and internationally integrated creditors' cartel. Research by Barclays Capital revealed that at the start of the crisis, some 80 percent of Greek bonds were held by only a handful of systematically important banks in the rich Eurozone countries, with the 10 biggest bondholders alone accounting for more than half of the country's outstanding obligations in mid-2011, and the 30 biggest accounting for over two-thirds.[4] Unlike the prewar decades or Argentina after its megaswap, the extent of noninstitutional ownership of Greek debt was relatively small.[5] Between 2009 and 2011, Greece's creditor composition therefore mirrored that of Mexico at the start of its crisis in the 1980s, easing the formation and strengthening the coherence of a European creditors' cartel of sorts. As before, high market concentration both strengthened the threat of a wholesale credit cutoff in the event of noncompliance, and eased creditor coordination in subsequent debt negotiations.

This answer, however, raises an additional puzzle: if international lending in the build-up to the European debt crisis took the form of bond finance, as it had in the 1930s, then why did the ownership structure of Greece's debt end up resembling the highly concentrated bank loans of the 1980s more than the dispersed bond holdings of the 1930s? There appear to be two possible explanations for this discrepancy. First, the high concentration of European bond finance seems to be a result of the peculiar structure of the continental European financial system, which like the Eurodollar markets of the 1970s remains heavily bank-centered, leaving private banks as the principal financiers of national governments.[6] Second, there is the perverse incentive structure of the regulatory regime inside the Eurozone, which does not have a capital requirement for sovereign debt, enabling private banks to pile up as many government bonds as they want without needing to raise their capital ratios.[7] Taken together, these two factors combined with the financialization-driven process of market centralization and the intermediary role fulfilled by the major investment banks to contribute to a highly concentrated European sovereign bond market.[8]

Beyond the relatively small number of banks involved in lending to Greece, there were a number of other factors that structurally interlocked creditor interests and thereby eased the formation of a coherent creditors' cartel. The first and most important concerns the exceptionally deep integration of EU capital markets, which opened up an additional line of systemic vulnerability: banks in the core were not only heavily exposed to peripheral governments but also to peripheral *banks and businesses*. Research by Silvia Ardagna of Bank of America Merrill Lynch and Francesco Caselli of the London School of Economics has found that "due to the close links among the financial markets of advanced economies, distress of one sovereign can spill over to other sovereigns and banks." The authors emphasize that "key channels—in addition to banks' direct holdings of foreign sovereign debt— are banks' cross-border interbank exposures and banks' claims on nonfinancial entities in countries affected by sovereign tensions."[9] Since domestic financial firms inside the debtor countries would have been the first to fold in the event of a peripheral default, European bankers and officials had every interest in the stability not just of the peripheral governments but also of the banking sectors in these countries. In short, the interests of European lenders were intertwined across the board, making it easier for the biggest ones among them to act in concert.

Another important factor that eased creditor coordination and strengthened the disciplinary force of finance was the rise of credit rating agencies and their central role as monitors of governments' creditworthiness. In recent decades, rating agencies have assumed a number of functions that had previously been firmly within the domain of the International Monetary Fund. We saw in the Mexican case study how the Fund had fulfilled the crucial task of a surveillance agency and a gatekeeper of private market access during the 1980s. Only with an IMF stamp of approval—in the form of a completed Stand-By Arrangement—could distressed debtors expect to return to international capital markets, and a debtor could only expect to obtain such a stamp of approval if it carried out "responsible" policies geared towards the freeing up of domestic resources for foreign debt servicing. This not only gave the IMF considerable leverage over the debtors' policies; it also helped the Fund coordinate creditor action by providing important nonprice signals beyond risk-based interest rate spreads. With the rise of the credit rating oligopoly from the 1990s onwards, these financial surveillance functions have since been replicated in private form by the so-called Big Three—Moody's, Standard & Poor's, and Fitch—whose entire business model rests on monitoring debtors and assessing their risk of default. The credit reports released by these agencies now effectively serve as a private stamp of approval for continued market access. Moreover, their ratings have been "hard-wired" into financial market regulations through Basel II and III rules and the eligibility criteria for collateral defined by the leading central banks, including the ECB.[10] Moody's word, in short, has become law.

Like the financial sector more generally, the credit rating industry is a highly concentrated business, with the Big Three together accounting for 95 percent of total world market share between them. This extremely high market concentration gives these companies considerable leverage over the governments whose various debt instruments they rate. Although an agency like Standard & Poor's cannot prevent default in a direct sense, its ratings do serve to shape the incentive structure for the buying and selling of government bonds, thus providing trusted nonprice signals to coordinate creditor action and prevent freeriding by individual lenders in the event of a default, as the average investor would not want to be seen holding junk bonds. Since both investors and regulators rely on these agencies' private credit ratings to assess default risk and determine whether a government's bonds are investment grade and can be used as collateral, a downgrade by a single agency can have far-reaching repercussions for an investor's ability to hold on to these bonds and for a government's ability to access international capital markets. This dynamic of centralized surveillance and monitoring, which is intrinsic to the contemporary global financial system, therefore creates a strong additional constraint on debtors, compelling them to continuously heed "investor demands" and impress "the markets" on the credibility of their commitments, lest they be punished with credit rating downgrades, higher borrowing costs, or even complete exclusion from international capital markets.[11] Taken together, the concentrated nature of international lending, the interlocked interests of private creditors, and the centralized monitoring of the credit rating agencies thus contributed to the emergence of a coherent creditors' cartel that could effectively enforce market discipline on the peripheral debtors and compel them to pursue strict austerity measures and repay their debts. The result of this strong market discipline was to greatly constrain the room for maneuver available to policymakers, leading to a situation in which, as we noted in the introduction to this book, "governments of different political orientations, of different political strength, with different capacities for concertation with the social partners found themselves implementing essentially the same structural adjustment program."[12]

This broad similarity in policy outcomes across divergent national contexts strongly hints at the existence of structural factors that overruled domestic party politics and national institutional idiosyncrasies by disciplining the political choices of national governments, circumscribing the policy options available to them, punishing divergent actions and ideas, and compelling policymakers to play by the rules of the game or face the wrath of the bond market. For Armingeon and Baccaro, the European debt crisis is therefore a clear "case in which domestic politics, either party- or interest group–based, does not matter: there is only one option—internal devaluation—and it is imposed from the outside."[13] The limited room for maneuver available to debtor states is clearly reminiscent of the developing country debt crises of the 1980s and 1990s; if anything, the constraints on national policy autonomy in the Eurozone periphery appear to be even greater, as governments lack control over monetary policy, forcing them to shift the full burden of adjustment onto wage earners and social welfare recipients. With the option of an external devaluation foreclosed, the only remaining choice is between internal devaluation or default. And since the spillover costs of the latter were widely considered to be too debilitating to countenance, policymakers in the periphery were left with austerity and structural adjustment as the only "permissible" policy response.[14]

## THE CREDIBLE THREAT OF A CREDIT CUTOFF

As in Mexico and Argentina, this market-based enforcement mechanism was most clearly on display at the start of the crisis, when Greece still had access to the bond market and increasingly depended on it to refinance its maturing obligations and make up for its widening budget shortfall. When the first signs of crisis began to manifest themselves from late-2009 onwards, the Greek government became increasingly concerned about its access to foreign credit. As Finance Minister George Papaconstantinou recalls, "the refrain was: above all, we needed to convince the markets and the rating agencies. . . . [W]e needed to send a strong signal of determination to reduce the deficit—in other words, announce more austerity."[15]

Unlike in Mexico and Argentina, where the option to suspend payments was at least briefly discussed within the government at the start of the crisis, in Greece this possibility was never even properly considered. Papaconstantinou notes that "there was no default scenario for the country. . . . [W]e wanted to continue borrowing on the market. If that failed, we wanted a European solution. Ideally a European lending facility needed to be announced, thereby convincing everyone that we would not default under any circumstances."[16] Above all, Greek officials feared that a "sudden stop" in credit provision would leave the government without sufficient financial resources to plug the enormous hole in its budget.[17] After all, with the government running a deficit of 15.4 percent of GDP in 2009 and of 4 percent in 2010, being locked out of capital markets in the wake of a default would have necessitated even more severe austerity measures than those demanded by official lenders, making a suspension of payments a comparatively unattractive option in the first year of the crisis.[18] Papaconstantinou himself argued that a "unilateral debt restructuring—simply deciding not to pay back our debt—would be catastrophic. It would at a stroke make Greece a pariah, shutting it out of all international markets, and would make it impossible to finance our large primary fiscal deficit."[19]

Nevertheless, Greek policymakers' fears of market discipline and their early moves to restore investor confidence by announcing far-reaching budget cuts could not prevent a cascade of credit rating downgrades between 2009 and 2011, which in turn caused borrowing costs to rise even further (see figure 16.4). Having belatedly recognized the error of their ways in the lead-up to the global financial crisis, the rating agencies—which had long given Greece a

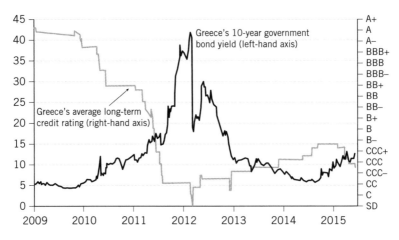

FIGURE 16.4. Greece's credit rating vs. borrowing costs (2009–2015). *Source*: Reuters (2015b); based on ratings by S&P, Moody's, and Fitch.

prime rating on a par with Germany's—now seemed determined to overcompensate for their earlier complacence by incessantly questioning the credibility of the government's commitments to push through the expected fiscal adjustments and honor its enormous €300 billion debt load. The result was a loss of investor confidence, leading to rising interest rate spreads (see figure 16.5) that forced the government to cut spending even further in the vain hope of reassuring the markets. As the crisis intensified, similar patterns began to unfold in Portugal and Ireland and to a lesser extent in Spain and Italy. Economists Paul de Grauwe and Yumei Ji have since argued that this self-reinforcing market dynamic resulted in the imposition of "excessive austerity" on the debtor states, showing that "the higher the spreads in 2011, the more intense were the austerity measures." In fact, "the intensity of the austerity can be explained almost uniquely *by the size of the spreads.*"[20]

The extent of Greece's commercial, financial, and monetary integration into the wider European economy made it particularly vulnerable to a sudden stop of capital inflows. In terms of international trade, Greece was—and remains—heavily dependent on imports of key goods like oil and pharmaceuticals. There were widespread fears that hospitals might run out of medicine or gas stations and power plants might run out of fuel in the event of a default, as the loss of access to trade credit and the lack of foreign currency reserves would have left the country unable to pay for the respective imports.[21] At the same time, the domestic financial sector was particularly vulnerable to a suspension of payments since Greek banks were exposed to their own government to the tune of €54.4 billion, and would have instantly collapsed if the state were to renege on these obligations.[22] This in turn motivated depositors to begin withdrawing

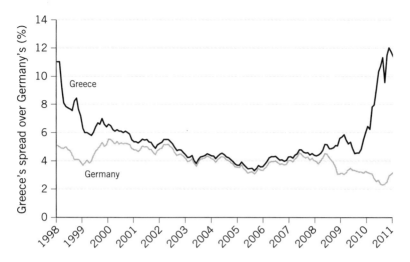

FIGURE 16.5. Rising spread on 10-year government bond yields, Greece vs. Germany, 1998–2011. *Source*: Federal Reserve Bank of St. Louis (2017).

their savings from these increasingly vulnerable banks—stuffing them in their mattresses or sending them abroad as a precautionary measure. Papaconstantinou recalls that "we were constantly worried that the 'bank jog' of the first months of 2010 . . . could become a full-fledged 'bank run.' Once that happened, there would be no way back and it would be necessary to close the banks and impose capital controls."[23]

Finally, concerns about spillovers into trade and banking were compounded by overarching monetary considerations, with Greece's Eurozone membership effectively hanging in the balance in the event of a default. While there are no legal provisions for removing a member state from the Economic and Monetary Union (EMU), there were widespread fears that a Greek default would inexorably lead to that outcome through a more informal mechanism. In short, a default would have led to the collapse of the main domestic banks, forcing the government to recapitalize them and pump liquidity into the financial system. Lacking control over its own central bank and autonomous monetary policy, the only way for the Greek government to do so would have been to resort to the issuing of IOUs, which would gradually come to displace the euro as a de facto means of payment inside Greece, ultimately compelling the government to formalize the transition back to a national currency. The threat of Grexit could therefore be considered another "spillover effect" of default—and since the country's main businesses, its wealthy elite and its relatively Europhile middle class were all strongly committed to Eurozone membership, the government desperately wanted to avoid setting in motion such a vicious spiral.

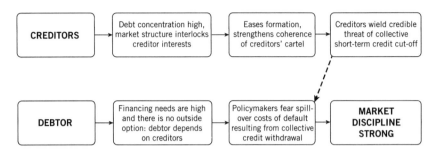

FIGURE 16.6. The first enforcement mechanism in Greece.

Taken together with the credit and trade dependencies mentioned above, the systemic vulnerability of the domestic banking system and the likely implications that a default would have had for Greece's EMU membership therefore greatly reduced the country's overall economic resilience, making its government much more susceptible to investor demands and market pressure.[24] The first enforcement mechanism of market discipline, in short, was exceptionally strong in the initial phase of the crisis, leaving the government with relatively little room for maneuver.

Just as in Mexico and Argentina, however, the sheer force of this first mechanism eventually risked undermining itself. Greece's rising borrowing costs, which originally compelled the incoming center-left government to tighten its belt and repay its debts, were now threatening to make it impossible for the country to borrow sufficient funds to refinance its maturing obligations. If the constantly rising interest rates and repeated credit rating downgrades were not counterbalanced in time with official-sector intervention, the investor panic would have resulted in a disorderly default, which neither the Greek government nor its international creditors desired. Once again, the market discipline imposed by a highly concentrated and structurally interlocked creditors' cartel turned out to be a necessary but insufficient condition for preventing default. As a result, in early 2010, it slowly began to dawn on European leaders that Greece would not be able to repay its creditors without some form of financial support. As Papaconstantinou put it, "everybody now realized we had reached the point where, however many measures we took, they would not be enough. The markets required a 'backstop' in case Greece stopped having market access."[25]

# SEVENTEEN

## Anatomy of a "Holding Operation"

By April 2010, Greece was teetering on the brink of bankruptcy. Skyrocketing borrowing costs had effectively excluded the country from international capital markets, and with only €12 billion left in its cash reserves and interest rates on two-year bonds breaching 12 percent, the government found it impossible to raise sufficiently affordable credit on international capital markets. The largest sovereign default in history now loomed as early as May 19, when a massive €8.9 billion bond payment was due. A belated realization of the seriousness of the situation finally seemed to concentrate the minds of European leaders, who had grown terrified at the prospect of uncontrollable contagion across the periphery and a forced Greek exit from the Eurozone—all with the global financial crisis still fresh in everyone's mind and investors constantly on edge in anticipation of the next systemic shock. Since Greece's principal lenders turned out to be a handful of systemically important French and German banks, each "dangerously overexposed to peripheral countries" (see figure 17.1 and table 17.1), the prospect of a Greek payment suspension and subsequent contagion across the periphery unleashing a crippling continental banking crisis—the second in just two years—looked particularly unattractive to the French and German governments.[1]

This is when the second enforcement mechanism of conditional lending kicked in. In the following chapter, we will see how the high concentration of Greece's debt among a number of big banks in the core countries eventually moved the creditor states and the ECB to join forces with the IMF and intervene aggressively on foreign bondholders' behalf, disbursing a series of record-breaking international bailout loans under strict policy conditionality to keep Greece solvent and servicing its external debts.

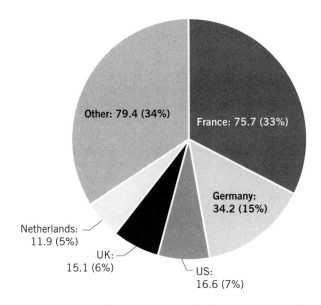

FIGURE 17.1. Bank holdings of Greek sovereign debt by country on April 30, 2010.
*Source*: Reuters; Bank for International Settlements.
*Note*: In U.S. $ billions and as a share of the $236 billion total.

TABLE 17.1.
Foreign claims on Eurozone periphery in third quarter of 2009 (US$ million)

|  | Greece | Ireland | Italy | Portugal | Spain | Total |
|---|---|---|---|---|---|---|
| *Germany* | 43,236 | 193,271 | 209,295 | 47,261 | 240,296 | 733,359 |
| *France* | 78,571 | 52,130 | 484,103 | 36,359 | 172,805 | 823,968 |
| *Austria* | 6,337 | 8,968 | 21,121 | 2,634 | 9,276 | 48,336 |
| *Belgium* | 8,292 | 42,443 | 52,457 | 11,707 | 47,389 | 162,288 |
| *Ireland* | 8,717 |  | 46,669 | 5,809 | 33,534 | 94,729 |
| *Italy* | 8,753 | 22,597 |  | 6,664 | 32,925 | 70,939 |
| *Japan* | 8,777 | 21,940 | 53,163 | 3,529 | 27,551 | 114,960 |
| *Netherlands* | 12,054 | 32,090 | 74,551 | 13,171 | 125,805 | 257,671 |
| *Portugal* | 10,453 | 4,857 | 5,722 |  | 30,116 | 51,148 |
| *Spain* | 1,157 | 14,612 | 51,376 | 87,403 |  | 154,548 |
| *UK* | 12,492 | 191,849 | 81,966 | 26,264 | 120,723 | 433,294 |
| *US* | 19,448 | 73,759 | 68,753 | 6,202 | 68,194 | 236,356 |

*Source*: Thompson (2015); Bank for International Settlements, International Banking Statistics.

## THE FIRST GREEK BAILOUT OF 2010

At the start of the crisis, it was estimated that over two-thirds of Greece's €300 billion debt load was held abroad. EU stress tests showed that Greek banks made up for €54.4 billion of the total share, indicating that the majority of the outstanding bonds were held by non-Greek banks (see figure 17.1).[2] Moreover, as we saw before, European banks also carried very large *indirect* exposures through their loans to and ownership shares in Greek banks and businesses. Since many Greek banks and firms would have gone bankrupt in the event of a government default, these private-sector exposures were an equally serious cause for concern. Investor fears of contagion across the Eurozone periphery added a further element of vulnerability, as major lenders like Deutsche Bank, Commerzbank, Société Générale, BNP Paribas, and Crédit Agricole carried large exposures to the governments and private sectors of Ireland, Portugal, Spain, and Italy as well, which were widely considered to be the next dominos to fall if Greece were to default on its debts. It is therefore safe to say that, even if it could have withstood a Greek default in isolation, the risk of contagion meant that the very survival of the European banking system was at stake in early 2010. Lee Buchheit of Clearly Gottlieb and his collaborator Mitu Gulati at Duke University point out the similarities with the crisis of the 1980s in this respect, as well as the important differences with the 1990s:

> The sovereign debt crises of the last 10 years or so have affected mostly nonbank creditors—hedge funds, pension funds, other institutional holders of emerging market sovereign debt, sometimes even individuals. Those crises did not threaten the stability of the banking sectors in creditor countries. A restructuring of Greek debt will, [by contrast], rekindle fretful memories of the global debt crisis of the 1980s.[3]

Despite the systemic threat posed by a disorderly Greek default, it was clear that official-sector intervention would come at a political cost. Especially in Germany, public opposition to financial support for "lazy" and "profligate" Southerners was high, as were concerns among leading German officials about inducing moral hazard. For months, the German government therefore wavered in its response to the crisis, kicking the can down the road and continuing to insist on the no-bailout clause of the Maastricht Treaty, which explicitly forbade the provision of bailout loans to a distressed fellow Eurozone government, while exerting various forms of political pressure on the Greek government behind the scenes. As the crisis deepened, however, the German position became increasingly untenable, and in April 2010 European leaders finally agreed on the necessity of official-sector intervention to avoid a cessation of payments.

A research note by Société Générale, which itself carried significant exposure to the Greek government, explained that "what seems to have galvanized

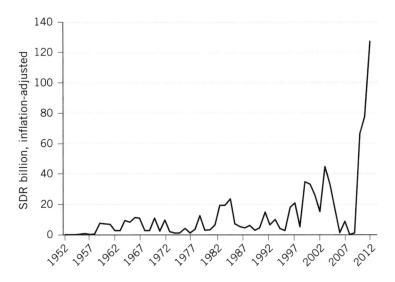

FIGURE 17.2. Value of new nonconcessional IMF lending commitments, 1952–2011.
*Source*: Edwards and Hsieh (2011); IMF.

minds is the realization that much of European banking is heavily exposed to Southern Europe and Greece in particular."[4] After an initial period of dithering and denial, the French and German governments therefore decided that they should prevent default at all costs: they would rather bail out their own banks indirectly, by providing an enormous emergency loan to the Greek government and subsequently forcing the country to repay its debts in full, than allow Greece to suspend payments and be forced to bail out their own banks directly.[5] By convincing the IMF and the other Eurozone countries to help them put up the funds required to keep Greece afloat, the German and French governments could share the costs and risks of a bailout with the taxpayers of other countries. The heavily exposed EU banks clearly shared this policy preference, as it helped them avoid both the costs and the blame of another financial meltdown while shielding shareholders from a dilution of their equity stake that would likely have accompanied further capital injections by their own governments.

And so, on May 2, 2010, just 2.5 weeks before the critical May 19 deadline on a major bond payment, European finance ministers and the Greek government finally agreed to the activation of a €110 billion emergency loan, €80 billion of which was to be provided by the EU member states and €30 billion by the IMF. It was the largest international bailout in history and the biggest single loan the Fund had ever made to a member state. Together with the later bailouts of Ireland and Portugal, it brought about an unprecedented increase in new IMF commitments (see figure 17.2).

The memorandum of understanding that was subsequently signed between the Greek government and its official lenders showed some striking similarities to past bailout programs in the Global South—but also a number of important differences. The Greek bailout was similar in that it hinged on the disbursement of large official-sector emergency loans under strict policy conditionality, combined with a staunch insistence on full and timely debt repayment and a wholesale rejection of upfront debt relief. It was different in that the emergency loans and the policy conditionality were unrivaled in their scope and severity, and in that the U.S. Treasury Department and the U.S. Federal Reserve played a marginal role in their disbursement and implementation. Instead, the initiative for the bailout was taken by the German and French governments, the European Commission, and the ECB, while the IMF—instead of assuming the international leadership it had provided in the crises of the 1980s and 1990s— was to play a more supportive role this time around.[6] Together, the tripartite committee of the European Commission, the IMF, and the ECB that was to execute the program and monitor Greece's compliance came to be known as the Troika of foreign lenders.

But there was another striking difference that set the Greek bailout apart from previous IMF interventions in the Global South: the fact that Greece was not only a developed country, but also a member of the largest currency union in the world. While developing countries have historically shared Greece's problem of borrowing abroad in a "foreign" currency that they do not control, and while Argentina in particular had experienced a similar lack of monetary policy autonomy as a result of its convertibility regime with the U.S. dollar, most of these countries generally had their own central bank and their own currency, allowing them to at least wield the tools of monetary policy and currency devaluation in the adjustment process. Greece, by contrast, suffered an additional layer of dependence as it did not control the money circulating through its economy and could not devalue its currency. Since unilateral default and a negotiated debt restructuring were systematically ruled out by the creditors, this left only the option of an "internal devaluation," shifting the burden of adjustment entirely onto the shoulders of Greek workers and taxpayers.

Moreover, Greece's domestic banking system acutely relied on ECB liquidity provision for its survival, providing the central bank with great leverage over the Greek government, which the ECB—as we will see later in this chapter— eventually wielded with strategic intent to enforce full compliance. In this sense, at least, we could say that Greece's Eurozone membership was a unique feature that set the country's debt crisis apart from most previous crises in the Global South. Nevertheless, the general power dynamic between Greece and its creditors, even with this additional layer of dependence, was fundamentally the same: official lenders, including the ECB, were capable of disciplining the Greek government through the threat of withholding further financing in the event of noncompliance, which was widely understood by all actors involved to inflict devastating spillover costs on the Greek economy. The monetary specificities of the Greek case may therefore make it appear highly idiosyncratic, but the underlying asymmetry in the balance of power between the heavily indebted Greek government and its official-sector creditors certainly recalls the experience of earlier debt crises in the developing world.

The funding provided by the EU and IMF as part of Greece's first bailout was intended to cover the country's external obligations and budget deficit for a period of three years, after which the government was expected to be able to return to the markets on its own. The memorandum of understanding with its creditors required the Greek government to enact one of the most severe front-loaded fiscal contractions of any developed country on record, to pursue deeply unpopular market reforms, reduce labor costs, slash pensions and unemployment benefits, lay off civil servants, and dismantle basic workers' rights like job protections and collective bargaining.[7] As in previous bailout programs in the Global South, creditors enforced these policy conditions by disbursing the bailout loan in tranches, always leaving the threat of a refusal of the next loan installment ominously lingering in the background. This option of "pulling the plug," which has been a key element of the IMF's Stand-By Arrangements ever since the 1980s, left the Greek government with little choice but to adhere to the specifics of the Troika's austerity and reform program, since a withdrawal of financial assistance would have left it without any external sources of financing.[8] Indeed, Greece's financial officials lived in constant fear of what Papaconstantinou called the "ultimate sanction: the withdrawal of financial support, leading to bankruptcy."[9] The enforcement of strict policy conditionality was therefore once again at the center of the creditors' approach to international crisis management. As ECB president Jean-Claude Trichet put it:

> Loans are not transfers, and loans come at a cost. They come not only at a financial cost; they also come with strict conditionality. This conditionality needs to give assurance to lenders, not only that they will be repaid but also that the borrower will be able to stand on its own feet over a multi-year horizon. In the case of Greece, this will require courageous, recognizable and specific actions by the Greek government that will lastingly and credibly consolidate the public budget.[10]

Seen in light of past adjustment programs, the austerity measures demanded of the Greeks were exceptionally tough.[11] In its highly critical 2016 review of the first Stand-By Arrangement, the IMF's Independent Evaluation Office (IEO) highlighted the program's "unusually strong, front-loaded fiscal adjustment," which was "among the largest in recent history."[12] Greece's projected budget cuts, averaging 4.5 percent of GDP per year over the course of the three-year program, were almost three times as large as the average 1.6 percent applied in the Latin American programs of the 1980s and 1990s. As a "crude measure of intensity," the IEO pointed out that the Greek program included an average of 22.5 structural measures to be applied per year—compared to 5.2 per year in the IMF programs of 2008 and 8.5 per year in 2010.[13] While Germany's total austerity amounted to 2 percent of GDP, Italy's to 3 percent, Portugal's to 5.4 percent, the UK's to 6.3 percent, Spain's to 6.8 percent, and Ireland's to 9 percent, Greece's total austerity during the crisis years amounted to a whopping 18 percent.[14]

Moreover, the austerity measures and structural reforms went hand in hand with a staunch refusal to consider the possibility of upfront debt restructuring. When Greece's finance minister George Papaconstantinou flew to Washington, D.C., on April 24, 2010, for an emergency meeting with the heads of the IMF and ECB and the EU Economic and Monetary Affairs commissioner at the sidelines of the annual IMF–World Bank spring meeting, he was told the exact same thing that Mexico's finance minister had been told when he made the same trip during the fateful Mexican Weekend of 1982: "debt restructuring was not on the table."[15] As Papaconstantinou himself recalls, it was said "in the most clear terms, aimed at me: 'George, do not open this issue' . . . I was not a fool. I would never have opened this issue unilaterally, and then be told, in the media, that it was not an option, and have all the investors running for cover in 24 hours."[16] As in 1982, in other words, official-sector intervention was made conditional on Greece rejecting unilateral action, freeing up the maximum amount of domestic resources for foreign debt servicing and maintaining a rigorous adherence to its external obligations.

## THE IMF'S AWKWARD ROLE IN THE TROIKA

From the very beginning, however, it was clear that the IMF's role in the Greek bailout was going to be different from its role in past debt crises. While in the 1980s and 1990s the Fund had—with the backing of the U.S. Treasury and Federal Reserve—taken up an active leadership role in international crisis management, the Europeans were very uneasy about outside interference into their monetary union. ECB President Trichet was particularly strongly opposed to IMF involvement, especially since some IMF officials continued to insist on the need for debt relief, which was out of the question for the ECB. The central bank attached great importance to Greece "honoring its sovereign signature," and it "strongly believed that any debt relief would in effect be the first step to the dissolution of the euro."[17] While Chancellor Merkel shared Trichet's opposition to debt relief, because of the weakness and exposure of Germany's banks, she eventually managed to convince the ECB chief of the need for IMF participation in the bailout.[18] Merkel insisted on IMF involvement because of the Fund's unrivaled expertise in conditional lending; the Europeans simply lacked the technical know-how and institutional capacity to administer conditionality and monitor fiscal policy and economic performance themselves.[19] Moreover, as an outside player with a credible exit threat, the IMF was more likely to discipline Greece by withholding future credit tranches in the event of noncompliance, thus improving the credibility of the Troika's ultimate threat.[20] Finally, bringing in the IMF would allow EU leaders to deflect at least part of the blame for painful adjustment measures onto a third party.[21] As Finland's finance minister, Alexander Stubb, later explained in relation to the third bailout of 2015, "we would prefer to have the IMF on board. It's not just because of its [financial] input into the program, but the credibility and tough conditionality the IMF approves in all of this."[22] And so the compromise that eventually emerged was for the IMF to participate in the bailout program as a "junior partner" of sorts, providing part of the loan and helping to design its conditionality, monitor performance, and enforce compliance, but without taking complete control of the wider Eurozone, as it was used to doing in the Global South.[23]

This awkward arrangement was to have serious repercussions for Greece. The most important was that the early calls for debt restructuring made by a number of high-ranking IMF officials were overruled in the face of staunch European opposition—especially from the French and the ECB—to forced bank losses. Certain departments within the Fund had been convinced from the very start that without meaningful debt relief the program had little chance of success. The Strategy, Policy & Review Department, in particular, was adamant that "an IMF loan to Greece must not go simply for payments to bondholders, as it had in Argentina's case, [since] giving Athens a big international rescue loan, with no haircut, would shift the burden to taxpayers."[24] To these staff members, the Greek crisis rekindled fretful memories of emerging market debt crises of the late 1990s. After the botched East Asian bailouts and the scandal of the IMF's record credit augmentations to Argentina, the Fund had drawn up a new set of rules on "exceptional access" to IMF facilities that set an annual limit on Fund disbursements of 200 percent of a member's IMF quota, and a cumulative limit of 600 percent of quota.[25] Programs were only allowed to exceed these limits if the Fund's experts found a "high probability" that the debt would indeed turn out to be sustainable.

But despite the fact that the IMF's own debt sustainability analysis did not find Greece's debt to be sustainable with "high probability," the Fund's management actively pushed for the Executive Board to agree to a €30 billion loan—amounting to an unprecedented 3,200 percent of Greece's quota, "the largest nonprecautionary Fund arrangement ever approved relative to quota."[26] Technically, the IMF's own rules prohibited the Executive Board from agreeing to such a large credit facility, so management simply changed the rules, adding a clause that "exceptional access would be justified if there is a high risk of international systemic spillovers."[27] The Independent Evaluation Office (IEO) later acknowledged that "perhaps no other IMF decision connected with the euro crisis has received more criticism than that of providing exceptional access financing to Greece when its sovereign debt was not deemed sustainable with high probability."[28] In its review of the 2010 Stand-By Arrangement, the IEO also found that the Fund's management did not adequately inform the

Executive Board on the decision to waver the debt sustainability criterion, and that "these governance and accountability issues . . . may have eroded the legitimacy and evenhandedness of the IMF."[29]

Yet despite this scathing criticism and the vocal misgivings of some of its own economists, the IMF's management insisted on participating in the Greek program—to vehement protests of some members of the board. Brazil's executive director complained that "debt restructuring should have been on the table" and argued that the bailout "may be seen not as a rescue of Greece, which will have to undergo a wrenching adjustment, but as a bailout of Greece's private debt holders, mainly European financial institutions." René Weber of Switzerland also voiced "considerable doubts about the feasibility of the program," asking: "Why has debt restructuring and the involvement of the private sector not been considered so far?" Executive directors from China, India, Argentina, and several other developing countries expressed similar concerns. The IMF's minutes of the 2010 board meeting further mention that "the exceptionally high risks of the program were recognized by staff itself, in particular in its assessment of debt sustainability."[30] But IMF chief Dominique Strauss-Kahn, who was keen to restore the Fund's international standing following its gradual marginalization during the liquidity-abundant opening decade of the twenty-first century, and who as the former French finance minister and aspiring presidential candidate was acutely aware of the losses that French banks would incur in a debt restructuring, pressed ahead with the Greek Stand-By Arrangement anyway. In effect, former IMF executive director Miranda Xafa writes, "the debt sustainability criterion was waived based on the systematic concerns arising from spillover risks if the program was not approved."[31]

And so the program went ahead, and Greece, even though it lagged behind on many of the required market reforms, dutifully carried out the budget cuts and tax hikes demanded by the Troika. In 2010 alone, the Greek government reduced total public spending by 5 percent of GDP. As the OECD acknowledged, "no other OECD country has achieved such a fiscal improvement in a single year over the past three decades."[32] A background paper for the IMF's Independent Evaluation Office agrees, noting that "the extent of the fiscal adjustment envisaged was exceptional by international and historical standards."[33] All in all, the Greek public deficit was reduced from over 15 percent of GDP in 2009 to less than 3 percent at the end of 2013—and further still after that. Yet the outcome of these unparalleled austerity measures was an unmitigated social and economic disaster, with the country entering a deep depression from which it has yet to recover. By early 2011, it was starting to become clear that the Greek economy was contracting much faster than the IMF had originally foreseen (see figure 17.3).[34]

Olivier Blanchard, the IMF's chief economist, later acknowledged that the Fund's unrealistic prognoses had hinged on a set of questionable assumptions about Greece's fiscal multipliers that underestimated the contractionary effects

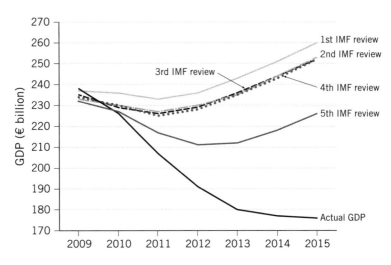

FIGURE 17.3. IMF growth projections vs. Greece's actual growth rate, 2009–2015. *Source*: Wyplosz and Sgherri (2016); IMF.

of the harsh austerity measures the IMF had helped to impose.[35] These incorrect multipliers were not just a product of innocent economic presuppositions, however. According to Susan Schadler, a former deputy director of the Fund's European Department, they were an outcome of "fundamental political pressures" that compelled IMF staff to paint a much rosier image of Greece's public finances and growth prospects than reality merited in order to be able to keep participating in the bailout program without falling foul of the IMF's own rules on bankrolling insolvent states.[36] In its review of the 2010 Stand-By Arrangement, the Fund acknowledged that "in retrospect, the [bailout] program served as a holding operation," buying time for private creditors to reduce their exposure and boost their capital ratios, ultimately "leaving the official sector on the hook" to bear the brunt of a future default or restructuring.[37] The banks used this time well: between the first quarters of 2010 and 2011, German lenders cut their exposure to Greek government debt by $9 billion and their overall lending by $19.8 billion, while the French reduced theirs by $13.6 billion and $14.16 billion, respectively.[38]

## THE SECOND PHASE OF THE CRISIS AND THE ROLE OF THE ECB

Nevertheless, European bank exposures remained significant in early 2011, and by the first anniversary of the first bailout agreement the austerity-induced collapse of the Greek economy raised the specter of a disorderly default anew. Moreover, having been battered by a full year of deposit withdrawals, the stability of the Greek banking system was now becoming a major issue of concern. "We are talking about June 2011," one Troika official said, "when Greeks were taking about one to two billion euros a day from the banking system. And the Greeks had to send military planes to Italy to get banknotes. It got to that point."[39] The renewed escalation in the debt crisis marked the start of the second phase of Eurozone crisis management, in which Greece's official lenders were to double down on their effort to enforce compliance. Despite the failure of the first bailout program to bring about debt sustainability and produce a return to the markets, European leaders saw a number of reasons to stay the course and begin negotiating a second bailout. According to Susan Schadler, "several interviewees suggested that apart from domestic political considerations, one reason the Europeans did not want to commit openly to absorbing the costs of the crisis and establishing an endgame [i.e., debt relief] was that they felt it necessary to perpetuate uncertainty as a method of holding the feet of the Greek government to the fire."[40] While international commentators widely criticized EU leaders for "muddling through" and "kicking the can down the road," in hindsight Europe's apparent wavering appears to have been less the result of indecision and more part of a deliberate strategy to buy time and allow their own banks to escape before the inevitable debt restructuring of 2012.[41]

The events of late 2011 clearly showed that EU leaders were in fact perfectly capable of organizing decisive action when confronted with an episode of noncompliance. On October 31, Prime Minister George Papandreou, having been backed into a corner by intensifying antiausterity protests at home, unexpectedly called a referendum on the Troika's conditions for a second bailout. Official-sector creditors immediately responded by closing ranks and flexing their structural power. The disbursement of the sixth loan installment was halted until after the referendum, and EU officials made it very clear "that the entire loan package would become obsolete if the plebiscite were to yield a negative result."[42] Papandreou was summoned to the G20 summit in Cannes on November 1, where—after being publicly humiliated by his European counterparts—he was told in no uncertain terms that he risked having his country cut off from all foreign credit and thereby pushed out of the Eurozone. Finance Minister Evangelos Venizelos, who accompanied Papandreou on the trip, recounts Merkel's message as follows: "either you cancel the referendum or you hold one, immediately, that asks: 'yes or no to the euro'. And after that we'll see if we'll go ahead with the [next] installment, the [bailout] program, the haircut."[43]

This explicit threat of a cutoff in foreign financing was compounded by the onset of pre-emptive spillover effects within the Greek banking system. Anticipating a potential financial collapse triggered by a government default and a forced exit from the Eurozone in the event of a "no" vote in the referendum, Greek citizens and firms began to pull billions of euros from their accounts. In the two preceding months, depositors had already withdrawn some €14 billion; a slow-motion bank run that intensified after Papandreou's referendum

FIGURE 17.4. Total corporate and household deposits in Greek banks, 2001–2012.
*Source*: Bank of Greece (2017).

announcement. George Provopoulos, governor of the Bank of Greece, informed parliament's economic affairs committee that "in the first 10 days of
November the decline continued on a large scale," bringing total deposits to
€170 billion by the end of 2011, down 30 percent from over €230 billion at the
start of 2010. Faced with the threat of a credit withdrawal and driven into a
corner by the escalating deposit flight and impending banking crisis, Papandreou finally buckled under the pressure and canceled his referendum, resigning from his post several days later. Venizelos later defended the government's
U-turn by explaining that it would have led to panic: "Imagine the reaction
of the markets. In three days we would have collapsed. We would never have
got to the referendum because there would have been a run on the banks."[44]
Deposit flight eventually stabilized as the perceived default risk subsided following the appointment of the technocratic prime minister Lucas Papademos
(see figure 17.4).[45]

Next to these increasingly aggressive moves by EU leaders to force Greece
back into the fold, the second phase of crisis management was also marked by
an increasingly important role for the European Central Bank. While the ECB,
as we saw earlier, had already played its part in opposing an early IMF-led debt
restructuring, its participation in the first bailout had mostly taken place behind
the scenes. As Papaconstantinou explains, "the ECB was putting no money on
the table. Their formal association with the program was awkward. . . . But they
wielded the ultimate weapon: control over the banking system; their rules on
collateral for lending to commercial banks meant they had plenty of weight in

the negotiations."[46] As the negotiations for a second bailout got underway in 2011–2012, the ECB readied this ultimate weapon and assumed a much more active role in the management of the crisis.[47] The first clear signs of central bank intervention came in the form of a handful of letters Jean-Claude Trichet sent to the finance ministers or heads of state of the peripheral countries, in which the ECB president threatened to withdraw various forms of ECB support.[48]

During the Troika's bailout talks with the Greek government, Trichet sent one such letter to George Papandreou—dated April 7, 2011—in which he explicitly threatened to revoke a suspension of rating requirements for privately held securities issued or guaranteed by the Greek government. Since this would have disqualified the country's systemic banks from using these securities as collateral for ECB loans, Trichet's letter effectively amounted to a threat to throttle the country's banking system, which completely depended on ECB support to stay afloat.[49] The announcement highlighted the central bank's preparedness to wield its structural power over the Greek banking sector—and hence over the Greek state, which depended on domestic banks to refinance its internal debt and keep credit circulating through the economy—to enforce compliance with the Troika's loan conditions.[50] As former IMF executive director Miranda Xafa writes, "essentially, Trichet informed the Greek government that even a [voluntary rescheduling] would lead the ECB to pull the plug on Greek banks, since they would lack appropriate collateral as well as the capital adequacy needed to access the ECB discount window. The consequence of such a move would be to force Greece to leave the euro area and print its own money."[51]

In addition to its disciplinary role with respect to the debtor countries, the ECB also organized what effectively amounted to an indirect bailout of private creditors through the mechanism of its bond-buying scheme. In May 2010, the ECB Governing Council had already signed off on the Securities Market Program (SMP), which revolved around the ECB purchasing the distressed bonds of peripheral governments on secondary markets. Since its statutes officially forbid monetary financing of member states, the ECB could not buy these bonds directly from distressed governments; what it could do, however, was to indirectly depress the interest rates on Greece's debt by entering into secondary markets and offering to buy up the securities held by private bondholders who could not otherwise get rid of them at good prices. After an initial wave of purchases starting in May 2010, the ECB intensified its bond-buying scheme in August 2011 (see figure 17.5), when market pressure on Spanish and Italian debt rose significantly with the escalation of the Eurozone crisis. Between May 2010 and September 2012, when SMP was replaced with the Outright Monetary Transactions (OMT) scheme, the ECB purchased a total of €210 billion in peripheral bonds on secondary markets, including half of Greece's outstanding obligations to foreign private creditors.[52] The result was to concentrate a large share of Greece's total outstanding debt on the ECB's balance sheet and to turn the central bank into Greece's single biggest bondholder in the short

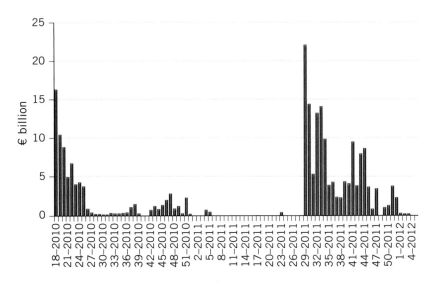

FIGURE 17.5. Weekly ECB bond purchases through SMP, May 2010 to Jan 2012.
*Source*: European Central Bank (2017).

term.[53] More importantly, SMP provided a source of demand—and hence an exit option—for private investors who could not otherwise reduce their exposure without taking significant losses.

Like the other ECB programs, SMP came under strict conditionality for the borrowing governments. As Trichet put it, "the first—and absolutely necessary—condition for success is that governments *accelerate* fiscal consolidation and are unwavering in their implementation of the tough measures that are indispensable."[54] Mario Draghi, who succeeded Trichet at the helm of the ECB in November 2011, later declared that "if the central bank were to intervene without any actions on the part of governments, without any conditionality, the intervention would not be effective and the Bank would lose its independence."[55] The implication of this insistence on conditionality was that ECB bond purchases could also be *withheld* if governments failed to meet the stated conditions, which is precisely what happened on a number of occasions during 2011, most importantly in November, when the Papandreou government in Greece and the Berlusconi government in Italy were brought to their knees by rising interest rate spreads after the European Central Bank temporarily suspended its bond-buying scheme to signal its displeasure over the inability of both governments to implement the demanded market reforms (and in Papandreou's case especially over his unexpected referendum announcement). As ECB Governing Council member Yves Mersch stated, "if we observe that our interventions are undermined by a lack of efforts by national governments then we have to pose

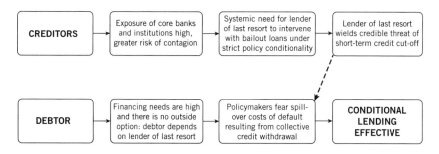

FIGURE 17.6. The second enforcement mechanism in Greece.

ourselves the problem of the incentive effect." When he was asked if this would involve withholding SMP, Mersch said: "If the ECB board reaches the conclusion that the conditions that led it to take a decision no longer exist, it is free to change that decision at any moment. We discuss this all the time."[56]

Combined, these three threats—the refusal to sign off on further loan disbursements by the Troika, the withdrawal of support for domestic banking systems, and the halting of its secondary market bond purchases—constituted the central bank's main stick in its dealings with peripheral debtors. At the same time, the ECB also held an important carrot, which it tellingly reserved for its dealings with private banks. When negotiations on a Greek debt restructuring with private sector involvement (PSI) got underway in 2011, the ECB decided "to compensate the damage . . . by introducing new measures in favor of the banking sector."[57] These took the form of two exceptional Long-Term Refinancing Operations (LTROs), allowing private banks to borrow an unlimited sum from the ECB at a fixed interest rate of 1 percent and with an unusually long three-year maturity. Both operations were heavily subscribed and allowed Eurozone banks to borrow over €1 trillion at negative real interest rates. LTRO constituted perhaps one of the clearest indications of the ECB's pro-creditor bias: while it only supported national governments under strict policy conditionality, threatening to cut off all external financing in the event of noncompliance, it simultaneously provided Eurozone banks with unlimited and unconditional liquidity at interest rates so low as to effectively constitute a free handout to private lenders, enabling them to engage in a lucrative carry trade between low-interest ECB loans and high-yielding peripheral debt instruments.

The most important effect of this cheap ECB liquidity was that it enabled banks in the periphery to increase their exposure to their own governments.[58] This in turn led to a repatriation of peripheral debt: as banks in the core reduced their exposure to the periphery, the ECB's interventions incentivized banks in the periphery to buy up their own governments' toxic bonds on secondary markets. This meant that, in the upcoming debt restructuring that was already being negotiated behind the scenes, Greece's private banks and pension funds were to be left holding the hot potato, while EU banks had already divested themselves of the majority of their holdings—a crucial point to which we will return in chapter 19, when we take a closer look at the 2012 debt restructuring.[59] For now, we can conclude that the second enforcement of conditional lending operated at full force in the first two years of the crisis, its effects enhanced by Greece's additional layer of dependence on the ECB for monetary policy and liquidity provision to its banks.

# EIGHTEEN

## The Establishment Digs In

B eyond the market discipline imposed by a highly concentrated international creditors' cartel and the Troika's conditional bailout loans, there was a third reason for Greece's continued compliance in the first years of its crisis: the eagerness with which the Greek political and financial establishment implemented the demanded austerity measures and kept servicing the foreign debt. Notwithstanding the inevitable frictions between Greek officials and the Troika, the fact remains that—apart from Papandreou's ill-fated referendum proposal and the shallow antimemorandum theatrics of Antonis Samaras while his rightwing New Democracy party was still in opposition—the Greek political establishment never truly defied its foreign lenders. Indeed, there was always a close level of collaboration between subsequent Greek governments and Troika officials, which was eased by the fact that Greece's growing dependence on credit and investment strengthened the hand of orthodox technocrats with close ties to the EU's financial establishment. Despite the cronyism and corruption of the Greek political elite, which was often criticized by European leaders from afar, the country's foreign creditors therefore had a powerful ally in the two establishment parties that had dominated the Greek political scene ever since the *metapolitefsi* period, or the transition to democracy in 1974. Both parties were closely intertwined with local business interests, meaning neither was willing to risk a suspension of payments on the government's debts.

To fully understand the logic of Greece's compliance in the first years of the crisis, we therefore need to analyze the domestic dynamics behind the country's decision to repay its debts. In this chapter, we will see how the state's growing dependence on credit strengthened the hand of the political and financial establishment in pursuing fiscal austerity and structural reform. The next chapter then takes a closer look at the 2012 debt restructuring and the outcomes of this first phase of the crisis, before we turn to the short-lived standoff between Syriza and the Troika in the first half of 2015.

## THE ENTANGLEMENT OF POLITICAL AND FINANCIAL ELITES

It is widely understood that the Greek political establishment has long been bound to a powerful elite constituency centered on a number of oligarchic clans with roots in shipping, construction, and banking—a phenomenon known as *diaploki* (διαπλοκή), or the "interweaving" of the public and private sectors. This phenomenon has historically endowed domestic elites with privileged access to financial policymaking, allowing them to act as a powerful force clamoring for full debt repayment. As the crisis took hold in 2010, local elites began to use their connections to the political class and their control over the media to champion the need for austerity, market liberalization, and the fire-sale privatization of state assets as a means of deflecting the burden of adjustment onto the rest of society. Just like Mexico's bankers' alliance and Argentina's *patria financiera*, a similar phenomenon can therefore be identified in Greece: the heterodox economist and later Greek finance minister Yanis Varoufakis has referred to it as an "establishment triangle" revolving around the political class, private bankers, and the financial technocrats at the Bank of Greece.[1] Elsewhere on the political spectrum, George Pagoulatos, who served as an advisor to the technocratic prime minister Lucas Papademos, makes a similar observation, pointing out how the country's banks have always been "run by prominent members of the political-economic elite."[2] Pagoulatos also stresses the fact that the bankers are powerful not just because of their personal connections to the political establishment; they are powerful because they fulfill "a crucial institutional role as intermediaries and distributors of developmental finance in the economy."[3] The deeper source of their power, in other words, is structural.

Moreover, just as Mexico and Argentina opened up to international capital under the structural adjustment programs of the 1980s and the influence of the Washington Consensus in the 1990s, so Greece underwent a neoliberal turn of its own under the center-left government of Prime Minister Costas Simitis, leader of the Panhellenic Socialist Movement (PASOK), around the turn of the century. In these early years of globalization, financialization, and European integration, the privileged position of the Greek banking establishment was further entrenched. As Fouskas and Dimoulas write, Prime Minister Simitis set out to create "a new type of social alliance, the 'social alliance of modernization,' gathered around the 'party of the stock exchange' and unified via a complex paralegal corruption network forming a new bipartisan consensus across the trembling [faultlines] of post-1974 Greek politics."[4] As a result, even if the two establishment parties alternated in office and competed fiercely on the electoral stage, the country's political reality after 1996 was thoroughly conditioned by the fact that both wings of the political establishment were structurally dependent on private credit to maintain their systems of patronage and their networks of clientelism. Euclid Tsakalotos, the Oxford-educated Marxist economist who took over from Varoufakis as Greece's finance minister in 2015, noted how "finance was central to both PASOK's and New Democracy's economic strategy." In fact, behind Simitis's vaunted "alliance of modernization" and the dominant two-party regime, "there was a growing symbiosis of financial and political power."[5] At the same time, as the Greek banks expanded their operations into Turkey and the Balkans and entrenched their ties with European finance after entry into the Eurozone, the Greek banking sector became deeply integrated into the continent's monetary and financial circuits and thus structurally bound up—through foreign ownership, shared investments, and other linkages like holding companies and subsidiaries—with some of the country's most important foreign creditors and trading partners. These structural ties ensured that the fate of Greece's banking oligarchy and domestic political elite became closely intertwined with the fate of European finance in general, providing a powerful "internal" incentive to honor the government's foreign obligations, maintain financial stability, and ensure Greece's continued membership of the Eurozone.

One of the most important elements binding Greek financiers to foreign lenders was the high *domestic* exposure to government debt, and the strong concentration of this debt among a small number of systemically important financial institutions: Greece's biggest banks and pension funds. EU stress tests showed that at the start of the crisis over €55 billion in Greek government bonds were held by domestic institutional investors, which given the small size of the Greek financial sector could be considered an astronomical amount.[6] Research undertaken by Marfin Investment Bank found that, in the spring of 2010, the holdings of the National Bank of Greece amounted to 88.6 of its investment portfolio; for Piraeus this share was 83 percent, for Eurobank 97.1 percent, for Postbank 98.5 percent, for Alpha Bank 87 percent, for the state-owned AteBank 75.6 percent, and for Emporiki Bank, then still owned by Crédit Agricole of France, 83.2 percent.[7] Since the top five commercial banks in Greece accounted for roughly 70 percent of the domestic liquidity market, the collapse of any one of these institutions as a result of a government default would have had far-reaching implications for private lending, leaving many domestic businesses and households unable to obtain credit.[8]

On top of this, as was briefly discussed in the previous section, something very significant happened as the crisis deepened in 2011: while banks in the core countries divested themselves of peripheral bonds through the ECB's Securities Markets Program, banks in the periphery stepped in to fill the void, borrowing cheaply through the ECB's Long-Term Refinancing Operations (LTRO) to purchase the high-yielding, high-risk bonds of their own governments, causing peripheral debt to partly migrate from the balance sheets of banks in the core towards the balance sheets of banks in the periphery itself—increasing domestic debt concentration and heightening overall financial vulnerability in these

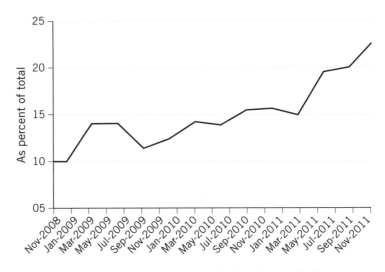

FIGURE 18.1. Share of Greek government bonds held by domestic banks, Nov. 2008 to Nov. 2011. *Source*: Bruegel database of sovereign bond holdings, developed by Merler and Pisani-Ferry (2012b).

countries. What this meant for Greece is that its debt was partly repatriated during the crisis: as inflows from abroad declined, Greek banks reduced their foreign investment and tapped into the ECB's LTRO to buy more of their own government's bonds (see figure 18.1).[9]

This experience appears to fit a broader pattern across the Eurozone periphery: the data show that "holdings of government debt by nonresidents have diminished in proportion for all the countries in trouble (Greece, Ireland, Portugal, Spain and to a lesser extent Italy), while more or less stable for France and the Netherlands, and increasing for Germany."[10] The obverse side of this development was the growing dependence of peripheral states on their own banking sectors—which, in Greece's case, also became increasingly concentrated at the crisis deepened, causing smaller banks to fail or be absorbed by bigger ones (see figure 18.2). A paper co-authored by some of the world's leading sovereign debt scholars explains how this process helped prevent a suspension of payments in the peripheral countries and, for a while at least, even forestalled an orderly renegotiation, as "any significant restructuring of the government's debt [would have led to] a domestic banking crisis," leaving officials exceedingly hesitant to inflict losses on private bondholders.[11]

For Greece, the outcome was a dynamic not unlike the one previously observed in Mexico and Argentina, where local bankers—in spite of the financial fragility of their firms—gained in political influence as the crisis deepened, at least in part because the government increasingly depended on highly concentrated domestic credit markets to refinance the *internal* debt. As in Mexico, where the foreign holding companies of Mexican banks acted as intermediaries for foreign bank syndicates, making it impossible to default on one without crippling the other, the Greek government was similarly constrained in its ability to pursue a selective default on German and French banks, since the cross-default clauses would have also affected the bonds held by its own banks.

This provided the Greek political and financial establishment with a strong incentive to accept the terms of the bailout as they were dictated by European lenders, even if this required major welfare losses for the general population and risked undermining popular and electoral support. The alternative—to default on all or part of the outstanding debt—would have likely led to a domestic banking collapse, with serious consequences for overall economic performance, at least in the short term. This observation helps explain why Greece kept servicing its debts even though it managed to establish a primary budget surplus by 2013, thereby removing its dependence on foreign creditors for the financing of current government expenditure. Clearly, it was not just the government's own credit access that Greek officials were worried about; the country's real Achilles heel was the state's dependence on the fragile domestic banking system. Again, this state dependence tended to increase the influence of those politicians and technocrats who maintained close ties to the domestic and international financial establishment.[12]

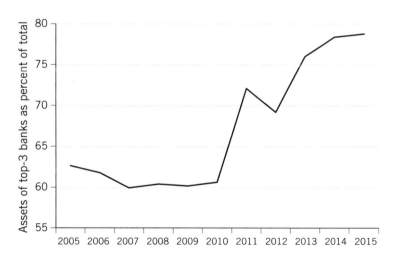

FIGURE 18.2. Bank concentration in Greece, 2005–2015. *Source*: Federal Reserve Bank of St. Louis (2017).

*Note*: Annual, not seasonally adjusted.

## THE STRENGTHENED POSITION OF THE "INTERNAL TROIKA"

Like Mexico and Argentina before it, Greece witnessed conflicting positions on how to deal with the country's enormous debt load, with some favoring full repayment and others favoring default. Unlike in Mexico and Argentina, however, those in favor of a suspension of payments did not find much support within the higher echelons of the establishment parties, which were under the sway of a broad elite consensus on the need for unflinching compliance. Out on the streets, hundreds of thousands of protesters demanded an end to austerity and an Argentina-style moratorium on the external debt, but of all the parties in parliament only the Communists and the still relatively marginal Coalition of the Radical Left (Syriza) were openly calling for such a unilateral default. Nevertheless, on a number of occasions, the extreme pressure exerted from below nearly pushed the country to the brink of a payment suspension anyway. Reflecting on the spectacular riots that broke out during the initial wave of antiausterity demonstrations in May 2010, Finance Minister Papaconstantinou relays the government's fears of a general popular insurrection: "This went beyond protesting against what were indeed harsh measures," he wrote in his personal memoirs. "It was wholesale rejection, a collapse of the political and social consensus formed since the end of the dictatorship in 1974. . . . For a while . . . there was a sense that the situation was now out of control, that we were close to a wholesale revolt, and a storming of parliament."[13]

After three bank employees, including a pregnant woman, died in a blaze following the firebombing of the Marfin Bank in downtown Athens, President Karolos Papoulias declared that "our country has reached the edge of the abyss."[14] The protests briefly subsided in the wake of the tragedy, but in the spring of 2011 another wave of mass demonstrations led to the weeks-long occupation of Syntagma Square in front of parliament and repeated clashes between protesters and police. Identifying the direct connection between the revolt on the Greek streets and the investor panic on the trading floors, the British journalist Paul Mason reflected that "Syntagma Square had become the frontline of the global financial system."[15] Nevertheless, despite the recurring mass demonstrations and the seemingly endless succession of violent clashes and general strikes, the establishment parties managed to cling to power and confine the popular indignation to the streets. As the state's dependence on credit increased, the establishment politicians who agreed with the Troika's austerity regime and who were adamant to avoid a default and Grexit at all costs even found their position strengthened, since they were seen to be most capable of fulfilling a bridging role to foreign lenders. Prime Minister George Papandreou, the Harvard-educated scion of a political dynasty that included two former prime ministers, always fell well within this clique. But as the antiausterity protests intensified over the course of 2011, a schism emerged between Papandreou and his new finance minister, Evangelos Venizelos, who made no secret of his ambitions to obtain the premiership for himself. After two years of mass protests, it was becoming clear that public trust in the embattled Papandreou—and in the political system more generally—had all but evaporated. By mid-2011, Greece had begun to eerily resemble the equally ungovernable Argentina of the previous decade. Amidst the political carnage, Venizelos began plotting the overthrow of his own party leader.

In September and October 2011, the Greek government was confronted with yet another wave of mass demonstrations. During a national holiday celebrating the rejection of Mussolini's ultimatum on October 28, 1940, a throng of protesters spontaneously disturbed a military parade in Thessaloniki, marching through the procession of soldiers towards the stand of dignitaries and forcing the president of the republic to make a hasty and humiliating retreat. The media widely reported the incident as the ultimate degradation of the national honor and a sign that the legitimacy of the post-1974 democratic order had sunk to previously unimaginable lows. The episode marked a highly symbolic turning point.[16] Papaconstantinou recalls that "we were facing an increasingly hostile political environment, economic disruption and social unrest. . . . We felt increasingly under siege at home and abroad."[17] It was in this context that Papandreou finally announced his plan to hold a referendum on the second bailout. As a government aide confided, "George has decided to go over everyone's head and take it to the people. To do otherwise would have meant death to the political system and economy by a thousand slices. No country could go on with strikes and protests on such a scale."[18] Papandreou himself later explained that "everybody was saying that the government [were] traitors. I realized the situation was getting out of control."[19]

In hindsight, the prime minister's decision to call a referendum can be seen, in a way, as analogous to the bombshell announcement by President López Portillo of Mexico in late 1982 that he would be nationalizing the country's banking sector: both were desperate gambles for resurrection by center-left leaders who were rapidly losing control over their respective parties and who felt compelled to make a dramatic last stand to save their political legacy. And just like López Portillo's fateful bank nationalization, Papandreou's referendum announcement ended up backfiring disastrously. Four days later the idea had been shelved, and within a week Papandreou had ceased to be prime minister. Remarkably, however, Papandreou's resignation did not give way to chaos and default, as De la Rúa's resignation had in Argentina after the riots of December 2001. It actually had the opposite effect: like López Portillo's last stand in Mexico, it led to a defeat of the center-left and the ultimate victory of the bankers' alliance. Papandreou's democratic brinkmanship, far from helping to build national unity around the reform and stabilization effort, as he had hoped, ended up isolating the prime minister within his own party. Kouvelakis notes how "domestically, Papandreou's gesture—followed swiftly by direct pressure from European lenders—indirectly strengthened the hand of the 'Internal Troika' faction of PASOK, who immediately rejected the idea of a referendum and instead called for a government of 'national unity.' "[20]

Finance Minister Venizelos, who gained the lenders' preference over Papandreou, found his position strengthened as well. When the two PASOK leaders were summoned to the G20 meeting in Cannes, those present noted that the prime minister "visibly deflated as the fight continued. As he fatigued, Mr Venizelos took up the battle, a sign many saw as the sudden realization by the Greek prime minister that he had become a spent political force—and Mr Venizelos, who had long coveted the premiership, was moving to exploit the change in circumstances."[21] European Commission President Manuel Barroso approached Venizelos at the gathering and agreed with the finance minister that "we have to kill this referendum."[22] As soon as this alliance between European leaders and PASOK's "internal Troika" was forged, Papandreou lost control over his own governing party. In discussions with aides, it was later revealed, Barroso personally handpicked former ECB vice-president Lucas Papademos to head a technocratic government of national salvation with the backing of Samaras' New Democracy and with Venizelos himself as finance minister and PASOK's new leader.[23] As Stathis Kouvelakis concludes, "thus the way was paved for the formation of a government headed by the banker Papademos—the natural incarnation of a ruling bloc that is entirely dominated by the interests of European finance."[24]

The rise of Papademos himself closely mirrored that of the technocratic governments in Latin America in previous decades. Like the banker-friendly De la Madrid in Mexico, Papademos was seen as ideologically close to the international financial establishment and uniquely capable of enhancing the credibility of Greece's commitment to its foreign obligations, and hence seeing to the state's structural dependence on credit.[25] In a telling sign of his loyalties, one of the first public statements by the new unelected prime minister was an opinion piece in the *Financial Times* in which he rejected the idea of a 50 percent haircut of Greece's privately held debt; a much more extreme position than that of the German government, whose proposal for a 50 percent write-down eventually prevailed in the debt restructuring of March 2012, by which time German banks had already reduced the bulk of their exposure.[26] Tellingly, Papademos' article stressed the spillover costs that a debt restructuring was likely to have on Greek banks, on investor confidence, and on the wider economy: "the adverse consequences for Greece of 'hard', involuntary debt restructuring and a sovereign default," he wrote, "are not limited to the costs of recapitalizing domestic banks and supporting pension funds. The effects on confidence, the liquidity of the Greek banking system and the real economy are likely to be substantial, though difficult to predict and quantify."[27]

Apart from strengthening the hand of the "internal Troika" and giving rise to an unprecedented coalition government under technocratic leadership, Greece's

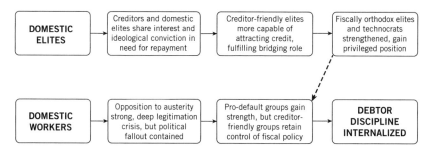

FIGURE 18.3. The third enforcement mechanism in Greece.

continued dependence on foreign creditors also strengthened the position of the governor of the Bank of Greece, George Provopoulos, who was himself a former CEO of Emporiki Bank and later Piraeus Bank. A *New York Times* report observed that "few hold as much power within their own country as [George Provopoulos], who has played a crucial role in keeping Greece out of bankruptcy and in the euro zone."[28] The waxing influence of the central bank within the establishment triangle was a direct outcome of its control over the flow of credit through the national economy and its role in keeping Greece's commercial banks—the state's principal source of private credit after 2011—afloat. "For decades," the *New York Times* article noted, "political influence in this country has been a direct function of a politician's ability to borrow and spend, with local banks, as the main buyers of Greek government bonds, acting as the primary facilitators. Under an austerity regime, such an approach is no longer possible. And as governments have come and gone . . . , the power of the Bank of Greece's governor has only solidified."

Thus, in the first two years of the crisis, the establishment triangle identified by Varoufakis, far from being weakened by the government's precarious fiscal position or the financial fragility of the Greek banks, actually managed to solidify its stronghold on financial policymaking through its capacity to fulfill a bridging role to foreign lenders and keep providing their fiscally distressed national government with much-needed short-term credit lines. The third enforcement mechanism, in short, was relatively effective. But while this helped internalize debtor discipline into the Greek state apparatus, it did not succeed in returning the country to solvency. If Greece was to avert a disorderly default, further emergency loans would be needed. Eventually, in October 2011, after more than half a year of painstaking negotiations, the EU and IMF finally agreed to a second €130 billion bailout, as part of a deal that also involved debt restructuring with private sector involvement (PSI), special funds earmarked for a Greek bank recapitalization, and a partial debt buyback. Beyond this, the

EU also upgraded its own financial defenses through the creation of the European Stability Mechanism, a permanent firewall for the monetary union with a total lending capacity of €500 billion. Having reinforced the resilience of the wider Eurozone and installed a creditor-friendly technocrat at the helm in Athens, European leaders finally felt at ease to begin discussing the technical specificities of what was to become the largest debt restructuring in history.

# NINETEEN

## The Socialization of Greece's Debt

In March 2012, Greece opened a tender for a voluntary bond exchange in which its private bondholders could swap their securities for a variety of re-denominated debt instruments carrying lower interest rates and longer maturities, but also significant up-front sweeteners and better protections from a possible future default. In agreeing to this negotiated debt restructuring, bondholders accepted a 53.5 percent haircut on the face value of their claims. By the time the tender closed, 97 percent of Greece's private creditors had exchanged €197 billion worth in debt, earning Greece net debt relief of around €107 billion, or a little over 50 percent of GDP—although it simultaneously took on an additional €130 billion in new loans from the Troika.[1] European officials and private bankers presented the private sector involvement as a major sacrifice to help Greece back on its feet and to allow it to grow again. But as in the case of the Brady deal of the late 1980s and the megaswap in Argentina in 2001, the total debt reduction Greece obtained in the restructuring turned out to be limited, while the EU banks that had overextended themselves on Greek bonds in the lead-up to the crisis managed to largely deflect the costs of PSI onto Greek taxpayers and small bondholders.

This chapter briefly presents the lead-up to and outcome of the 2012 debt restructuring, showing how the debt swap was specifically designed to spare the biggest private bondholders—EU banks—while leaving Greek taxpayers and pensioners to foot the bill for the subsequent hit taken by their own banks and pension funds. Most importantly, for the purposes of the next chapter on Syriza's standoff with the Troika in 2015, we will see how the debt restructuring of 2012 led to a radical shift in Greece's debt profile and creditor composition: from bonds held by private EU banks to official-sector loans from the EU member states and the IMF. By the end of PSI, in short, both the adjustment costs for the crisis and the risk of a future default had been fully socialized.

## THE TRANSFORMATION OF GREECE'S CREDITOR COMPOSITION

The first thing to note in relation to PSI is that Greece's debt profile and creditor composition had already begun to change very rapidly between the onset of the crisis in late 2009 and the conclusion of the debt restructuring in early 2012, with European banks using the time that had been bought with the two successive bailouts to sell the majority of their Greek government bonds, boost their overall capital ratios, and mark the remaining debt to market.[2] As a study for the IMF's Independent Evaluation Office notes, "expectations of future debt restructuring were widely held by private investors. . . . [B]y the time the PSI was finally implemented in spring 2012, most large foreign banks had sold their stakes."[3] Figure 19.1 reveals the sharp reduction in foreign banks' exposures to Greece over the course of the crisis, leaving them much less exposed by the time PSI came around. Table 19.1 illustrates how German banks were particularly successful at reducing their exposure, dropping their total claims from around €43 billion in late 2009 to €6.3 billion in early 2012, although other EU banks also greatly reduced their exposure, mostly by selling them to Greek banks or the ECB.[4] As John Kay of the *Financial Times* noted, "when Europe's leaders claim the continent is now better placed to withstand a crisis they mean only that this accumulation [of Greek bonds] has been largely transferred from the

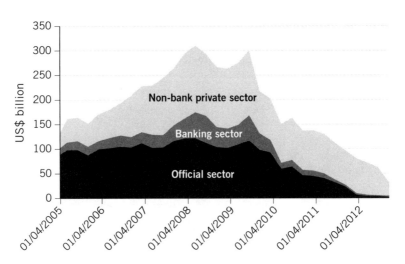

FIGURE 19.1. Foreign banks' consolidated exposures to Greece, 2005–2013.
*Source*: Bank for International Settlements (2017); idea for graph derived from Wyplosz and Sgherri (2016).
*Note*: Total claims outstanding by sector, on ultimate risk basis.

TABLE 19.1.
Reduction of foreign claims on Greece between start of crisis and PSI (in $ millions)

|  | 2009 Q3 | 2011 Q3 | 2012 Q1 | Reduction (%) |
|---|---|---|---|---|
| *France* | 78,571 | 47,899 | 41,725 | 47% |
| *Germany* | 43,236 | 18,636 | 6,319 | 85% |
| *UK* | 12,492 | 11,546 | 8,503 | 32% |
| *US* | 19,448 | 6,007 | 3,897 | 80% |

*Source*: Thompson (2015); Bank for International Settlements, International Banking Statistics.

private to the public sector, mainly the European Central Bank."[5] In chapter 17 we already saw how the ECB had been buying up peripheral junk bonds from European commercial banks through its Securities Market Program (SMP) ever since May 2010, enabling major bondholders like Commerzbank and Crédit Agricole to dump their exposure onto the central bank for much better money than they could possibly have obtained on the secondary bond market. After enabling these banks to offload their toxic assets onto the central bank's balance sheet at above-market prices, the ECB then insisted that it could not participate in PSI. The perverse outcome of SMP was thus to greatly reduce the share of Greece's total outstanding debt that was eligible for PSI, thereby diminishing the overall relief that Greece obtained in the restructuring.

The debt that could not be dumped on the ECB or sold to Greek banks was eventually marked to market.[6] Bloomberg data revealed that by early 2012 the biggest European banks had already written down their Greek bonds by over 70 percent. PSI, which would bring about an estimated 74 percent loss on the net present value of these bonds, forced bondholders to subtract only a little bit more, leaving "Europe's largest lenders and insurers . . . likely to accede to the Greek debt swap because they've already written down their sovereign holdings and want to avert the risk of a default."[7] Even the French banks, which had been most heavily exposed at the start of the crisis and which still carried much larger exposure than their German counterparts in early 2012, had already written down their holdings of Greek bonds to 25 percent of nominal value, rendering the haircut involved in PSI insignificant in terms of the banks' overall profits. For BNP Paribas, for instance, the losses were estimated to be in the range of €300 million—a relatively small amount for a bank that raked in €6.5 billion in profits in 2012, up from €6 billion in 2010, making it Europe's most profitable financial institution that year. For other big lenders like Deutsche Bank and Commerzbank exposures were similarly small. Analysis by Kepler Capital Markets confirmed that "European banks have had a long time to prepare and many already have the losses behind them."[8] Moreover, it should be noted that these write-downs did not involve real capital destruction but simply a downward adjustment of prospective profits.[9] To the banks, then, the idea of a debt restructuring was actually starting to look like an increasingly attractive option as it would provide them with a convenient exit from the crisis.

It was in this context that the main representatives of the creditors' cartel—the Institute of International Finance (IIF) and a steering committee made up of some of Europe's largest banks—finally agreed to start negotiations with the Greek government and the European creditors on the exact shape of PSI. The IIF's leading role in the negotiations was particularly notable because the banking lobby, headed by Deutsche Bank CEO Joseph Ackermann, had been formed during the Mexican debt crisis of the 1980s to defend the interests of the commercial banks and to coordinate creditor action in rescheduling negotiations with Latin American governments. Together with the bondholder steering committee, the IIF now helped Greece's private creditors present a unified front in its talks with Greek and European officials. A report by the international law firm Allen & Overy notes that this "was a remarkable innovation since it is believed that there has been no major steering committee for bondholders since perhaps the nineteenth century, although there have been steering committees for bank lenders."[10] Moreover, the steering committee explicitly "took [its] cue from the last great steering committees of international banks established in the 1980s to deal with the bankruptcy of Mexico in 1982 and many other emerging countries."[11] A direct connection can therefore be established between the highly concentrated bank lending and coordinated creditor action in Mexico in 1982, and the concentrated form of bond finance and coordinated creditor action in Greece in 2012. In both cases, the banks managed to prevent a unilateral default, buy crucial time to reduce their exposure and build up their capital reserves, and finally coordinate an orderly creditor-led restructuring that helped them divest of their toxic assets without having to accept significant losses. Moreover, in both cases, the coordinating role of the IIF and the bondholder steering committee enabled international banks not only to delay the inevitable debt restructuring as long as possible, but also to extract significant concessions from the debtor and official creditors alike. Needless to say, the experience in both of these cases contrasts sharply to the highly dispersed bond holdings and poorly coordinated creditor action in Argentina after mid-2001, which ended in unilateral default and a coercive debtor-led restructuring.[12]

Taken together, these developments helped pave the way for a remarkable shift in the Eurozone's position on debt restructuring. The German government and its allies in Austria, Finland, and the Netherlands—which had long been among the most vocal opponents of debt relief—suddenly reversed course and began to openly push for private sector involvement. "Europe is prepared," Finland's finance minister Alexander Stubb declared in early 2012. "A hell of a lot better prepared than it was on May 9, 2010—and a hell of a lot better prepared than it was last year."[13] Greece's official lenders had now reached the conclusion that a voluntary debt write-down no longer constituted an existential threat to the European banking system. Moreover, beside reducing their exposure, increasing their capital ratios, and marking their remaining bonds to market, most banks had also bought sufficient credit-default swaps to insure themselves against the eventuality of a Greek credit event, meaning the costs of the restructuring would instead be borne by the systemically less important and politically less influential insurance companies that had sold these swaps.[14]

And so the PSI restructuring was finally allowed to go ahead in March 2012, providing the misleading impression that private creditors had now shared in the burden of adjustment for the crisis. The reality was very different. After the deal was concluded, one senior Eurozone official acknowledged that the bondholders "got a good deal. They get nearly 50 percent back. Given the alternative, that's good."[15] In fact, the restructuring turned out to be a boon for many of the original investors. For one thing, Greece's lenders were offered an "exceptionally large cash sweetener, in the form of highly rated EFSF notes. . . . Regardless of what happened in Greece, participating investors would have this 'bird in hand.'"[16] Moreover, their freshly restructured bonds were now denominated under English as opposed to Greek law, making it impossible for future Greek governments to retrofit different conditions onto these claims or denounce the debts by passing a repudiation bill through parliament—a legal insurance policy that seemed particularly attractive in light of an increasingly likely electoral victory for the radical left Syriza party, which at that point still openly called for a unilateral debt moratorium.

## WINNERS AND LOSERS FROM THE PSI DEBT RESTRUCTURING

The big losers from PSI were the Greek pension funds, which according to the *Financial Times* took a €22 billion hit on their holdings of government bonds—losses corresponding to around one-tenth of GDP.[17] The Greek banks, of course, were also badly damaged by the haircut. By the time the debt restructuring came around, Greek banks constituted the single largest group of private creditors to the Greek government and took a massive €37.7 billion hit on their holdings. Unlike the average Greek pensioner, however, Greek bankers received ample compensation for these losses. The second EU-IMF bailout specifically earmarked €48.2 billion for the purpose of recapitalizing and stabilizing the domestic banking system. The money that was used was subsequently added to the country's foreign debt, thus reducing the net relief obtained in the restructuring by €37.3 billion (the remaining €10.9 billion was never used).

The result was to shift the costs of adjustment from private shoulders into public hands: while PSI reduced the state's obligations to domestic banks, the subsequent recapitalization *increased* Greece's debts to the Troika, imposing a much heavier burden on taxpayers and pensioners just to make their domestic banks whole again.[18] Despite the fact that the Greek state thus ended up covering 90 percent of the total capital injection into its own banking system, it never asserted ownership rights over the banks; the bank owners themselves only put up 10 percent of the injected funds, but were left untouched and remained in full control of their firms. And that was not all. As a report in the *New York Times* noted:

> The banks' top executives are poised to potentially strike it rich. The plan developed by the Greek government and its international creditors to recapitalize the country's banks involves an unusual twist as stock offerings go: the new shares in the banks will give investors free and potentially lucrative warrants that will entitle them to buy many more shares in the future at a predetermined price.[19]

Given the rising stock valuation of the banks post-PSI, these warrants constituted yet another official-sector handout to private bankers.[20] The perverse incentives generated in the process also allowed speculative investors like John Paulson, the U.S. hedge fund billionaire, to pick up Greek bank shares at greatly deflated prices with a view to collecting easy profits a few years out, once the banks' stock valuations had risen again following the pre-announced bank recapitalization—a development that triggered an anomalous stock exchange bubble in bank shares between mid-2012 and late 2014, even as the Greek economy was mired in depression. As another report in the *New York Times* noted, "the biggest winners [of the second bailout with PSI] were hedge funds, which pocketed higher profits than many had expected, in yet another Greek bailout financed by European taxpayers."[21]

In stark contrast to this preferential treatment for international and domestic financiers, the country's pension funds and the 15,000 retail investors who held government bonds were never compensated for their losses.[22] In fact, the Eurogroup explicitly vetoed the Greek government's plan to exempt small bondholders from the haircut.[23] PSI, in other words, far from constituting a gesture of benevolence by Greece's lenders, mostly served to deflect the costs of the crisis from private lenders onto Greek taxpayers and pensioners, endowing the former with ample opportunities for financial speculation while raising taxes and imposing an endless succession of tax hikes, budget cuts, and pension reductions on the latter. As a final affront, the Troika then pushed the Greek government to further consolidate its already highly concentrated banking system, with the country's biggest banks absorbing the smaller ones until there were only four systemic lenders left: Piraeus, Alpha, Eurobank, and National Bank of Greece.[24] Together, the Big Four now accounted for 90 percent of market share between them, leaving future Greek governments—including Syriza's—much more exposed to concentrated financial power at home.

The most consequential result of the Troika's approach to crisis management, however, was the complete transformation of Greece's debt profile and creditor composition. In fact, while the pre-PSI period had already witnessed a marked shift in the ownership structure of Greek bonds, the post-PSI transformation

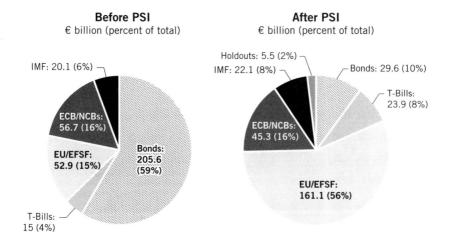

FIGURE 19.2. Greece's public debt profile pre- and post-PSI. *Source*: Wyplosz and Sgherri (2016).

*Note reproduced from source*: "Greek government and government-guaranteed debt owed to private creditors [striped] and official creditors [solid]. 'ECB/NCBs' debt refers to ECB SMP holdings as well as holdings by national central banks in the euro area. 'EU/EFSF' loans include the GLF loans as well as the EFSF loans. 'T-bills' are privately held short-term debt instruments. 'Bonds' include also guaranteed debt issued by banks" (Wyplosz and Sgherri 2016).

was so stark that some of the world's leading sovereign debt scholars felt compelled to point out that "we are not aware of any other similarly drastic case of 'credit migration' from private into official hands in the history of sovereign debt."[25] While in 2010 nearly 80 percent of Greece's government debt had been in foreign private hands, by late 2012 this was only 20 percent, with most of the remainder now held in foreign *official* hands—marking a perfect inversion of the country's creditor composition in the space of just two years (see figure 19.2). As in Argentina's megaswap, institutional investors once again managed to divest from their junk bonds by dumping their exposure onto third parties in a voluntary debt restructuring. This time, however, the debt was not dispersed among hundreds of thousands of overseas retail investors, but *socialized* by the rest of the Eurozone.[26]

The process through which this socialization occurred was twofold, going back to the official-sector intervention mentioned earlier in this chapter. First, the lion's share of the two EU-IMF bailouts was spent on foreign debt servicing, which automatically led to a gradual replacement of Greece's privately held foreign debt with officially held foreign debt. Since the Greek government did not regain market access by the date foreseen in the original EU-IMF program, it simply kept accumulating new obligations to the Troika in order to repay its maturing debts to European banks. Research by the European School of

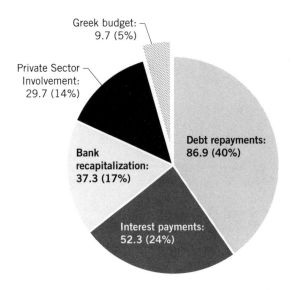

In € billion (percent of total)

Greek budget:
9.7 (5%)

Private Sector
Involvement:
29.7 (14%)

Debt repayments:
86.9 (40%)

Bank
recapitalization:
37.3 (17%)

Interest payments:
52.3 (24%)

FIGURE 19.3. Where did the Greek bailout money go? *Source*: Rocholl and Stahmer (2016).

*Note*: Use of funds from first and second EU/IMF/ECB bailout program.

Management and Technology in Berlin has found that only 5 percent of the total international bailout funds actually went to Greek government expenditure; the remaining 95 percent went straight back to the country's bondholders, including domestic banks, which needed to be compensated for PSI, amounting to a de facto bailout of private creditors in all but name (see figure 19.3).[27]

The second process through which Greece's sovereign debt was socialized was the ECB's securities markets program (SMP), which, as we saw before, provided European banks with an outlet to dump their peripheral junk bonds, causing the respective obligations to migrate from the balance sheets of some of the continent's biggest private financial institutions to the balance sheet of the European Central Bank.

The outcome of all this was arguably even more consequential than Argentina's infamous megaswap of mid-2001: not only did private bondholders manage to shift the burden of adjustment onto the people of Greece and the risks of a future default or debt write-down onto European taxpayers, thereby avoiding foreseeable future losses; they also found a way to subtly obscure that fact by pretending they had now shared in the costs of the crisis by providing voluntary debt relief.[28] The fact that official-sector creditors actively assisted in furthering and obscuring this socialization of Greece's debts eventually unleashed a storm of criticism—not just from the usual suspects on the left, but from within the IMF as well. As the Fund's own auditors concluded in a highly critical review of the IMF's role in the management of the crisis:

> Private creditors were able to significantly reduce their exposure. . . . There was a large-scale substitution from privately-held to publicly-held debt. Part of this was by design—program financing was to be used to repay maturing bonds in 2010 and 2011—but the shift was intensified by market access not being regained in 2012, as well as by SMP. Purchases of Greek government bonds under SMP created rigidities when debt was restructured as a result of the decision to exclude [ECB] bond holdings from the PSI.[29]

Taking into account all the above, it would not be an exaggeration to claim that PSI was deliberately delayed and specifically designed with the interests of the major European bondholders in mind. Lee Buchheit, the sovereign debt lawyer who helped deliver PSI on Greece's behalf, would later tell Yanis Varoufakis that, when the Papademos government first approached him about the restructuring, he was skeptical and insisted they should demand a better deal than the one the Germans were offering. But Greek officials insisted that they would go along with the German plan. "It was a terrible thing to have done to the people of Greece," Buchheit confessed to Varoufakis, "and an excellent opportunity to cut your debt was wasted, with my participation."[30] The net debt reduction from PSI turned out to be negligible. As William Cline, a senior fellow at the Peterson Institute for International Economics who also studied Mexico's Brady deal in 1989, points out, "the overall effect of the large PSI of April 2012 was . . . to reduce total Greek debt by slightly less than one-fourth. It is perhaps not surprising that once the country had plunged into the insolvency mode, a debt reduction by only one-fourth would not have been sufficient to reestablish solvency decisively."[31] Others, including a Goldman Sachs analyst, concluded that "the PSI component of the deal was little more than symbolic, and provided no meaningful debt relief."[32] Moreover, the socialization of Greece's debt by the EU meant that if the country was to ever default on its debts in the future, the costs would now no longer fall on the banks that had taken the risks of lending to Greece in the first place, but on the European taxpayers who—mostly without being aware of it—had already bailed them out.[33]

A few months after the completion of Greece's debt restructuring and the subsequent parliamentary elections that brought the right-wing New Democracy party of Antonis Samaras to power, market pressures on Spain and Italy led to renewed fears of a possible peripheral default and Eurozone meltdown. It was at this point that the ECB finally stepped into the breach to calm the restive European bond market once and for all. On July 26, 2012, Mario Draghi made his famous pledge that the central bank would do "whatever it takes to preserve the euro"—a statement that was followed up on September 6 by a Governing Council decision to terminate SMP and replace it with an even more ambitious program called Outright Monetary Transactions (OMT). The latter never even needed to be activated: the sheer force of Draghi's statement, backed by the financial firewall of the European Stability Mechanism and possible resort to OMT, was enough to pacify the markets and restore at least a semblance of normalcy to the Eurozone—even as the Greek economy continued to implode under the Troika-mandated austerity regime. By that point, however, the bankers had already won.

## HIGHLY UNEQUAL DISTRIBUTION OF ADJUSTMENT COSTS

Given the strong procreditor bias in the management of the crisis, it should not come as a surprise that the distribution of adjustment costs between Greece and its lenders ended up being heavily skewed towards the former, with ordinary Greeks shouldering most of the burden. We have already seen how private bondholders escaped from PSI unscathed and how a number of hedge funds made windfall profits from the deal. To this we can now add the highly asymmetric distribution of adjustment costs between Greece and its *official* creditors. The IMF, for one, earned some €3.5 billion in interest payments and fees from the first two Greek bailouts, amounting to 37 percent of the Fund's total net income between 2010 and 2015 and making up for 79 percent of its internal expenses during this period.[34] The European Central Bank also made €7.8 billion in profits between 2012 and 2016 from the Greek bonds it acquired through SMP; profits it promised at various stages in the crisis to return to the Greek government, but which at the time of writing it still held on to.[35] The German government, for its part, turned out handsome gains as well. In addition to an estimated €1.34 billion in interest gained from Greece's EU/EFSF bailout loans, as well as the SMP profits collected by the Bundesbank, Germany also benefited spectacularly from the investor flight to safety. A study by the Halle Institute for Economic Research has found that the German government saved over €100 billion—or 3 percent of GDP—on interest payments between 2010 and 2015, with most of these reduced expenditures attributable "Greece flight" alone. The authors specify that "these benefits . . . tend to be larger than the expenses, even in a scenario where Greece does not repay any of its debts."[36]

Beyond this asymmetric international distribution, the burden of adjustment *within* Greece was also heavily skewed towards workers, pensioners, the youth, small businesses, the unemployed, and the poor—as opposed to the owners of the big banks and shipping companies, or wealthy elites more generally.[37] Just as in past debt crises in the Global South, the adjustment process centered almost exclusively on aggressive wage, pension, and welfare cuts, regressive tax hikes, public sector layoffs, and the privatization of public assets— all of which disproportionately harmed lower- and middle-income households that depend on income from wages or welfare spending for their livelihoods. To provide just one particularly striking example: the poorest Greeks witnessed a 333.7 percent increase in their tax burden between 2009 and 2013, contrasting sharply to the 9 percent increase for the tax-evading upper decile.[38] At the same time, the extreme austerity measures imposed by the creditors aggravated the economic contraction and contributed to unprecedented unemployment rates of over 25 percent (more than 60 percent for the young), while average wages were cut by over a quarter. Although the labor share of income had increased from 34 percent to 35.7 percent between 2008 and 2010, it dropped back to 32.3 percent in 2013, while the absolute amount of wages fell by over a quarter, from €82.4 billion in 2008 to €59.3 billion in 2013. The average income of the poorest fell by an astonishing 45.2 percent over this period.[39] Aside from the Balkan wars and the traumatic economic transition of the postcommunist states in the early 1990s, such extreme relative depravation is probably unprecedented in postwar Europe. Indeed, it is difficult to think of any other case in which popular living standards in an advanced capitalist country have collapsed so dramatically outside of wartime.

The sacrifices of Greek workers, pensioners, and the unemployed contrast sharply to the preferential treatment and financial privileges of the country's wealthy elite, most of whom were able to evacuate their wealth from Greek banks by depositing it in Swiss bank accounts or routing their incomes via various tax havens like Cyprus, Luxembourg, and the Netherlands, avoiding both taxes and a possible post-Grexit devaluation in the process. In the end, perhaps the most damning conclusions about the management of the Greek debt crisis were those reached by the IMF itself in its 2013 review of the first bailout program. The report noted that "the actual decline in GDP was so much greater than anticipated [because] the fiscal multipliers were too low"; "the burden of adjustment was not shared evenly across society"; "ownership of the program was limited"; "the program was based on a number of ambitious assumptions"; "the risks were explicitly flagged"; and "ex-ante debt restructuring was not attempted."[40] The most remarkable admission in the IMF report is that there was actually an alternative at the outset of the crisis—upfront debt relief—but that this was not pursued because of political pressure exerted by the European governments whose banks carried the largest exposures. IMF officials recognized that "many commentators considered debt restructuring to be inevitable," but this was simply not an option to the Fund's European member states.[41] And so, the IMF's auditors noted, "with debt restructuring off the table, Greece faced two alternatives: default immediately, or move ahead as if debt restructuring could be avoided. The latter strategy was adopted, but in the event, this only served to delay debt restructuring and allowed many private creditors to escape."[42]

In the end, it turns out that much of the suffering was in fact unnecessary. "Earlier debt restructuring," the IMF concludes, "could have eased the burden of adjustment on Greece and contributed to a less dramatic contraction in output."[43] A counterfactual analysis by the Hans Böckler Stiftung's Macroeconomic Policy

Institute in Germany found that "austerity explains almost the entire collapse of Greek GDP," and suggests that "in the absence of austerity, the Greek economy would have entered a prolonged period of stagnation, rather than a depression," as up to 80 percent of the contraction would have been avoided.[44] Although European officials and the ECB were loath to admit it themselves, an official inquiry by the European Parliament on the Troika's role in the management of the crisis recognized the undue procreditor bias in the successive Eurozone bailout programs, noting that "the protection of bondholders was seen as an EU necessity in the interests of financial stability." The European Parliament's Budget Committee reached a similar conclusion, adding that "we have in fact transferred the wild card from private banks to governments."[45]

We can therefore conclude that, despite the superficial differences, especially in terms of the idiosyncrasies of Greece's Eurozone membership, the management of the Greek debt crisis shows some striking underlying similarities to the management of previous debt crises in the Global South. Indeed, both in terms of the type of policies pursued, the creditor-friendly outcomes of crisis management, and the underlying enforcement mechanisms of debtor discipline, the official response to the threat of a Greek default resembled a number of patterns that had first been established in Mexico during its lost decade of the 1980s (see table 19.2). Both countries suffered a "lost decade" of depressed growth and escalating poverty and unemployment as a result of the wrenching budget cuts, tax hikes, and structural adjustments imposed by foreign lenders. But there was also one very important difference: unlike Mexico in the 1980s, in Greece popular opposition to the continued imposition of structural adjustment from abroad was fierce, leading to a citizens' revolt that shook the political system to its very core and eventually upended the two-party status quo that had characterized Greek politics since the transition to democracy in the 1970s. After five long years of deepening economic depression, growing political disaffection, and mounting social discontent, the start of 2015 finally witnessed the ouster of the old establishment parties and the formation of a left-led antiausterity coalition—raising concerns among creditors that Greece might go Argentina's way after all and defy its foreign lenders. It is to this standoff between the radical left Syriza government and its European creditors that we turn next.

TABLE 19.2.
Comparison between the debt crises in Mexico and Greece

| Mexico in the 1980s | Greece before 2012 |
|---|---|
| **Syndicated bank lending:** | **Concentrated bond finance:** |
| Debt concentration high | Debt concentration high |
| Interlocked lending structure | Interlocked lending structure |
| Creditor coordination easy | Creditor coordination easy |
| Credible threat of credit cut-off | Credible threat of credit cut-off |
| *Market discipline strong* | *Market discipline strong* |
| | |
| **Active U.S/IMF intervention:** | **Active EU/IMF intervention:** |
| Sizeable international bailout loans | Record international bailout loans |
| Coordinated roll-overs to keep debtors solvent | Coordinated delay of PSI enables debt socialization |
| IMF monitoring/supervision of debtor policies | Troika monitoring/supervision of debtor policies |
| Policy conditionality enforces discipline | Policy conditionality enforces discipline |
| *Effective conditional lending* | *Effective conditional lending* |
| | |
| **Limited debtor autonomy:** | **Limited debtor autonomy:** |
| Growing dependence on foreign credit and capital | Growing dependence on credit and ECB liquidity |
| Bridging role for domestic elites and technocrats | Bridging role for domestic elites and technocrats |
| Popular opposition forestalled through cooptation | Powerful opposition, but political fallout contained |
| Strengthened bankers' alliance | Strengthened establishment triangle |
| *Internalization of debtor discipline* | *Internalization of debtor discipline* |
| | |
| **OUTCOME:** | **OUTCOME:** |
| *No unilateral default* | *No unilateral default* |
| Room for maneuver constrained | Room for maneuver constrained |
| Mexico develops into "model debtor" | Greece pursues harshest fiscal adjustment in history |
| Creditors only restructure debt after divesting | Creditors only restructure debt after divesting |
| Highly unequal distribution of adjustment costs | Highly unequal distribution of adjustment costs |

# TWENTY

## The Defeat of the Athens Spring

While the two subsequent bailouts, the aggressive ECB intervention, and the voluntary debt restructuring of 2012 had done little to resolve Greece's seemingly interminable debt crisis, they did remove the existential threat the country had once posed to the European banking system, causing market fears to subside and Greece to temporarily disappear from the international newspaper headlines. But even as the world seemed to briefly forget about the country's travails and turned its attention to what appeared to be more pressing concerns, a massive time bomb was softly ticking away below the surface of Greek politics. By shifting the entire burden of adjustment onto Greek society, the creditors had successfully transformed a financial and economic crisis into a full-blown social and political crisis—one that would soon produce the first in a series of many electoral upsets across the Western world, ousting the centrist establishment parties from office and bringing to power a radical left coalition that was at least nominally committed to ending austerity and renegotiating Greece's obligations to its European creditors. The standoff between the Syriza-led government and its foreign lenders finally culminated in the momentous referendum of July 5, 2015, in which an overwhelming majority of Greeks voted to reject the creditors' terms for further bailout financing. Yet just a week later, Prime Minister Alexis Tsipras found himself back in Brussels capitulating to his European counterparts and signing up to a third bailout whose terms were widely considered to be even worse than those he had just called on his own people to reject.

This dramatic turn of events raises what is by now a familiar question: why did the Syriza-led government not simply suspend payments and pursue an aggressive debt restructuring, as Argentina had in the wake of its own anti-austerity revolt in December 2001? The short-lived standoff between Syriza and the Troika in the first half of 2015 presents a unique test of the structural power hypothesis, precisely because it concerns a case in which the stated preferences of foreign lenders visibly clashed with the stated preferences of the debtor country, allowing us to examine in relatively straightforward terms how one side was able to impose its will on the other.[1] This chapter argues that the ultimate reasons for Greece's continued compliance in 2015 must be sought in a combination of two factors: first and foremost, the extremely hostile response and overwhelming structural power of the country's foreign lenders, operating through the two international enforcement mechanisms spelled out in previous chapters; and second, the internal divisions within the Syriza government, which gradually led to a reassertion of the third enforcement mechanism of internalized debtor discipline following its partial and temporary breakdown after Syriza's ascent to government.

In the end, the profound asymmetry in the international balance of power and the diminished autonomy on the part of the Greek government heightened a number of pre-existing contradictions within Syriza's political program and strengthened the position of those Syriza officials who were seen to be close to the domestic financial establishment and who were in favor of a more conciliatory line towards foreign lenders, culminating in Tsipras's stunning *kolotoumba*—Greek for "somersault," or political volte-face—after the referendum. As we will see, however, this outcome was by no means predetermined or inevitable; rather, it was the result of fierce internal power struggles, which after months of political contestation were finally settled in favor of Syriza's business-friendly party leadership.

## THE LEAD-UP: THE THIRD MECHANISM BREAKS DOWN

In chapter 18 we already saw how the first years of the crisis had witnessed the gradual internalization of debtor discipline into the Greek state apparatus through the strengthening of domestic elites and technocrats with close ties to the European financial establishment and a shared interest in full repayment. As in Argentina, however, this process was contradictory in nature. On the one hand, the state's growing dependence on private credit endowed the "establishment triangle" with an important bridging role towards foreign creditors and a privileged position in economic policymaking; on the other, a deepening legitimation crisis and intense popular opposition to further adjustment and reform weakened it from below. In the first years of the crisis, the former mechanism was strong enough to marginalize domestic opposition to austerity and keep the antagonism confined to the streets. But as the economy languished and social discontent intensified, the countervailing latter dynamic—the strong popular resistance emerging from below—eventually gained the upper hand in electoral politics as well.

The antiausterity movement clearly had economic logic on its side. By 2014, it was clear to most international observers, including many IMF officials, that the two successive bailouts had only made Greece's debt problems worse, contributing to an economic contraction that was even more extreme than that experienced by the United States during the Great Depression, with all the attendant social and political consequences (see figures 20.1, 20.2, 20.3, and 20.4). Ashoka Mody, who earlier served as the deputy director of the IMF's research and European departments, noted that "almost everyone now agrees that pushing Greece to pay its private creditors was a bad idea. The required fiscal austerity was simply too great, causing the economy to collapse."[2] Similarly, in a critical report on the IMF's handling of the crisis, the Fund's own Independent Evaluation Office concluded that the two subsequent bailouts of 2010 and 2012 "ultimately failed to restore Greece to financial and macroeconomic stability":

> In 2013, real GDP was 77 percent of the 2009 level, and the rate of unemployment rose from 9.6 percent to 27.5 percent over the same period [60 percent for young people]. The initial goal of placing the debt-to-GDP ratio on a declining trend from 2014 was not achieved. Investor confidence was shattered and deposit withdrawals accelerated amid a political and social crisis.[3]

Eventually, as the social consequences of the internal devaluation became unbearable, the Greek people rapidly lost trust in the political establishment, and the perceived legitimacy of democratic institutions—already feeble for a variety of historical and institutional reasons—all but evaporated (see figure 20.5). The enormous antiausterity demonstrations and the succession of general strikes that had rocked the country in 2010–2012 were an early expression of this escalating crisis of representation. But even if the mass mobilizations eventually subsided after the parliamentary elections of 2012, the incidence of popular protest remained strikingly high by international standards. Official data from the Ministry of Public Order put the total number of protest actions and demonstrations between 2010 and 2014 at 20,210. As a report in the establishment newspaper *Kathimerini* pointed out, "this translates into 5,100 protests per year, or approximately 14 marches and rallies on a daily basis, including Sundays."[4] As in Argentina, the country's burgeoning social movements were able to mobilize a broad cross-section of society against the external imposition of structural adjustment and the collusion of domestic elites with foreign lenders. Developing innovative solidarity networks and democratic forms of local self-organization outside of established political institutions, activists and ordinary citizens led a powerful grassroots response to the social consequences of repeated wage cuts, welfare retrenchment, and mass unemployment.[5]

Although this budding citizens' revolt did not immediately find a reflection in government policy, over time the widespread social discontent and the immense popular pressure from below translated into the collapse of public support for the two establishment parties, which fell from a combined 77 percent of the vote in 2009 to 32 percent in the first election round of 2012, and which continued to fall from there. The wholesale implosion of the center-left PASOK, in particular, irreversibly tainted by its implication in both bailout programs, paved the way for the Coalition of the Radical Left, or Syriza, to firmly establish itself as the country's main opposition party and Greece's next

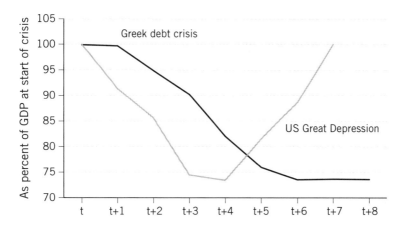

FIGURE 20.1. Comparison of Greece's output loss (2007–2015) vs. U.S. Great Depression (1929–1936). *Source*: International Monetary Fund (2017b).

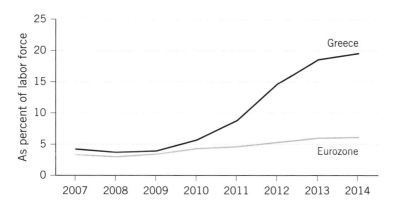

FIGURE 20.2. Greece's long-term unemployment rate compared to the Eurozone's, 2007–2014. *Source*: Eurostat.

government-in-waiting. It was a remarkable transformation. Having emerged from a broad range of socialist and (ex-)communist currents in the wake of the antiglobalization protests of the late 1990s and early 2000s, Syriza was still a small and marginal left-wing formation when the crisis first struck in 2010. By mid-2012, however, they had already overtaken the once-dominant PASOK to become the main force on the Greek left.

The elections of 2012 were to become a barometer of simmering antiausterity sentiment, and the response on the part of the Troika and domestic elites

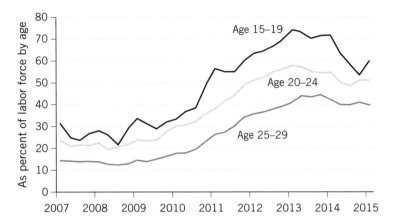

FIGURE 20.3. Greece's youth unemployment rate (by age group), 2007–2015.
Source: Hellenic Statistical Authority.

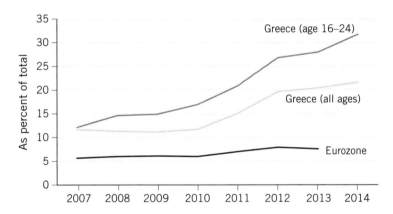

FIGURE 20.4. Share of the population experiencing severe deprivation, 2007–2014.
Source: Eurostat.

to the threat of a Syriza victory would reveal the basic contours of the eventual containment strategy they would pursue in 2015. In June 2012, having ended the inconclusive first round of voting neck-and-neck with New Democracy, the leftists were leading the polls up to mere days before the second round of voting. The European creditors and the domestic establishment answered this prospect of a leftist government with a campaign of fear, warning voters that a Syriza victory would inevitably lead to a domestic banking collapse and a forced exit from the Eurozone. These predictions subsequently fed into a self-fulfilling prophecy that propelled depositors to begin withdrawing their savings and send them abroad *en masse*. As bank deposits fell to €159 billion, demand for paper money trebled, causing total cash in circulation to reach €48 billion, or 24.8 percent of GDP—an extraordinary figure in light of the 4–7 percent average for developed economies. George Provopoulos, the central bank director, later said that "in a matter of a few days, a full-blown banking crisis could have erupted," while a Troika official claimed that "there would have been complete and immediate panic" in the event of a Syriza victory.[6]

In another interview, Provopoulos stated that "if this phenomenon had gone on, there would have been no reason but to go into a full bank run. That would have resulted in the exit of the country from the euro area."[7] The former central banker and technocratic prime minister Papademos said he was so concerned about the possible repercussions of a Syriza victory "that he remained in his office on the Sunday night of the elections to prepare for the market shock."[8] In the end, the sense of financial panic generated by increasingly apocalyptic media reports helped New Democracy catch up with Syriza and narrowly defeat the leftists in the repeat elections. The conservatives eventually formed an uneasy pro-establishment coalition with their historic archrivals PASOK, causing the risk of default to recede and depositor fears to subside.

In hindsight, the events of June 2012 served as a harbinger of the bank run that would eventually undermine Syriza's short-lived antiausterity experiment in 2015. The anticipatory spillover effects surrounding the elections of 2012 also had a more immediate consequence, however, convincing Tsipras of the need to moderate Syriza's policy proposals. Up until its narrow last-minute defeat by New Democracy, the leftists had consistently called for a unilateral moratorium on external debt service followed by a citizens' audit of the national debt

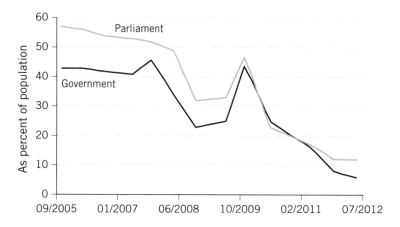

FIGURE 20.5. Public trust in Greece's political institutions, 2005–2012. *Source*: Exadaktylos and Zahariadis (2013); Eurobarometer.

and a repudiation of all government obligations found to be acquired through odious or illegal means. But after witnessing the incipient bank run triggered by the anticipation of a possible Syriza victory, Tsipras and his key advisers began to tone down this prodefault rhetoric, much as Lula had in Brazil, in an attempt to win over middle-class voters who remained fearful of the spillover costs of default and the risk of a potential Grexit in particular.

This experience thus demonstrates how the structural power of foreign creditors can exert its influence even over *opposition* parties, compelling them to fall in line with the expectation of uninterrupted debt servicing. With its vague and inconsistent new pledge to "end austerity" and "renegotiate the debt" while at the same time avoiding unilateral action and staying inside the Euro-zone, Syriza managed to gain growing electoral support and finally won the snap elections of January 25, 2015, forming a national-popular antiausterity coalition with the far-right Independent Greeks. Its contradictory new strategy on the external debt, however, also laid the trap that would eventually ensnare the young prime minister: in trying to shore up domestic support, Tsipras had greatly raised popular expectations of a meaningful break with the creditors' austerity regime, while simultaneously foreclosing the only option—a credible and demonstrated preparedness to pursue unilateral action—that could have en-dowed him with some real leverage in his negotiations with the lenders.

Although he proceeded to adopt the fierce anticreditor rhetoric of the Kirchners, regularly railing against the death of democracy in the Eurozone and Greece's degraded status as a European "debt colony," Tsipras therefore did not possess anything like the substantive bargaining power that Kirchner had enjoyed in his negotiations with private bondholders between 2003 and 2005. First of all, Kirchner had acceded to power two years *after* Argentina's origi-nal default and exit from the convertibility regime, meaning he no longer had to contend with major bond payments, while the painful short-term spillover costs of the payment suspension and subsequent currency devaluation had al-ready begun to subside and given way to a rapid economic recovery, greatly expanding the government's room for maneuver in the process. Syriza, by con-trast, faced a particularly onerous repayment schedule in 2015, and Tsipras seemed to be concerned about being held personally responsible for the socio-economic and monetary fallout of a failure to meet these payments, making him much more susceptible to the sway of his creditors.[9] Second, Kirchner had enjoyed a much more favorable international economic environment while in power, including ample foreign-exchange earnings owing to the commodity boom, self-sufficiency in the production of key commodities like food, as well as an outside option for external financing—all of which greatly reduced his de-pendence on foreign trade, global capital markets, and international financial institutions. Greece, by contrast, was acutely dependent on key imports, had no major export industries to speak of, and did not have any foreign-exchange reserves, which in light of its exclusion from global capital markets rendered it much more dependent on its official-sector creditors for external financing to be able to keep its hospitals and power plants up and running. Third, and most important, Greece did not possess its own independent currency or central bank. Unlike Kirchner in Argentina, the Syriza government faced the crucial challenge of Greece's dependence on a "foreign" entity—the European Central Bank—to maintain its payments system and keep its fragile domestic banks afloat; a key factor to which we will return later in this chapter.

Finally, while Kirchner had squared off against a dispersed panoply of small bondholders and an IMF that had been greatly weakened by its overexposure to emerging market debt and strong U.S. opposition to further international bailouts, Greece actually faced a highly coordinated cartel of official-sector creditors that, despite their internal differences, managed to present a relatively unified front through the institutions formerly known as the Troika. Since these institutions now collectively held 85 percent of Greece's total outstanding debt, any leverage the country's government might have had in 2010 or 2011—when Europe's banks were still dangerously overexposed and likely to collapse in the event of a Greek default—had now effectively evaporated. By the time Syriza came to power in January 2015, the big European banks carried only negligible exposures to Greece. As the head of the German banking association BdB put it, "the credit exposure of German banks in Greece is low. That's why, should it come to insolvency for Greece, the direct effects on German banks could be overcome." Consolidated exposure to Greek banks and companies was also down sharply compared to 2011. An emailed report by J. P Morgan showed that the cutting of links to Greek units and the systematic dumping of Greek bonds on the ECB left Europe's biggest banks with "limited risk to Greece." The total amount owed to the major European banks like BNP Paribas, Crédit Agricole, Société Générale, Deutsche Bank, Commerzbank, and ING—which had once been among Greece's main creditors—were said to range between 0.1 and 0.9 percent of these banks' total outstanding loans; "very limited" and "immaterial" for the banks' profits, according to Bloomberg.[10] European banks, in short, no longer had a real stake in the outcome of the crisis.

All of this radically changed the nature of the game. By the time Syriza acceded to government, the struggle over the burden of adjustment was no longer a question of how much European bankers would have to pay for the excessive lending they had engaged in during the lead-up to the crisis, but how much European *taxpayers* should be made to pay to alleviate the burden on their Greek counterparts—or, as the narrative was generally construed in the creditor countries, how much the supposedly "industrious" and "parsimonious" northerners would have to cough up for the *Schnapps und Frauen* of their "profligate" and "tax-evading" southern neighbors.[11] By early 2015, the U.S. government and IMF were starting to openly suggest that the Eurozone should pursue a more equitable distribution of adjustment costs, but Germany and its allies would have none of it, fiercely resisting any form of debt relief. The reasons for the lenders' intransigence were clearly political. Domestically, the creditor governments feared the electoral repercussions of being made to look soft on Greece after insisting for over five years that "every last cent" of the successive Greek bailouts would be coming back to taxpayers. Internationally, they feared that acceding to Syriza's demands would embolden and empower antiausterity forces elsewhere in the Eurozone periphery, especially Podemos in Spain and the Movimento Cinque Stelle in Italy. In sum, debt forgiveness was not on the agenda; Tsipras and his comrades could not be allowed to overturn the regime of fiscal control that had been so painstakingly devised over the past half-decade of European crisis management. If further antiausterity rebellions were to be prevented or contained, Tsipras would have to be crushed and humiliated.[12] And so it came to pass.

## THE STAND-OFF: EXCLUDED FROM FOREIGN FINANCING

Although Tsipras's government explicitly rejected unilateral action on the debt, preferring instead to raid the public sector—requisitioning the last-remaining cash reserves of pension funds, hospitals, schools, universities, and municipalities—to remain current on its foreign obligations, it did pursue a number of symbolic antiausterity measures during its first days in office, like reinstating the laid-off cleaners of the finance ministry and refusing to meet Troika officials on Greek soil. Official creditors responded to these unilateral moves by immediately declaring the government in violation of the conditions spelled out in the memorandum of understanding, disqualifying it from the last loan tranche of the second bailout and leaving it at the mercy of the ECB's Governing Council for further liquidity support to its fragile domestic banking system—the government's real Achilles' heel. Anticipating correctly that Tsipras would seek to avoid an outright payment suspension for fear of having Greek banks cut off from ECB support and thereby being forced out of the Eurozone, the creditors knew they could simply play for time and bleed the leftists dry ahead of the massive €6.7 billion euro bond payments that were falling due to the ECB over the summer. In pursuing this approach, Greece's official lenders made astute use of the fact that the first two enforcement mechanisms of debtor discipline remained fully operative throughout 2015, while the third mechanism remained partly operative and could eventually be reconsolidated after Greece had been sufficiently starved of funds and enough external pressure had been brought to bear on the fledgling Syriza government.

The effects of the first mechanism of market discipline kicked in even before the leftists had properly assumed office. Although Greece had been locked out of international capital markets ever since its first bailout in early 2010, the Samaras government had managed to float a small and mostly symbolic number of bonds in April 2014. Investors charged an exorbitant interest rate, and

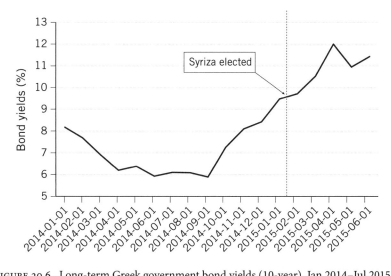

FIGURE 20.6. Long-term Greek government bond yields (10-year), Jan 2014–Jul 2015. *Source*: Federal Reserve Bank of St. Louis (2017).

the sale was mostly intended to bolster Samaras' questionable claim to have restored the government's solvency and investor confidence in Greece; yet the bond auction did raise the prospect—however remote—of an eventual exit from the bailout program and a return to the markets. Later in the year, however, as Samaras plummeted in the polls and as it became clear that he would not be able to muster the parliamentary supermajority required to nominate a new presidential candidate in early-2015, making new elections inevitable, Greece's borrowing costs skyrocketed in anticipation of a likely Syriza victory, and any prospects of a return to the markets evaporated overnight (see figure 20.6). Completely locked out of international capital markets, a future Syriza government would have to either pivot around on its own political axis and convince foreign investors and official creditors of its commitment to austerity and reform, or somehow manage to survive without any external financing.

The prospect of a radical left government increased market pressures in other areas as well. Most importantly, deposit flight and capital flight returned with a vengeance in the last weeks of 2014 and the first weeks of 2015 (see figures 20.7 and 20.8). Some €12 billion was withdrawn from the banks in January alone, causing total deposits to fall to below €150 billion.[13] Meanwhile, domestic businesses and elites began to rapidly divest in anticipation of the negative economic spillover costs of a prolonged standoff with foreign creditors. A report in *The Guardian* noted that "Greek investors, led by shipowners and other industrialists, have stepped up transfers of funds. One insider said bankers were being instructed to make multimillion-euro transfers daily."[14] Economist

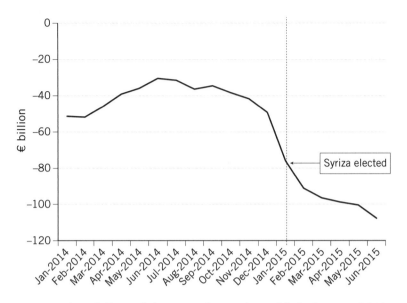

FIGURE 20.7. Greece's Target2 balance as indicator of capital flight, Jan 2014–Jul 2015.
*Source*: Steinkamp and Westermann (2017).

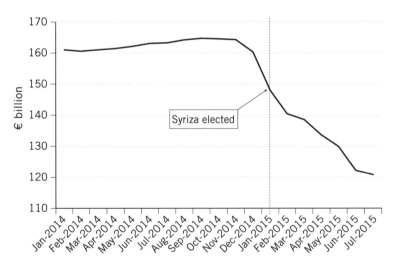

FIGURE 20.8. Total corporate and household deposits in Greek banks, Jan 2014–Jul 2015.
*Source*: European Central Bank (2017).

Theodore Pelagidis relayed that "the rich and affluent have been telling their private bankers to transfer funds, and that reflects the mounting concern over how Syriza will behave after the election."[15]

As a result of the rapid fall in corporate and household deposits, Greece's four systemic banks were forced to re-apply for emergency liquidity assistance (ELA) from the Greek central bank, with a senior banker in Athens explaining that ELA "is seen as a buffer against a growing liquidity squeeze on the banks, caused by political uncertainty over the election outcome."[16] During the week of the elections Alpha, Piraeus, Eurobank, and National Bank each lost over 20 percent in market capitalization. "This is a massacre," another Athens banker said. "Markets are panicking. . . . They're trying to preempt a crisis on banks' liquidity. They know the crisis will be centered around the banks."[17]

And so it was. The moment Syriza was elected, the bank jog intensified, and the stock market lost a further 41.5 percent in the first quarter alone, with bank shares leading the downward spiral. By April, total bank deposits had fallen to €133.7 billion; their lowest level in a decade, even below the previous nadir reached in 2011–2012. All of this rendered the Syriza-led government acutely vulnerable to a withdrawal of Troika loans and ECB liquidity support; a fact that Alexis Tsipras appeared to be strangely oblivious to, but the European lenders were clearly well-aware of.[18] It was in this context of growing state dependence on European financing that the second mechanism kicked in with full force, as the creditors simultaneously strangled Greece's leftists along four different dimensions. First, the Eurogroup responded to Syriza's defiance by immediately withholding the last €7 billion credit tranche of the 2012 bailout, while the ECB also withheld the €2 billion in retained profits that it had made from the Greek bonds it acquired through SMP, even though it had previously agreed to return this sum to the Greek government. The IMF continued to withhold its disbursements as well. In doing so, the three arms of the Troika robbed the Tsipras government of the external financing it needed in order to meet its exceptionally onerous repayment schedule for 2015 (see figure 20.9), with a total sum of €17 billion falling due over the course of the year and a series of large ECB payments coming up in July and August in particular—obligations the government would never be able to honor without the disbursement of the last tranche of the second bailout. The withholding of these funds therefore raised the prospect of a disorderly default on the country's biggest and most powerful creditors.[19]

Second, the ECB excluded Greece from its expanded assets purchases, or quantitative easing program (QE), which would see the central bank buy up to €60 billion in securities a month on secondary markets. Given the prohibitive borrowing costs it faced, the Greek government acutely depended on the inclusion of its bonds in QE to depress interest rates and allow for an eventual return to the markets. The ECB, however, announced that inclusion would depend on the government's compliance with the terms of the second bailout, with

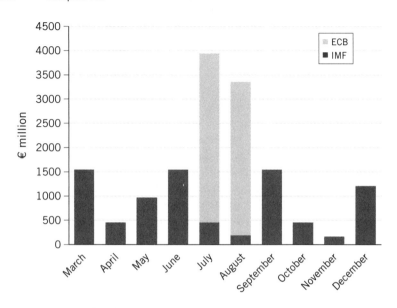

FIGURE 20.9. Greece's official-sector repayment schedule for 2015. *Source*: Varoufakis (2017).

Mario Draghi stating that "there are obviously some conditions before we can buy Greek bonds."[20] Exclusion from QE thus served as an additional disciplining mechanism in the hands of the ECB Governing Council, just as exclusion from SMP had during an earlier stage of the crisis. Perhaps even more importantly, however, the fact that the ECB did begin to buy up the bonds of *other* peripheral borrowers through QE helped to build up the Eurozone's defenses and insulated countries like Spain and Portugal from possible contagion. "QE had been hugely unpopular with conservatives and most notably in Germany," Adam Tooze notes. "But it was behind the shield of Draghi's QE that they were able to lay siege to Athens without fear of greater destabilization. They could prioritize the fight against political contagion without having to worry about the financial kind."[21]

Third, to further compound the pressure on the Greek government's liquidity, the ECB banned Greek banks from buying their own government's T-bills (short-term IOUs that are crucial for a government's ability to maintain current expenditure and roll over maturing short-term obligations). Supposedly on the grounds that these T-bills had become too risky now that investor demand had dried up in the wake of Syriza's election, the ECB's decision effectively served to cut the government off from its main source of short-term credit. While Draghi claimed that the decision was a purely technical matter, made in accordance with the ECB's own rules and mandate, this treatment of the Syriza government contrasted sharply to the central bank's treatment of the previous Samaras government, which was actually granted an *increase* in its T-bill limit from €15 billion to €18.3 billion after it was elected.[22] Varoufakis argues that, "by reversing the direction of causality, [Draghi] created a legal weapon against us. . . . The reason demand [for T-bills] dried up was the anticipation, fueled by leaks from within the ECB, that the ECB would squeeze our government's liquidity, thus bringing Greece to the verge of bankruptcy."[23]

Finally, in its most momentous decision of all, the ECB then announced that it would no longer be accepting Greek government bonds as collateral for access to the central bank's discount window, thereby forcing Greece's private banks to turn to the national central bank for emergency liquidity assistance (ELA) instead. Because the ECB retains control over the maximum amount that national central banks can provide under this procedure (the so-called ELA ceiling), its Governing Council "could use this control to exert significant pressure on the Greek government in its negotiations with the Troika."[24] As Benjamin Braun notes in a critical Transparency International report on the ECB's role in the management of the Greek crisis, "the peculiar architecture of the monetary and financial system of the euro area means that whoever calls the shots on ELA . . . is calling the shots on the euro-area membership of the country in question. No other central bank in the world holds that power."[25] As the standoff between Syriza and the Troika intensified, the ECB displayed its willingness to wield this structural power with strategic intent, squeezing the amount of emergency financing available to Greek banks by surgically raising the ELA ceiling—providing just enough support to keep them going from week to week. This drip-feed strategy of "liquidity asphyxiation," as Varoufakis called it, constantly left the threat of an ECB-provoked banking collapse hanging over the head of the Syriza government like a Sword of Damocles. After all, a simple refusal to increase the ELA ceiling next time around would instantly set in motion a self-reinforcing bank run that could end up with Greece being forced out of the Eurozone; an outcome Tsipras had explicitly and repeatedly pledged to avoid.

The combined effect of these four maneuvers—the withholding of the Troika's last loan tranche and the ECB's SMP profits, the exclusion from QE, the limit on T-bill purchases by Greek banks, and the liquidity asphyxiation through ELA—was to further increase market pressures on the Syriza government, showing how the first and second enforcement mechanisms became deeply intertwined over the course of 2015. "In short," Varoufakis summarizes the Troika's logic, "we shall squeeze you so much and so publicly that investors will pull out of Greece, depositors will accelerate their bank run, and your government will suffocate"—resulting in crippling economic spillover costs, aimed at bringing the leftists to their knees.[26] Despite the defiant moves of its first days in office, then, the Troika managed to easily force Syriza into its first capitulation by February 20, when the government signed a preliminary agreement that would extend the second bailout program to June 30 and allow a slight increase in the government's T-bill limit, but without the lenders disbursing the remaining loan tranche or the ECB raising the ELA ceiling. The agreement was furthermore made conditional on Greece taking a cooperative stance towards its creditors, with the government pledging "to refrain from any roll-back of measures and unilateral changes to the policies and structural reforms that would negatively impact fiscal targets, economic recovery or financial stability, as assessed by the institutions." The Dutch finance minister and Eurogroup chairman, Jeroen Dijsselbloem, noted that "the biggest driver" behind the deal—which did not offer any concessions on debt relief, privatizations, or fiscal surpluses, as Tsipras had hoped—were "fears that Greece might experience a full-blown bank run."[27] Michala Marcussen, head of economics at Société Générale bank, noted that "Greece is being kept on an incredibly tight leash," and stated that the Eurozone's refusal to disburse further credit or to provide additional liquidity was "clearly intended to keep Greece under pressure and keep things moving forward in the negotiations."[28] This pressure was kept up over the next months, as Eurozone finance ministers systematically refused to give in to Greek demands for leniency during their lengthy Eurogroup sessions. By June, the government had practically depleted all public-sector cash reserves and a disorderly default on the IMF and ECB seemed inevitable. Faced with the unyielding stance of his counterparts and the unwillingness of a large part of his own party to agree to his creditors' demands, Tsipras eventually opted for a cataclysmic last stand. Days before a critical June 30 deadline, when the second bailout was set to expire and a major (partially delayed) IMF payment was falling due, the negotiations collapsed—finally causing the crisis to come to a head.

In the early hours of June 27, Tsipras announced a referendum on the terms of the creditors' final offer. The economic consequences were nothing short of dramatic. Two-year bond yields shot up 14 percentage points to 34 percent and the slow-motion bank jog that, with the ECB's acquiescence, had been slowly gaining steam for months turned into a full-blown ATM run overnight.[29] As lines formed in front of cash machines and banks across the country rapidly ran out of bills, a wholesale financial implosion now seemed imminent. The next day, in a final confirmation that it was willing to aggressively use its control over the supply of emergency liquidity as a political weapon, the ECB refused to raise the ELA ceiling. Draghi himself denied that there were political motivations behind this controversial maneuver, reiterating that "the ECB is a rules-based institution"—but the figures belied an important shift in the central bank's approach towards the leftist government. While the ECB had provided almost €110 billion in emergency liquidity assistance to Greek banks to stem the bank jog under the technocratic Papademos government in 2012, it actually capped this amount at €86.8 billion under the Tsipras government by June 28, 2015, even though the banks' needs were even more pressing this time around (figure 20.10 shows how total central bank funding to Greek banks was

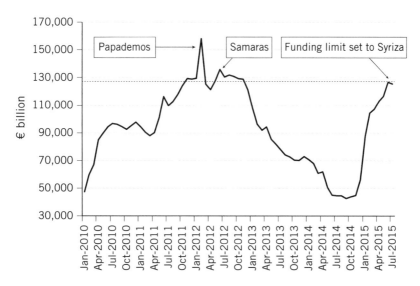

FIGURE 20.10. Central bank funding (including ELA) to Greek banks, Jan 2010–Jul 2015. *Source*: Bank of Greece (2017), aggregated balance sheet MFIs.

significantly lower under Syriza than it had been under Samaras and especially Papademos).[30] To many observers, the political overtones of this decision were self-evident. As one senior international banker put it, "they are squeezing them on everything, it's part of a system to suffocate them, to make them realize the end is coming, to realize it is time to get on their knees."[31] In a matter of hours, the government was forced to declare a bank holiday, shut down the stock exchange, and impose far-reaching capital controls, including an ATM withdrawal limit of €60 per day and an outright ban on bank transfers abroad. On June 30, the second bailout program expired, and Greece missed a €1.5 billion payment to the IMF, becoming the first developed country ever to go into arrears on the Fund.[32]

The wholesale cutoff from foreign financing unleashed debilitating economic spillover costs, as a result of which trade, production, and credit circulation effectively ground to a halt. The head of the Hellenic Chamber of Commerce stated that "there is no system in place for Greek companies to transfer money abroad. Our lifeblood has been shut off. People are depleting their stocks. We are going to start seeing shortages of meat by the end of the week. . . . The ferry operators are demanding cash up front to bring in fuel and supplies."[33] With firms unable to pay their foreign suppliers, imports dropped, and domestic production stalled. The Purchasing Managers' Index (PMI), a key indicator of the health of the manufacturing sector, fell from 46.9 to 30.2 in July (its lowest point on record) while new orders fell from 43.2 to 17.9.[34] An economist at Markit, the private firm compiling PMI data, explained that "factories faced a record drop in new orders and were often unable to acquire the inputs they needed, particularly from abroad, as bank closures and capital restrictions badly hampered normal business activity."[35] While Greece had been projected to emerge from its depression in 2015, the European Commission estimated that it would now face a GDP contraction of up to 4 percent as a result of the capital controls and the collapse in business confidence.[36] Cut off from foreign credit and liquidity, the Greek economy underwent a massive seizure.

This was the dramatic backdrop against which voters were asked to give their verdict on the Troika's terms for further emergency financing. With the government calling on voters to reject the creditors' ultimatum and with the polls showing the referendum result to be poised on a knife's edge, it suddenly seemed very plausible that Greece might default on its summer payments to the ECB and come crashing out of the Eurozone. It was under these circumstances that the third enforcement mechanism, which had partially broken down with the leftists' ascent to government, began to reassert itself with a vengeance. To understand why, we now have to take a closer look at Syriza's complex internal party politics and its internecine struggles over the appropriate course of action to be taken in the face of imminent financial meltdown.

## THE RIFT: SYRIZA'S INTERNAL CONFLICTS ON THE DEBT QUESTION

In truth, although Syriza's rise to power had certainly disturbed the creditors' relatively stable form of indirect rule in Greece, the third enforcement mechanism of internalized debtor discipline had never fully broken down. Despite the radical change in government, large parts of the financial bureaucracy either remained ideologically aligned with proestablishment forces or had already been put under the de facto control of the creditors themselves. The Bank of Greece, for one, was still headed by Samaras' former finance minister Yannis Stournaras, who had been appointed to the position by the previous administration in what some saw as a deliberate attempt to obstruct a future Syriza government by maintaining a powerful foothold inside the state-finance nexus. Meanwhile, as part of the conditions for the second bailout, the administration of key elements of the finance ministry—including its tax office, its statistics office and the bank bailout authority—had been transferred directly to the Troika.[37]

Even the elements of the state within the government's own remit were subject to intense proestablishment pressure from within. The new Syriza ministers bitterly complained that career bureaucrats inside their ministries, aligned through nepotistic arrangements and clientelistic networks with the old establishment parties, regularly refused to follow their orders, or withheld crucial information and resources from Syriza officials, leaving the government blind-sided and ineffective in the face of a chaotic and highly uncertain political and economic environment. Combined with the external pressure exerted by for-eign creditors through the first two enforcement mechanisms, the establish-ment's bureaucratic bridgehead inside the state apparatus greatly reduced the government's room for maneuver and—as we will see—gradually strengthened the position of those officials inside the governing party who favored a more conciliatory approach to foreign lenders and domestic elites. Both the Troika and the Greek oligarchs were acutely aware of the internal divisions within Syriza, and strategically made use of them by embracing the shell-shocked Tsipras, who they saw as willing to compromise, while pressuring him to ditch the more con-frontational Varoufakis and the left-wing elements inside his own party.[38] As Va-roufakis himself writes in his memoirs of the crisis, "our government's election had broken the [establishment] triangle and wounded its machinery. The Troika now had to divide our government in order to reassert its rule."[39]

These divide-and-rule efforts were eased by the fact that the ruling party itself was already deeply divided within. As in Mexico in the early days of 1982, there were conflicting positions inside the government on how to respond to the creditors' demands. On the one hand, as the standoff intensified and the do-mestic banking crisis deepened, a more business-friendly and careerist faction inside Syriza—headed by the powerful deputy prime minister Yannis Dragasa-kis and an influential group of close ministerial aides, including Tsipras's child-hood friend and closest confidant, Nikos Pappas—started pushing for a strategy of appeasement in an anxious bid to unlock the remaining funds from the pre-vious bailout and avoid a disorderly default and Grexit. Within leftist circles in Greece, it was widely rumored that the excommunist Dragasakis, through his personal connections with the old *nomenklatura* and new economic elites of the Eastern European countries, had developed close ties to Greek bankers and businessmen, who aggressively expanded into the region following the collapse of the Soviet Union.[40] Together with George Stathakis, the party's other main economist, Dragasakis represented what could be considered the "right wing" of Syriza. According to central committee member Stathis Kouvelakis, this fac-tion, which was close to Tsipras, "developed their own distinctive approaches to the economic issues, which were systematically different from the decisions of party congresses or the official position of the party."[41] Thanks to his close ties to the business world and his creditor-friendly stance on the debt, "the Greek eco-nomic establishment considered Dragasakis a point-man in Syriza they could trust."[42] Dragasakis thus came to fulfill a crucial bridging role between the new Syriza-led government and the financial establishment.

This powerful right-wing faction inside the party squared off against a siz-able internal opposition revolving around the Left Platform, led by Energy Minister Panagiotis Lafazanis, which controlled about a third of the party and favored a radical rupture with foreign creditors, a unilateral default on the external debt, and an exit from the Eurozone. As the standoff with the Troika intensified after the initial agreement of February 20, a number of prominent Syriza officials and MPs on the left of the presidential faction of the party—the so-called Group of 53—broke with Tsipras's increasingly subservient line and became openly critical of the leadership's faltering strategy in the negotiations, joining the Left Platform in opposing further concessions to the creditors. These groups soon found support from a growing chorus of grassroots activists and a number of iconic party members and government supporters, including the legendary 92-year-old World War II resistance hero and Syriza MEP Mano-lis Glezos and the 89-year-old composer and long-time political activist Mikis Theodorakis. Zoe Konstantopoulou, the popular speaker of parliament who created and presided over the Truth Committee on Public Debt—which in a preliminary report found Greece's obligations to be "illegal, illegitimate, odious and/or unsustainable"—also called on the government to declare a moratorium on further repayments followed by a full citizens' audit of the debt and an out-right repudiation of all obligations confirmed to be odious, or illegitimate.

Meanwhile, Yanis Varoufakis, increasingly exasperated by the unyielding position of his fellow Eurozone finance ministers, began to push for a more confrontational line as well. In his memoirs, Varoufakis claims that the party leadership had initially signed off on his strategy of "constructive disobedience." Once in power, however, Tsipras and his inner circle quickly began to waver. Taken aback by the aggressiveness of the creditors' response and feeling in-creasingly trapped by the deadlock in the negotiations, they eventually yielded to Dragasakis's insistence on de-escalation and appeasement. This rightward creep of the party leadership was eased by the fact that the social mobilizations had largely subsided in anticipation of a Syriza victory after mid-2012, which meant that Tsipras took power in a very different environment from the one he would have inherited in 2012. Unlike Argentina's Peronist establishment in late-2001, which was overwhelmed by civil disorder upon taking office and ef-fectively forced through pressure from below to take a more confrontational stance towards its foreign creditors, Tsipras could afford to limit himself to mostly symbolic and rhetorical interventions while gradually backpedaling on his prior pledges, precisely because large parts of Greek society were already in an advanced state of disempowerment and demobilization. Moreover, Tsipras had made it his strategy after 2012 to win over middle-class voters, which in his view required a more moderate political line on the debt and the euro.[43] At the same time, he had pushed through a reform of Syriza's organizational structure and political culture, away from a diverse coalition of left-wing forces towards a more unified, leader-centric party. According to Kouvelakis, "the aim was to move from a militant party of the left, with a strong culture of internal debate, heterogeneity, involvement in social movements and mobilizations, to a party with a passive membership which could be more easily manipulated by the center, and keener to identify with the figure of the leader. . . . The leadership clearly wanted to . . . move to a top-down electoral machine."[44]

In the process of these internal transformations, the party's leadership was effectively cut loose and rendered autonomous not just from its more militant base, but also from its own general membership. No longer having to answer to a disparate array of radical left-wing forces, Tsipras had now freed his own hand to respond to the changing international environment in a way that befitted his opportunistic and ambitious political style. In practice, this meant that, as the spillover costs of Varoufakis's confrontational line began to make themselves felt, and as Dragasakis and his business-friendly associates found their internal position strengthened by the bridging role they fulfilled to foreign creditors and domestic elites, Tsipras increasingly began to lean towards a strategy of de-escalation. There was nothing inevitable about this move; it was a political decision by the prime minister and his closest advisors. But it was one that contributed decisively to Syriza's rightward drift on the debt, and one that would eventually set the government on course for its unconditional surrender to the Troika.[45] Bypassing Varoufakis, Tsipras established a direct line of communication with Merkel. "By the end of March," Varoufakis writes, "and certainly by the beginning of April, the impartial spectator within me was telling me that our opponents had succeeded in intimidating [Tsipras] . . . I sensed that Alexis had succumbed to the chancellor's spell."[46]

On April 27, three days after the Eurogroup finance ministers had effectively stonewalled their Greek counterpart at the Riga summit, Tsipras sidelined Varoufakis from the technical discussions with the Brussels Group, which would now be coordinated by Tsakalotos and key members of Dragasakis's creditor-friendly team, led by George Chouliarakis. Meanwhile, Varoufakis recounts that the war cabinet—the six-member team deciding on the government's negotiating strategy—"had been turned, with a large majority now favoring wholesale capitulation and seeing me as the main impediment."[47]

## The Climax: "We Underestimated Their Power"

This was the domestic political background against which the Troika launched its final offensive. During the Eurogroup meeting on June 18, it fiercely resisted any attempts by the Greek government to reach a mutually acceptable compromise. In the subsequent weekend of June 20 and 21, an exasperated Tsipras instructed Dragasakis's negotiating team to draft up a proposal that practically amounted to a declaration of surrender. The government was now openly backtracking on its election promises to end austerity, pledging to maintain an implausible and at any rate highly destructive primary budget surplus of 3.5 percent for the next decade—a feat no other country, with the exception of Singapore and Norway, had ever achieved. Nevertheless, two days later, the Greek proposal came back marked in "red ink," with Eurozone officials striking through most of the Greek proposals as inadequate, replacing them with their own words and leaking the document to the press. The combination of the creditors' intransigence and their insistence on his public humiliation reportedly infuriated Tsipras. According to Tsakalotos, who accompanied the prime minister during the late-night emergency talks in Brussels on June 22, "Alexis did everything in his power to surrender, but . . . Merkel would not allow him to. His concessions were dismissed as insufficient and he was told to return to the Troika, conclude a further agreement with them and then pass that through another Eurogroup in two days' time."[48]

After this rejection, the sequence of events unfolded in rapid succession. First, at the EU leaders summit on June 26, billed as the "last chance" to prevent Greece from going into arrears on the Fund and crashing out of the Eurozone, EU leaders made Greece an offer it could not refuse, in the form of the so-called Juncker package—a take-it-or-leave-it deal demanding much tougher measures than Syriza had previously been asked to sign up to in return for a bridging loan. Purportedly incensed by the creditors' ultimatum, Tsipras stormed out of the Brussels negotiating room and flew back to Athens to inform his cabinet that he would be activating the referendum plan he had long been contemplating, ostensibly in a bid to strengthen his negotiating position. In reality, however, the call for a plebiscite was probably more like a last-ditch attempt by the flailing prime minister to save face and extricate himself from the Catch-22 into which he had maneuvered himself. Backed into a corner by his European counterparts and in full awareness that Syriza's internal opposition and the Greek population would never allow him to accept their demands for an unconditional surrender, Tsipras took the decision to the people, urging them to vote against the Troika's demands with the promise that this would allow him to extract greater concessions in further debt talks.

We may never know what was really going through Tsipras's mind at the time, and it remains unclear whether he even wanted to win the referendum or not. But what we do know is that Dragasakis and the majority of the war cabinet fiercely opposed the prime minister's high-risk gamble and, in a heated cabinet discussion on June 30, even tried to convince him to cancel it. Refusing to go down in history as another Papandreou, Tsipras upheld his decision but abandoned the defiant tone he had struck since the failed EU summit on June 26, insisting once again that he would not take unilateral action and that Greece's position within the Eurozone was not in question. To give substance to this pledge and to please the moderates inside his government, Tsipras authorized Dragasakis' negotiating team to draft a conciliatory new proposal to the Eurogroup—remarkably similar to the one he was calling on voters to reject, and thus effectively signaling his willingness to surrender. All it accomplished was to further confuse both the lenders and his supporters. The proposal was rejected out of hand, and EU leaders insisted that there would be no further negotiations until after the July 5 referendum. In an ironic twist, the best Dragasakis and his allies could hope for now was for the government's "preferred" outcome to be defeated at the polls, thus legitimizing an honorable retreat. As Dragasakis himself put it, "we need an emergency exit."[49]

This turned out to be a tragic miscalculation on at least two counts. First, the creditor response to the referendum announcement ended up being much more aggressive than the Greek government had anticipated. Despite Tsipras's repeated claims to the contrary, European leaders instantly declared the referendum to constitute a vote on Greece's Eurozone membership—thus explicitly threatening a forced Grexit in the event of a victory for the *oxi* campaign. Jeroen Dijsselbloem reiterated his long-standing calls for further austerity and declared that "if [the Greek] people say they don't want that, there is not only no basis for a new program, there is also no basis for Greece in the Eurozone."[50] EU officials immediately cut off the official talks on further financing and refused to agree to a five-day bridging period requested by the Greek government to be able to carry out the referendum in peace. As we saw before, the ECB refused to increase the ELA ceiling, which, in the face of the incipient bank run that had started overnight following Tsipras's referendum announcement, amounted to a de facto decision to cut the Greek banking system off from central bank support. The government was forced to close the banks, and a senior advisor at the finance ministry reported that in a matter of days large parts of the economy and the state apparatus were already starting to "die off" or malfunction as a result of the debilitating spillover costs:

> Companies [that] do not pay their employees through bank accounts cannot pay cash to employees—and there are many. . . . So we have a situation which is escalating into a chain reaction . . . like having a heart attack . . . if you view cash liquidity as the blood of the economy. On the weekend when the ECB stopped, we had the heart attack. Now [the week before the referendum] we are having its after-effects. Different organs are getting numb. Some stop working, others are trying but they don't have enough blood.[51]

These unprecedented events in turn fed into the second point on which the Syriza leadership had spectacularly miscalculated—namely the fact that the creditors' aggression, far from browbeating the Greek people into submission, actually ended up fanning the flames of popular indignation, unleashing long-repressed social energies and pent-up frustrations that quickly overflowed the government's capacity to contain or direct them. Suddenly everything came to a head: the Troika's total credit embargo and liquidity asphyxiation from above had brought Greece to the brink of financial collapse, while the people's irrepressible desire for dignity and self-determination exploded into one of the largest demonstrations in modern Greek history, with an estimated 500,000 people taking to Syntagma Square and the surrounding streets on Friday, July 3 to demand that their government stand up to the Troika's intimidation tactics and reject the imposition of further austerity. Two days later, an overwhelming 61.8 percent of Greeks, far more than the government or any official poll had anticipated, defied the threats made by the lenders and the Greek establishment and voted to reject the creditors' terms. A geographical analysis of the referendum result showed that the poorer areas in Athens had overwhelmingly voted against, while the wealthier areas had overwhelmingly voted in favor, highlighting a deep class divide over the issues of austerity and the national debt.[52]

As can be seen in Paul Mason's behind-the-scenes documentary, #ThisIsACoup, the announcement of the referendum result shook Syriza's top government officials to their very bones. In his memoirs, Varoufakis writes that the prime minister's residence "felt as cold as a morgue, as joyful as a cemetery. . . . The ministers and functionaries I encountered looked numb, uncomfortable in my presence, as if they had just suffered a major electoral defeat."[53] At the war cabinet meeting that night, Varoufakis presented a plan to capitalize on the spectacular energy generated by the popular mobilizations and the resounding no-vote through the activation of a two-pronged deterrent he had been quietly preparing for months: to issue euro-denominated IOUs through a parallel payments system, and to declare a unilateral haircut on the Greek SMP bonds held by the European Central Bank.[54] The proposal was defeated by a four-to-two majority in the six-member inner-cabinet. Realizing that his position had become untenable, Varoufakis tendered his resignation. One of the biggest obstacles on the road to capitulation had now been removed. He was replaced by his old friend Tsakalotos.

Within a week Tsipras found himself back at the negotiating table in Brussels signing up to a new three-year, €86 billion bailout agreement—€25 billion of which was to be set aside for bank recapitalization—under conditions that were widely considered to be even worse than the ones he had just convinced his own people to reject. As one senior Syriza official put it, "It is a total capitulation. We never had a 'Plan B' for what to do if the [ECB] cuts off liquidity and the creditors simply destroyed our country, which is what they are doing."[55] An EU official confided that Tsipras had been "crucified" by his Eurozone counterparts during the postreferendum negotiations, while a diplomat from a hardline creditor country described the terms of surrender as "akin to turning Greece into an economic protectorate."[56] As he later passed the third bailout bill through Parliament, Tsipras himself acknowledged that he was not without options: "I had a choice between a deal I did not agree with," he said, "or a disorderly default." It was his failure to adequately prepare for the latter, and his refusal to even consider the possibility of admitting defeat and resigning, that ultimately left him with no choice but to embrace the former. As a Greek finance ministry official explained afterwards, when asked about the reasons for the prime minister's stunning *kolotoumba*: "we underestimated their power."[57]

TABLE 20.1.
Comparison between the debt crises in Argentina and Greece

## Argentina in 2001

**Decentralized bond finance:**
Debt concentration low
Bondholders atomized/dispersed
Creditor coordination difficult
No new credit forthcoming
*Market discipline weak*

**No U.S./IMF intervention:**
IMF pulls plug on Argentina's bailout program
No official coordination of small bondholders
U.S. isolationists push for reduced IMF role abroad
Policy conditionality breaks down
*No more conditional lending*

**Relative debtor autonomy:**
Lenient int'l conditions, relative self-sufficiency
Sidelining of domestic elites and technocrats
Legitimation crisis leads to antiausterity revolt
Strengthened national-popular coalition
*Breakdown of debtor discipline*

**OUTCOME:**
*Unilateral default*
Exceptional room for maneuver postdefault
Argentina becomes most defiant debtor by far
Debtor initiates aggressive debt restructuring
Move towards more equitable redistribution

## Greece in 2015

**Excluded from markets:**
Debt almost entirely socialized
Bondholders relatively unified
Official creditor coordination easy
Only prospect of new credit if compliant
*Market discipline strong*

**Active EU/IMF intervention:**
Troika withholds further credit but still engaged
Particularly aggressive intervention by ECB (ELA)
Continued Troika monitoring/surveillance of policy
Policy conditionality enforces discipline
*Continued conditional lending*

**Limited state autonomy:**
Unforgiving int'l conditions, limited self-sufficiency
Sidelining of prodefault radicals inside government
Legitimation crisis leads to antiausterity referendum
Syriza's "internal Troika" cuts itself loose from base
*Re-internalization of debtor discipline*

**OUTCOME:**
*No unilateral default*
Room for maneuver remains severely constrained
Greece caves in to Troika's terms for third bailout
Tsipras waits forever for creditors to "forgive" debt
Continued immiseration of Greek population

# CONCLUSION

## Shaking Off the Burden

Placed in a long-term historical perspective, the outcome of the Greek debt crisis—and, indeed, of most international debt crises of the past four decades—appears as a striking anomaly. Never before have so many highly indebted sovereign borrowers been so insistent on avoiding a unilateral suspension of payments in the wake of a major global financial crisis, and never before have private and official creditors been so successful in enforcing compliance with their cross-border debt contracts amid such widespread fiscal distress.[1] While the three main international debt crises before World War II all witnessed widespread sovereign default, the declaration of such unilateral debt moratoriums has been an exceedingly rare phenomenon during the crises of the post-1982 period. This development has been particularly striking in the decade since 2008, which unlike the 1820s, the 1870s, and the 1930s did not see any outright payment suspensions by heavily indebted peripheral borrowers. Today, international lending thus appears to be governed by the widespread assumption that even crisis-ridden borrowers always will—and always should—try their very best to continue servicing their foreign debts; an assumption that has become so deeply entrenched as to now be considered the norm.

Of course, highlighting and seeking to understand this striking decline in the incidence of sovereign default is not to say that the problem of government insolvency or the possibility of future payment suspensions has been eradicated altogether. Indeed, isolated default scenarios are likely to remain an important fixture of international finance in the future, as further financial cataclysms are inevitable and the enforcement mechanisms of debtor compliance are bound to one day fail again, just as they did in Argentina in 2001. What is clear, however, is that there has been a marked transition from unilateral debtor action toward more "orderly" multilateral solutions revolving around the negotiated rescheduling or restructuring of distressed borrowers' foreign obligations. There is significant evidence that, as a result of these developments, the outcomes of international crisis management have become much friendlier to private creditors in recent decades, leaving the debtors to shoulder the bulk of the burden of adjustment for recurring international debt crises.[2] As I have argued in this book, this shift towards more creditor-friendly outcomes can largely be attributed to the vast increase in the structural power of finance since the 1970s—an increase that has been underpinned by the growing concentration and centralization of international credit markets, by the active intervention of creditor states and the IMF, and by the growing state dependence on private credit, which has tended to strengthen the position of orthodox technocrats and financial elites inside the borrowing countries who share with their foreign creditors a material interest and ideological conviction in the desirability of full repayment. Together with the increased mobility of capital and the growing centrality of finance in the process of capital accumulation, these developments have greatly amplified the economic spillover costs of default and progressively disempowered those social groups who are seen to champion a more heterodox policy response and a more equitable distribution of adjustment costs, contributing to a gradual internalization of debtor discipline. As Charles Lipson noted early on, "this political structure for collective action ensures that no state will default unless it is insolvent or is willing to accept a radical rupture with the capitalist world economy."[3] Occasionally, debtor revolts still manage to rattle the informal regime of cross-border contract enforcement from within, but the general pattern is now unmistakable: "in a big crisis, creditors rule."[4]

All of this tells us important things about the fraught relationship between capitalism and democracy under conditions of globalization and financialization. In the three in-depth case studies of Mexico, Argentina, and Greece, we saw how the newfound insistence on full and uninterrupted debt service has had far-reaching social implications, leading to a very skewed distribution of adjustment costs between private financiers in the advanced capitalist countries and working people inside the peripheral borrowing countries. These distributional consequences have in turn gone hand in hand with momentous political implications for the debtor countries. Compared to both the prewar era and the immediate postwar decades, the national autonomy of heavily indebted peripheral borrowers has been steadily hollowed out by the resurrection of global finance and the aggressive interventions of creditor states and international financial institutions. Seen in this light, the Latin American debt crisis of the 1980s was the signal event highlighting the start of a new era in international lending; a phase that has been marked by the growing capacity of international creditors—especially the big private banks—to shape the outcomes of major financial disturbances to their own advantage. This has in turn greatly undermined the quality of democracy in the debtor states, leading to ever more intrusive forms of creditor control and ever greater disregard for established democratic procedures, as evidenced by the concerted turn toward less accountable and more technocratic modes of government and the systematic insulation of political institutions and economic policymaking from popular pressures for a more equitable distribution of adjustment costs. Nowhere have these antidemocratic tendencies of neoliberal crisis management been more clearly on display than in Greece, whose political independence and fiscal autonomy have been all but sacrificed at the altar of the European bond market in recent years. It is therefore worth considering the political repercussions of the Eurozone's response to the crisis in some greater detail.

## Throttling Democracy

When the Syriza-led government pivoted around on its political axis in the summer of 2015 and stunned its own supporters by signing a new memorandum of understanding with the Troika of foreign lenders, the agreement literally stipulated that "no unilateral fiscal or other policy actions will be taken by the authorities which would undermine the liquidity, solvency or future viability of the banks."[5] Greece's national sovereignty, in other words, was officially suspended insofar as the interests of the banks were concerned. The *Financial Times* concluded that Greece had "pledged to accept a level of external oversight of its economy unprecedented of an EU member," and noted that "this can be seen as a hard-nosed programme in which the principal authors sit not in Mr Tsipras's cabinet but in the offices of the IMF, the EU and the creditors, led by Germany."[6] In a striking historical echo of the regime of international financial control that was established in Athens by the imperialist creditor powers of the late-nineteenth century, Greece once again finds itself under the tutelage of its European lenders, with little or no freedom to determine its own fiscal policy priorities.

This outcome casts particularly strong doubts on one widespread explanation for debtor compliance in the institutionalist political science and economics literature: the so-called democratic advantage hypothesis that was briefly outlined in chapter 1.[7] This hypothesis would lead us to expect Greece's compliance to have been the result of significant legislative and judicial checks on the executive, limiting the latter's ability to act unilaterally and compelling it to credibly commit to "creditor rights." The evidence, however, suggests the exact opposite: the credibility of Greece's commitments was strengthened not by limits on the executive but by what some have called "an extension of autocratic executive power."[8] As the crisis deepened, subsequent Greek governments frequently resorted to emergency decrees and executive edicts to bypass parliament and neutralize widespread social and political opposition to further austerity and neoliberal reform. Prior to the 2015 elections, Dimitris Dalakoglou remarked that "for the last two years Greece has been governed almost exclusively with decrees that were designed to be emergency provisions for use in extreme cases such as war or natural disasters. Since June 2012, twenty-five [such decrees] have been issued. Hardly any of the major structural adjustment measures were approved by the normal parliamentary process."[9] These antidemocratic tendencies intensified with the deepening of the social and economic crisis, which led to an increasingly unilateral approach on the part of the executive. In 2013, the *New York Times* reported that Prime Minister Samaras "stepped up his use of emergency decrees and edicts to impose changes that other political parties and Greece's unions have a long history of trying to thwart," including edicts to prevent and end strike actions by schoolteachers, seamen and metro workers, as well as executive decrees "imposing stricter supervision on ministries and state bodies."[10]

At the same time, many long-standing constitutional provisions—especially those guaranteeing labor and pension rights, the minimum wage and collective bargaining—were aggressively dismantled at the orders of the Troika and at the behest of private creditors, who at times openly expressed their opposition to the legal protections afforded by the postdictatorship settlement. In one report, J. P. Morgan complained that the constitutions of the Southern European countries displayed too much of a "socialist influence," with "weak executives; weak central states relative to regions; constitutional protection of labor rights; consensus building systems that foster clientelism; and the right to protest if unwelcome changes are made to the political status quo."[11] Many of these provisions, of course, were important checks and balances introduced to reduce the concentration of executive power following the abuse of governmental authority by past military dictatorships. Rather than asking for these democratic checks to be strengthened, the creditors explicitly indicated their desire to see such provisions weakened. As a result, the legislative power became increasingly sidelined as the crisis deepened.[12]

These domestic political developments were cemented with a set of institutional changes at the European level. The European Fiscal Compact, in particular, was unambiguously intended to impose budgetary discipline on the deficit states of the periphery and to limit the national sovereignty of individual Eurozone members in determining budgetary priorities. Legal scholars have observed that the treaty "basically entrenches a certain economic theory at the level of constitutional law" and point out that, "while it elevates the austerity paradigm . . . to the status of 'unbreakable law', it basically outlaws Keynesianism and its counter-cyclical economic policies."[13] Loïc Azoulai, who previously held the chair of Law at the European University Institute, has referred to the pact as a "legal monster" for its far-reaching encroachment on national sovereignty and fundamental constitutional provisions.[14] An editorial in the *European Constitutional Law Review*, the leading journal in the field, declared that the fiscal compact "strikes at the heart of the institutions of parliamentary democracy by dislocating as a matter of constitutional principle the budgetary autonomy of the member states."[15] Debtor states like Greece now have little choice but to abide by the rules laid down by the creditor states. As the former German finance minister Wolfgang Schäuble candidly put it, the Greeks "can vote however they want, but whatever election result we have will change nothing about the actual situation in the country."[16] Democracy suspended, political leaders could carry on with the more urgent task of servicing their debts.

The evidence is therefore clear on this point: Greece's creditors—both private and official—had remarkably little faith in the ability of representative institutions and the democratic process to ensure credible commitment. Insofar as Greece's political system, its political culture, and its postdictatorship constitution were to be reformed to ensure continued repayment, the creditors' priority was not to limit executive power but to elevate it; not to strengthen the role of parliament but to sideline it; not to defend hard-fought labor rights but to upend them; not to increase national ownership over the reform effort but to eliminate it; not to force Greek leaders to respect the popular will but to insulate them from it. The result, as we have seen, was a deep legitimation crisis, with public trust in the political system and EU institutions collapsing, a massive wave of protests, strikes, and riots rocking the country, and a neo-Nazi criminal gang entering parliament as the country's third-largest party. The irony in all this is hard to overstate: the democratic process was throttled in the very place where its ancient ancestor was born, all to repay a debt that many international experts—including those at the IMF—long considered to be unsustainable to begin with; a debt that likely included many obligations acquired through the illegitimate means of corruption, embezzlement, and graft; and a debt whose oppressive burden has fallen almost entirely on the shoulders of those who had least to do with causing the crisis in the first place: the poorest Greeks.

Again, there are strong historical echoes here—and not just with the creditors' financial control of the late-nineteenth century or the structural adjustment programs that were imposed on the Global South in the 1980s and 1990s.[17] The throttling of Greek democracy in its classical birthplace in the name of continued debt servicing also recalls a very different set of lessons from a much earlier historical epoch: that of Solon the Athenian, the classical Greek poet and statesman who is credited with proclaiming the ancient city-state's first democratic constitution in the sixth century B.C. While some today may have heard of the famous Solonian reforms, which repealed many of the cruel—"draconian"—laws that had been laid down by his predecessor Draco, fewer are likely to be aware that Solon's protodemocratic constitution actually had its origins in the crippling debt crisis and the revolutionary upheavals that had rocked the classical Greek world in the preceding decades. In the *Constitution of the Athenians*, Aristotle tells us that during this period "the poor with their wives and children were in servitude to the rich," and that "there was for a long time civic struggle between the nobles and the people." According to Plutarch, "the whole demos was in debt to the rich."[18] When the social crisis deepened, indentured peasants across Greece took up arms and rose up against their creditor landlords. As the German historian Victor Ehrenberg writes in his classic study, *From Solon to Socrates*, "the rule of an oligarchy of noble and wealthy landowners had become so oppressive that a revolution did not seem far away."[19]

It was in this context that Solon was elected archon, and it was in this context that he pronounced his celebrated democratic reforms. Among his first acts upon assuming power, he canceled all outstanding debts, freed the enslaved and indentured debtors, and outlawed the widespread institution of debt bondage—a radical set of measures that together came to be known as the *seisachtheia* (σεισάχθεια), or the "shaking-off of burdens." What Solon and the rebelling debt slaves realized, in other words, was that there could be no democracy without freedom, and no freedom without liberation from "debt's oppressive load."[20] Debt relief as a precondition for universal emancipation: this is the specter of Solon that has haunted Europe for the better part of the past decade, from the squares of Athens and Madrid to the offices of Brussels and Berlin—all the way to the trading floors of Frankfurt, Paris, and London. If European unity and Greek democracy are to stand any chance of surviving the tumultuous opening decades of the twenty-first century, this is the specter we will now have to revive.

## SHAKING OFF THE BURDEN

There are many different ways to go about securing debt relief. The first and most straightforward would be for creditors to come to their senses and recognize the necessity of cancelling at least part of the outstanding obligations in order to free the debtor from an unsustainable debt burden and thereby avert a deeper social crisis. While such an appeal to the moral instincts and economic reason of the creditors may seem outlandish in the present context, the voluntary provision of debt relief is by no means unprecedented; in fact, the practice stretches all the way back to the early civilizations of ancient Mesopotamia. In his magisterial study, *Debt: The First 5,000 Years*, anthropologist David Graeber recounts how Sumerian and Babylonian kings regularly wiped the slates clean, cancelling all outstanding personal obligations and freeing the debt slaves to mark a fresh start upon taking the throne, or to stave off the risk of social breakdown during periods of war, crisis, and natural catastrophe. The first known word for freedom, the Sumerian term *amargi*, literally means "return to mother," and referred to the ability of indentured laborers to finally go home after being freed from debt servitude.[21] The Code of Hammurabi, dating back to the year 1754 BC, stipulated that "if anyone owes a debt for a loan, and a storm prostrates the grain, or the harvest fails, or the grain does not grow for lack of water, in that year he need not give his creditor any grain, he washes his debt-tablet in water and pays no rent for this year." Later, the biblical Law of Jubilee, cited in Leviticus, even decreed the automatic cancellation of all debts on the seventh (or fiftieth) year, along with the liberation of all those held in bondage. Debt relief, in short, was not only foundational to the development of the concept of freedom, but has long played an important role in maintaining social harmony as well.

From the twentieth century onwards, starting with the cancellation of allied wartime debts to the United States during the interwar period, the demand for debt relief has increasingly begun to be applied to the sovereign obligations of heavily indebted states. The first country to have its debts voluntarily canceled after World War II was the perpetrator itself: Germany. Adamant to avoid the mistakes of the Versailles Treaty, the U.S. government coaxed its allies—including war-ravaged Greece—into signing the London Debt Agreement of 1953, which at the stroke of a pen eliminated half of West-Germany's external obligations and allowed the country to repay the remainder under highly favorable terms. Subsequent research has found that the benefits of debt relief—lowering borrowing costs, freeing up fiscal space for public investment, and stabilizing inflation—were foundational to the country's postwar *Wirtschaftswunder*.[22] Several years later, in 1956, the major creditor countries came together in Paris to renegotiate the debts of Argentina, giving rise to the Paris Club, which was to be tasked with finding ad hoc solutions to debt servicing problems through the coordination of voluntary reschedulings and restructurings of bilateral loans made by the rich countries. Since then, the Paris Club has concluded 433 agreements with 90 different debtor countries, involving a total amount of $583 billion in debt.[23] In 1976, the more informal London Club of private creditors came together for the first time to renegotiate the debts of Zaire, and has since served as a platform for the renegotiation of foreign claims held by private creditors.

More recently, in the wake of the developing country debt crises of the 1980s and 1990s, the Jubilee 2000 coalition helped popularize the modern-day notion of a debt jubilee for heavily indebted poor countries (HIPCs) through a sustained international campaign for the cancellation of low-income country debts. The political pressure exerted by a wide array of civil society organizations and the mass protests by the alter-globalization movement eventually propelled the leaders of the wealthy G7 countries to agree to the Multilateral Debt Relief Initiative (MDRI) for some of the world's poorest debtor states. So far, thirty-six developing countries, thirty of them in Africa, have thus received a combined $76 billion in debt reduction through the World Bank's and IMF's HIPC and MDRI initiatives, amounting to roughly two-thirds of their total external obligations. Although the HIPC programs have been criticized for moving too slowly, for not providing sufficient relief, for not including enough countries, for failing to live up to their promises, and for imposing the same damaging policy conditionality as the IMF's and World Bank's original loan agreements, they have nevertheless set an important precedent by demonstrating that creditor claims on foreign sovereigns can by no means be considered inviolable. In sum, between the smashing of cuneiform tablets in ancient Mesopotamia and the more recent mobilizations for a modern-day debt jubilee, there is nothing particularly unusual about the demand for voluntary debt relief; there are plenty of historical precedents attesting to both the possibility and the desirability of this outcome in the event of a deep social crisis caused by unbearable overindebtedness.

In today's fragile and highly interconnected global political economy, the multilateral solution of a negotiated debt restructuring has the added advantage of being "orderly" and thereby avoiding both the chaotic spillover costs of default for the debtor and the risk of financial contagion for the creditors. In Greece's case, almost all of the country's debts, roughly 85 percent, are now held in official hands—by the European creditor states, the EU bailout funds, the ECB, and the IMF—which, in theory at least, should make it relatively easy to coordinate an orderly write-down. Even the IMF officially favors this outcome, although as a senior creditor it still systematically refuses to write down its own holdings and has so far gone along with its European partners in opposing a formal haircut and pushing back the inevitable debt restructuring as far as possible. In practice, the hard reality of international power politics therefore tends to interfere with the presumed benefits of ad hoc multilateral solutions.[24] Unsurprisingly, it turns out that leaving the initiative to the creditors—whether private or official—enables them to shape the outcome to their own advantage, delaying and designing inevitable debt restructurings in such a way as to spare themselves from real losses. In the words of the IMF itself, creditor-led debt restructurings are therefore often "too little, too late" from the perspective of debt sustainability, which is precisely the lesson that emerged from our case studies of Mexico's Brady Deal, Argentina's megaswap, and Greece's PSI.[25] As far as international crisis management is concerned, it is clear that moral considerations and economic reason ultimately count for far less than the power of finance and the narrow self-interest of the dominant creditor states and international financial institutions.

This observation has led some to advocate the replacement of the current ad hoc approach to multilateral debt restructuring with the statutory solution of a sovereign bankruptcy regime, which would arguably provide for a more neutral arbitration process and thereby lead to more equitable outcomes in international crisis management.[26] The basic idea is that by institutionalizing bankruptcy procedures at the global level (possibly modeled on the provisions of chapter 9 of the U.S. Bankruptcy Code, which deals with insolvent municipalities), debtor states can be protected from the predatory behavior of speculative investors—especially vulture funds—demanding "the last pound of flesh." The problem with this proposal, however, is that it ultimately encounters the same hard reality of international power politics as the ad hoc approach; a fact that became very clear when IMF deputy managing director Anne Krueger launched an ambitious proposal for a sovereign debt restructuring mechanism (SDRM) following the Argentine debacle of 2001.[27] By 2003, the SDRM proposal had effectively been scuppered as a result of fierce opposition from Wall Street, which wielded both its instrumental power over the U.S. government (through aggressive lobbying) and its structural power over the debtors (through the internalization of market discipline among important borrowers like Mexico, which ended up opposing the SDRM for fear that it would raise its borrowing costs) in order to defeat the proposal before it even saw the light of day.[28] More recently, the Greek debt crisis and Argentina's protracted battle with the vulture funds have put the notion of a sovereign bankruptcy regime back on the agenda, but it remains unclear how such an initiative could ever be successfully implemented without the active support of the dominant creditor states, which in turn are unlikely to ever push for it as long as their own powerful banks and financial institutions remain firmly opposed to it.

## BITING THE BULLET

How, then, are heavily indebted states like Greece to extricate themselves from this conundrum? The only option, it seems, would be to simply default anyway. If multilateral solutions—whether ad hoc or statutory—are incapable of providing timely and sufficient debt relief, the debtor can always bite the bullet and *take* it. The most straightforward approach would be for the debtor to prepare as thoroughly as possible for the economic fallout before unilaterally suspending its external debt service, signaling clearly to its creditors that it is unable to pay and will only resume its debt service following a successful restructuring of the outstanding obligations to reach a sustainable new level of indebtedness. Ordinary citizens in the debtor country could be insulated from the resultant spillover costs through special exemptions, guarantees, and compensations for depositors and small investors like pensioners. When they repudiated the tsar's debt in 1918, for instance, the Bolsheviks explicitly exempted small bondholders, which shielded ordinary workers from some of the immediate costs of the default. More recently, Thomas Piketty has suggested raising a one-off tax on capital to repay the public debt in one fell swoop—although a similar exceptional tax on capital could also be used ex post to compensate small bondholders for their losses in the event of a default.[29] In sum, governments do have some tools at their disposal to ensure that the poor do not end up paying for a crisis caused by the speculative investments of the rich.

Although any sovereign default nowadays is likely to cause significant short-term disruption, the historical chapters and the Argentine case study have shown how the declaration of a unilateral debt moratorium has the added advantage of restoring the initiative in future debt negotiations to the debtor: while creditors are unlikely to agree to meaningful debt relief as long as they are receiving 100 cents on the dollar, they may reconsider their position after several years of receiving nothing at all. If a borrower resolves to halt its debt service and manages to cushion the immediate economic impact and bridge the brief period that it is likely to be locked out of international capital markets, it can therefore wield its unilateral default to extract better terms in subsequent debt negotiations, possibly leading to a more debtor-friendly outcome overall. The immediate spillover costs of default are likely to be very painful, but if historical experience is anything to go by they will likely give way to recovery within six months to one or two years at most. Since foreign investors tend to have relatively short memories, long-term exclusion from international capital markets should not be an issue of concern; indeed, history confirms that even following an exceptionally coercive restructuring the money will quickly start flowing in again once debt service is resumed. While this book has amply demonstrated how the short-term spillover costs of default generally make an outright suspension of payments a highly unattractive option for policymakers, a good argument could be made that in exceptional cases—like Argentina's in 2001 or Greece's in 2015—it may still be preferable to the long-term consequences of endless austerity and fire-sale privatizations, whose costs may never be recovered in full.

Alternatively, or in addition, a sovereign borrower could even opt to repudiate or reject liability over certain obligations outright. In the years since the developing country debt crisis of the 1980s, a growing number of scholars and activists have advocated such an approach on the basis of the idea that many heavily indebted countries' obligations are in fact "odious." The concept of odious debt was first developed by the legal theorist Alexander Sack in 1927, who argued that a loan cannot be considered binding upon the nation if it was contracted without the consent and benefit of the general public. The basic idea is that, insofar as it can be proven that creditors were aware of this fact when they first extended the loan, the debt fails to qualify as an obligation of the nation and instead constitutes a personal debt of the ruler, meaning that its binding nature legally expires along with the fall of the regime or government that contracted the original loan.[30] In recent years, the concept of odious debt was perhaps most prominently drawn upon by Rafael Correa in an attempt to legitimize the Ecuadorian payment suspension and debt buyback of 2008. After a debt audit commission made up of representatives from grassroots movements, civil society organizations, and government institutions concluded that part of the country's obligations concluded since the 1970s were indeed odious, Correa declared a unilateral moratorium on two-thirds of Ecuador's outstanding foreign commercial obligations; an uncompromising position his government maintained for six months, during which it secretly instructed the U.S. investment bank Lazard to begin buying back its defaulted bonds on secondary markets at discounts as low as 20 cents on the dollar. Through this neat trick, the government succeeded in purchasing over 90 percent of its own worthless obligations, extinguishing $3.2 billion in external debt in the process, for a cost of only $900 million. According to Éric Toussaint, spokesperson of the Committee for the Abolition of Third World Debt (CADTM) who also served on the Ecuadorian audit committee, the total savings from the default (including interest) amounted to $7 billion, "which became available for social spending for items such as health care, education and infrastructure development."[31]

Today, Ecuador's default stands out as an exceptional case in which a developing country defied its foreign creditors without suffering debilitating economic spillover costs. The fact remains, however, that the relatively successful outcome of Correa's confrontational debt strategy occurred under the same favorable external conditions as Argentina's debt restructuring of 2005. As in the latter case, the international commodity boom rendered Ecuador much less dependent on international capital markets and international financial institutions, contributing to a breakdown of the first and second enforcement mechanisms. Combined with intense popular pressure from below, in the form of mass mobilizations that contributed to the ouster of several presidents in the years preceding the default, disarming the third mechanism of internalized debtor discipline in the process, these external conditions greatly expanded the government's room for maneuver compared to the capital-scarce environment it had encountered in the 1980s and 1990s. Under less forgiving external conditions, the situation might have been very different, leaving Ecuador considerably more vulnerable to a strong market reaction and aggressive official creditor intervention.

In normal circumstances, unilateral default strategies therefore run into the same set of constraints that all other solutions to debt cancellation have encountered over the past four decades: the structural power of finance. Clearly, unilateral solutions alone cannot resolve the systemic problem of the debtors' limited policy autonomy—at least not in the absence of a broader shift in the international balance of forces underpinning the creditor-friendly status quo.

Again, nowhere were the asymmetric power dynamics between debtors and creditors more clearly on display than in Greece in 2015, during the standoff between the Syriza government and the Troika of foreign lenders. Earlier that year, the same Éric Toussaint of the CADTM had been appointed spokesperson of the Greek Truth Committee on Public Debt, which in a preliminary report found the majority of the country's obligations to be "illegal, illegitimate, odious and/or unsustainable," recommending a unilateral payment suspension followed by a full citizens' audit of the debt.[32] As we saw in the last chapter of this book, however, the absence of adequate preparations on the part of the Greek government meant that the balance of forces—both between Greece and the Troika, and within Syriza itself—remained fundamentally stacked against such radical unilateral measures. While a plausible case can be made that Greece would indeed have been better off suspending payments rather than swallowing the draconian conditions of a third EU bailout, having economic reason and international law on one's side is clearly not enough to bring about a positive outcome in the realm of domestic and international power politics, where right generally fails to automatically translate into might. In the absence of a broader international *political* response, little is likely to change at the level of individual policy outcomes.

In sum, for a formal debt repudiation to be both declared and accepted, without the debtor suffering debilitating spillover costs, and for the doctrine of odious debt to have any legal effect beyond the parliament or courts of the borrowing state itself, it would have to be recognized by debtor and creditor countries alike. This reality once again leaves the borrower at the whim of its lenders. It is perhaps no surprise, then, that the doctrine of odious debt has not been formally enshrined in international law and has never been officially invoked by any debtor country in a multilateral restructuring process. British and New York law, under which most peripheral states' sovereign bonds are contracted, simply do not recognize the concept. As a result, even countries like South Africa and Iraq, which were often said to have an exemplary right to the cancellation of odious debts contracted under defunct despotic regimes, explicitly declined to invoke the doctrine: after the U.S. occupation and the overthrow of Saddam Hussein, Iraq obtained 80 percent debt relief from the Paris Club on grounds of "necessity," while South Africa continued to service the debts of the Apartheid regime. Even legal scholars who are otherwise sympathetic to debtor interests therefore tend to conclude that, "although the doctrine may provide a useful platform for political rhetoric or to sway public opinion, alone it has not proved to be a basis for debt repudiation."[33]

## "Taking Back Control"

If both multilateral and unilateral solutions ultimately run up against the limits set by international finance, how are we to address the enormous challenges posed to social justice and democracy by towering public debt loads and recurring financial crises? As I have sought to demonstrate in this book, there are structural factors at play behind the prevailing outcomes of international crisis management. It therefore follows that both isolated unilateral action and ad hoc multilateral renegotiations, even if they may certainly offer a short-term palliative for a distressed sovereign borrower, ultimately cannot provide a general solution to the contemporary problem of sovereign debt bondage. The only enduring solution would be a *structural* solution flowing from a concerted bottom-up challenge to the asymmetric power relations at the heart of the global political economy. Instead of seeking to redress the inequities wrought by globalization, financialization and neoliberal crisis management purely at the level of legal solutions or individual policy outcomes, future political action will have to confront these problems at the level of their underlying causes and the overarching systemic frameworks in which they arose in the first place.

Without a determined international pushback against the structural power of finance, building on mass social mobilizations and active popular participation in both the creditor and the debtor countries, working people everywhere— North and South alike—are likely to continue to foot the bill for repeated financial boom-and-bust cycles. Only through a transformative political project that resolves to overcome humanity's collective dependence on highly concentrated international credit markets, and only with an emancipatory and strategic political vision that transcends national boundaries and brings together what the

Burkinabé revolutionary Thomas Sankara once called a "united front against debt," can we begin to make serious inroads against the ascendancy of finance and the turbulent world it has created in its image.

While transformative structural change will inevitably take time, the basic contours for a democratic countermovement are already beginning to emerge from below. Its battle cries resounded from the occupied squares of Athens and Madrid during the European antiausterity demonstrations, and even made their way into the wolf's lair at Wall Street, Frankfurt, and the City of London for a few short weeks in late 2011. Although these mobilizations against the privileges of the "1 percent" eventually petered out, it is clear that politics in the advanced capitalist democracies—in debtor and creditor states alike—has not been the same since. Most of the countries that experienced large-scale protests in the crisis years are now witnessing the rise of powerful antiestablishment forces, including a raft of progressive political formations whose eyes are firmly set on the exorbitant privileges of the financial elite. Buoyed by the groundwork of a wide array of activist groups, grassroots movements, and heterodox think tanks and civil society organizations, as well as a growing number of publications scrutinizing the untrammeled concentration of wealth and power in the hands of the few, a new democratic politics is starting to take shape that has the potential to gravely upset the neoliberal status quo not just in the debtor countries, but even in some of the most powerful creditor countries. Critical scholarship will undoubtedly have an important role to play in this process of political recomposition moving forward, not just in terms of refining our collective understanding of the inner workings of contemporary capitalism, but also in providing concrete proposals on how to confront the deepening crisis of liberal democracy and the structural power of finance in our time.

One of the first main challenges in this respect will be to devise innovative and productive new ways to bring finance under democratic control, so that it can finally begin to fulfill its public function of credit allocation and financial intermediation without subjecting entire populations to the profit motive of a handful of private banks and institutional investors. Needless to say, the social and political struggle for such a profound transformation of the global political economy will encounter fierce opposition from those who continue to benefit from the status quo, and there can be no guarantees that any of these objectives will ever see the light of day. But in the context of an imploding neoliberal center and a newly empowered xenophobic far-right, the radical demand for a modern-day *seisachtheia*—shaking off the burden of oppressive debt loads while "taking back control" over international finance and bringing an end to the nefarious practice of sovereign debt bondage—may now offer the only remaining bulwark against those who would usurp democracy in the name of authoritarian nationalism. Under the fading shadow of the Great Recession, amid the political tumult of a new wave of antiestablishment revolts, the specter of Solon abides.

# APPENDIX

## A Word on Methodology

The research project behind this book built on a qualitative methodological approach that combined comparative-historical methods with intensive case studies, process tracing, and structural power analysis. Such a qualitative framework has some advantages over the formal theoretical modeling and quantitative methods that are generally deployed by economists working on sovereign debt and default. First of all, small-N case study methods tend to be better suited for grasping complex causation in social reality.[1] Rather than establishing a mere coincidence of hypothesized causes and outcomes, this study's main interest was in the exact causal *mechanisms*—mostly invisible from the bird's eye view of regression analysis—that connect hypothesized causes (the structural power of finance) to real-world outcomes (the relative decline in the incidence of unilateral default). Secondly, leading methodologists in the social sciences have convincingly argued that the conceptual validity gained from the qualitative approach tends to feed into more reliable and more innovative results.[2] Since parsimonious modeling generally compels economists to prioritize the operationalization of variables over the more analytical and qualitative task of conceptualization, their results are often plagued by a misspecification of theoretical microfoundations—hence the attempt to develop a new typology of default in chapter 2. A third reason to embrace a qualitative approach is that the concept of power is notoriously difficult to operationalize in any type of research, especially in large-N studies, moving most economists to ignore this thorny subject altogether. And yet the study of sovereign debt will have to somehow confront the "essentially contested concept" of power, providing an opening for comparative-historical methods that can produce a more fine-grained understanding of the way power operates within specific cases and across different structural contexts.[3]

This research project therefore combines three different methods:

1. *Comparative-historical analysis*: Comparative-historical case study methods are generally considered well-suited for addressing the "big questions" of structural change in the social world. As Mahoney and Rueschemeyer

put it, "big processes and structures were—and still are—most appropriately studied through explicit comparisons that transcend national or regional boundaries [and] could not—and cannot—be analyzed without recognizing the importance of temporal sequences and the unfolding of events over time."[4] This research project built on both a historical dimension contrasting the crises of the prewar and the postwar periods, and in-depth comparative case studies of three contemporary debt crises. The historical dimension is intended to capture important changes in the structure of the global political economy over time, which in turn have important consequences for the explanatory variable (the structural power of finance) and the outcome of interest (the relative decline in the incidence of sovereign default). The contemporary case studies are intended to uncover the complex ways through which the explanatory variable brings about (or fails to bring about) the outcome of interest. The main findings of these comparisons are summarized in the tables at the end of each of the case studies (chapters 11, 15, 19, and 20).

2. *Systematic process analysis*: In recent years, comparative social science methodologists have increasingly come to recognize the need to combine traditional cross-case comparisons with systematic within-case analysis.[5] One particularly prominent within-case method in the political sciences is systematic process analysis, or process tracing, as it is more commonly known.[6] In this method, the researcher postulates a specific causal mechanism linking a hypothesized explanatory variable to the outcome of interest, and then investigates whether the causal processes implied by a specific theory hold up against diagnostic pieces of evidence derived from a variety of sources pertaining to the case in question. As such, process tracing is "an indispensable tool for theory testing and theory development not only because it generates numerous observations within a case, but because these observations must be linked in particular ways to constitute an explanation of the case."[7] In chapter 1, I developed a set of flowcharts representing the causal mechanisms implied by each of the traditional hypotheses in the economics literature, and then tested the different "moments" within these causal chains against the empirical evidence, finding the first three explanations (reputation, sanctions, and institutions) to be unconvincing. In chapters 2 and 3, I integrated the causal process implied by the spillover costs hypothesis into a critical political economy framework highlighting distributional conflicts and power asymmetries, and incorporated this into a theory of the structural power of finance. In chapter 4, I then outlined the three enforcement mechanisms through which I hypothesize this power to operate, as well as the conditions under which these are likely to be effective or not. In the remainder of the book, I tested these propositions against both the his-

torical evidence and the contemporary evidence from three of the most important debt crises of recent decades. The findings are summarized in the flowcharts at the end of the first three chapters of each of the case studies.

3. *Structural power analysis:* Susan Strange once quipped that comparativists often tend to contrast more than they compare; an observation that has more recently been echoed by Wolfgang Streeck.[8] In the political economy literature, this tendency is perhaps most clearly reflected in the influential Varieties of Capitalism (VoC) literature, which has generally emphasized the former (varieties) at the expense of the latter (capitalism). While the study of diverging policy responses to common economic shocks can undoubtedly yield interesting and important theoretical and empirical insights, a pattern of *similar* policy responses across different contexts should equally fascinate the genuine comparativist. While both approaches are valid (since there will always be both differences and similarities), some scholars have suggested that the dominant emphasis on diverging outcomes should be complemented with a more systematic attempt to "demonstrate that certain relationships among variables hold true in a wide variety of cases."[9] It is precisely in this area that structural power analysis—with its focus on the bigger picture—comes in as a useful theoretical approach. Past research drawing on structural power analysis, however, mostly steered clear of the question of methodology—an oversight that left this body of literature at a significant scholarly disadvantage with respect to the more methodologically sophisticated approach of the VoC literature. In this research project, I have sought to ground structural power analysis within a somewhat more reflexive methodological and theoretical framework, involving a systematic attempt to identify the *exact mechanisms* through which structural power operates, and the precise conditions and countervailing mechanisms under which it is likely to be effective or not. Again, these are summarized in the flowcharts in chapter 4 and tested in the case studies.

*A final word on case selection:* The contemporary cases selected for this study (Mexico, Argentina, and Greece) were chosen for a combination of substantive and theoretical reasons. Substantively, these three countries were central to their respective international crisis cycles. Mexico was at the heart of the Latin American debt crisis of the 1980s in much the same way that Greece has been at the heart of the more recent European debt crisis. Argentina's crisis came at the tail-end of the emerging-market financial crises of the late 1990s; moreover, its default was the largest in history, and therefore poses an important contrast to the prevalent pattern in international crisis management over the past four decades. Theoretically, the cases also present a sufficient degree of variation in outcomes to allow for a meaningful comparison between a "typical case" of compliance (Mexico in the 1980s) and a "deviant case" of noncompli-ance (Argentina in late-2001). On the basis of the insights derived from this comparison, we can then approach the case of greatest substantive interest (the ongoing debt crisis in Greece, which has been vacillating between compliance and noncompliance for the better part of a decade) from an original, histori-cally informed angle.[10]

# NOTES

## INTRODUCTION: THE SOVEREIGN DEBT PUZZLE

1. Bank of Canada (2017).

2. This puzzle was first identified by Eaton and Gersovitz (1981), to whose work we return in chapter 1.

3. Hickel (2017). For up-to-date numbers, see the World Bank's (2017) international debt statistics.

4. It should be emphasized from the start that default is not a binary category or a black-and-white proposition. In chapter 2, I will discuss the meaning of default and the different forms that it can take in practice, ranging from negotiated debt reschedulings at one end to outright debt repudiations on the other.

5. The quote is from a conference presentation by Ocampo (2013). Eichengreen (1991, 154) confirms: "In contrast with the 1980s, outright default was common in the era of bond finance."

6. Winkler (1933, 1).

7. Flandreau and Flores (2009, 659).

8. Marichal (1989, 66).

9. Hobson (1902); Hilferding (1910); Luxemburg (1913); Lenin (1917); Bukharin (1918).

10. Mitchener and Weidenmier (2011, 156). These findings have been contested by Tomz (2007).

11. Polanyi (1944, 14).

12. Winkler (1933, xvi).

13. Eichengreen and Portes (1990); Jorgensen and Sachs (1989).

14. In his review of five centuries of sovereign lending, for instance, Dyson (2014, 323) notes that "the absence of sovereign default became the new norm."

15. Eichengreen and Bordo (2003).

16. Bank of Canada (2017).

17. Eaton and Gersovitz (1981); Tomz (2007).

18. Bulow and Rogoff (1989).

19. North and Weingast (1989); Schultz and Weingast (2003).

20. Panizza, Sturzenegger and Zettelmeyer (2009, 693).

21. Well-known contributions to the political economy of the Latin American debt crisis include those by Stallings (1987); Griffith-Jones (1988); Frieden (1991a); Haggard and Kaufman (1992). Others, like Gourevitch (1986), did not look specifically at sovereign debt crises but made important contributions to the political economy of comparative policy responses to international economic crises.

22. For more on these distributional conflicts and power struggles, see Streeck (2013) and Frieden (2015).

23. For example, Lindblom (1977); Block (1987); Strange (1986). A more extensive discussion follows in chapter 3.

24. For example, Culpepper (2015); Culpepper and Reinke (2014); Hager (2016); Brooks and Lombardi (2016); Helleiner (2014); Woll (2014); Winecoff (2015); Fairfield (2015); Bell and Hindmoor (2016); Moran and Payne (2014).

25. This was one of the main insights from the literature on the Latin American debt crisis of the 1980s, which I will now seek to expand into a broader argument about the historical development of international credit markets and the structural power of finance in the recent European debt crisis.

26. See, for instance, Streeck (2013; 2014).

27. See Lazzarato (2012). For an anthropological discussion of the morality of debt, see Graeber (2011). For a social-theoretical treatment of this theme, see the chapter on debt in Dodd (2014). For a related history and critique of the creditor morality surrounding the "dangerous idea" of austerity, see Blyth (2013).

28. Winkler (1933, 136).

29. Borchard (1951, 243).

30. There is a large literature on the consequences of financial globalization and international capital mobility for state autonomy and governments' room of maneuver, which we will briefly discuss in chapter 3.

31. Cited in Donadio and Erlanger (2012).

32. Armingeon and Baccaro (2012, 182).

# 1: WHY DO COUNTRIES REPAY THEIR DEBTS?

1. "The most radical way of posing the question is to ask whether there would be a sovereign debt market [at all] if creditors had no direct power to enforce repayment whatsoever" (Panizza et al. 2009, 9).

2. Buchheit and Gulati (2009, 1). Similarly, Lienau (2014, 1) observes that international lending is governed by a simple rule: "sovereign debtors must repay, regardless of the circumstances of the initial debt contract, the actual use of loan proceeds, or the exigencies of any potential default."

3. Kruger and Messmacher (2004, 3).

4. "The central issue," Martínez and Sandleris (2011, 909) write, "is not why governments default, but quite the opposite: why they usually choose not to do it."

5. Eaton and Gersovitz (1981).

6. Eaton and Gersovitz (1981, 290).

7. This is the version of the reputation argument adopted and further developed by Tomz (2007).

8. Lindert and Morton (1989, 40) concluded that "investors seem to pay little attention to the past repayment record of the borrowing governments," while Eichengreen and Portes (1989, 3) found "little evidence that countries which defaulted in the 1930s suffered inferior capital market access after World War II." Indeed, "they were offered virtually identical access to the capital market as were countries which had maintained debt service without interruption." While Ozler (1992) found that defaults after the 1930s did affect interest rates, the effect does not appear to be strong enough to deter default.

9. Jorgensen and Sachs (1989).

10. Even Cuba was able to accumulate a debt of $3.2 billion to non-U.S. banks and Western governments. As Kaletsky (1985, 88) notes, "Cuba's ability to borrow as much per head as Indonesia or Thailand, in a period of twenty years after a major debt repudiation and foreign asset confiscation, provides an eloquent example of the lack of solidarity among creditor nations and private banks in response to defaults."

11. Cited in Kraft (1984, 19, 35).

12. Oliveri (1992, 16).

13. Reinhart, Rogoff and Savastano (2003).

14. Cited in Blustein (2005, 30–31).

15. Eichengreen and Portes (2000); Obstfeld and Taylor (2003); Gelos, Sahay and Sandleris (2004); Datz (2013).

16. In the Bonar V and VI auctions, for instance, 70 and 80 percent of bonds, respectively, were sold to international investors (Gelpern 2005, 1).

17. Datz (2009, 470).

18. "[T]he amount of credit declined dramatically in 2001 and reached a low point in 2005. . . . Credit began to flow in again in 2005 and by 2006 reaching the levels of 1994–5. Thus these type of sanctions were of short duration and one can conclude that the evidence shows a myopic view of the default" (Baer et al. 2010, 13).

19. Gibson, Hall, and Tavlas (2011, 9–10).

20. Eaton and Fernandez (1995, 31).

21. Das, Papaioannou, and Trebesch (2012, 60). Cruces and Trebesch (2013), by contrast, find that larger defaults do lead to higher borrowing costs and longer exclusions from capital markets, indicating some long-term reputational consequences of default. Tomz' (2007) book currently stands as the most important and most sophisticated defense of the reputation hypothesis in the political science and IR/IPE literature.

22. Gelos, Sahay, and Sandleris (2004, 1), for instance, find that it only took past defaulters an average of 4.5 years to regain full capital market access in the 1980s. By the 1990s, this duration had been reduced to 0 to 2 years, with an average of just 3.5 months, leading the authors to conclude that "we are unable to detect strong punishment of defaulting countries by credit markets" (ibid.). Similarly, Borensztein and Panizza (2008) find that yield spreads tend to stabilize one or two years after default.

23. Bulow and Rogoff (1989).

24. Reinhart and Rogoff (2009, 54).

25. Kolb (2011, 9).

26. Reinhart and Rogoff (2009, 57).

27. Eichengreen (2002).

28. Moody's (2000).

29. "As an initial matter," Choi, Gulati, and Posner (2012, 133) point out, "one can wonder why anyone pays attention to sovereign contracts at all, [since] it will almost always be impossible for creditors to march into a country and simply repossess the assets of the sovereign even if a contract so allows."

30. Mauro, Sussman, and Yafeh (2006, 133).

31. Borchard (1951, 172).

32. Kaletsky (1985, 21).

33. Griffith-Jones (1988, 360).

34. Panizza, Sturzenegger, and Zettelmeyer (2009, 9).

35. Cited in Gelpern (2005, 4).

36. Buchheit and Gulati (2009, 1).

37. As Buchheit and Gulati (2010, 2) pointed out early on, "from the legal standpoint, the salient feature of Greece's bond debt is that approximately 90% of the total is governed by Greek law."

38. Allen & Overy (2012, 11); see also Choi, Gulati, and Posner (2011).

39. Ahmed, Alfaro, and Maurer (2010, 45). A more recent paper by Schumacher, Trebesch, and Enderlein (2014) challenges this perspective, finding a "drastic rise of sovereign debt litigation" and "significant externalities" outside of the courtroom.

40. Eichengreen (1992, 260); Jorgensen and Sachs (1989, 66); Skiles (1988, 24).

41. Diaz-Alejandro (1983, 29).

42. This argument is developed by Tomz (2007).

43. See Helleiner (2005) and the Argentine case study in Part IV of this book.

44. Rose (2005, 205).

45. "Contrary to the prediction of the trade sanction argument," Martínez and Sandleris (2011, 911) find, "there seems to be no significant decline on bilateral trade between the defaulting country and defaulted creditor countries in the aftermath of defaults." Given these unambiguous findings, the authors conclude that "trade sanctions can be ruled out as the enforcement mechanism for sovereign debt repayment." See also Das, Papaioannou, and Trebesch (2012, 61–2).

46. Panizza, Sturzenegger, and Zettelmeyer (2009, 29).

47. Mitchener and Weidenmier (2005); Ahmed, Alfaro, and Maurer (2010).

48. Mitchener and Weidenmier (2011, 156).

49. Mitchener and Weidenmier (2011, 163). The historical case studies by Borchard (1951) and Wynne (1951) also appear to confirm the effectiveness of financial control and military sanctions in enforcing repayment.

50. Tomz and Wright (2008, 6–7).

51. Tomz (2007).

52. Mauro, Sussman, and Yafeh (2006); Finnemore (2003). As Panizza et al. (2009, 28) write, "regardless of how the debate between Tomz (2007) and Mitchener and Weidenmier (2005) is resolved, there does not appear to be any recent evidence for supersanctions."

53. North and Weingast (1989).

54. North and Weingast (1989, 808).

55. North and Weingast (1989, 829).

56. Schultz and Weingast (2003).

57. Schultz and Weingast (2003, 11).

58. Eichengreen, Haussman, and Panizza (2005). Buckley (2009, 2) explains the notion of original sin in simple terms: "As a nation can only print its own currency, and as poor countries invariably can only borrow abroad in other nation's currencies, sovereign debtors can be unable to service their foreign-currency denominated debts as they fall due."

59. Robinson (1998).

60. Stasavage (2002). While Robinson and Stasavage call into question the internal validity of the democratic advantage hypothesis, a number of other studies have challenged its external validity (e.g., Brewer and Rivoli 1990; Sussman and Yafeh 2000; Tomz 2002; Saiegh 2005).

61. Stasavage (2007a; 2007b; 2011).

62. Flandreau and Flores (2009, 679).

63. Balcerowicz (2010, 4–5).

64. Archer, Biglaiser, and DeRouen (2007); Saiegh (2005).

65. Mauro, Sussman, and Yafeh (2006, 1).

66. Enderlein, Trebesch, and Von Daniels (2011, 24).

67. Oliveri (1992, 163, 165).

68. Bailey and Cohen (1987).

69. Middlebrook (1989).

70. Roddick (1988, 49).

71. Cited in Berg (1984, 4).

72. Kaufman (1985, 474).

73. Cited in Tussie (1988, 293).

74. Ferreira Rubio and Goretti (1995, 2).

75. Rose-Ackerman, Desierto, and Volosin (2010). Stinga (2009) shows that the use of law-making NUDs (as compared to simple presidential decrees) increased sharply after 1994 to 30 percent of total decrees issued (up from 13 percent before 1994). He moreover notes how this "confirm[s] the important role of institutional veto powers exclusively in favor of the President."

76. Schamis (2002a, 87).

77. Rose-Ackerman, Desierto, and Volosin (2010, 1).

78. Tomz (2002).

79. Beaulieu, Cox, and Saiegh (2012, 709–10).

80. Archer, Biglaiser, and DeRouen (2007, 341).

81. Saiegh (2005, 20).

82. Reinhart and Rogoff (2009, 57).

83. e.g., Cole and Kehoe (2000); Dooley (2000); Gelos, Sahay, and Sandleris (2004); Alfaro and Kanczuk (2005); Sandleris (2008; 2014); and Mendoza and Yue (2011).

84. Mengus (2014).

85. Kaminsky and Schmukler (2002); Levy-Yeyati and Panizza (2011); Borensztein, Cowan, and Valenzuela 2007; Borensztein and Panizza (2008).

86. Gennaioli, Martin, and Rossi (2013, 1); see also Angeloni and Wolff (2012).

87. Brutti (2011). See also Bank for International Settlements (2011).

88. Cruces (2007); Arteta and Hale (2005); Das, Papaioannou, and Trebesch (2012; 2011); Fuentes and Saravia (2010); Cohen (1991); Rogoff (1999, 31); Panizza et al. (2009).

89. Borensztein and Panizza (2010); Fuentes and Saravia (2010, 337), "if there are any costs derived from default, it is likely that they last only for a limited number of periods [sic.]."

90. Lanau (2008).

91. Rabobank (2011, 1).

## 2: A Critical Political Economy Approach

1. This assumption can be summarized as follows: "the borrower country, conceptualized as a unitary agent, compares the relative utility of repaying its debt and of defaulting on its debt; as a rational agent, it defaults when the utility from default is larger" (Dimsky 2011, 119).

2. The political economy scholarship on Latin American debt (e.g., Stallings 1987; Griffith-Jones 1988; Frieden 1991a; Haggard and Kaufman 1992) has done much to illuminate this dimension. As Frieden (1989, 24) has noted, for instance, "foreign debt is often a source of domestic political conflict, for it can raise important redistributive issues." I propose to follow this line of analysis, placing distributional conflict at the heart of the analysis of sovereign debt repayment (see also the more recent work by Frieden 2015).

3. Streeck (2014) has recently developed a political economy approach to public debt that accords central importance to such distributional conflicts and power differentials, although he mostly focuses on the wealthy OECD countries, especially those in the Eurozone, whose debts tend to be domestically held. Streeck pays less attention to developing countries and middle-income peripheral borrowers, whose debts are more likely to be held by foreign creditors in the wealthy countries, adding a key international dimension. In a similar vein, Hager (2016) has recently published a fascinating study on public debt, power, and inequality in the United States that successfully manages to incorporate the international dimension of Chinese debt ownership, but the "exorbitant privilege" of seigniorage renders the U.S. case very distinct from any other. I build and expand on such analyses, while looking more explicitly at peripheral borrowers, whose defining structural weakness ("original sin") is often their dependence on foreign sources of credit.

4. Lienau (2014, 37) has criticized a similar conception in the International Relations literature: "[I]n the preferred metaphor of international relations theory, this account of sovereignty conceives of the state as a 'unitary black box' whose internal machinations are irrelevant to its foreign interactions."

5. As Guembel and Sussman (2008, 3) have rightly noted, "this aggregation ignores important conflicts of interests within the debtor country, [arising] because some agents, presumably those who are better off, are invested in their own country's sovereign bonds, while poor agents have no such positions."

6. Tomz (2002, 2); Drazen (1998); Beetsma (1994); Calvo (1988).

7. As Streeck (2013, 14) has put it, "the politics of public debt may be conceived in terms of a *distributional conflict between creditors and citizens*," with both constituencies laying a claim on scarce public funds "in the form of contractual-commercial and political-social rights, respectively." Frieden (1991a) developed a more specific approach looking at the interaction between class-based and sector-based conflict and cooperation.

8. Waldenström (2011, 287–288).

9. Tomz (2002); Saiegh (2005); Lapavitsas et al. (2012). Of course, there are important countervailing factors here. Workers' bank deposits or pension funds may be at risk in the event of a default, for instance, or their employers may go bankrupt leaving them without a job. For this reason, workers can never simply be assumed to automatically support a unilateral default strategy.

10. Streeck (2011, 9) remarks that "standard economic theory treats social structure and the distribution of interests and power vested in it as exogenous, holding them constant and thereby making them both invisible and, for the purposes of economic 'science', naturally given."

11. As Lipson (1981, 606) pointed out years ago in a seminal article, "the metaphor of anarchy, so often used to describe the underlying conditions of international rela-

tions, should not be interpreted as an absence of structures that constrain state behavior and give rise to stable expectations. What must be explored . . . is the character of the international political structures that have thus far prompted debt service by sovereigns, even when they have found it onerous to continue payments." These structures include both global capital markets and international financial institutions. As Lipson notes, "what is most compelling about these structures is that sovereigns are constrained less by other sovereigns than by sanctions and incentives organized primarily by multinational banks and official multilateral lenders."

12. Streeck (2011, 9–10).

13. Kolb (2011, 7) perfectly illustrates this tendency when he writes that "default by a sovereign borrower is almost always a choice, and because the default is by a government, such a choice necessarily has a political component."

14. Lienau (2014, 5).

15. For an example of this, see Reinhart and Rogoff (2009, 54).

16. For example, Eaton, Gersovitz and Stiglitz (1986, 29) write that, since national wealth is always greater than the total outstanding debt, "it seems implausible that lending to developing countries is constrained by their ability to pay. Long before a country's ability to pay would become relevant, its willingness to pay constrains its access to credit." More recently, Mauro and Yafeh (2003, 11) reached a similar conclusion, arguing that "willingness to pay seems to have been more important than ability to pay."

17. Choi, Gulati, and Posner (2012, 132–133). Panizza, Sturzenegger, and Zettelmeyer (2009, 668) claim that ability to pay is of limited import "since even crises that are triggered by a bad shock could be viewed as 'willingness to pay' crises in the sense that, with sufficient adjustment (e.g., a large decline in consumption), repayment would be feasible."

18. Das, Papaioannou, and Trebesch (2012, 67); Cooper and Sachs (1985).

19. Winkler (1933, 31) observed early on that "Defaults on the part of nations seem to occur either immediately preceding a boom or immediately following." For more recent evidence on this, see Reinhart, Reinhart, and Trebesch (2016); Accominotti and Eichengreen (2016); Kaminsky and Vega-Garcia (2016).

20. Eichengreen, Hausmann, and Panizza (2005).

21. Kaminsky and Vega-Garcia (2016, 81, 82).

22. Manasse and Roubini (2009) and Catão and Milesi-Ferretti (2014) are notable exceptions.

23. Grossman and Van Huyck's (1985) recognition of "excusable defaults" is a notable exception to this tendency.

24. Reinhart and Rogoff (2009, 11); Wright (2010, 3); Tomz and Wright (2007, 353); Beers and Chambers (2006, 22).

25. Sartori (1970).

26. Enderlein, Trebesch, and Von Daniels (2011), for instance, criticize the literature's implicit conceptualization of default as a binary variable (default vs. nondefault), and develop a more nuanced approach based on nine different indicators that can account for different gradations of coerciveness. In a similar vein, Arellano, Mateos-Planas, and Ríos-Rull (2013) have sought to define the concept of a partial default to break out of the stark full repayment vs. full default dichotomy.

27. Das, Papaioannou, and Trebesch (2012, 9). Borchard (1951, 129) made a similar distinction between outright repudiation ("a refusal to admit the binding character of

an obligation") and simple default ("which admits the binding character of the debt but pleads inability to meet its terms"). The International Swaps and Derivatives Association (ISDA) defines debt repudiation as "a situation in which an authorized officer rejects or challenges the validity of one or more obligations."

28. A further distinction that is not recognized in the tables needs to be made between domestic and external default, whereby the focus of this book—as was already established in the introduction—is firmly on the latter: external default on cross-border loans.

29. See the volume by Guzman, Ocampo, and Stiglitz (2016) for more on this.

30. This formulation is due to Marks (1978, 231).

## 3: The Structural Power of Finance

1. Donadio and Povoledo (2011). In the online version of the report, this sentence was later changed to: "roiling financial markets have upended traditional democratic processes." See Rachel Donadio and Elisabetta Povoledo, "Berlusconi Steps Down, and Italy Pulses with Change," *New York Times*, November 12, 2011, https://www.nytimes.com/2011/11/13/world/europe/silvio-berlusconi-resign-italy-austerity-measures.html.

2. Bennhold (2012).

3. Wolf (2012).

4. Altman (2011).

5. For example, Marx (1867; 1894; 1939); Hilferding (1910); Lenin (1917); Bukharin (1918); Harvey (1982); Arrighi (1994).

6. Mills (1956).

7. Dahl (1961).

8. Dahl (1959, 36). Moreover, he reasoned that "none of these aggregates is homogeneous for all purposes; that each of them is highly influential over some scopes but weak over many others; and that the power to reject undesired alternatives is more common than the power to dominate over outcomes directly."

9. Miliband (1969, 23).

10. Barrow (1993, 25).

11. Gilens and Page (2014, 1).

12. Poulantzas (1969, 70).

13. Poulantzas (1969, 73).

14. Poulantzas (1969, 70).

15. Barrow (1993, 46).

16. Poulantzas (1978, 129).

17. Lindblom (1977).

18. Lindblom (1977, 168).

19. Lindblom (1982).

20. Lindblom (1982, 237).

21. Block (1987, 8).

22. Culpepper (2008, 7). "As long as the process of accumulation is private," Adam Przeworski (1980, 55) wrote, "the entire society is dependent upon maintaining private profits and upon the actions of capitalists allocating these profits."

23. Lindblom (1977, 175).

24. In an early critique, Holloway and Picciotto (1978, 3) argued that both Poulantzas and Miliband suffered from "an inadequate theorization of the relation between the economic and the political as discrete forms of capitalist social relations." By failing to articulate how capital and the state are actually interrelated, both ended up *reifying* the duality. If we are to take our political economy seriously, Holloway and Picciotto insisted, we should "break out of this dichotomy by developing an adequate theory of this relation."

25. Goldscheid (1919); Schumpeter (1918, 100–01).

26. O'Connor (1973, 6).

27. "On the one hand," O'Connor (1973, 188) wrote, "the growth of state debt gives the treasury more power in monetary and fiscal planning. On the other, the institution of the debt normally tightens capital's grip on the state." See also Dyson (2014, 34).

28. Mandel (1971, 16).

29. Previous Marxist studies referred to the "structural dependence of the state on capital" (e.g., Przeworski and Wallerstein 1988).

30. As Culpepper (2015, 399) notes, "the structure of the capitalist system is one in which each [state and finance] depends on the other. Studying structural power means being attentive to the political implications of both elements of this mutual dependency."

31. See Dahl (1957). This conception of power was criticized early on by Bachrach and Baratz (1962) for eliminating the possibility of analyzing less direct forms of power, most importantly agenda-setting power, which has since become known as the "second face" of power. In another important contribution, Lukes (1974) subsequently took Bachrach and Baratz to task for not going far enough, proposing a third face of power that allowed for the internalization of discipline, in much the same way as Foucault had theorized.

32. Barnett and Duvall (2005, 53).

33. Strange (1988, 31). See also: Waltzenbach (2000); Lawton, Rosenau, and Verdun (2000, 5); Kirshner (2009, 208).

34. Strange (1994, 31).

35. Culpepper (2015); Culpepper and Reinke (2014).

36. Frieden (2015, 6) similarly notes that "debtors have powerful weapons in their arsenal, in particular the threat of suspending service on their debts—of defaulting. Creditors can threaten to cut borrowers off from financing, but debtors can threaten to cut creditors off from their earnings."

37. McKinsey (2013). They have since fallen dramatically: by 2012 they were 60 percent below their peak.

38. Hirschman (1970, 82) already argued that voice is "appreciably strengthened if [it] is backed up by the *threat of exit* . . . whether it is made openly or whether the possibility of exit is merely well understood to be an element in the situation by all concerned." There is a large literature highlighting the constraining effects of financial globalization on democratic responsiveness (e.g., Frieden 1991b; Helleiner 1994; Cerny 1995; Mahon 1996; Rodrik 1997), although some have sought to add nuance or question the notion that increased capital mobility constrains policy autonomy (e.g., Garrett 1998; Mosley 2000).

39. Andrews (1994, 199). Hacker and Pierson (2002, 282) similarly argue that "capital mobility is a key—and highly variable—element of business' structural position."

40. For example, "financial globalization enhances the authority of market agents at the expense of sovereign governments" (Cohen 2012, 175). See also Underhill and

Zhang (2008); Rodrik and Subramanian (2009). For a contrarian view, see Mosley (2003), who argues that globalization does not lead to a "race to the bottom."

41. Strange (1998, 25). For more on this "strange power," see Keohane (2000); Lawton, Rosenau, Verdun (2000).

42. Strange (1998, 18).

43. "What has been much less obvious to IPE scholars," Strange (1991, 35) lamented after the international debt crisis of the 1980s, "was the structural power exercised by whoever or whatever determined the financial structure, especially the relations between creditors and debtors."

44. Leander (2000, 350); Strange (1998, 180).

45. Strange (1996).

46. For example, Krippner (2011); Duménil and Levy (2011); Panitch and Gindin (2013).

47. Sassen (1996).

48. As Lapavitsas (2013, 194) notes, the period of globalization has principally been characterized by the "ascendancy of finance," which is precisely what the concept of financialization aims to capture.

49. Definitions include "the increasing importance of financial markets, financial motives, financial institutions, and financial elites in the operation of the economy and its governing institutions, both at the national and international level" (Epstein 2001, 1); "a pattern of accumulation in which profits accrue primarily through financial channels rather than through trade and commodity production" (Krippner 2005, 174, see also Arrighi 1994); "a process whereby financial markets, financial institutions, and financial elites gain greater influence over economic policy and economic outcomes" (Palley 2007, 1); "a broad-based transformation in which financial activities . . . become increasingly dominant" (Krippner 2011, 2); "a systemic transformation of capitalism, as a historical period" (Lapavitsas 2014).

50. Zingales (2012).

51. Haldane (2010, 5–6).

52. Haldane (2010, 5–6).

53. Uhde and Heimeshoff (2009).

54. Santillán Salgado (2011).

55. Haldane (2010, 6).

56. Wolf (2010).

57. Harvey (2010).

58. The quote is from Foster (2007, 6).

59. Lapavitsas (2008, 3); Krippner (2011).

60. Bhagwati (1998); Wade and Veneroso (1998). For more on the debates surrounding the IMF's role in the East Asian crisis of the late-1990s, see for instance Stiglitz (2002) and Noble and Ravenhill (2000).

61. Streeck (2014, 72)

62. "In contrast to the *Staatsvolk* of the tax state," Streeck (2014, 73) writes, "the *Marktvolk* of the debt state is transnationally integrated. They are bound to national states purely by contractual ties, as investors rather than citizens."

63. On the latter point, Streeck (2014, 80) notes that creditors "cannot vote out a government that is not to their liking; they can, however, sell off their existing bonds or

refrain from participating in a new auction of public debt," thereby punishing government through higher borrowing costs.

64. Streeck (2014, 80–81).

65. Streeck (2014, 93).

66. Streeck (2014, 83–84).

## 4: THREE ENFORCEMENT MECHANISMS

1. See, for instance, Keohane (2000, x); Lawton, Rosenau, and Verdun (2000); Verdun (2000, 78).

2. Culpepper (2011, 185).

3. Even though Lindblom explicitly recognized the possibility that policymakers sometimes decide to face down market discipline—noting that wherever there are prisons there will also be prison breaks—he never really specified when business interests are likely to win out and when they are not.

4. Helleiner (2006, 84).

5. Cohen (2000, 99).

6. e.g., Culpepper (2015); Culpepper and Reinke (2014); Helleiner (2014); Woll (2014); Winecoff (2015); Emmenegger (2015); Fairfield (2015); Bell and Hindmoor (2016); Moran and Payne (2014).

7. Culpepper and Reinke (2014, 6).

8. My theoretical approach, especially the argument that follows—about the concentrated nature of credit markets easing the formation of an international creditors' cartel—is greatly indebted to some of the important contributions on the Latin American debt crisis made by scholars like Griffith-Jones and Sunkel (1986), Stallings (1987), Marichal (1989) and others.

9. Suter and Stamm (1992, 648) already hypothesized that "the degree of creditors' influence [is] determined by the actor structure or, more specifically, by the actor structure on the creditors' side. . . . [T]he capability of creditors to exert far-reaching influence on debtor countries and to enforce hard terms of debt settlements against the interests of debtor countries, depends upon the establishment of strong cooperative networks among creditors. The institutionalization of such creditor clubs on their part presupposes that a relatively few actors dominate a dense interaction structure."

10. Kaplan (2013), for instance, finds that decentralized bond markets increase market discipline on the fiscal policies of Latin American borrowers. "Compared to vested bankers," Kaplan and Thomsson (2017, 606) reason, "bondholders can more readily exit their lending relationships, leaving governments with less room to manage the economy. Their constant threat of capital withdrawal compels sovereign debtors to pursue austerity with commitments to balanced budgets and low inflation." The authors present convincing evidence for their claims. It should be noted, however, that Kaplan and Thomsson are primarily concerned with market discipline as it relates to *fiscal policy*, or government spending more specifically. The research presented in this book looks at a different dependent variable (debt repayment), which may help explain the diverging findings. In the following passages, I will seek to explain why concentrated markets tend to improve creditors' capacity to make debtors repay their debts.

11. In this respect, my argument is similar to Frieden's (1991a), when he notes that highly concentrated sectors tend to find it easier to cooperate, avoid collective action problems, and exert political influence.

12. Soederberg (2005, 935).

13. There is an extensive body of literature on the politics of IMF lending. Much of this work is concerned with the question who drives IMF policy: the Fund's own staff and management, its most powerful shareholders (the United States and Western Europe), ideological considerations, or private financial interests. Answering this question is unfortunately beyond the scope of this study. The point I make here has less to do with the *determinants* of IMF policy and more with its *consequences*, i.e., the credit-enforcement role that its lending, monitoring, and surveillance activities have fulfilled within the global financial architecture since the early 1980s. In short, I propose to look at what the IMF actually does (to provide conditional lending to distressed borrowers) and the central role that this activity plays in keeping debtors solvent and servicing their debts. There is unfortunately no space here to discuss the related debates on the determinants of IMF policy, but the interested reader should certainly consult past studies by Pastor (1987); Thacker (1999); Vreeland (2003); Babb (2003); Broz (2005); Broz and Hawes (2006); Copelovitch (2010); as well as more recent studies by Kentikelenis, Stubbs and King (2016) and the forthcoming monograph by Kentikelenis.

14. This is another important point derived from the literature on the Latin American debt crisis. It is also made by the IMF's in-house historian, Boughton (2001), in his extensive study of the Fund's role in the international crisis management during the 1980s and 1990s.

15. Broz (2005).

16. Maxfield (1990, 93).

17. Maxfield (1990); Streeck (2014).

18. Streeck (2015) refers to this process as the rise of the "consolidation state."

19. One such study finds that "the willingness of a government to repay its debts, and thus its ability to borrow in the first place, depends on the development of private financial markets. More developed financial markets translate into more severe consequences of public defaults, thereby providing governments with stronger incentives to repay" (Gennaioli, Martin, and Rossi 2013, 34).

## 5: THE MAKING OF THE INDEBTED STATE

1. Hamilton (1947, 118).

2. Fratianni and Spinelli (2006, 262).

3. Stasavage (2011, 31).

4. Dyson (2014).

5. Marx (1867, 919).

6. Pezzolo (2005, 147); on the interrelated nature of war-making, state-formation, and credit access, see Tilly (1982). Drelichman and Voth (2014, 27) note that "successful European powers typically spent around three-quarters of tax revenue on war and related activities."

7. Richard Ehrenberg wrote that "regular revenues, often very large, were never sufficient to produce the enormous sums needed. The credit of the cities therefore was

accordingly their most powerful weapon in the struggle for their freedom" (cited in Stasavage 2011, 28).

8. Pezzolo (2007, 4). Dyson (2014, 107) makes a similar observation: "Above all, the development of public debt was rooted in the evolution of a rentier class."

9. Pezzolo (2007, 15–16). He further notes that, "If this hypothesis is plausible, it is then necessary to reconsider the classic model put forward by North and Weingast."

10. Stasavage (2011, 2–3). Dyson (2014, 123, 126) also writes that "oligarchic structures of rule entrenched creditor power. . . . The concept of public debt disguised the grip of a small social oligarchy on fiscal government."

11. Cited in Dyson (2014, 18).

12. Pezzolo (2005, 157–158).

13. Pezzolo (2005, 163).

14. Pezzolo (2007, 15). Dyson (2014, 108) refers to this as "the private management of the public debt."

15. Fratianni (2006, 494).

16. Braudel (1972).

17. As Stasavage (2011, 14) notes, "merchants tended to own debt whereas members of the craft guilds bore a significant part of the tax burden necessary to service this debt." Pezzolo (2005, 160) reports that "Florentines clearly felt that the lower classes paid creditors through the taxes on consumption."

18. Marx (1867, 919; 1852).

19. Stasavage (2011, 21): "With some risk of simplification, we can speak of an underlying conflict between mercantile groups who held public annuities and who sought to ensure that taxes would be levied to service these obligations, and other social groups who protested against heavy indirect taxes on common consumption goods. Disputes about public finance were often coupled with conflict over the structure of representative institutions in each city and with the question of which social groups should be represented on city councils. Should these bodies retain an oligarchical form with a small number of individuals in control, or should they instead be opened to other groups and in particular craft guild representatives?"

20. By weakening the existing oligarchy, the revolt cleared the way for the rise of the Medici as the city's dominant family (Pezzolo 2005, 149).

21. Arrighi (1994, 325–326).

22. Stasavage (2011, 21).

23. O'Brien (2001), for instance, notes that the English Civil War started off as a tax revolt in response to a rising sovereign debt burden. Historian John Shovlin (2006, 9) writes that "it is a truism that the French Revolution was touched off by the near bankruptcy of the state." On the Whiskey Rebellion and fiscal conflict in the United States more generally, see the fascinating recent study by Hager (2016). The Dutch case will be briefly discussed toward the end of this chapter.

24. "The small percentage of foreign investors suggests that the government credits market did not extend beyond the city walls" (Pezzolo 2005, 156–157).

25. Winkler (1933, 28–29).

26. Hunt (1990) has contested the notion that Edward III's default provoked the collapse of the Bardi and Peruzzi, arguing that a homegrown banking crisis was to blame.

27. Arrighi (1994).

28. Both cited in Arrighi (1994, 126, 98).

29. Drelichman and Voth (2014, 6).

30. Drelichman and Voth use the term "lenders' coalition" to refer to this unified creditor front. I will use the term "creditors' cartel" instead to dovetail with the literature on the 1980s debt crisis (see Part III of this book). The term "cartel" in this case does not refer to the creditors' pricing power but rather to their capacity to act in unison and prevent any one lender from breaking ranks. As for the concentration of the debt, the Spinola, Grimaldo, and Fugger families accounted for 40 percent of all loans (Drelichman and Voth 2014, 146).

31. Drelichman and Voth (2014, 38).

32. Drelichman and Voth (2014, 208).

33. Drelichman and Voth (2014, 38).

34. Tracy (1985, 217).

35. Tracy (1985, 217). As Fratianni (2006, 403–404) writes, citing Parker (1975), "Like in Genoa, creditors in the United Provinces had a high degree of protection because: '. . . the chief investors ran the government.'"

36. Braudel (1984, 246–247). Riley (1980, 15, 16) notes that "By the 1780s every major power in Europe, with the sole exception of Prussia, and many of the secondary powers had found it expedient to supplement ordinary revenues either with loans raised directly in the Dutch Republic or by attracting Dutch capital to domestic issues. . . . In terms both of the frequency of issue and the volume of capital moving abroad, Amsterdam's most intensive activity occurred between 1780 and 1793."

37. "[The] individualistic character [of its capital market] made Amsterdam susceptible to liquidity crises that tended to be prolonged because of the lack of effective management in their early stages. . . . As the capital market shifted toward government lending, the individualistic credit structure of commercial finance remained intact" (Riley 1980, 32, 35).

38. Riley (1980, 37, 38) refers to "a limited number of firms" and a "select company of bankers" that "controlled the issue of most loans to European governments."

39. "There was little leeway for firms excluded from that circle to acquire entry to it, although there was sometimes intense competition within the circle to acquire or retain agencies" (Riley 1980, 42).

40. Only Britain and France were able to float a sizable domestic debt, although even here Dutch capital inflows played an important role, as Dutch investors would simply invest their surplus capital into the London or Paris capital market through various local intermediaries.

41. Arrighi, Hui, Ray, and Reifer (1999, 54); see also Braudel (1984, 248, 273, 276).

42. Riley (1980, 173).

## 6: The Internationalization of Finance

1. Neal (1990); Carlos and Neal (2011); Bank of England (2017).

2. Dickson (1967); Arrighi (1994, 211).

3. As Winkler (1933, 34–35) notes, "in the course of the nineteenth century, the policy of lending abroad made considerable progress, and we gradually begin to observe the development of internationalism and banking and finance. It was in the course of this period that defaults became more numerous."

4. As Marichal (1989, 14) notes, "the allure of Latin American riches, real or imaginary, was a major factor in one of the earliest stock and bond crazes of modern capitalism."

5. Marichal (1989, 43). Bolívar's letter to de Larrea is cited in Marichal (1989, 33). See also Winkler (1933), Borchard (1951), and Wynne (1951).

6. Marichal (1989, 43, 55, 67).

7. Spain in 1834, Portugal in 1837 and 1841, Greece in 1843 (see Reinhart and Rogoff 2009).

8. Wynne (1951, 288–90).

9. Borchard (1951, 240).

10. Strong (2002).

11. Feis (1930, 102–103, 104–105).

12. Marichal (1989, 61).

13. Marichal (1989, 66).

14. As Borchard (1951, 241–242) notes, "thus we can observe the progression of a policy over a relatively short span of years."

15. Feis (1933, 105); Marichal (1989, 102); Luxemburg (1913, 405–406).

16. Luxemburg (1913, 401). See also Hobson (1902); Hilferding (1910); Bukharin (1918).

17. Feis (1930, 105).

18. Marichal (1989, 121).

19. *Twycross v. Dreyfus*, 5 Ch. D 605, 616 (C. A. 1877), cited in Kaletsky (1985, 7–8).

20. "The state of disunity and the lack of coordination among the bondholder groups was one of the major problems in the enforcement of sovereign compliance with debt contracts. The lack of coordination among the bondholders not only allowed for new loans to defaulters but also raised the risk premiums on foreign loans" (Birdal 2010, 47).

21. Feis (1930, 114–115).

22. Borchard (1951, xxiv).

23. Polanyi (1944, 14).

24. Borchard (1951, 172). Feis (1930, 105) also notes that bondholders were "backed by punitive powers of the stock exchange."

25. Borchard (1951, 178).

26. Marichal (1989, 121–122) notes that "the suspension of interest payments provided breathing room for the suffocating economies of the smaller countries of Central and South America."

27. Feis (1930, 12).

28. Wynne (1951, 313–414).

29. Winkler (1933, 147–148).

30. Wynne (1951, 296, 344).

31. The first citation is from Wynne (1951, 335), the second from Feis (1930, 292).

32. Ahmed, Alfaro, and Maurer (2010). For an extensive treatment of this episode, see Hood (1975).

33. Both cited in Tomz (2007, 136).

34. Tomz (2007, 138). Feis (1930, 109) also notes that "a dozen issues divided the British and Venezuelan governments, defaulted government bonds, unpaid contract claims,

reparations for property seized or damaged in civil war, and matters more indisputably in the realm of government concern—ship seizures and delays. . . . In Parliament, which had not been given explanatory papers before action, Lord Lansdowne emphasized the personal injury done to British subjects, the affront to English sovereignty, rather than the direct pecuniary claims—though the collection of these, too, he defended."

35. "Thereafter Europe could, by proper planning, collect its debts through the United States" (Feis 1930, 109).

36. Winkler (1933, 137); see also Borchard (1951, 4–7).

37. Cited in Winkler (1933, 137–138).

38. Marichal (1989, 174) writes that "powerful financial groups of the United States" played an important role in shaping this regime, "impos[ing] a tight grip over fiscal and monetary policy as well as over the public and private financial machinery of each of these nations . . . 'dollar diplomacy' was here equivalent to a symbiosis of financial and military colonialism."

39. Feis (1930, 109–11).

40. Cited in Feis (1930, 110).

41. Tomz (2007). See also Borchard (1951, 269, 273): "The cases which are usually considered as examples of military intervention in support of bondholders are rare. In fact, even they are not exclusively illustrations of military protection of bondholders but involve other types of claimants as well. . . . [A]rmed intervention for the collection of bond obligations is not likely to occur. If such intervention does occur, it will most probably have political objectives, to which economic considerations are secondary."

42. Cited in Lindert (1989, 236).

43. For a treatment of the role of bondholder organizations prior to World War I, see Esteves (2007).

44. Flandreau and Flores (2012, 21–22).

45. Flandreau and Flores (2009, 647).

46. Polanyi (1944, 10–11).

47. Nasar (2000). Flandreau and Flores (2009, 4–7): "Just as today's IMF usually makes a last-ditch effort to shore up a failing country, intermediaries in the past were involved at the early stages of any crisis."

48. Flandreau and Flores (2009, 663–667).

49. Cited in Fishlow (1989, 92).

50. Flandreau and Flores (2011, 4).


## 7: From Great Depression to Financial Repression

1. Arrighi (1994).

2. Stallings (1987); Papadia (2017).

3. As Winkler (1933, xvi) put it, the outcome of the Great Depression "tells of how little the investor has learned from the past experiences of earlier creditors, thus proving once again the truth of the Hegelian dictum that 'We learn from history that we learn nothing from history.'"

4. Eichengreen (2008, 67–69).

5. Eichengreen and Portes (1985, 16).

6. Eichengreen (2008, 70).

7. Reinhart and Rogoff (2009); Eichengreen and Portes (1985).

8. Borchard (1951, 224).

9. Papadia (2017, 9).

10. Marichal (1989, 203–204).

11. Marichal (1989, 103).

12. Marichal (1989, 208). Diaz-Alejandro (1983) and Fishlow (1989) have also highlighted the collapse in the terms of trade as an important external factor leading to the defaults of the 1930s.

13. Winkler (1933, xvi, 47).

14. Accominotti and Eichengreen (2016). Of course there were important variations in how this systemic crisis impacted individual countries (see Papadia 2017).

15. Borchard (1951, 143).

16. The term "excusable default" was coined by Grossman and Van Huyck (1985).

17. Cited in Borchard (1951, 243).

18. Cited in Winkler (1933, 63–64).

19. Ocampo (2013).

20. Cited in Tomz (2007, 105).

21. As Feis (1930, 464) remarked in relation to corporate bond finance during this period, "securities changed hands daily, unremarked amidst the multitude of similar transactions. The investment had become large-scale, and anonymous. Thousands of individuals unknown to each other joined to support a company of whose existence a periodical report would be their most direct proof. History was being made without a signature."

22. Fishlow (1985, 429).

23. Jorgensen and Sachs (1989, 49).

24. Frieden (2015).

25. Marichal (1989, 228).

26. Winkler (1933, 51). "Such supervision," he added (ibid.), "might be exercised directly by governments, by the central banks of the various countries, or by special organizations sponsored by the private banks."

27. Kindleberger (1988, 175). While he referred specifically to the absence of a central bank able to maintain monetary and financial stability, the same observation applies to the solvency of sovereign borrowers.

28. Kindleberger (1988, 177, 179).

29. Maxfield (1990).

30. Eichengreen (2008). While Eichengreen specifically refers to external *monetary* discipline in relation to the international gold standard, the same principle applies to external debt service.

31. "In numerous instances such protests led to outright default" (Marichal 1989, 11).

32. Papadia (2017, 19), for instance, stresses this interplay between domestic and international conditions in shaping the variation in the severity of defaults. Interestingly, he finds that "reliance on external sources of finance made countries more reluctant to renege on their foreign payments and face the possibility of being cut off from international financial markets."

33. Dyson (2014).

34. Harvey (2010).

35. "This comparison suggests that countries that opted for default recovered more successfully from the ravages of the Great Depression. . . . [H]eavy defaulters recovered more quickly from the Depression" (Eichengreen and Portes 1990, 77, 80).

36. Jorgensen and Sachs (1989, 78); Bertola and Ocampo (2012, 13). See also Marichal (1989, 228): "While the Great Depression and World War II severely dislocated the Latin American economies, the defaults helped pave the way for recovery. By unilaterally freezing their external financial commitments, a large number of republics were able to attenuate the impact of the international financial and commercial crisis that had originated with the crash of 1929. The defaults did not lead to economic independence, but they did reduce financial dependency during more than a decade."

37. Ruggie (1982).

38. Lemoine (2013); Ali Abbas et al. (2014).

39. Reinhart and Sbrancia (2011, 4).

40. Blyth (2013, 240).

41. Reinhart and Rogoff (2009).

42. For extensive treatments of the resurrection of global finance, see, for instance, Helleiner (1994); Duménil and Levy (2004); Krippner (2011); Panitch and Gindin (2012).

43. Unlike Reinhart and Rogoff (2009), whose book provides a wealth of statistical data to make short shrift of the misleading notion that "this time is different"—i.e., the persistent idea that *this time* rising debt levels will not lead to widespread crisis and default—I focus not on the recurring nature of crises (which is indeed inherent to financial capitalism), but on the *differences in the prevailing policy response*. As I will show in the three contemporary case studies that follow, the postwar experience in international crisis management is qualitatively distinct from the prewar pattern in crisis management. In this sense, it would be fair to say that—despite the recurring nature of international debt crises—the changing outcomes of these crises seem to confirm the fact that this time actually *is* different. The rest of this book will demonstrate why.


## 8: Syndicated Lending and the Creditors' Cartel

1. Cited in Kraft (1984, 3).

2. Marichal (1989).

3. "The option of unilateral action (leading to default or extended moratoria) has not been officially adopted by any major debtor since 1982" (Griffith–Jones 1988, 7–8).

4. Bertola and Ocampo (2012, 18).

5. Oliveri (1992, 2).

6. Cited in Quirk (1983, 10).

7. Harvey (2005, 29).

8. George (1988, 67). Or see Branford and Kucinski (1988, 133): "why have the governments of the big Latin American debtors been so reluctant to build up a debt strategy based on default? And why have the governments of the smaller nations been so slow to create an effective debtors' cartel that would give them the collective leverage to default?"

9. Griffith-Jones (1988, 6).

10. Stallings (1987, 1–2).

11. These observations constitute a challenge to the reputation hypothesis, according to which we would expect defaulters to face higher borrowing costs than non-

defaulters, or to be excluded from credit markets altogether. In reality, creditors did not heed countries' previous repayment records—they were relatively myopic in their risk assessment and purely in the game for short-term profits.

12. Branford and Kucinski (1988, 95).

13. Gurría (1995b, 191).

14. Kraft (1984, 35).

15. Griffith-Jones and Sunkel (1986, 110).

16. Silva Herzog (1991, 53).

17. Maxfield (1990, 111).

18. Cited in Kraft (1984, 4).

19. Oliveri (1992, 93).

20. World Bank (2017).

21. Silva Herzog (1991, 58).

22. Silva Herzog (1991, 58).

23. Interview with the author (Gurría 2013).

24. First citation from interview with the author (Gurría 2013); second citation from Kraft (1984, 3–4).

25. Babb (2001, 21).

26. Interview with the author (Gurría 2013).

27. Cited in Kraft (1984, 4).

28. Silva Herzog (1991, 59).

29. Interview with the author (Gurría 2013).

30. As Aggarwal (1987, 21) notes, "the oligopolistic nature of the banking community and the acute overexposure of large banks facilitated cooperation."

31. Lipson (1985, 210).

32. Oliveri (1992, 61, 72). Marichal (1989, 236–237) notes that "the coordination among these financial monoliths is not perfect because they are rivals, but generally they act in concert, using their considerable political influence to get the respective national governments to support their financial strategies."

33. Devlin and Ffrench-Davis (1995, 129).

34. Cited in George (1988, 68).

35. Teichman (2001, 49).

36. Tussie (2013).

37. Canak (1989, 20).

38. The first quote is from Stallings (2013); the second from Stallings (1987, 4).

39. Lipson (1981, 622).

40. Marichal (1989, 236–237).

41. Cited in Roodman (2006, 16–17).

42. Cited in Kraft (1984, 39).

## 9: The IMF's "Triumphant Return" in the 1980s

1. "Whereas intervention in the 1930s was sporadic," Eichengreen and Lindert (1989, 20) write, "in the 1980s it has been systematic."

2. Jorgensen and Sachs (1989, 48).

3. Lindert (1989, 238).

4. Kraft (1984, 9); Sachs and Huizinga (1987, 555).

5. Cline (1995, 6–7).

6. Lissakers (1983, 164).

7. Lissakers (1983, 160).

8. Interview with the author (Van Wijnbergen 2013).

9. Boughton (2001, 290).

10. Teichman (2001, 48).

11. Cited in Kraft (1984, 7).

12. Boughton (2001, 297).

13. See Reinhart and Rogoff (2009) for the most prominent example.

14. Gurría (1988, 75).

15. Interview with the author (Gurría 2013).

16. Cited in Helleiner (1994, 176).

17. Bailey and Cohen (1987, 24).

18. Kindleberger (1973).

19. Wood (1984, 705).

20. Delamaide (1984, 111).

21. "It is the catalysing effect of IMF agreements which gives the fund its real powers. . . . [T]he loans negotiated after an IMF agreement are far greater than the IMF loan itself" (Körner, Maass, et al. 1986, 65).

22. Helleiner (1994); Harvey (2005). Also see Bhagwati (1998) and Wade and Veneroso (1998) on the emergence of a Wall Street-IMF-Treasury complex during the management of the crises of the 1990s.

23. Lipson (1985, 223); Delamaide (1984, 112).

24. Griffith-Jones (1988, 3).

25. Cited in Bernal (1982, 82).

26. Cited in Delamaide (1984, 221).

27. Roddick (1988, 38).

28. Lipson (1981, 623).

29. Branford and Kucinski (1988, 111).

30. Branford and Kucinski (1988, 18).

31. Cited in Roddick (1988, 44).

32. Cited in Leslie (1983, 24).

33. Pastor (1989, 91). Others, however, have argued that these conditions were still regularly flouted by the debtor country governments in the 1980s.

34. Chahoud (1991, 31).

35. Cited in Wood (1984, 706). Haggard (1985) and Edwards (1989) have shown how debtors did not always necessarily live up to the word of their Stand-By Arrangements.

36. Wood (1984, 707).

37. Lindert (1989, 227).

38. Boughton (2001, 290–291); Lissakers (1983, 167).

39. Kraft (1984, 8).

## 10: The Rise of the Bankers' Alliance

1. Maxfield (1990).

2. Maxfield (1990).

3. Silva Herzog (1991, 57).

4. Silva Herzog (1991, 57).

5. Silva Herzog (1991, 58); Maxfield (1990).

6. As Aggarwal (1996, 363) has noted, Mexico's "economic recovery depended on trade and foreign investment," and the country's position "was further weakened by its dependence upon maintaining amicable relations with the international financial community."

7. Alvarez (2014, 1).

8. Alvarez (2014, 26).

9. Boughton (2001, 540).

10. Maxfield (1990, 144).

11. Delamaide (1984, 103).

12. Tello (1984, 45), cited in Cypher (1990, 123).

13. Marois (2007, 7).

14. Blanco, cited in Maxfield (1990, 144).

15. Cypher (1990, 123).

16. Maxfield (1990, 144).

17. Cited in Kraft (1984, 39).

18. Cited in Maxfield (1992, 75).

19. Boughton (2001, 300).

20. Maxfield (1990, 146). Mexico's president was not the only one who depended on Silva Herzog's bridging role. In a sign that Mexico's creditors had come to rely on his creditor-friendly leadership as well, U.S. Treasury Secretary Donald Regan actively pressed his Mexican colleague not to resign. "It was a critical moment for Mexico and for the international financial system," Boughton (2001, 302) recalls, "and Silva Herzog's resignation would have left a huge vacuum in the [creditors'] circle of power and influence."

21. Bailey and Cohen (1987, 20–21).

22. Maxfield (1990, 160).

23. Diaz-Alejandro (1984, 378).

24. Buffie (1990, 526).

25. Alvarez (2014, 26).

26. Cypher (1990, 175).

27. Cypher (1990, 163).

28. Maxfield (1992, 76).

29. Cited in Kraft (1984, 46).

30. Bailey and Cohen (1987, 32).

31. Cypher (1990, 163).

32. Teichman (2001, 131).

33. Babb (2001, 20).

34. *Economist* (1984, 60); *Economist* (1981, 68).

35. Bailey and Cohen (1987, 21).

36. Walton and Ragin (1989, 218).

37. Middlebrook (1989, 196).

38. As Middlebrook (1989, 196) notes, the Confederation of Mexican Workers and the Mexican Labor Congress "have not mobilised union members to challenge openly policies that harm workers' interests. Instead, organised labour has persisted in a well-established tradition of incremental, intra-elite bargaining with government officials on

a wide range of economic and political issues—despite irrefutable evidence that this approach has failed to provide benefits to compensate for workers' sacrifices."

39. King (1989, 1).
40. Cited in Teichman (2001, 60).
41. Oliveri (1992, 41).
42. Lissakers (1983, 175).

## 11: "THE RICH GOT THE LOANS, THE POOR GOT THE DEBTS"

1. For a related argument about IMF conditionality and development policy space, see Kentikelenis, Stubbs, and King (2016).
2. Pastor (1987, 13); Gurría (1995a, 36).
3. Boughton (2001, 371).
4. Gurría (1988, 89–90).
5. Gurría (1988, 90).
6. Gurría (1995a, 36).
7. Bailey and Cohen (1987, 42); Roddick (1988, 114).
8. Roddick (1988, 114); Boughton (2001, 439).
9. Teichman (2001, 135).
10. Cited in Pastor (1989, 79).
11. Boughton (2001, 276).
12. Interview with the author (Gurría 2013).
13. Roddick (1988, 49).
14. Cited in Berg (1984, 4).
15. Tussie (1988, 286).
16. Oliveri (1992, 163). In a rebuttal of the democratic advantage hypothesis, Kaufman observed that "the new democratic government of Argentina . . . was by far the most defiant, [while] Mexico's party-based authoritarian regime has been most compliant" (Kaufman 1985, 474). After a meeting with Argentine negotiators, one senior U.S. banker even exclaimed that "we expected to get facts and figures, a detailed picture of the country's medium- to long-term economic plans. All we got were some platitudes about Argentina's new democracy" (cited in Tussie 1988, 293).
17. *Wall Street Journal*, June 6, 1984.
18. Cited in Aggarwal (1996, 351).
19. Cline (1983); Tussie (1988, 286–287).
20. Roddick (1988, 49).
21. Interview in *Business Week*, August 12, 1985.
22. Cited in Roddick (1988, 50).
23. Cited in Solanas (2004).
24. Branford and Kucinski (1988, 116).
25. Tussie (2013).
26. Cited in Berg (1985, 21); Roddick (1988, 14).
27. "Quotation of the Day," *New York Times*, November 30, 1987, Page A00002 of the national edition.
28. Aggarwal (1996, 40, 361).
29. Aggarwal (1996, 334).

30. Boughton (2001, 491); see also Gurría (1995a, 36); Claessens, Diwan and Fernandez-Arias (1992, 20).

31. Cline (1995, 71, 76).

32. Cline (1995, 216).

33. *New York Times,* January 6, 1989; Aggarwal (1996, 364).

34. Cited in Oliveri (1992, 73).

35. Aggarwal (1990, 26).

36. Van Wijnbergen (1991, 17).

37. Dooley (1995, 279); Dooley, Fernandez-Arias, and Kletzer (1994, 7).

38. Claessens, Diwan, and Fernandez-Arias (1992, 37).

39. Armendariz and Armendariz (1995, 138).

40. Jorgensen and Sachs (1989, 79).

41. Cline (1995, 220). He ascribes the Fund's refusal to press the banks to the Treasury's insistence that the IMF should not take a side against Wall Street in its negotiations with Mexico.

42. Claessens, Oks, and Van Wijnbergen (1993, 1).

43. Crowley (1993, 26).

44. Cline (1995, 43).

45. Aggarwal (1996, 351).

46. e.g., Dooley (1995, 275); Griffith-Jones (1988, 9); Sachs (1986, 406); Bertola and Ocampo (2012, 16).

47. Branford and Kucinski (1988); George (1988).

48. Roodman (2006, 17); Frieden (1991a, 218).

49. As Marois (2011, 18–19) puts it, "the wealthy have been able to avoid taxation through institutionalized loopholes and weak enforcement, but average wage earners cannot easily escape income tax and have therefore borne the brunt of income tax payments."

50. Lomnitz-Adler (2004, 47), cited in Harvey (2005, 100).

51. Middlebrook (1989, 198–199).

52. Pastor (1987, 249); Garuda (2000); Vreeland (2001).

53. Robinson (2004, 144).

54. Fischer (1989, 363).

55. World Bank (1983).

56. Cypher (1990, 155).

57. Pastor (1989, 98).

58. UNICEF (1989, 11).

## 12: THE EXCEPTION THAT PROVES THE RULE

1. Mortimore and Stanley (2006, 16). The total defaulted debt included $82 billion owed to private creditors, $6.3 billion to the Paris Club countries, and $9.5 billion to the IMF (Datz 2013, 12). The IMF was eventually repaid in full in 2006, following the successful private-sector debt renegotiation of 2005.

2. For example, Friedman (1995); Pauly (1997); Strange (1998); Hardt and Negri (2000); Stiglitz (2002).

3. Cooper and Momani (2005, 306), for instance, have argued that "the notion of structural discipline sets the 'reach of coercion' at a level that, at least in the Argentine

case, failed to match realities. . . . The power of international creditors' discipline appears to be far more elusive in practice than might be expected."

4. This moratorium was upheld by President Duhalde in early 2002 and only overcome after a successful debt restructuring by President Kirchner in 2005—more on which in chapter 15.

5. Rubin's former employer—Goldman Sachs—was significantly exposed to Mexican and developing country debt, leading to accusations of a possible conflict of interests.

6. Rambarran (2004, 40).

7. Dominguez and Tesar (2004, 5).

8. Epstein and Pion-Berlin (2006, 6).

9. Baer, Margot, and Montes-Rojas (2010, 11–12).

10. As Setser and Gelpern (2006, 31) have pointed out, "continued support for the status quo reflected a key economic reality: all other policy options carried higher short-term costs than trying to muddle through."

11. Cited in Setser and Gelpern (2006, 475).

12. See, for example, Wade and Veneroso (1998); Stiglitz (2002).

13. Blustein (2005, 30–31).

14. Gelpern (2005, 3).

15. These higher interest rates are clearly reflected in the sudden spike in interest payments in the second half of 2001, depicted in figure 12.5.

16. Blustein (2005, 125).

17. Lewis (2009, 133).

18. Cited in Cooper and Momani (2005, 316).

19. Teubal (2004, 182).

20. Rambarran (2004, 6).

21. Lewis (2009, 157).

22. Blustein (2005, 162).

## 13: From IMF Poster Child to Wayward Student

1. Cibils, Weisbrot, and Kar (2002, 6).

2. Lewis (2009, 56).

3. Cibils and LoVuolo (2012, 768) referred to the invitation of De la Rúa as "a clear sign of [the IMF's] approval and support for the economic policies implemented in Argentina during the 1990s."

4. Cibils and LoVuolo (2012, 755).

5. Cited in Blustein (2005, 58).

6. International Monetary Fund (1999).

7. See Broz (2005) on the role of conservative U.S. lawmakers in opposing further bailouts.

8. Cooper and Momani (2005, 313); Helleiner (2005, 963).

9. Setser and Gelpern (2006, 474).

10. Cooper and Momani (2005, 308).

11. See, e.g., Mussa (2002).

12. Díaz-Cassou, Erce-Domínguez and Vázquez-Zamora (2008, 16).

13. Helleiner (2005, 362).
14. Setser and Gelpern (2006, 474).
15. Blustein (2005, 117).
16. Cibils, Weisbrot, and Kar (2002); Helleiner (2005).
17. Corrales (2002, 35).
18. Corrales (2002, 35–36).
19. Cited in Blustein (2005, 142).
20. Blustein (2005, 175).
21. Corrales (2002, 36).
22. Wucker (2003, 50).
23. Damill, Frenkel, and Rapetti (2005, 74).
24. Blustein (2005, 98).
25. Cited in Blustein (2005, 122).
26. Schamis (2002a, 87).
27. Setser and Gelpern (2006, 475).
28. Cavallo (2004, 147).

## 14: THE RISE AND FALL OF THE *PATRIA FINANCIERA*

1. "Argentina became one of the most highly liberalized financial systems in the world" (O'Connell 2005).
2. Schamis (2002b, 129).
3. Cited in Schamis (2002a, 82).
4. Cooper and Momani (2005, 308).
5. Mussa (2002).
6. Lewis (2009, 130).
7. Blustein (2005, 13); Rock (2002).
8. Schamis (2002a, 87).
9. Setser and Gelpern (2006, 472) point out that "the institutional power of the economy ministry in particular hinged in no small part on its ability to deliver external financing."
10. "The technocratic Cavallo demanded vast discretionary powers over economic policy, just as he had done under Menem. This . . . reinforced a policymaking process already heavily dependent on executive degrees, marginalized Congress, and devalued the overall process of representation" (Schamis 2002a, 87).
11. Setser and Gelpern (2006, 475–476).
12. Blustein (2005, 168) confirms this: "more worrisome than litigation . . . was the concern about the banking system."
13. Cited in Blustein (2005, 168).
14. Cavallo (2002, 1–2).
15. Cavallo (2002, 2).
16. Epstein and Pion-Berlin (2006, 7).
17. Epstein and Pion-Berlin (2006, 8).
18. Klein (2004, 3).
19. Epstein and Pion-Berlin (2006, 9).

20. "El 70% está insatisfecho con las instituciones políticas," *La Nación,* October 28, 2001.

21. Tomz (2002, 14–15).

22. Tomz (2002, 14–15).

23. Schuster (2008, 165).

24. Tomz (2002, 15).

25. Tomz (2002, 15).

26. Tomz (2002, 15).

27. Cited in Tomz (2002, 15).

28. Tomz (2002, 13–14).

29. Hausman and Velasco (2002, 11).

30. Schuster (2008, 167).

31. See, for instance, Colectivo Situaciones (2002); Zibechi (2003); Sitrin (2012).

32. Rambarran (2004, 6–7).

33. Cited in Ariso and Jacobo (2002, 159).

34. Lewis (2009, 135–136).

35. Malamud (2006, 13).

36. Malamud (2006, 13–14).

37. Lewis (2009, 136).

38. Malamud (2006, 14).

39. Tomz (2002, 15–16).

40. Cited in Tomz (2002, 15–16).

## 15: "Even in a Default There Is Money to Be Made"

1. Levitsky and Murillo (2003, 155).

2. Lewis (2009, 147).

3. Lewis (2009, 146).

4. Baer, Margot, and Montes-Rojas (2010, 8).

5. Weisbrot and Cibils (2002, 4); Cibils, Weisbrot, and Kar (2002, 20).

6. Lewis (2009, 145–146).

7. Grugel and Riggirozzi (2007, 10).

8. Klein (2004, 4).

9. Llach (2004); Rock (2002, 56).

10. This is why Schuster (2008, 168) argues that "the power of protest has been perhaps one of the most important lessons derived from the events of December 2001."

11. Cited in Fiorentini (2012).

12. Levitsky and Murillo (2003, 155).

13. Turner and Carballo (2005, 175–176).

14. Epstein and Pion-Berlin (2006, 12).

15. Féliz (2012, 5).

16. Corrales (2002, 38–39).

17. Cited in Helleiner (2005, 954).

18. Both cited in Zibechi (2003).

19. Schuster (2008, 176).

20. Lewis (2009, 156).

21. Baer, Margot, and Montes-Rojas (2010, 12).
22. Lewis (2009, 158).
23. Gelpern (2005, 3).
24. Mortimore and Stanley (2006, 20).
25. Gelpern (2005, 3).
26. Ocampo (2013).
27. Datz (2013, 474).
28. Cited in Datz (2013, 465).
29. Lewis (2009, 158).
30. Helleiner (2005, 956).
31. All cited in Helleiner (2005).
32. Mortimore and Stanley (2006, 20).
33. Cited in Moffett (2004).
34. Cited in Moffett (2004).
35. Lewis (2009, 157).
36. Díaz-Cassou, Erce-Domínguez, and Vázquez-Zamora (2008, 15).
37. Cited in Helleiner (2005, 954).
38. Helleiner (2005, 955)
39. All cited in Helleiner (2005, 955).
40. Baer, Margot, and Montes-Rojas (2010, 12); Mortimore and Stanley (2006).
41. Cibils, Weisbrot, and Kar (2002, 21).
42. Weisbrot and Cibils (2002, 3).
43. World Bank (2017).
44. Lewis (2009, 162); Datz (2013, 472).
45. Scott (2006, 6).
46. Mortimore and Stanley (2006, 20).
47. Roubini (2005).
48. Williamson (2002, 12).
49. Williamson (2002, 11).
50. Miller, Thampanishvong, and Zhang (2004, 3–4).
51. *Economist* (2003).
52. Cited in Miller, Thampanishvong, and Zhang (2004, 24).
53. Roubini (2005).
54. Dominguez and Tesar (2004, 15–16).
55. Roubini (2005). President Macri repaid the holdouts in 2016 after a prolonged legal standoff.
56. Datz (2013, 474).
57. Moffett (2004).
58. Santiso (2003, 190), cited in Datz (2013, 474).
59. *Economist* (2005).

## 16: The Power of Finance in the Eurozone

1. This number was eventually revised upwards to €36 billion, or 15.4 percent of GDP.

2. As we saw in the historical discussion, Greece defaulted in the debt crises of the 1820s, the 1890s, and the 1930s. For more on "debt intolerance" and "serial default" see Reinhart, Rogoff, and Savastano (2003).

3. Altman (2011).

4. Barclays Capital (2011). A variety of European institutional investors (including mutual funds, pension funds, and hedge funds) also had some exposure.

5. Buchheit and Gulati (2010); Moore and Hope (2014).

6. Merler and Pisani-Ferry (2012a).

7. Boone and Johnson (2012, 4).

8. A study by Boermans and Vermeulen (2016, 12) finds that "the average market concentration in individual bonds [in the Eurozone] is generally high, especially among sovereign debt and bank bonds. We also find that the European banking sector tends to hold bonds with the lowest levels of dispersion of ownership."

9. Ardagna and Caselli (2014, 25).

10. Dyson (2014, 391).

11. As Dyson (2014, 391) puts it, "the disciplinary power of the credit rating agencies derives from the way in which the ratings that they choose to assign to states provide the signals that prompt bond and foreign exchange markets to discriminate fiscal saints from sinners."

12. Armingeon and Baccaro (2012, 182).

13. Armingeon and Baccaro (2011, 31).

14. See Blyth (2013).

15. Papaconstantinou (2016, 66, 78).

16. Papaconstantinou (2016, 69, 72).

17. These fears were not entirely unjustified. For the risk of so-called sudden stops in the context of the Eurozone, see Merler and Pisani-Ferry (2012a).

18. Ardagna and Caselli (2014, 6).

19. Papaconstantinou (2016, 188).

20. De Grauwe and Ji (2013, 3).

21. Allen & Overy (2012, 8).

22. These numbers are from the European Banking Authority's EU-wide stress test results, cited in Rocholl and Stahmer (2016).

23. Papaconstantinou (2016, 102).

24. Rommerskirchen (2015).

25. Papaconstantinou (2016, 101).

## 17: Anatomy of a "Holding Operation"

1. Buchheit and Gulati (2012, 2); Buchheit (2011, 4). As Thompson (2015, 856) puts it, "German banks were structurally hugely vulnerable to crisis once the financial boom ended because of their funding models and high leverage . . . German and French banks were also the most exposed in 2009 to the periphery."

2. European Banking Authority (2011) stress test results. Wyplosz and Sgherri (2016, 13) refer to €56 billion.

3. Buchheit and Gulati (2010, 6).

4. Cited in Fuhrmans and Moffett (2010).

5. "With the onset of the Greek crisis the German government . . . faced a serious dilemma. If it upheld the Maastricht principle of no bailouts for euro-zone states, it would either have to let the support system it had erected for Germany's banks unravel or engage in a further round of direct bailouts of these banks. If, by contrast, it accepted bailouts for other euro-zone member states, it could secure a less transparent bailout of German banks at the expense of having to re-secure domestic support for monetary union on new terms" (Thompson 2015, 858).

6. Blustein (2015).

7. Independent Evaluation Office (2016).

8. Ardagna and Caselli (2014, 13).

9. Papaconstantinou (2016, 130).

10. European Central Bank (2010a).

11. "There is only one precedent of a country succeeding in implementing an average annual primary deficit reduction larger than the one Greece was to undertake, and none that has achieved a comparable cumulative reduction over a similar number of years. Recall that the comparison programmes are the most aggressive on record in the OECD in the last 40 years" (Ardagna and Caselli 2014, 16–17).

12. Independent Evaluation Office (2016, 27).

13. Independent Evaluation Office (2016, 32).

14. Varoufakis (2017, 132).

15. Papaconstantinou (2016, 116).

16. Cited in Blustein (2015, 1).

17. "Debt restructuring was strictly off limits" (Papaconstantinou 2016, 126).

18. Thompson (2015).

19. Blustein (2015, 6) writes that "the German public . . . would never accept an emergency loan unless it came with severe conditions, enforced by arbiters with recognized neutrality and competence—and the IMF was the only institution that came close to that description."

20. "An external player with less of a political stake in the EU was expected to boost creditors' efforts of surveillance and be more effective in imposing sanctions in the case of incompliance with conditionality, for example by holding back a credit tranche. . . . [T]he IMF was seen as having the advantage of an 'exit threat,' that is, it could withhold a credit tranche or even withdraw from a programme, measures the European Commission and member states could not credibly threaten to take" Schwarzer (2015, 611).

21. Rogers (2012).

22. Cited in Robinson, Wagstyl, and Milne (2015).

23. Blustein (2016).

24. Blustein (2015, 6).

25. De Las Casas (2016).

26. Wyplosz and Sgherri (2016, 1).

27. Schadler (2016).

28. Independent Evaluation Office (2016, 15).

29. "IEO interviews and the sequence of events suggest that the Executive Board's decision-making and advisory roles were undermined, rather than strengthened as intended under the exceptional access policy procedures. Information reached Directors

practically at the same time as decisions were publicly announced by management and the IMF's European partners, leaving little room for the Board to provide real input or to influence decisions. . . . [D]elayed information and involvement deprived the Board of the ability to direct and monitor management and staff, making it difficult to hold them accountable. Thus, management's discretion and decision-making powers were left effectively unchecked" (De las Casas 2016, 14–15).

30. The minutes were leaked and published by the *Wall Street Journal* (2013).

31. Xafa (2014, 14).

32. OECD (2011).

33. Wyplosz and Sgherri (2016, 25).

34. Cline (2013, 2).

35. Blanchard and Leigh (2013).

36. Schadler (2013, 12).

37. IMF (2013). As a background paper for the IMF's Independent Evaluation Office later concluded, "debt restructuring was delayed until spring 2012, allowing private foreign creditors to reduce exposures and shift the bulk of sovereign debt into official hands" (Wyplosz and Sgherri 2016, viii).

38. Badkar (2011).

39. Cited in Islam (2013, 2–3).

40. Schadler (2013, 12).

41. As Ardagna and Caselli (2014, 10) note, "default delayed could conceivably turn into default avoided . . . , and perhaps more importantly, delaying default . . . would give core-country banking sectors time to reduce their own exposure to Greece."

42. Roth (2013, 21).

43. Cited in Smith (2014).

44. Cited in Smith (2014).

45. Weeks and Ziotis (2012).

46. Papaconstantinou (2016, 145).

47. Dyson (2014, 384) notes that the years 2011–2012 marked "a tipping point for the ECB" during which it "embraced unlimited, three-year liquidity provisions to euro area banks [and] committed to unlimited, if conditional, intervention in sovereign bond secondary markets." In the process, "the euro area sovereign debt crises catapulted the ECB into a broader role in crisis management."

48. The Irish, Italian and Spanish press have since released Trichet's letters addressed to their respective governments over the course of 2011.

49. As Papaconstantinou (2016, 191) put it, "Translation: cease and desist, or we will pull the plug on your banking system. . . . One year later, with significant fiscal consolidation behind us, with goodwill at least partially returned and with debt restructuring being openly discussed in the Eurogroup, the ECB was still threatening to use the nuclear option."

50. Parts of Trichet's letter to Papandreou have since been published in the Greek press (Palaiologos 2014).

51. Xafa (2014, 15).

52. Truth Committee on Public Debt (2015, 24); Dyson (2014, 387).

53. The European Financial Stability Fund (EFSF) and the IMF held a greater share of Greece's total debt load today, but the maturities of these obligations extend much further into the future.

54. European Central Bank (2010b). Elsewhere, Trichet stated: "It is crucial that governments implement rigorously the measures needed to ensure fiscal sustainability. It is in the context of these commitments only that we have embarked on an intervention programme in the securities markets" (European Central Bank 2010c).

55. European Central Bank (2012).

56. Cited by Reuters (2011).

57. Panico and Purificato (2013, 5).

58. Dyson (2014, 386).

59. "The SMP and then the LTFO [LTRO] provided mechanisms by which German [and other European] banks could dispose of periphery assets. The LTFO gave periphery banks the money to buy German holdings of periphery bonds. German banks were also able to use subsidiaries in the periphery to secure LTFO funding. The result was a sharp repatriation of capital from the periphery to the core of the eurozone and, by 2012, a significant inflow of capital into Germany" (Thompson 2015, 861).

## 18: The Establishment Digs In

1. Varoufakis (2013).

2. Pagoulatos (2003).

3. Pagoulatos (2003, 74).

4. Fouskas and Dimoulas (2013, 157).

5. Laskos and Tsakalotos (2013, 30).

6. Wyplosz and Sgherri (2016, 13).

7. Manolopoulos (2011); Fouskas and Dimoulas (2013, 153–154).

8. Fouskas and Dimoulas (2013, 153–154).

9. Brutti and Sauré (2014, 6–7) explicitly position their "secondary markets" hypothesis as an answer to the traditional "enforcement problem" of sovereign debt, highlighting the importance of high domestic debt concentration in preventing default.

10. Merler and Pisani-Ferry (2012a, 4).

11. Buchheit, Gelpern, Gulati, Panizza, Weder, and Zettelmeyer (2013, 25–26). The authors note that "domestic banks are relatively immune from restructurings because they expect to be recapitalized, for financial stability reasons, if their losses from domestic sovereign bond holdings are sufficiently high. Indeed, if the holdings of the banking system as a whole are high enough, the restructuring will likely not happen at all."

12. These observations differ in important respects from the conclusion reached by Pagoulatos (2014), who argues that the Greek banks lost their structural power in the crisis. Pagoulatos bases this argument narrowly on the capital mobility hypothesis, arguing that high mobility provides bankers with an exit option, whereas low mobility erodes their power. Since their mobility was reduced as they became more exposed to their own government, Pagoulatos reasons that the banks lost their privileged position. The sources of the structural power of finance, however, cannot be reduced to capital mobility alone; they must be traced back to the structural dependence of the state on credit—a dependence that in the case of Greece greatly increased as the crisis deepened and the state came to rely more and more on its domestic banks to refinance the *internal* debt, even if these banks lost their exit threat. Moreover, Pagoulatos does not spell out the relative nature of the banks' reduced power. It is one thing to note that the

banks became vulnerable and structurally constrained over the course of the crisis; it is quite another to argue that therefore the banks lost their privileged position in economic policymaking, or that the state was able to exert greater control over the banking sector. While it is certainly true that the Greek banks were weakened by their financial vulnerability, this was a weakening vis-à-vis European creditors—above all the European Central Bank, on which Greece's private banks relied for liquidity support. It does not automatically follow from this, however, that the Greek state thereby regained control over the banks; in fact, the dependence of the Greek state and banks was mutual, their fate intertwined—a phenomenon analysts refer to as the "doom loop" between sovereign and banking risk. The banks remained structurally powerful over their highly dependent national government, even as the ECB and the European creditor states wielded ultimate structural power over the banks themselves.

13. Papaconstantinou (2016, 105–106).

14. Papaconstantinou (2016, 137).

15. Mason (2013, 99).

16. Kouvelakis (2011, 19) notes that "a symbolic threshold had been crossed. . . . It was in response to this situation that a shaken Papandreou suggested his high-risk referendum initiative."

17. Papaconstantinou (2016, 159, 193).

18. Cited in Smith (2011).

19. Cited in Spiegel (2014).

20. Kouvelakis (2011, 25).

21. Spiegel (2014).

22. Papaconstantinou (2016, 225).

23. Spiegel (2014).

24. Kouvelakis (2011, 26); Papademos had notably served as governor of the Bank of Greece when, in 2002, Goldman Sachs paddled an infamous "cross-currency swap" to the Greek government that infused $1 billion of funding without this sum showing up as debt on Greece's balance sheet, thus allowing the country to borrow while still meeting the criteria for Eurozone membership.

25. As Laskos and Tsakalotos (2013, 92) write, "Papademos was chosen for his technocratic prowess and his affinity with financial markets" and he was "a favorite of both the Troika and important business and media interests within Greece itself."

26. Thompson (2015).

27. Papademos (2011).

28. Thomas (2013a).

## 19: The Socialization of Greece's Debt

1. This was followed in December 2012 by a bailout-funded debt buyback that resulted in further debt reduction of 6–11 percent of GDP (depending on the presumed discount rate).

2. Allen & Overy (2012, 13); Angeloni and Wolff (2012, 9).

3. Wyplosz and Sgherri (2016, 22).

4. As Helen Thompson notes, "for the most part this reduction in exposure occurred without the German banks incurring significant losses" (Thompson 2015, 859).

5. Kay (2012).

6. Roth (2013, 19).

7. Benedetti-Valentini and Kirchfeld (2012).

8. Benedetti-Valentini and Kirchfeld (2012).

9. Roth (2013).

10. Allen & Overy (2012, 9).

11. Allen & Overy (2012, 9).

12. "In the 1980s, it was possible to organise bank creditors because typically the number of really major banks involved was not more than a couple of dozen. With the re-opening of the bond market for emerging countries in the 1990s, there was no mechanism whereby bondholders were sufficiently organised to form a representative group. There were too many bondholders and some were not subject to official pressures" (Allen & Overy 2012, 9).

13. Cited in Chaffin (2012).

14. Papaconstantinou (2016, 236).

15. Cited in Baker and Sassard (2012).

16. Zettelmeyer, Trebesch, and Gulati (2013, 26).

17. Hope (2017).

18. The figures are from Rocholl and Stahmer (2016).

19. "Because many of the investors who are expected to participate in the stock program are the same executives who were running the banks at the time of their near collapse, critics see it as a case of bankers being rewarded despite their management missteps. And they say the Greek government is forgoing billions of euros in potential revenue with the way the stock offering is being handled. To date, of the 206 billion euros . . . that the troika has dispensed to bail out Greece, an estimated 58 billion euros—all of which comes from European taxpayers—has been spent propping up the country's banks" (Thomas 2013b).

20. Varoufakis (2014).

21. Thomas (2012).

22. "Among the losers of PSI were public entities which suffered losses of €16.2 billion. Most of these losses accrued to pension schemes, with losses of €14.5 billion. . . . Another group, which registered significant losses, were the small bondholders. It is estimated that more than 15,000 families lost their life savings" (Truth Committee on Public Debt 2015, 17, 20).

23. Papaconstantinou (2016, 233).

24. Papaconstantinou (2016, 251–252).

25. Zettelmeyer, Trebesch and Gulati (2013, 34).

26. "[S]tarting in May 2010, Greece began drawing down on its official sector loans, partly to cover its budget deficits, but mostly to repay its bondholders at par. The liabilities thus inexorably began to migrate out of the hands of the folks who had lent the money and taken the commercial risk (the bondholders) and into the hands of Greece's official (taxpayer funded) sponsors. It was a policy that lasted . . . until the summer of 2011. It seems belatedly to have dawned on the official sector players that they were gradually displacing their private sector counterparts as the principal lenders to Greece" (Buchheit and Gulati 2012, 4).

27. Rocholl and Stahmer (2016).

28. Roubini (2012); Buchheit and Gulati (2012, 4); Eiffel Group & Glienicker Group (2015); Mody (2015). A background paper for the IMF's Independent Evaluation Office

noted: "The burden of adjustment was not sufficiently spread across different strata of the society" (Wyplosz and Sgherri 2016, 37).

29. IMF (2013a, 17).

30. Cited in Varoufakis (2017, 533).

31. Cline (2013, 4).

32. Ardagna and Caselli (2014, 17).

33. This outcome is precisely what IMF programs are formally supposed to avoid. As a paper for the IMF's Independent Evaluation Office notes, "the socialization of private losses is commonly seen as a cardinal sin that financial assistance programs should try to prevent" (Wyplosz and Sgherri 2016, 22–23).

34. Varoufakis (2017, 491).

35. See the *Financial Times* report by Khan (2017), who also cites the ECB's response: "'This is a matter of national competence and falls outside the remit of the ECB,' said the central bank. It added that decisions about what to do with the profits would be taken by national member states. 'Any future decisions on the transfer to the Greek State of amounts equivalent to the National Central Bank's (NCB) income do not fall within the remit of the ECB or the NCBs, but rather that of the national governments of the euro area Member States,' said the letter signed by ECB president Mario Draghi."

36. Dany, Gropp, Littke, and Von Schweinitz (2015).

37. "The measures taken so far place the burden of adjustment almost exclusively on the crisis countries, despite that they are not solely responsible for the crisis. Even worse, within these countries, the burden is borne disproportionately by the weakest and least-responsible for the crisis" (Antzoulatos 2012, 531).

38. Giannitsis and Zografakis (2015, 17).

39. Giannitsis and Zografakis (2015, 36, 63).

40. IMF (2013a, 21–27).

41. Xafa (2014, 14).

42. IMF (2013a, 27).

43. IMF (2013a, 33).

44. Gechert and Rannenberg (2015, 1).

45. Cited in Truth Committee on Public Debt (2015).

## 20: The Defeat of the Athens Spring

1. Culpepper (2015) has usefully pointed out that future structural power scholarship should precisely focus on such situations of clashing preferences. Although he focuses explicitly on the structural power of business, we can apply the same principle to the study of the structural power of official-sector creditors.

2. Mody (2015).

3. Independent Evaluation Office (2016, 36). For more on the social crisis, see for instance the important work done on the health effects of austerity by Stuckler and Basu (2014) and Kentikelenis et al. (2014).

4. Stangos (2014).

5. See, for instance, Vradis and Dalakoglou (2011); Sitrin and Azzellini (2014); Kentikelenis (2017).

6. First quote cited in Spiegel (2014); second quote cited in Islam (2013, 4).

7. Cited in Reguly (2013).

8. Spiegel (2014).

9. A former Syriza comrade who had known Tsipras since his adolescent days told Reuters that: "He has grown in leaps politically, but his decisions are a result of his fears. Fear that he will be the prime minister who led Greece out of the euro, fear his party will split, and also fear he is betraying the ideology he has fought for and believed in since he was a child" (Kyriakidou 2015).

10. Bloomberg (2015).

11. This is a reference to Jeroen Dijsselbloem, the Dutch finance minister and chairman of the Eurogroup, who infamously accused Southern European countries of spending their money on "booze and women."

12. Varoufakis (2017) has a similar interpretation of the events leading up to his own defeat and resignation.

13. Chrysoloras, Ziotis, and Bensasson (2015); Chrysoloras and Bensasson (2015).

14. Smith (2015).

15. Cited in Smith (2015).

16. Cited in Hope and Wagsty (2015).

17. Cited in Thompson, C. (2015).

18. When personally confronted by the author, at a gathering of the European Left in Florence in November 2014, with the question what he would do if Greece's creditors refused to give in to his demands for a renegotiation of Greece's debts, Tsipras simply laughed off the possibility: "This is a game of chicken," he replied, "and we won't blink first." To the author, it already seemed clear at this point that Tsipras woefully underestimated the prevailing balance of power within the Eurozone.

19. The amount of €17 billion excludes treasury bills, which are regularly rolled over by the domestic banks that hold them. If these bills are included the total amount that was due in 2015 rises to €37.5 billion.

20. Cited in Bensasson and Chrysoloras (2015).

21. Tooze (2017).

22. Varoufakis (2017, 311–312).

23. Varoufakis (2017, 311–312). He concludes that, "far from being apolitical, the ECB's huge discretionary power over when to enforce its rules and when to circumvent them—when to strangle a government and when not to—make it the most political central bank in the world . . . Draghi ended up making our government the exception by imposing upon us rules that had been waived for everyone else."

24. Braun (2017, 49).

25. Braun (2017, 49).

26. Varoufakis (2017, 136).

27. Giugliano (2015); Spiegel (2015).

28. Chrysoloras and Bensasson (2015).

29. Jolly and Bradsher (2015).

30. Eurobank (2016, 39).

31. Cited in Barker and Hope (2015).

32. The missed payment did not technically constitute a default since the IMF operates a 30-day grace period before declaring a government to be in default.

33. Cited in Evans-Pritchard (2015).

34. Any value over 50.00 marks an expansion of output and anything below 50.00 marks a contraction.

35. Cited in Hannon (2015).

36. European Commission (2015); Strupczewski (2015).

37. Varoufakis (2017, 162–163).

38. Confirmed by Peter Spiegel (2015): "Many officials—up to and including some eurozone finance ministers—have suggested privately that only a decision by Alexis Tsipras, Greek prime minister, to jettison the far left of his governing Syriza party can make a bailout agreement possible."

39. Varoufakis (2017, 306).

40. Varoufakis (2017, 86) recounts that he had been told by a friend inside the party that "it is commonly known that [Dragasakis] has made it his business, even back in his communist party days, to keep the bankers close." Kouvelakis (2016, 51–52), who served on Syriza's central committee, confirms that Dragasakis "eventually used the connections he had with the *nomenklatura* in Eastern European countries to facilitate business arrangements between Greek entrepreneurs and the new economic elites emerging there in the 1990s. So he had close relations with Greek business circles, especially bankers."

41. Kouvelakis and Budgen (2015).

42. Kouvelakis (2016, 52).

43. Kouvelakis (2016, 50–51).

44. Kouvelakis (2016, 48–49).

45. The story of Syriza's internal evolution is recounted in greater detail by Kouvelakis (2016).

46. Varoufakis (2017, 321, 347).

47. Varoufakis (2017, 394).

48. Tsakalotos' words here are cited by Varoufakis (2017, 443–444).

49. According to Varoufakis (2017, 443–444), this is what Dragasakis responded to his question, at the emergency cabinet meeting on June 26, whether the government had called the referendum to win it or to lose it. "[U]nlike me," Varoufakis writes, "Dragasakis wanted to lose so as to legitimize our acceptance of the Troika's terms." See also Kouvelakis (2016, 63–64).

50. Cited in Sterling (2015).

51. Cited in Salmon (2015).

52. Galatsidas and Arnett (2015).

53. Varoufakis (2017, 467).

54. Lambert (2015).

55. Cited in Evans-Pritchard (2015).

56. Cited in Spiegel and Wagstyl (2015).

57. Cited in Salmon (2015).

## CONCLUSION: SHAKING OFF THE BURDEN

1. Reinhart and Rogoff (2009, xxxi) also note this "fairly recent quiet spell in which governments have generally honored their debt obligations," and point out how this in-

sistence on full repayment in the wake of the global financial crisis of 2008 "is far from the norm" from a long-term historical point of view.

2. See, for instance, the previously cited contributions by Jorgensen and Sachs (1989), who found that the terms of the rescheduling deals of the 1980s became considerably more creditor-friendly than the unilateral defaults of the 1930s, or Lindert (1989), who found that in the 1980s official intervention became "far less concessionary" than it had been in the 1930s. More recently, Guzman, Ocampo and Stiglitz (2016) have argued that contemporary debt restructurings are often "too little, too late" from the perspective of the debtor country. An anonymous reviewer of this manuscript has pointed out that Meyer, Reinhart, and Trebesch offer a different perspective, finding remarkable similarity in haircuts over 200 years of debt restructuring. Their study was ongoing and unpublished at the time that this book went to press, though, which meant that I was unfortunately unable to assess Meyer, Reinhart, and Trebesch's findings and compare them to the evidence presented by the other scholars cited above and elsewhere in this book.

3. "The debts are politically secure because they are backed by a network of multilateral banks, private lenders, and . . . advanced capitalist states. They are jointly capable of consolidating debt in emergencies and severely punishing those who default lightly" (Lipson 1981, 629).

4. Wolf (2012).

5. The document is available at: http://online.wsj.com/public/resources/documents /greecedoc.pdf.

6. Wagstyl and Robinson (2015).

7. Schultz and Weingast (2003).

8. Watkins (2014, 14).

9. Dalakoglou (2014).

10. Alderman (2013).

11. J.P. Morgan (2013).

12. To give some concrete examples: an emergency act passed along with the first memorandum of understanding in 2010 (s.1.4 law 3845/2010) provides government ministers with a "*carte blanche*" to "issue executive decrees which can cover all aspects of economic and social policy, repeal pre-existing laws and sign further binding agreements giving away parts of national sovereignty without Parliamentary approval." Another act (s.1.9 law 3847/2010) states that memorandums and agreements with foreign creditors become binding upon their signing and "are introduced in Parliament later just for 'debate and information' " (both cited in Douzinas 2013).

13. Bugaric (2013, 25).

14. Cited in Kocharov (2012).

15. ECLR (2012, 5–6).

16. Cited in Donadio and Erlanger (2012).

17. Historian Jamie Martin is currently working on a book on the continuities between nineteenth-century financial control and contemporary IMF programs. See his short blog post on "the colonial origins of the Greek bailout" for a basic outline of this research project (Martin 2015).

18. Cited in Ehrenberg (1968, 46–47).

19. Ehrenberg (1968, 49).

20. See Solon's poem at the beginning of the book, which reached us via Aristotle.

21. Graeber (2011).

22. Galofré-Vilà, McKee, Meissner, and Stuckler (2016). See also Ritschl (2012).

23. See www.clubdeparis.org.

24. Varoufakis (2016) makes the same observation.

25. See IMF (2013b, 1, 7, 15). For more on the "too little, too late" phenomenon, see Ocampo (2016) and the other contributions in the edited volume by Guzman, Ocampo, and Stiglitz (2016).

26. Again, see the recent volume by Guzman, Ocampo, and Stiglitz (2016).

27. The IMF had already been discussing such an SDRM scheme internally for quite some time. The Argentine crisis and default provided extra impetus, as did pressure by U.S. Treasury Secretary Taylor, who saw an orderly sovereign bankruptcy regime as a possible way to avoid further international bailouts.

28. Krueger (2002). As Brooks and Lombardi (2016) put it, "the evidence indicates that private creditor power, especially the structural kind, has been an important force behind the more widespread opposition to a sovereign debt restructuring mechanism."

29. Piketty (2014).

30. See Lienau (2014).

31. Toussaint (2017).

32. Truth Committee on Public Debt (2015).

33. Damle (2007).

## Appendix: A Word on Methodology

1. As Datz (2009, 2) writes, "What is clear is that it has been increasingly difficult to treat debt restructuring episodes as homogenous developments amendable to parsimonious and generalizable models. Despite their undeniable importance in creating and analyzing datasets that track correlations among key variables, large-N analyses and formal models cannot condense in agglomerating exercises all the nuances that compose different restructuring scenarios, which, to a large extent, may determine default costs in the short and long-terms." More generally, Hall (2006, 26) has observed that, "despite the continuing popularity of regression analysis, recent theoretical developments in social science tend to specify a world whose causal structure is too complex to be tested effectively by conventional statistical methods."

2. McKeown (2004); Mahoney (2007).

3. A potential drawback of such comparative case study methods is that there is a risk of researchers cherry-picking their cases to fit a particular theory. In this case, the project sought to ward off this danger of confirmation bias by deliberately selecting the two most prominent historical cases along the dependent variable—a point to which I will return later—to ensure that there were two contrasting outcomes under investigation (Mexico's compliance vs. Argentina's defiance), allowing for careful empirical scrutiny of the underlying causal mechanisms that produced these outcomes. The lessons from this comparison were subsequently applied to the Greek case, whose outcome was still largely unknown at the outset of this research project in 2011.

4. Mahoney and Rueschemeyer (2003, 7). George and Bennett (2005, 21) argue that, "compared to the shortcomings of regression-analysis and the [deductive-nomological

model developed by King, Keohane and Verba], the advantages of such comparative-historical methods include much higher conceptual validity, the ability to derive new hypotheses from the observations, the exploration of new causal mechanisms, and the modeling of complex causal relations."

5. Collier (1993, 17) argues that "within-case comparisons are critical to the viability of small-N analysis." George and Bennett (2005, 18) identify a "growing consensus that the strongest means of drawing inferences from case studies is the use of a combination of within-case analysis and cross-case comparisons."

6. Hall (2006).

7. George and Bennett (2005, 207).

8. See chapter 9, "How to Study Contemporary Capitalism?" in Streeck (2016).

9. Peters (1998, 26).

10. For the distinction between typical and deviant cases, and a methodological treatment of case selection more generally, see Gerring (2007). Argentina is probably better defined as a specific subtype of the deviant case—a so-called influential case—which at first glance appears to call into question or even invalidate a theory's predictions, but which upon closer inspection ends up confirming that theory. As Gerring (2007, 108) puts it, "the influential case is the 'case that proves the rule.'" In some circles, there is a view that scholars should always avoid selection along the dependent variable, but leading methodologists have convincingly argued that for small-N studies it is much wiser to deliberately select cases with a view to obtaining a representative sample of outcomes. Collier and Mahoney (1996, 21) stress that "in small-N studies, random sampling may produce more problems than it solves." Instead, they propose theoretically informed nonrandom case selection as "an alternative approach . . . that deliberately produces a sample in which the variance on the dependent variable is similar to its variance in the larger set of cases."

# REFERENCES

Accominotti, Olivier, and Barry Eichengreen. 2016. "The Mother of All Sudden Stops: Capital Flows and Reversals in Europe, 1919–32." *Economic History Review* 69, no. 2: 469–492.

Aggarwal, Vinod K. 1987. "International Debt Threat: Bargaining among Creditors and Debtors in the 1980s." Policy Papers in International Affairs, no. 29, University of California, Berkeley, Institute of International Studies.

———. 1990. "Foreign Debt: The Mexican Experience." *Relazioni Internazionali*, September: 26–33.

———. 1996. *Debt Games: Strategic Interaction in International Debt Rescheduling*. Cambridge: Cambridge University Press.

Ahmed, Faisal Z., Laura Alfaro, and Noel Maurer. 2010. "Lawsuits and Empire: On the Enforcement of Sovereign Debt in Latin America." *Law and Contemporary Problems* 73, no. 39: 39–46.

Alderman, Liz. 2013. "Wave of Protests Engulfs Greece." *New York Times*, June 17, 2013.

Alfaro, Laura, and Fabio Kanczuk. 2005. "Sovereign Debt as a Contingent Claim: A Quantitative Approach." *Journal of International Economics* 65, no. 2: 297–314.

Ali Abbas, S. M., Laura Blattner, Mark De Broeck, Asmaa El-Ganainy, and Malin Hu. 2014. "Sovereign Debt Composition in Advanced Economies: A Historical Perspective." IMF Working Paper 14/162. International Monetary Fund, Washington, DC.

Allen & Overy. 2012. "How the Greek Debt Reorganisation of 2012 Changed the Rules of Sovereign Insolvency." Report by Allen & Overy's Law Intelligence Unit, London.

Altman, Roger. 2011. "We Need Not Fret over Omnipotent Markets." *Financial Times*, December 1, 2011.

Alvarez, Sebastian. 2014. "The Untold Story of the Mexican Debt Crisis: Domestic Banks and External Debt, 1977–1989." EABH Working Paper No. 14-03. European Association for Banking and Financial History, Frankfurt am Main.

———. 2016. "The Mexican Debt Crisis of 1982 Redux: Domestic Banks, International Interbank Markets and Debt Renegotiation." PhD dissertation, University of Geneva. Geneva.

———. 2017. "Venturing Abroad: The Internationalisation of Mexican Banks Prior to the 1982 Crisis." *Journal of Latin American Studies* 49, no. 3: 517–548.

———. 2018. "A Fatal Flaw: Domestic Banks and Mexico's International Negotiating Position in the 1982 Debt Crisis." *Revista de Historia Económica / Journal of Iberian and Latin American Economic History*. Advance online publication, doi: 10.1017 /S0212610918000113.

Andrews, David M. 1994. "Capital Mobility and State Autonomy: Toward a Structural Theory of International Monetary Relations." *International Studies Quarterly* 38, no. 2: 193–218.

Angeloni, Chiara, and Guntram B. Wolff. 2012. "Are Banks Affected by Their Holdings of Government Debt?" Bruegel Working Paper 2012/07. Bruegel, Brussels.

Antzoulatos, Angelos A. 2012. "Policy Responses to the European Debt Crisis Treating the 'Symptoms' or the 'Disease?'" *Panoeconomicus* 5: 529–552.

Archer, Candace C., Glen Biglaiser, and Karl DeRouen Jr. 2007. "Sovereign Bond Ratings and Democracy: The Effects of Regime Type in the Developing World." *International Organization* 61, no. 1: 341–365.

Ardagna, Silvia, and Franceso Caselli. 2014. "The Political Economy of the Greek Debt Crisis: A Tale of Two Bailouts." *American Economic Journal: Macroeconomics* 6, no. 4: 291–323.

Arellano, Cristina, Xavier Mateos-Planas, and Jose-Victor Rios-Rull. 2013. "Partial Default." Paper presented at NBER Summer Institute, July 2013.

Ariso, Guillermo, and Gabriel Jacobo. 2002. *El Golpe S.A.* Buenos Aires: Grupo Editorial Norma.

Armendariz, Beatriz, and Patricia Armendariz. 1995. "Debt Relief, Growth and Price Stability in Mexico." *Journal of Development Economics* 48, no. 1: 135–149.

Armingeon, Klaus W., and Lucio Baccaro. 2011. "The Sorrows of Young Euro: Policy Responses to the Sovereign Debt Crisis." Paper presented at CES conference, Barcelona, June 2011.

———. 2012. "The Sorrows of Young Euro: The Sovereign Debt Crisis of Ireland and Southern Europe." In *Coping with Crisis: Government Reactions to the Great Recession*, edited by Nancy Bermeo and Jonas Pontusson, 162–198. New York: Russell Sage Foundation.

Arrighi, Giovanni. 1994. *The Long Twentieth Century: Money, Power, and the Origins of Our Times*. London and New York: Verso.

Arrighi, Giovanni, Po-keung Hui, Krishnendu Ray, and Thomas Erlich Reifer. 1999. "Geopolitics and High Finance." In *Chaos & Governance in the Modern World System*, edited by Giovanni Arrighi and Beverly J. Silver, 37–96. Minneapolis: University of Minnesota Press.

Arteta, Carlos, and Galina Hale. 2005. "Are Private Borrowers Hurt by Sovereign Debt Rescheduling?" Unpublished manuscript. www.aeaweb.org/annual_mtg_papers/2006/0108_1300_1303.pdf.

Babb, Sarah. 2001. "The Rise of the New Money Doctors in Mexico." Paper presented at Financialization of the Global Economy Conference, Political Economy Research Institute (PERI), University of Massachusetts, Amherst, December 7–8. 2001.

———. 2003. "The IMF in Sociological Perspective: A Tale of Organizational Slippage." *Comparative Studies in International Development* 38, no. 2: 3–27.

Bachrach, Peter, and Morton S. Baratz. 1962. "Two Faces of Power." *American Political Science Review* 56, no. 4: 947–952.

Badkar, Mamta. 2011. "How Exposure to Greece Has Changed in the Last Year." *Business Insider*, September 19. http://www.businessinsider.com/greece-exposure-2010-2011-default-2011-09.

Baer, Werner, Diego Margot, and Gabriel Montes-Rojas. 2010. "Argentina's Default and the Lack of Dire Consequences." Department of Economics Discussion Paper 10/09. City, University of London, London.

Bailey, Norman A., and Richard Cohen. 1987. *The Mexican Time Bomb*. New York: Priority Press.

Baker, Luke, and Sophie Sassard. 2012. "How the Greek Debt Puzzle Was Solved." *Reuters*, February 29, 2012.

Balcerowicz, Leszek. 2010. "Sovereign Bankruptcy in the EU in the Comparative Per-spective." PIEE Working Paper 10/18, Peterson Institute for International Economics, Washington, DC.

Bank for International Settlements. 2011. "The Impact of Sovereign Credit Risk on Bank Funding Conditions." CGFS Paper 43, Bank for International Settlements, Basel.

———. 2017. BIS Statistics (consolidated positions on counterparties resident in Greece). http://stats.bis.org/statx/srs/table/B4?c=GR&p=20171&m=S.

Bank of Canada. 2017. Database of Sovereign Defaults, 2017. http://www.bankofcanada .ca/2014/02/technical-report-101/.

Bank of England. 2017. "History of the Bank of England." http://www.bankofengland .co.uk/about/Pages/history/default.aspx.

Bank of Greece. 2017. Monetary and Banking Statistics. http://www.bankofgreece.gr /Pages/en/Statistics/sdds.aspx

Barclays Capital. 2011. "Greece: The (Long) Countdown to Restructuring." *Economics Research Briefing*, May 11. Barclays Capital, London.

Barker, Alex, and Kerin Hope. 2015. "Greek Banks Pin Hopes on Political Accord." *Financial Times*, February 18, 2015.

Barnett, Michael, and Raymond Duvall. 2005. "Power in International Politics." *International Organization* 59, no. 1: 39–75.

Barrow, Clyde W. 1993. *Critical Theories of the State: Marxist, Neo-Marxist, Post-Marxist*. Madison: University of Wisconsin Press.

Beaulieu, Emily, Gary W. Cox, and Sebastian Saiegh. 2012. "Sovereign Debt and Regime Type: Re-considering the Democratic Advantage." *International Organization* 66, no. 4: 709–738.

Beers, David, and J. Chambers. 2006. "Sovereign Defaults at 26-Year Low, To Show Little Change in 2007." *Standard & Poor's Commentary*, September 18, 2006.

Beetsma, Roel. 1994. "Servicing the Public Debt: Comment." Working Paper No. 9477. Center for Economic Research, Tilburg University, Tilburg.

Bell, Stephen, and Andrew Hindmoor. 2016. "Structural Power and the Politics of Bank Capital Regulation in the United Kingdom." *Political Studies* 65, no. 1: 103–121.

Benedetti-Valentini, Fabio, and Aaron Kirchfeld. 2012. "Greek Debt Swap Seen Win-ning Support from Europe's Banks." *Bloomberg*, February 21, 2012.

Bennhold, Katrin. 2012. "Bond Traders in Europe Deal in High Expectations, and Fear." *New York Times*, August 3, 2012.

Bensasson, Marcus, and Nikos Chrysoloras. 2015. "Draghi Pressures Tsipras as Greece Hung Outside QE Plan." *Bloomberg*, January 22, 2015.

Berg, Vin. 1984. "Argentina's Rebuff to the IMF Panics Bankers. *EIR Economics* 11, no. 25: 4–7.

———. 1985. "Pragmatic Concessions to IMF May Kill Debtor Nations." *EIR Economics* 12, no. 1: 20–22.

Bernal, Richard. 1982. "Transnational Banks, the International Monetary Fund and External Debt of Developing Countries." *Social and Economic Studies* 31, no. 4: 71–101.

Bertola, Luis, and Jose Antonio Ocampo. 2012. "Latin America's Debt Crisis and Lost Decade." Unpublished manuscript. Institute for the Study of the Americas. University of London, London.

Bhagwati, Jagdish N. 1998. "The Capital Myth: The Difference Between Trade in Widgets and Dollars." *Foreign Affairs* 77, no. 3: 7–12.

Birdal, Murat. 2010. *The Political Economy of Ottoman Public Debt: Insolvency and European Financial Control in the Late Nineteenth Century*. London: Tauris.

Blanchard, Olivier J., and Daniel Leigh. 2013. "Growth Forecast Errors and Fiscal Multiplier." IMF Working Paper 13/1. International Monetary Fund, Washington, DC.

Block, Fred. 1987. *Revising State Theory: Essays in Politics and Postindustrialism*. Philadelphia: Temple University Press.

Bloomberg. 2015. "European Banks Have Limited Greek Exposure, JP Morgan Says." *Bloomberg Business*, January 5, 2015.

Blustein, Paul. 2005. *And the Money Kept Rolling In (and Out): Wall Street, the IMF, and the Bankrupting of Argentina*. New York: Public Affairs.

———. 2015. *Laid Low: The IMF, the Euro Zone and the First Rescue of Greece*. CIGI Paper 61, April. Center for International Governance Innovation, Waterloo, ON.

———. 2016. *Laid Low: Inside the Crisis That Overwhelmed Europe and the IMF*. Waterloo, ON: Center for International Governance Innovation.

Blyth, Mark. 2013. *Austerity: History of a Dangerous Idea*. Oxford: Oxford University Press.

Boermans, Martijn, and Robert Vermeulen. 2016. "Market Concentration in the Euro Area Bond Markets: An Application with Granular Sectoral Securities Holdings Statistics." *Irving Fischer Committee Bulletins* 2016, no. 41. Bank for International Settlements, Basel.

Boone, Peter, and Simon Johnson. 2012. "It's Not About Greece Anymore." *New York Times Economix blog*, May 6, 2015. http://economix.blogs.nytimes.com/2010/05/06/its-not-about-greece- anymore/.

Borchard, Edwin M. 1951. *State Insolvency and Foreign Bondholders*. Vol. 1, *General Principles*. London: Oxford University Press.

Borensztein, Eduardo, Kevin Cowan, and Patricio A. Valenzuela. 2007. Sovereign Ceilings 'Lite'? The Impact of Sovereign Ratings on Corporate Ratings in Emerging Market Economies. IMF Working Paper 07/75. International Monetary Fund, Washington, DC.

Borensztein, Eduardo, and Ugo Panizza. 2008. "The Costs of Sovereign Default." IMF Working Paper 08/238. International Monetary Fund, Washington, DC.

Borensztein. Eduardo, and Ugo Panizza. 2010. "Do Sovereign Defaults Hurt Exporters?" *Open Economies Review* 21, no. 3: 393–412.

Boughton, James M. 2001. *Silent Revolution: The International Monetary Fund, 1979–1989*. Washington, DC.: International Monetary Fund.

Branford, Sue, and Bernando Kucinski. 1988. *The Debt Squads: The US, the Banks and Latin America*. London: Zed Books.

Braudel, Fernand. 1972. *The Mediterranean and the Mediterranean World in the Age of Philip II*. Vol. 1. Berkeley: University of California Press.

———. 1984. *Civilization and Capitalism, 15th–18th Century*. Vol. 3, *The Perspective of the World*. New York: Harper & Row.

Braun, Benjamin. 2017. *Two Sides of the Same Coin? Independence and Accountability of the European Central Bank*. Brussels: Transparency International.

Brewer, Thomas L., and Pietra Rivoli. 1990. "Politics and Perceived Country Credit-worthiness in International Banking." *Journal of Money, Credit, and Banking* 22, no. 3: 357–369.

Brooks, Skylar, and Domenico Lombardi. 2016. "Private Creditor Power and the Politics of Sovereign Debt Governance." In *Too Little, Too Late: The Quest to Resolve Sovereign Debt Crises*, edited by Martin Guzman, Jose Antonio Ocampo, and Joseph E. Stiglitz (eds.), 56–75. New York: Columbia University Press.

Broz, J. Lawrence. 2005. "Congressional Politics of International Financial Rescues." *American Journal of Political Science* 49, no. 3: 479–496.

Broz, J. Lawrence, and Michael Brewster Hawes. 2006. "Congressional Politics of Financing the International Monetary Fund." *International Organization* 60, no. 2: 367–399.

Brutti, Filippo. 2011. "Sovereign Defaults and Liquidity Crises." *Journal of International Economics* 84, no. 1: 65–72.

Brutti, Filippo, and Phillip Sauré. 2014. "Repatriation of Debt in the Euro Crisis: Evidence for Secondary Market Theory." SNB Working Paper 3/14. Swiss National Bank, Zurich.

Buchheit, Lee C. 2011. "The Eurozone Debt Crisis in Historical Perspective." Unpublished manuscript. http://www.hoover.org/sites/default/files/buchheit.pdf.

Buchheit, Lee C., Anna Gelpern, G. Mitu Gulati, Ugo Panizza, Beatrice Weder di Mauro, and Jeromin Zettelmeyer. 2013. *Revisiting Sovereign Bankruptcy*. Report by the Committee on International Economic Policy and Reform. Washington, DC.: Brookings Institution.

Buchheit, Lee C., and G. Mitu Gulati. 2009. "The Coroner's Inquest: Ecuador's Default and Sovereign Bond Documentation." *International Financial Law Review* 29, no. 9: 22–25.

Buchheit, Lee C., and G. Mitu Gulati. 2010. "How to Restructure Greek Debt." Duke Law Working Paper 47. Duke University, Durham, NC.

——. 2012. "The Eurozone Debt Crisis: The Options Now." Unpublished manuscript. http://ssrn.com/abstract=2158850.

Buckley, Ross P. 2009. "The Bankruptcy of Nations: An Idea Whose Time Has Come." *The International Lawyer* 43, no. 3: 1189–1216.

Buffie, Edward. 1990. "Debt Management and Negotiations." In *Developing Country Debt and Economic Performance*. Vol. 2, *The Country Studies—Argentina, Bolivia, Brazil, Mexico*, edited by Jeffrey D. Sachs, 517–528. Chicago: University of Chicago Press.

Bugaric, Bojan. 2013. *Europe Against the Left? On Legal Limits to Progressive Politics.* LEQS Discussion Paper 61/2013. London School of Economics and Political Science, London.

Bukharin, Nikolai. 1918. *Imperialism and World Economy*. London: Martin Lawrence.

Bulow, Jeremy I., and Kenneth Rogoff. 1989. "Sovereign Debt: Is to Forgive to Forget?" *The American Economic Review* 79, 1: 43–50.

Calvo, Guillermo A. 1988. "Servicing the Public Debt: The Role of Expectations." *The American Economic Review* 78, no. 4: 647–661.

Canak, William L. 1989 *Lost Promises: Debt, Austerity, and Development in Latin America*. Boulder, CO: Westview Press.

Carlos, Ann M., and Larry Neal. 2011. "Amsterdam and London as Financial Centers in the Eighteenth Century." *Financial History Review* 18, 1: 21–46.

Catão, Luis, and Gian M. Milesi-Ferretti. 2014. "External Liabilities and Crises." IMF Working Paper 13/113. International Monetary Fund, Washington, DC.

Cavallo, Domingo F. 2002. "An Institutional Coup." Declaration to Judge Responsible for Investigating Events of 2001. http://www.cavallo.com.ar/wp-content/uploads/an_in situtional.pdf.

———. 2004 "Argentina and the IMF during the Two Bush Administrations." *International Finance* 7, no. 1: 137–150.

Cerny, Philip G. 1995. "Globalization and the Changing Logic of Collective Action." *International Organization* 49, 4: 595–625.

Chaffin, Joshua. 2012. "Athens Rehearses the Nightmare of Default." *Financial Times*, February 17, 2012.

Chahoud, Tatjana. 1991. "The Changing Roles of the IMF and the World Bank." In *The Poverty of Nations: A Guide to the Debt Crisis from Argentina to Zaire*, edited by Elmar Altvater et al. London: Zed Books.

Choi, Stephen J., G. Mitu Gulati, and Eric A. Posner. 2011. "Pricing Terms in Sovereign Debt Contracts: A Greek Case Study with Implications for the European Crisis Resolution Mechanism." Working Paper 541, John M. Olin Law & Economics, University of Chicago, Chicago, IL.

———. 2012. "The Evolution of Contractual Terms in Sovereign Bonds." *Journal of Legal Analysis* 4, no. 1: 131–79.

Chrysoloras, Nikos, and Bensasson, Marcus. 2015. "Greek Deposit Outflows Said to Slow to 3 Billion Euros." *Bloomberg*, April 1, 2015.

Chrysoloras, Nikos, Christos Ziotis, and Marcus Bensasson. 2015. "Greek Bank Deposit Flight Said to Accelerate to Record." *Bloomberg*, January 28, 2015.

Cibils, Alan B., and Ruben LoVuolo. 2012. "At Debt's Door: What Can We Learn from Argentina's Recent Debt Crisis and Restructuring?" *Seattle Journal for Social Justice* 5, no. 2: 755–795.

Cibils, Alan B., Mark Weisbrot, and Debayani Kar. 2002. "Argentina Since Default: The IMF and the Depression." CEPR Briefing Paper. Center for Economic and Policy Research, Washington, DC.

Claessens, Stijn, Ishac Diwan, and Eduardo Fernandez-Arias. 1992. "Recent Experience with Commercial Bank Debt Reduction." Working Paper 995. World Bank, Washington, DC.

Claessens, Stijn, Daniel Oks, and Sweder van Wijnbergen. 1993. "Interest Rates, Growth and External Debt: The Macroeconomic Impact of Mexico's Brady Deal." Working Paper 1147. World Bank, Washington, DC.

Clement, Piet, and Yvo Maes. 2013. "The BIS and the Latin American Debt Crisis of the 1980s." Working Paper 247. National Bank of Belgium, Brussels.

Cline, William R. 1983 "International Debt and the Stability of the World Economy." Policy Analyses in International Economics Series, Policy Brief 4/31. Institute for International Economics, Washington, DC.

———. 1995. *International Debt Reexamined*. Washington, DC.: Institute of International Economics.

———. 2013. "Debt Restructuring and Economic Prospects in Greece." Policy Brief Pb13-3. Peterson Institute for International Economics, Washington, DC.

Cohen, Benjamin J. 2000. "Money and Power in World Politics." In *Strange Power: Shaping the Parameters of International Relations and International Political Economy*, edited by Thomas C. Lawton, James N. Rosenau, and Ann Verdun, 91–114. Farnham: Ashgate.

———. 2012. *The Future of Global Currency: The Euro Versus the Dollar*. London: Routledge.

Cohen, Daniel. 1991. *Private Lending to Sovereign States*. Cambridge, MA: MIT Press.

Cole, Harold L., and Timothy J. Kehoe. 2000. "Self-fulfilling Debt Crises." *Review of Economic Studies* 67, no. 1: 91–116.

Colectivo Situaciones. 2002. *19 & 20: Notes for a New Social Protagonism*. New York: Minor Compositions.

Collier, David. 1993. "The Comparative Method." In *Political Science: The State of the Discipline II*, edited by Ada W. Finifter, 105–119. Washington, DC: American Political Science Association.

Collier, David, and James Mahoney. 1996. "Insights and Pitfalls: Selection Bias in Qualitative Research." *World Politics* 49, no. 1: 56–91.

Cooper, Andrew F., and Bessma Momani. 2005. "Negotiating Out of Argentina's Financial Crisis: Segmenting the International Creditors." *New Political Economy* 10, no. 3: 305–320.

Cooper, Richard N., and Jeffrey D. Sachs. 1985. "Borrowing Abroad: The Debtor's Perspective." In *International Debt and the Developing Countries*, edited by Gordon W. Smith and John T. Cuddington, 21–60. Washington, DC: World Bank.

Copelovitch, Mark S. 2010. "Master or Servant? Common Agency and the Political Economy of IMF Lending." *International Studies Quarterly* 54, no. 1: 49–77.

Corrales, Javier. 2002. "The Politics of Argentina's Meltdown." *World Policy* 19, no. 3: 29–42.

Crowley, Thomas. 1993. "The Role of the Commercial Banks in the Latin American Debt Crisis." *Trocaire Development Review*, 1993–94: 9–29.

Cruces, Juan J. 2007. "The Value of Pleasing International Creditors." Unpublished manuscript. Department of Economics, Universidad Torcuato di Tella, Buenos Aires.

Cruces, Juan J., and Christoph Trebesch. 2013. "Sovereign Defaults: The Price of Haircuts." *American Economic Journal: Macroeconomics* 5, no. 3: 85–117.

Culpepper, Pepper D. 2008. "Business Power, Policy Salience, and the Study of Politics." *European Studies Forum* 38, no. 2: 5–11.

———. 2011. *Quiet Politics and Business Power: Corporate Control in Europe and Japan*. Cambridge: Cambridge University Press.

———. 2015. "Structural Power and Political Science in the Post-Crisis Era." *Business and Politics* 17, no. 3: 391–409.

Culpepper, Pepper D., and Rafael Reinke. 2014. "Structural Power and Bank Bailouts in the United Kingdom and the United States." *Politics & Society* 42, no. 4: 427–454.

Cypher, James M. 1990. *State and Capital in Mexico: Development Policy Since 1940*. Boulder, CO: Westview Press.

Dahl, Robert A. 1957. "The Concept of Power." *System's Research and Behavioral Science* 2, no. 3: 201–215.

———. 1959. *Social Science Research on Business: Product and Potential*. New York: Columbia University Press.

———. 1961. *Who Governs? Democracy and Power in an American City*. New Haven: Yale University Press.

Dalakoglou, Dimitris. 2014. "The Real Reasons Bailout Talks Took Place in Paris – And What It All Means for Greece." *The Conversation*, September 5, 2014. http://thecon versation.com/the-real-reasons-bailout-talks-took-place-in-paris-and-what-it-all -means-for-greece-31314.

Damill, Mario, Roberto Frenkel, and Martín Rapetti. 2005. "The Argentinean Debt: History, Default and Restructuring." Paper prepared for Sovereign Debt Project of the Initiative for Policy Dialogue (IPD). Columbia University, New York.

Damle, Jai. 2007. "The Odious Debt Doctrine After Iraq." *Law and Contemporary Problems* 70, no. 4: 139–156.

Dany, Geraldine, Reint E. Gropp, Helge Littke, and Gregor von Schweinitz. 2015. "Germany's Benefit from the Greek Crisis." IWH Working Paper 7/2015. Leibniz Institut für Wirtschaftsforschung, Halle.

Das, Udaibir S., Michael G. Papaioannou, and Christoph Trebesch. 2011. "Spillovers of Sovereign Default Risk: How Much Is the Private Sector Affected?" In *Sovereign Debt: From Safety to Default*, edited by Robert W. Kolb, 33–42. New York: Wiley.

———. 2012. "Sovereign Debt Restructurings 1950–2010: Literature Survey, Data, and Stylized Facts." IMF Working Paper 12/203. International Monetary Fund, Washington, DC.

Datz, Giselle. 2009. "Held Out? Reputation, International Litigation, Financial Incentives and Domestic Debt in Sovereign Restructurings." Paper presented at the Annual Convention of the International Studies Association. San Francisco, April 3–6, 2009.

———. 2013. "What Life after Default? Time Horizons and the Outcome of the Argentine Debt Restructuring Deal." *Review of International Political Economy* 16, no. 3: 456–484.

De Grauwe, Paul, and Yuemei Ji. 2013. "Mispricing of Sovereign Risk and Multiple Equilibria in the Eurozone." CEPS Working Paper 361. Centre for European Studies, Brussels.

De Las Casas, Miguel. 2016. "The IMF Executive Board and the Euro Area Crisis—Accountability, Legitimacy and Governance." IEO Background Paper 16-02/02. Independent Evaluation Office of the International Monetary Fund, Washington, DC.

Delamaide, Darrell. 1984. *Debt Shock: The Full Story of the World Debt Crisis*. New York: Doubleday.

Devlin, Robert, and Ricardo Ffrench-Davis. 1995. "The Great Latin American Debt Crisis: A Decade of Asymmetric Adjustment." *Revista de Economia Política* 15, no. 3: 117–142.

Diaz-Alejandro, Carlos F. 1983. "Stories of the 1930s for the 1980s." In *Financial Policies and the World Capital Market: The Problem of Latin American Countries*, edited by Pedro Aspe Armella, Rudiger Dornbusch, and Maurice Obstfeld, 5–40. Chicago: University of Chicago Press.

———. 1984. "Latin American Debt: I Don't Think We're in Kansas Anymore." *Brookings Papers on Economic Activity* 15, no. 2: 335–403.

Díaz-Cassou, Javier, Aitor Erce-Domínguez, and Juan J. Vázquez-Zamora. 2008. "Recent Episodes of Sovereign Debt Restructurings: A Case-Study Approach." Documentos Ocasionales 0804. Banco de España, Madrid.

Dickson, Peter G. M. 1967. *The Financial Revolution in England: A Study in the Development of Public Credit 1688–1756*. New York: St. Martin's Press.

Dimsky, Gary. A. 2011. "The International Debt Crisis." In *The Handbook of Globalisation (Second Edition)*, edited by Jonathan Michie, 90–103. Cheltenham: Edward Elgar.

Dodd, Nigel. 2014. *The Social Life of Money*. Princeton: Princeton University Press.

Dominguez, Kathryn M. E., and Linda L. Tesar. 2004. "International Borrowing and Macroeconomic Performance in Argentina." Paper presented at the NBER conference on International Capital Flows, National Bureau of Economic Research, Cambridge, MA, December 17–18, 2004.

Donadio, Rachel, and Steven Erlanger. 2012. "As Greeks Head to Polls Again, a Fear That No One Will Win." *New York Times*, June 16, 2012.

Donadio, Rachel, and Elisabetta Povoledo. 2011. "Berlusconi Steps Down, and Italy Pulses with Change." *New York Times*, November 12, 2011.

Dooley, Michael P. 1995. "A Retrospective on the Debt Crisis." NBER Working Paper 4963. National Bureau of Economic Research, Cambridge, MA.

———. 2000. "International Financial Architecture and Strategic Default: Can Financial Crises Be Less Painful?" *Carnegie-Rochester Conference Series on Public Policy* 53, no. 1: 361–377.

Dooley, Michael P., Eduardo Fernandez-Arias, and Kenneth M. Kletzer. 1994. "Recent Private Capital Inflows to Developing Countries: Is the Debt Crisis History?" NBER Working Paper 4792. National Bureau of Economic Research, Cambridge, MA.

Douzinas, Costas. 2013. *Philosophy and Resistance in the Crisis*. Cambridge: Polity Press.

Drazen, Allan. 1998. "Towards a Political Economic Theory of Domestic Debt." In *The Debt Burden and its Consequences for Monetary Policy*, edited by Guillermo Calvo and Mervyn King, 159–176. London: Macmillan.

Drelichman, Mauricio, and Hans-Joachim Voth. 2014. *Lending to the Borrower from Hell: Debt, Taxes and Default in the Age of Philip II*. Princeton: Princeton University Press.

Duménil, Gérard, and Dominique Lévy. 2004. *Capital Resurgent*. Cambridge, MA: Harvard University Press.

———. 2011. *The Crisis of Neoliberalism*. Cambridge, MA: Harvard University Press.

Dyson, Kenneth. 2014. *States, Debt, Power: "Saints" & "Sinners" in European History & Integration*. Oxford: Oxford University Press.

Eaton, Jonathan, and Raquel Fernandez. 1995. *Sovereign Debt*. NBER Working Paper 5131. National Bureau of Economic Research, Cambridge, MA.

Eaton, Jonathan, and Mark Gersovitz. 1981. "Debt with Potential Repudiation: Theoretical and Empirical Analysis." *The Review of Economic Studies* 48, no. 2: 289–309.

Eaton, Jonathan, Mark Gersovitz, and Joseph E. Stiglitz. 1986. *The Pure Theory of Country Risk*. NBER Working Paper 1894. National Bureau of Economic Research, Cambridge, MA.

ECLR Editorial. 2012. "The Fiscal Compact and the European Constitutions: 'Europe Speaking German.'" *European Constitutional Law Review* 8, no. 1: 1–7.

Economist. 1981. "The New Hero." March 10: 68–69.

———. 1984. "Mexico's Happy Creditors." April 8: 60.

———. 2003. "Hard or Soft?" September 25. https://www.economist.com/node/2088974/.

———. 2005. "Argentina's Debt Restructuring: A Victory by Default?" March 3. https://www.economist.com/node/3715779/.

Edwards, K., and Hsieh, W. (2011) "Recent Changes in IMF Lending." *RBA Bulletin*, December Quarter. Sydney: Reserve Bank of Australia.

Edwards, Sebastian. 1989. "The International Monetary Fund and the Developing Countries: A Critical Evaluation." *Carnegie-Rochester Conference Series on Public Policy* 31: 7–68.

Ehrenberg, Victor. 1968 [2011]. *From Solon to Socrates*. London: Routledge.

Eichengreen, Barry J. 1991. "Historical Research on International Lending and Debt." *The Journal of Economic Perspectives* 5, no. 2: 149–169.

———. 1992. *Golden Fetters: The Gold Standard and the Great Depression, 1919–1939*. Oxford: Oxford University Press.

———. 2002. *Financial Crises and What to Do About Them*. Oxford: Oxford University Press.

———. 2008. *Globalizing Capital: A History of the International Monetary System*. Princeton: Princeton University Press.

Eichengreen, Barry J., and Michael D. Bordo. 2003. "Crises Now and Then: What Lessons from the Last Era of Financial Globalization." In *Monetary History, Exchange Rates and Financial Markets: Essays in Honor of Charles Goodhart*, Vol. 2, edited by Paul Mizen, 52–91. London: Edward Elgar.

Eichengreen, Barry J., Ricardo Hausmann, and Ugo Panizza. 2005. "Currency Mismatches, Debt Intolerance, and Original Sin: Why They Are Not the Same and Why It Matters." In *Capital Controls and Capital Flows in Emerging Economies: Policies, Practices and Consequences*, edited by Sebastian Edwards, 121–169. Chicago: University of Chicago Press.

Eichengreen, Barry J., and Peter H. Lindert. 1989. *The International Debt Crisis in Historical Perspective*. Cambridge, MA: MIT Press.

Eichengreen, Barry J., and Richard Portes. 1985. "Debt and Default in the 1930s: Causes and Consequences." NBER Working Paper 1772. National Bureau of Economic Research, Cambridge, MA.

———. 1989. "Dealing with Debt: The 1930s and the 1980s." NBER Working Paper 2867. National Bureau of Economic Research, Cambridge, MA.

———. 1990. "The Interwar Debt Crisis and Its Aftermath." *The World Bank Research Observer* 5, no. 1: 69–94.

———. 2000. "Debt Restructuring With and Without the IMF." Unpublished manuscript, University of California, Berkeley.

Eiffel Group & Glienicker Group. 2015. "Giving Greece a Chance." *Bruegel blog*, May 21, 2015. http://bruegel.org/2015/05/giving-greece-a-chance/.

Emmenegger, Patrick. 2015. "The Long Arm of Justice: U.S. Structural Power and International Banking." *Business and Politics* 17, no. 3: 473–493.

Enderlein, Henrik, Cristoph Trebesch, and Laura von Daniels. 2011. "Sovereign Debt Disputes: A Database on Government Coerciveness During Debt Crises." *Journal of International Money and Finance* 31, no. 2: 250–266.

Epstein, Edward, and David Pion-Berlin. 2006. "The Crisis of 2001 and Argentine Democracy." In *Broken Promises? The Argentine Crisis and Argentine Democracy*, edited by Edward Epstein and David Pion-Berlin, 3–28. Lanham, MD: Lexington Books.

Epstein, Gerald A. 2001. "Introduction: Financialization and the World Economy." In *Financialization and the World Economy*, edited by Gerald A. Epstein, 3–16. Cheltenham: Edward Elgar.

Esteves, Rui Pedro. 2007. "Quis Custodiet Quem? Sovereign Debt and Bondholders' Protection Before 1914." Discussion Paper No. 323. Oxford: Oxford University.

Eurobank. 2016. *Third Quarter 2016 Results*. Report by Eurobank, Athens. https://www .eurobank.gr/Uploads/pdf/3Q2016_Results_Presentation_Final.pdf

European Banking Authority. 2011. EU-wide stress test results. European Banking Authority, London. http://www.eba.europa.eu/risk-analysis-and-data/eu-wide-stress-testing /2011/results.

European Central Bank. 2010a. Keynote speech at the 9th Munich Economic Summit. European Central Bank, Frankfurt, April 29, 2010. https://www.ecb.europa.eu/press /key/date/2010/html/sp100429.en.html.

———. 2010b. Interview with Frankfurter Allgemeine Zeitung (FAZ). European Central Bank, Frankfurt, May 21, 2010. https://www.ecb.europa.eu/press/inter/date/2010/html /sp100521.en.html.

———. 2010c. "The ECB's Response to the Recent Tensions in Financial Markets." Speech by Jean-Claude Trichet at the 38th Economic Conference of the Oesterrichische National-bank. Vienna, 31 May 2010. https://www.ecb.europa.eu/press/key/date/2010/html /sp100531_2.en.html.

———. 2012. Introductory statement to the press conference. European Central Bank, Frankfurt, September 6, 2012. https://www.ecb.europa.eu/press/pressconf/2012/html /is120906.en.html.

European Commission. 2015. *European Economic Forecast: Winter 2015*. Brussels: European Commission. http://ec.europa.eu/economy_finance/publications/european _economy/2015/pdf/ee1_en.pdf.

European Parliament. 2014. "Report on the Enquiry on the Role and Operations of the Troika (ECB, Commission and IMF) with Regard to the Euro Area Programme Coun-tries." Report A7-0149/2014. http://www.europarl.europa.eu/sides/getDoc.do?pubRef =-//EP//TEXT+REPORT+A7-2014-0149+0+DOC+XML+V0//EN.

Eurostat. 2017. General Government Gross Debt. http://ec.europa.eu/eurostat/tgm/table .do?tab=table&init=1&language=en&pcode=teina225&plugin=1.

Evans-Pritchard, Ambrose. 2015. "Crippled Greece Yields to Overwhelming Power as Deal Looms." *The Telegraph*, July 11, 2015.

Exadaktylos, Theofanis, and Nikos Zahariadis. 2013. "The Lack of Public Trust in Po-litical Institutions Is a Massive Obstacle to Public Policy Change in Greece." *LSE EUROPP blog*, January 17, 2013. http://blogs.lse.ac.uk/europpblog/2013/01/17/greece -trust-institutions/.

Fairfield, Tasha. 2015. "Structural Power in Comparative Political Economy: Perspectives from Policy Formulation in Latin America." *Business and Politics* 17, no. 3: 411–441.

Federal Reserve Bank of Dallas. 2012. "Choosing the Road to Prosperity: Why We Must End Too-Big-to-Fail—Now." Annual report, Federal Reserve Bank of Dallas.

Federal Reserve Bank of St. Louis. 2017. Federal Reserve Economic Data (FRED). https://fred.stlouisfed.org/.

Feis, Herbert. 1930. *Europe, The World's Banker: 1870–1914*. New Haven: Yale University Press.

Féliz, Mariano. 2012. "Neo-Developmentalism: Beyond Neoliberalism? Capitalist Crisis and Argentina's Development since the 1990s." *Historical Materialism* 20, 2: 1–19.

Ferreira Rubio, Delia, and Matteo Goretti. 1995. "Gobernar la emergencia. Uso y abuso de los decretos de necesidad y urgencia (1989–1993)." *Agora* 1, no. 3: 75–94.

Finnemore, Martha. 2003. *The Purpose of Intervention: Changing Beliefs about the Use of Force*. Ithaca, NY: Cornell University Press.

Fiorentini, Francesca. 2012. "Argentina: Que Se Vayan Todos—They All Must Go!" *Red Pepper*, May 4, 2012.

Fischer, Stanley. 1989. "Resolving the International Debt Crisis." In *Developing Country Debt and Economic Performance*, edited by Jeffrey D. Sachs, 359–385. Chicago: University of Chicago Press.

Fishlow, Albert. 1985. "Lessons from the Past: Capital Markets During the 19th Century and the Interwar Period." *International Organization* 39, no. 3: 383–439.

———. 1989. "Conditionality and Willingness to Pay: Some Parallels from the 1890s." In *The International Debt Crisis in Historical Perspective*, edited by Barry J. Eichengreen and Peter H. Lindert, 86–105. Cambridge, MA: MIT Press.

Flandreau, Marc, and Juan H. Flores. 2009. "Bonds and Brands: Foundations of Sovereign Debt Markets, 1820–1830." *The Journal of Economic History* 69, no. 3: 646–684.

———. 2011. "Bondholders vs. Bond-Sellers? Investment Banks and Conditionality Lending in the London Market for Foreign Government Debt, 1815–1913." Working Paper No. 0002, European Historical Economics Society (EHES).

———. 2012. "The Peaceful Conspiracy: Bond Markets and International Relations During the Pax Britannica." *International Organization* 66, no. 2: 211–241.

Foster, John Bellamy. 2007. "The Financialization of Capitalism." *Monthly Review*, 58, no. 11.

Fouskas, Vassilis K., and Constantine Dimoulas. 2013. *Greece, Financialization and the EU*. London: Palgrave.

Fratianni, Michele. 2006. "Government Debt, Reputation and Creditors' Protections: The Tale of San Giorgio." *Review of Finance* 10, no. 4: 487–506.

Fratianni, Michele, and Franco Spinelli. 2006. "Italian City-States and Financial Evolution." *European Review of Economic History* 10, no. 3: 257–278.

Frieden, Jeffry A. 1989. "Winners and Losers in the Latin America Debt Crisis: The Political Implications." In *Debt and Democracy in Latin America*, edited by Barbara Stallings and Robert R. Kaufman, 23–37. Boulder, CO: Westview Press.

———. 1991a. *Debt, Development, and Democracy: Modern Political Economy and Latin America, 1965–1985*. Princeton: Princeton University Press.

———. 1991b. "The Politics of National Economic Policies in a World of Global Finance." *International Organization* 45, no. 4: 425–451.

———. 2015. "The Political Economy of Adjustment and Rebalancing." *Journal of International Money and Finance* 52 (April): 4–14.

Friedman, Thomas L. 1995. "Don't Mess with Moody's." *New York Times*, February 22, 1995.

Fuentes, Miguel, and Diego Saravia. 2010. "Sovereign Defaulters: Do International Capital Markets Punish Them?" *Journal of Development Economics* 91, no. 2: 336–347.

Fuhrmans, Vanessa, and Sebastian Moffett. 2010. "Exposure to Greece Weighs on French, German Banks." *Wall Street Journal*, February 17, 2010.

Galatsidas, Achilleas, and George Arnet. 2015. "Greek Referendum: How Athens Voted – Interactive Map." *The Guardian datablog*, July 9, 2015. http://www.theguardian.com /.news/datablog/nginteractive/2015/jul/09/greek-referendum-how-athens-voted-interactive-map.

Galofré-Vilà, Gregori, Martin McKee, Christopher M. Meissner, David Stuckler. 2016. "The Economic Consequences of the 1953 London Debt Agreement." NBER Working Paper 22557. National Bureau of Economic Research, Cambridge, MA.

Garrett, Geoffrey. 1998. "Global Markets and National Politics: Collision Course or Virtuous Circle?" *International Organization* 52, no. 4: 787–824.

Garuda, Gopal. 2000. "The Distributional Effects of IMF Programs: A Cross-Country Analysis." *World Development* 28, 6: 1031–1051.

Gechert, Sebastian, and Ansgar Rannenberg. 2015. "The Costs of Greece's Fiscal Consolidation." Policy brief, March 2015, Institut für Makroökonomie und Konjunkturforschung. Hans Böckler Stiftung, Düsseldorf. http://www.boeckler.de/pdf/p_imk_pb_1_2015.pdf.

Gelos, R. Gaston, Ratna Sahay, and Guido Sandleris. 2004. "Sovereign Borrowing by Developing Countries: What Determines Market Access?" IMF Working Paper 04/221. International Monetary Fund, Washington, DC.

Gelpern, Anna. 2005. "After Argentina." Policy Brief PB05-2. Peterson Institute for International Economics, Washington, DC.

Gennaioli, Nicola, Alberto Martin, and Stefano Rossi. 2013. "Sovereign Default, Domestic Banks and Financial Institutions." Citation based on working paper, later published as Nicola Gennaioli, Alberto Martin, and Stefano Rossi. 2014. "Sovereign Default, Domestic Banks and Financial Institutions." *Journal of Finance* 69, no. 2: 819–866.

George, Alexander L., and Andrew Bennett. 2005. *Case Studies and Theory Development in the Social Sciences.* Cambridge, MA: MIT Press.

George, Susan. 1988. *A Fate Worse Than Debt.* London: Penguin.

Gerring, John. 2007. *Case Study Research: Principles and Practices.* Cambridge: Cambridge University Press.

Giannitsis, Tassos, and Stavros Zografakis. 2015. "Greece: Solidarity and Adjustment in Times of Crisis." Study 38, Institut für Makroökonomie und Konjunkturforschung, Hans Böckler Stiftung, Düsseldorf.

Gibson, Heather D., Stephen G. Hall, and George S. Tavlas. 2011. "The Greek Financial Crisis: Growing Imbalances and Sovereign Spreads." Working Paper 124, Bank of Greece, Athens.

Gilens, Martin, and Benjamin I. Page. 2014. "Testing Theories of American Politics: Elites, Interest Groups and Average Citizens." *Perspectives on Politics* 12, no. 3: 564–581.

Giugliano, Ferdinando. 2015. "Athens Faces Uphill Struggle Despite Eurozone Deal." *Financial Times*, March 4, 2015.

Goldscheid, Rudolf. 1919. *Sozialisierung der Wirtschaft oder Staatsbankrott: Ein Sanierungsprogramm.* Vienna: Anzengruber Verlag: Brüder Suschitzky.

Gourevitch, Peter. 1986. *Politics in Hard Times: Comparative Responses to International Economic Crises.* Ithaca, NY: Cornell University Press.

Graeber, David. 2011. *Debt: The First 5,000 Years.* London: Melville House.

Griffith-Jones, Stephany (ed.). 1988. *Managing World Debt.* New York: St. Martin's.

Griffith-Jones, Stephany, and Osvaldo Sunkel. 1986. *Debt and Development Crises in Latin America: The End of an Illusion.* Oxford: Clarendon Press.

Grossman, Herschel I., and John B. Van Huyk. 1985. "Sovereign Debt as a Contingent Claim: Excusable Default, Repudiation, and Reputation." NBER Working Paper 1673, National Bureau of Economic Research, Cambridge, MA.

Grugel, Jean, and Maria Pia Riggirozzi. 2007. "The Return of the State in Argentina." Working Paper WEF0018, World Economy and Finance Research Programme, University of Sheffield.

Guembel, Alexander, and Oren Sussman. 2008. "Sovereign Debt without Default Penalties." *Review of Economic Studies* 76, 4: 1296–1320.

Gurría, J. Ángel. 1988. "Debt Restructuring: Mexico as Case Study." In *Managing World Debt*, edited by Stephany Griffith-Jones, 64–112. New York: St. Martin's.

———. 1995a. "The Mexican Debt Strategy." *Challenge* 38, no. 2: 34–38.

———. 1995b. "Capital Flows: The Mexican Case." In *Coping with Capital Surges: The Return of Finance to Latin America*, edited by Ricardo Ffrench-Davis, and Stephany Griffith-Jones, 189–224. Boulder, CO: Lynne Riener.

———. 2013. Interview with the author. OECD Headquarters, Paris, January 2013.

Guzman, Martin, Jose Antonio Ocampo, and Joseph E. Stiglitz (eds.). 2016. *Too Little, Too Late: The Quest to Resolve Sovereign Debt Crises*. New York: Columbia University Press.

Hacker, Jacob S., and Paul Pierson. 2002. "Business Power and Social Policy: Employers and the Formation of the American Welfare State." *Politics and Society 30*, no. 2: 277–325.

Hager, Sandy Brian. 2016. *Public Debt, Inequality, and Power: The Making of a Modern Debt State*. Oakland: University of California Press.

Haggard, Stephan. 1985. "The Politics of Adjustment: Lessons from the IMF's Extended Fund Facility." *International Organization* 39, no. 3: 505–534.

Haggard, Stephan, and Robert R. Kaufman (eds.). 1992. *The Politics of Economic Adjustment: International Constraints, Distributive Conflicts and the State*. Princeton: Princeton University Press.

Haldane, Andrew G. 2010. "The $100 Billion Question." Speech at the Institute of Regulation & Risk, North Asia (IRRNA), Hong Kong, March 30, 2010. https://www.bis.org/review/r100406d.pdf.

Hall, Peter A. 2006. "Systematic Process Analysis: When and How to Use It." *European Management Review* 3, no. 1: 24–31.

Hamilton, Earl J. 1947. "Origin and Growth of the National Debt in Western Europe." *The American Economic Review* 37, no. 2: 118–130.

Hannon, Paul. 2015. "Eurozone PMI Survey Shows Collapse in Greek Manufacturing Output." *Wall Street Journal*, August 3, 2015.

Hardt, Michael, and Antonio Negri. 2000. *Empire*. Cambridge, MA: Harvard University Press.

Harvey, David. 1982. *The Limits to Capital*. London: Verso.

———. 2005. *A Brief History of Neoliberalism*. Oxford: Oxford University Press.

———. 2010. *The Enigma of Capital and the Crises of Capitalism*. London: Profile.

Hausman, Ricardo, and Andrés Velasco. 2002. "Hard Money's Soft Underbelly: Understanding the Argentine Crisis." *Brookings Trade Forum 2002*. Washington, DC: Brookings Institute.

Helleiner, Eric. 1994. *States and the Reemergence of Global Finance: From Bretton Woods to the 1990s*. Ithaca, NY: Cornell University Press.

———. 2005. "The Strange Story of Bush and the Argentine Debt Crisis." *Third World Quarterly* 26, no. 6: 951–969.

———. 2006. "Below the State: Micro-Level Monetary Power." In *International Monetary Power*, edited by David M. Andrews, 72–90. Ithaca, NY: Cornell University Press.

———. 2014. *The Status Quo Crisis: Global Financial Governance after the 2008 Financial Meltdown*. Oxford: Oxford University Press.

Hickel, Jason. 2017. "Aid in Reverse: How Poor Countries Develop Rich Countries." *The Guardian*, January 14, 2017.

Hilferding, Rudolf. 1910 [1981]. *Finance Capital: A Study of the Latest Phase of Capitalist Development*. London: Routledge.

Hirschman, Albert O. 1970. *Exit, Voice and Loyalty: Responses to Decline in Firms, Organizations, and States*. Cambridge, MA: Harvard University Press.

Hobson, J. A. (1902 [2011]) *Imperialism: A Study*. Nottingham: Spokesman.

Holloway, John, and Sol Picciotto. 1978. "Introduction: Towards a Materialist Theory of the State." *In State and Capital: A Marxist Debate*, edited by John Holloway and Sol Picciotto, 1–31. London: Edward Arnold.

Hood, Miriam. 1975. *Gunboat Diplomacy, 1895–1905: Great Power Pressure in Venezuela*. Crows Nest: Allen & Unwin.

Hope, Kerin. 2017. "Greek Bankers Face Charges over Financial Crisis Bond Swaps." *Financial Times*, April 23, 2017.

Hope, Kerin, and Stefan Wagsty. 2015. "Two Greek Banks Seek Emergency Funds from ECB." *Financial Times*, January 16, 2015.

Hunt, Edwin S. 1990. "A New Look at the Dealings of the Bardi and Peruzzi with Edward III." *Journal of Economic History* 50, no. 1: 149–162.

Independent Evaluation Office. 2016. *The IMF and the Crises in Greece, Ireland, and Portugal*. IEO Evaluation Report. Washington, D.C.: Independent Evaluation Office of the International Monetary Fund.

International Monetary Fund. 1999. "IMF Completes Third Review under EFF for Argentina." IMF News Brief 99/24, International Monetary Fund, Washington, DC.

———. 2013a. "Greece: Ex Post Evaluation of Exceptional Access Under the 2010 Stand-by Arrangement." IMF Country Report 13/156, International Monetary Fund, Washington, DC.

———. 2013b. "Sovereign Debt Restructuring: Recent Developments and Implications for the Fund's Legal and Policy Framework." IMF Policy Paper, April 26, 2013, International Monetary Fund, Washington, DC.

———. 2017a. International Financial Statistics. http://www.imf.org/en/Data.

———. 2017b. "2016 Article IV Consultation." IMF Country Report 17/40. International Monetary Fund, Washington, DC.

Islam, Faisal. 2013. *The Default Line: The Inside Story of People, Banks and Entire Nations on the Edge*. London: Head of Zeus.

J. P. Morgan. 2013. "The Euro Area Adjustment: About Halfway There." Europe Economic Research Note, May 28, 2013. https://culturaliberta.files.wordpress.com/2013/06/jpm-the-euro-area-adjustment-about-halfway-there.pdf.

Jolly, David, and Keith Bradsher. 2015. "Greece's Debt Crisis Sends Stocks Falling Around the Globe." *New York Times*, June 29, 2015.

Jorgensen, Erika, and Jeffrey D. Sachs. 1989. "Default and Renegotiation of Latin American Foreign Bonds in the Interwar Period." In *The International Debt Crisis in Historical Perspective*, edited by Barry J. Eichengreen and Peter H. Lindert. Cambridge, MA: MIT Press.

Jubilee Debt Campaign. 2015. "ECB to Make between €10 and €22 Billion Profit out of Loans to Greece." *Jubilee Debt Campaign blog*, July 10, 2015. jubileedebt.org.uk/blog/ecb-to-make-between-e10-billion-and-e22-billion-out-of-loans-to-greece/.

Kaletsky, Anatole. 1985. *The Costs of Default*. New York: Priority Press.

Kaminsky, Graciela L., and Sergio L. Schmukler. 2002. "Emerging Market Instability: Do Sovereign Ratings Affect Country Risk and Stock Returns?" *The World Bank Economic Review* 16, no. 2: 171–195.

Kaminsky, Graciela L., and Pablo Vega-Garcia. 2016. "Systemic and Idiosyncratic Sovereign Debt Crises." *Journal of the European Economic Association* 14, no. 1: 80–114.

Kaplan, Stephen B. 2013. *Globalization and Austerity Politics in Latin America*. Cambridge: Cambridge University Press.

Kaplan, Stephen B., and Kaj Thomsson. 2017. "The Political Economy of Sovereign Debt: Global Finance and Electoral Cycles." *The Journal of Politics* 79, no. 2: 605–623.

Kaufman, Robert R. 1985. "Democratic and Authoritarian Responses to the Debt Issue: Argentina, Brazil, Mexico." *International Organization* 39, no. 3: 473–503.

Kay, John. 2012. "Some Euros Are More Equal than Others." *Financial Times*, May 22, 2012.

Kentikelenis, Alexander E. 2017. "The Social Aftermath of Economic Disaster: Karl Polanyi, Countermovements in Action, and the Greek Crisis." *Socio-Economic Review*, online prepublication, doi: 10.1093/ser/mwx031.

Kentikelenis, Alexander E., M. Karanikolos, A. Reeves, M. McKee, and D. Stuckler. 2014. "Greece's Health Crisis: From Austerity to Denialism." *The Lancet* 383, no. 9918: 748–753.

Kentikelenis, Alexander E., Thomas H. Stubbs, and Lawrence P. King. 2016. "IMF Conditionality and Development Policy Space." *Review of International Political Economy* 23, no. 4: 543-582.

Keohane, Robert. 2000. "Foreword." In *Strange Power: Shaping the Parameters of International Relations and International Political Economy*, edited by Thomas C., James N. Rosenau, and Amy Verdun, ix–xvi. Farnham: Ashgate.

Khan, Mehreen. 2017. "ECB Made €7.8bn Profits from Greek Bond Holdings." *Financial Times*, October 10, 2017.

Kindleberger, Charles P. 1973. *The World in Depression*. Berkeley: University of California Press.

———. 1988. "The Financial Crises of the 1930s and the 1980s: Similarities and Differences." *Kyklos* 41, no. 2: 171–186.

King, Robin A. 1989. "The Mexican Proposal for a Continent-Wide Debt Moratorium: Lessons from the 1930s, Contrasts with the 1980s." Working Paper 89/10, Department of Economics, University of Texas at Austin.

Kirshner, Jonathan. 2009. "After the (Relative) Fall: Dollar Diminution and the Consequences for American Power." In *The Future of the Dollar*, edited by Eric Helleiner and Jonathan Kirshner, 191–215. Ithaca, NJ: Cornell University Press.

Klein, Marcus. 2004. "Stumbling on the Verge of the Abyss (Without Falling into It): Argentina and Its Crisis of the Millennium." In *The Argentine Crisis at the Turn of the Millennium*, edited by Flavia Fiorucci and Marcus Klein, 1–14. Amsterdam: Aksant.

Kocharov, Anna (ed.). 2012. "Another Legal Monster? An EUI Debate on the Fiscal Compact Treaty." EUI Working Paper Law 2012/9, European University Institute, Florence.

Kolb, Robert W. (ed.). 2011. *Sovereign Debt: From Safety to Default*. New York: John Wiley.

Körner, Peter, Gerp Maass, Thomas Siebold, and Rainer Tetzlaff. 1986. *The IMF and the Debt Crisis: A Guide to the Third World's Dilemma*. London: Zed Books.

Kouvelakis, Stathis. 2011. "The Greek Cauldron." *New Left Review* 72, November-December: 17–32.

———. 2016. "Syriza's Rise and Fall." *New Left Review* 97, January-February: 45–70.

Kouvelakis, Stathis, and Sebastian Budgen. 2015. "Greece: Phase One." *Jacobin*, January 22, 2015. https://www.jacobinmag.com/2015/01/phase-one/.

Kraft, Joseph. 1984. *The Mexican Rescue*. New York: Group of 30.

Krippner, Greta R. 2005. "The Financialization of the American Economy." Socio-Economic Review 3, no. 2: 173–208.

———. 2011. Capitalizing on Crisis: The Political Origins of the Rise of Finance. Cambridge, MA: Harvard University Press.

Krueger, Anne O. 2002. *A New Approach to Sovereign Debt Restructuring*. Washington, D.C.: International Monetary Fund.

Kruger, Mark, and Miguel Messmacher. 2004. Sovereign Debt Defaults and Financing Needs. IMF Working Paper 04/53. International Monetary Fund, Washington, DC.

Kyriakidou, Dina. 2015. "The Man Who Cost Greece Billions." *Reuters Special Report*, July 20, 2015.

Lambert, Harry. 2015. "Yanis Varoufakis full transcript: our battle to save Greece." *New Statesman*, July 13, 2015. http://www.newstatesman.com/world-affairs/2015/07/yanis-varoufakis-full-transcript-our-battle-save-greece.

Lanau Grau, Sergi. 2008. "Essays on Sovereign Debt Markets." http://tesisenred.net/bit stream/handle/10803/7380/tsl.pdf.

Lapavitsas, Costas. 2008. "Financialised Capitalism: Direct Exploitation and Periodic Bubbles." Unpublished manuscript, University of London, School of Oriental and African Studies. http://leftlibrary.com/lapavitsas1.pdf.

———. 2013. *Profiting without Producing: How Finance Exploits Us All*. London and New York: Verso.

———. 2014. "The Era of Financialization: An Interview with Costas Lapavitsas." *Dollars and Sense*, May/June 2014. http://www.dollarsandsense.org/archives/2014/0414 lapavitsas.html.

Lapavitsas, Costas, et al. (eds.). 2012. *Crisis in the Eurozone*. London and New York: Verso.

Laskos, Christos, and Euclid Tsakalotos. 2013. *Crucible of Resistance: Greece, the Eurozone and the World Economy*. London: Pluto.

Lawton, Thomas C., James N. Rosenau, and Amy C. Verdun. 2000. "Introduction: Looking Beyond the Confines." In *Strange Power: Shaping the Parameters of International Relations and International Political Economy*, edited by Thomas C. Lawton, James N. Rosenau, and Amy C. Verdun, 1–16. Farnham: Ashgate.

Lazzarato, Maurizio. 2012. *The Making of the Indebted Man: An Essay on the Neoliberal Condition*. Los Angeles, CA: Semiotext(e).

Leander, Anna. 2000. "Strange Looks on Developing Countries: A Neglected Kaleidoscope of Questions." In *Strange Power: Shaping the Parameters of International Relations and International Political Economy*, edited by Thomas C. Lawton, James N. Rosenau, and Amy C. Verdun, 343–365. Farnham: Ashgate.

Lemoine, Benjamin. 2013. "The Politics of Public Debt Structures: How Uneven Claims on the State Colonize the Future." *Near Futures Online* 1, March. http://nearfutures online.org/wp-content/uploads/2016/03/Lemoine_10.pdf.

Lenin, Vladimir Ilyich. 1917 [1939]. *Imperialism, the Highest Stage of Capitalism*. New York: International Publishers.

Leslie, Peter. 1983. "Techniques of Rescheduling: The Latest Lessons." *The Banker* 133, no. 686: 23–30.

Levitsky, Steven, and María Victoria Murillo. 2003. "Argentina Weathers the Storm." *Journal of Democracy* 14, no. 4: 152–166.

Levy-Yeyati, Eduardo, and Ugo Panizza. 2011. "The Elusive Costs of Sovereign Defaults." *Journal of Development Economics* 94, no. 1: 95–105.

Lewis, Paul H. 2009. *The Agony of Argentine Capitalism: From Menem to the Kirchners.* Santa Barbara, CA: ABC-CLIO.

Lienau, Odette. 2014. *Rethinking Sovereign Debt: Politics, Reputation, and Legitimacy in Modern Finance.* Cambridge, MA: Harvard University Press.

Lindblom, Charles E. 1977. *Politics and Markets: The World's Political-Economic Systems.* New York: Basic Books.

———. 1982. "The Market as Prison." *The Journal of Politics* 44, no. 2: 324–336.

Lindert, Peter H. 1989. "Response to Debt Crisis: What Is Different about the 1980s?" In *The International Debt Crisis in Historical Perspective*, edited by Barry J. Eichengreen and Peter H. Lindert, 227–276. Cambridge, MA: MIT Press.

Lindert, Peter H., and Morton, P. J. 1989. "How Sovereign Debt Has Worked." In *Developing Country Debt and Economic Performance*. Vol. 1, *The International Financial System*, edited by Jeffrey D. Sachs, 39–806. Chicago: University of Chicago Press.

Lipson, Charles. 1981. "The International Organization of Third World Debt." *International Organization* 35, no. 4: 603–631.

———. 1985. "Bankers' Dilemmas: Private Cooperation in Rescheduling Sovereign Debts." *World Politics* 38, no. 1: 200–225.

Lissakers, Karin. 1983. "Dateline Wall Street: Faustian Finance." *Foreign Policy*, March 16, 1983.

Llach, Lucas. 2004. "A Depression in Perspective: The Economics and the Political Economy of Argentina's Crisis of the Millennium." In *The Argentine Crisis at the Turn of the Millennium: Causes, Consequences and Explanations*, edited by Flavia Fiorucci, and Marcus Klein, 40–63. Amsterdam: Aksant.

Lomnitz-Adler, Claudio. 2004. "The Depreciation of Life During Mexico City's Transition into the Crisis." In *Wounded Cities: Destruction and Reconstruction in a Globalized World*, edited by Jane Schneider, and Ida Susser, 47–70. New York: Berg.

Lukes, Steven. 1974. *Power: A Radical View.* Basingstoke: Macmillan.

Luxemburg, Rosa. 1913 [2003]. *The Accumulation of Capital.* London: Routledge.

Maddison, Angus. 1985. *Two Crises: Latin America and Asia, 1929–38 and 1973–83.* Paris: Development Center of the Organization for Economic Cooperation and Development.

Mahon, James E. 1996. *Mobile Capital and Latin American Development.* University Park, PA: Pennsylvania State University Press.

Mahoney, James. 2007. "Qualitative Methods and Comparative Politics. *Comparative Political Studies* 40, no. 2: 122–144.

Mahoney, James, and Dietrich Rueschemeyer (eds.). 2003. *Comparative-Historical Analysis in the Social Sciences.* New York: Cambridge University Press.

Malamud, Andrés. 2006. "Social Revolution or Political Takeover? The Argentine Collapse of 2001 Reassessed." Paper presented at the XXVI Latin American Studies Association Congress (LASA), San Juan, Puerto Rico, March 15–18.

Manasse, Paolo, and Nouriel Roubini. 2009. "'Rules of Thumb' for Sovereign Debt Crises." *Journal of International Economics* 78, no. 2: 192–205.

Mandel, Ernest. 1971. *The Marxist Theory of the State*. New York: Pathfinder Press.

Manolopoulos, Jason. 2011. *Greece's "Odious" Debt: The Looting of the Hellenic Republic by the Euro, the Political Elite and the Investment Community*. London: Anthem Press.

Marichal, Carlos. 1989. *A Century of Debt Crises in Latin America*. Princeton: Princeton University Press.

Marks, Sally. 1978. "The Myths of Reparations." *Central European History* 11, no. 3: 231–255.

Marois, Thomas. 2007. "The Lost Logic of State-Owned Banks: Mexico, Turkey, and Neoliberalism." Paper presented at Canadian Political Science Association 79th annual conference, University of Saskatchewan, May 31, 2007.

———. 2011. "The Socialization of Financial Risk in Mexico." Research on Money and Finance Discussion Paper 25. School of Oriental and African Studies, University of London, London.

Martin, Jamie. 2015. "The Colonial Origins of the Greek Bailout." *Imperial & Global Forum*, July 27, 2015. https://imperialglobalexeter.com/2015/07/27/the-colonial-origins-of-the -greek-bailout/.

Martínez, Jose Vicente, and Guido Sandleris. 2011. "Is It Punishment? Sovereign Defaults and the Decline in Trade." *Journal of International Money and Finance* 30, no. 6: 909–930.

Marx, Karl. 1867 [1990]. *Capital*, Vol. 1. London: Penguin.

———. 1894 [1991]. *Capital*, Vol. 3. London: Penguin.

———. 1939 [1993]. *Grundrisse*. London: Penguin.

Mason, Paul. 2013. *Why It's (Still) Kicking Off Everywhere*. London: Verso.

Mauro, Paolo, Nathan Sussman, and Yishay Yafeh. 2006. "Bloodshed or Reforms? The Determinants of Sovereign Bond Spreads in 1870–1913 and Today." CEPR Discussion Paper 5528. Center for Economic Policy Research, London.

Mauro, Paolo, and Yishay Yafeh. 2003. "The Corporation of Foreign Bondholders." IMF Working Paper 03/107. International Monetary Fund, Washington, DC.

Maxfield, Sylvia. 1990. *Governing Capital: International Finance and Mexican Politics*. Ithaca, NY: Cornell University Press.

———. 1992 "The International Political Economy of Bank Nationalization: Mexico in Comparative Perspective." *Latin American Research Review* 27, no. 1: 75–104.

McKeown, Timothy J. 2004. "Case Studies and the Limits of the Statistical Worldview." In *Rethinking Social Inquiry: Diverse Tools, Shared Standards*, edited by Henry Brady, and David Collier, 139–167. Lanham, MD: Rowman and Littlefield.

McKinsey Global Institute. 2013. *Financial Globalization: Retreat or Reset?* MGI Global Capital Markets 2013 report. Seoul and San Francisco: McKinsey and Company.

Mendoza, Enrique G., and Vivian Z. Yue. 2011. "A General Equilibrium Model of Sovereign Default and Business Cycles." IMF Working Paper 11/166. International Monetary Fund, Washington, DC.

Mengus, Eric. 2014. "Honoring Sovereign Debt or Bailing Out Domestic Residents: A Theory of Internal Costs of Default." Banque de France Working Paper 480, Bank of France, Paris.

Mercado, P. Ruben. 2007. "The Argentine Recovery: Some Features and Challenges." VRP Working Paper, University of Texas at Austin, Austin, TX.

Merler, Silvia, and Jean Pisani-Ferry. 2012a. "Sudden Stops in the Euro Area." Policy Brief 2012/06, Bruegel, Brussels.

——. 2012b. "Who's Afraid of Sovereign Bonds?" *Bruegel Policy Contribution* 2012, no. 2 (February).

Middlebrook, Kevin J. 1989. "The Sounds of Silence: Organised Labour's Response to Economic Crisis in Mexico." *Journal of Latin American Studies* 21, 2: 195–220.

Miliband, Ralph. 1969. *The State in Capitalist Society*. New York: Basic Books.

Miller, M. Thampanishvong, K. and Zhang, L. 2004. *Learning to Trust Lula: Contagion and Political Risk in Brazil*. Working Paper, University of Warwick, Coventry.

Miller, Marcus, Javier García Fronti, and Lei Zhang. 2006. "Contractionary Devaluation and Credit Crunch: Analysing Argentina." CSGR Working Paper Series 190/06, Centre for the Study of Globalisation and Regionalisation, University of Warwick, Coventry.

Mills, C. Wright. 1956. *The Power Elite*. New York: Oxford University Press.

Mitchener, Kris James, and Marc D. Weidenmier. 2005. "Supersanctions and Sovereign Debt Repayment." NBER Working Paper 11472, National Bureau of Economic Research, Cambridge, MA.

——. 2011. "Supersanctions and Sovereign Debt Repayment." In *Sovereign Debt: From Safety to Default*, edited by Robert W. Kolb, 155–167. New York: Wiley.

Mody, Ashoka. 2015. "The IMF's Big Greek Mistake." *Bloomberg View*, April 21, 2015.

Moffett, Matt. 2004. "After Huge Default, Argentina Squeezes Small Bondholders." *Wall Street Journal*, January 14, 2004.

Moody's. 2000. "How to Sue a Sovereign: The Case of Peru. New York: Moody's Investors Service." Special Comment, Moody's Investors Service Global Credit Research, New York, November 2000.

Moore, Elaine, and Kerin Hope. 2014. "Size of Greece's Debt Limits Scope for Solutions." *Financial Times*, January 13, 2014.

Moran, Michael, and Anthony Payne. 2014. "Introduction: Neglecting, Rediscovering and Thinking Again about Power in Finance." *Government and Opposition* 49, no. 3: 331–341.

Mortimore, Michael, and Leonardo Stanley. 2006. "Has Investor Protection Been Rendered Obsolete by the Argentine Crisis?" *CEPAL Review* 88: 15–31. Mexico City: United Nations Center for the Study of Latin America and the Caribbean.

Mosley, Layna. 2000. "Room to Move: International Financial Markets and National Welfare States." *International Organization* 54, no. 4: 737–773.

——. 2003. *Global Capital and National Governments*. Cambridge: Cambridge University Press.

Mussa, Michael. 2002. "Argentina and the Fund: From Triumph to Tragedy." *Policy Analyses in International Economics* 67. Washington, DC: Peterson Institute.

Nasar, Sylvia. 2000. "Masters of the Universe." *New York Times*, January 23, 2000.

Neal, Larry. 1990. *The Rise of Capitalism: International Capital Markets in the Age of Reason*. Cambridge: Cambridge University Press.

New Internationalist. 1990. "World Bank: The Facts." *New Internationalist* 214 (December).

Noble, Gregory W., and John Ravenhill (eds.). 2000. *The Asian Financial Crisis and the Architecture of Global Finance*. Cambridge: Cambridge University Press.

North, Douglas C., and Barry R. Weingast. 1989. "Constitutions and Commitment: The Evolution of Institutions Governing Public Choice in Seventeenth-Century England." *Journal of Economic History* 49, no. 4: 803–832.

O'Brien, Patrick. 2001. "Fiscal Exceptionalism: Great Britain and Its European Rivals: From Civil War to Triumph at Trafalgar and Waterloo." LSE Working Paper 65/01, Department of Economic History, London School of Economics and Political Science, London.

O'Connell, Arturo. 2005. "The Recent Crisis—and Recovery—of the Argentine Economy: Some Elements and Background." In *Financialization and the World Economy*, edited by Gerald A. Epstein, 289–313. Cheltenham: Edward Elgar.

O'Connor, James. 1973. *The Fiscal Crisis of the State*. New York: St. Martin's Press.

Obstfeld, Maurice, and Alan M. Taylor. 2003. "Globalization and Capital Markets." In *Globalization in Historical Perspective*, edited by Michael D. Bordo, Alan M. Taylor, and Jeffrey G. Williamson, 121–187. Chicago: University of Chicago Press.

Ocampo, José Antonio. 2013. "La crisis de la deuda a la luz de la historia latinoamericana." Presented at CEPAL conference: La crisis de la deuda: 30 años después, UN Economic Commission for Latin America and the Caribbean, Mexico City, February 18–19, 2013.

———. 2016. "A Brief History of Sovereign Debt Resolution and a Proposal for a Multilateral Instrument." In *Too Little, Too Late: The Quest to Resolve Sovereign Debt Crises*, edited by Martin Guzman, José Antonio Ocampo and Joseph E. Stiglitz, 189–205. Columbia University Press.

OECD. 2011. "Greece: Review of the Central Administration." Organization for Economic Cooperation and Development, Paris. http://www.oecd-ilibrary.org/governance/greece-review-of-the-central-administration_9789264102880-en.

———. 2017. OECD Economic Outlook Data. http://www.oecd.org/eco/outlook/economic-outlook/.

Oliveri, Ernest J. 1992. *Latin American Debt and the Politics of International Finance*. Westport, CT: Praeger.

Ozler, Sule. 1992. "Have Commercial Banks Ignored History?" NBER Working Paper 3959, National Bureau of Economic Research, Cambridge, MA.

Pagoulatos, George. 2003. *Greece's New Political Economy: State, Finance and Growth from Postwar to EMU*. London: Palgrave McMillan.

———. 2014. "Structural Limitations of Financial Power in Greece." *Government and Opposition* 49, no. 3: 452–482.

Palaiologos, Yannis. 2014. "How Trichet Threatened to Cut Greece Off." *Kathimerini*, March 11, 2014.

Palley, Thomas I. 2007. "Financialization: What It Is and Why It Matters." Working Paper 525, Levy Economics Institute, Bard College, Annandale-on-Hudson, New York.

Panico, Carlo, and Francesco Purificato. 2013. "The Debt Crisis and the European Central Bank's Role of Lender of Last Resort." PERI Working Paper 306, Political Economy Research Institute, University of Massachusetts Amherst, Amherst, MA.

Panitch, Leo, and Sam Gindin. 2012. *The Making of Global Capitalism: The Political Economy of American Empire*. New York and London: Verso.

Panizza, Ugo, Federico Sturzenegger, and Jeromin Zettelmeyer. 2009. "The Economics and Law of Sovereign Debt and Default." *The Journal of Economic Literature* 47, no. 3: 1–47.

Papaconstantinou, George. 2016. *Game Over: The Inside Story of the Greek Crisis*. Athens: Papadopoulos Publishing.

Papademos, Lucas. 2011. "Forcing Greek Restructuring Is Not the Answer." *Financial Times*, October 21, 2011.

Papadia, Andrea. 2017. "Sovereign Defaults During the Great Depression: The Role of Fiscal Fragility." Working Paper 255/2017, Department of Economic History, London School of Economics and Political Science, London.

Parker, Geoffrey. 1975. "War and Economic Change: The Economic Costs of the Dutch Revolt." In *War and Economic Development*, edited by David Joslin, 49–71. Cambridge: Cambridge University Press.

Pastor Jr., Manuel. 1987. "The Effects of IMF Programs in the Third World: Debate and Evidence from Latin America." *World Development* 15, no. 2: 249–262.

———. 1989. "Latin America, the Debt Crisis, and the International Monetary Fund." *Latin American Perspectives* 16, no. 1: 79–110.

Pauly, Louis W. 1997. *Who Elected the Bankers? Surveillance and Control in the World Economy*. Ithaca, NY: Cornell University Press.

Perry, Guillermo, and Luis Servén. 2003. "The Anatomy of a Multiple Crisis: Why Was Argentina Special and What Can We Learn From It?" World Bank Policy Research Working Paper 3081. World Bank, Washington, DC.

Peters, B. Guy. 1998. *Comparative Politics: Theory and Methods*. New York: NYU Press.

Pezzolo, L. 2005. "Bonds and Government Debt in Italian City States, 1250–1650." In *The Origins of Value: The Financial Innovations That Created Modern Capital Markets*, edited by W. N. Goetzmann and K. G. Rouwenhorst, 145–163. Oxford: Oxford University Press.

Pezzolo, Luciano. 2007. "Government Debts and Credit Markets in Renaissance Italy." Working Paper 05/2007, Department of Economics, Ca' Foscari University of Venice, Venice.

Piketty, Thomas. 2014. *Capital in the Twenty-First Century*. Cambridge, MA: Belknap/ Harvard University Press.

Polanyi, Karl. 1944 [2001]. *The Great Transformation: The Political and Economic Origins of Our Time*. Boston, MA: Beacon Press.

Poulantzas, Nikos. 1969. "The Problem of the Capitalist State." *New Left Review* 58: 67–78.

———. 1978. State, Power, Socialism. London: New Left Books/Verso.

Przeworski, Adam. 1980. "Social Democracy as a Historical Phenomenon." *New Left Review* 122: 27–58.

Przeworski, Adam, and Michael Wallerstein. 1988. "Structural Dependence of the State on Capital." *The American Political Science Review* 82, no. 1: 11–29.

Quirk, W. J. 1983. "Will an Underdeveloped Countries' Debtors' Cartel Squeeze the Big Banks?" *Business and Society Review* 47, no. 1: 10.

Rabobank. 2011. "To Default or Not to Default? What Are the Economic and Political Costs of Sovereign Default?" Rabobank Economic Research Department, Utrecht. https://economics.rabobank.com/PageFiles/7288/SP1102ska%20To%20default%20 or%20not%20to%20default_tcm64-138583.pdf.

Rambarran, Jwala. 2004. Argentina's Sovereign Default and the IMF: Global Financial Governance in a Tailspin. Unpublished manuscript. University of the West Indies, St. Augustine. https://sta.uwi.edu/conferences/financeconference/Conference%20Papers /Session%2010/Argentina%20Sovereign%20debt%20default%20and%20teh%20 IMF%20Global%20Financial%20Governance%20in%20a%20Tailspin.pdf.

Reguly, Eric. 2013. "George Provopoulos: Facing a Run on Greek Banks, He Never Blinked." *Globe & Mail*, April 19, 2013.

Reinhart, Carmen M., Vincent Reinhart, and Christoph Trebesch. 2016. "Global Cycles: Capital Flows, Commodities, and Sovereign Defaults, 1815–2015." *The American Economic Review: Papers and Proceedings* 106, no. 5: 574–180.

Reinhart, Carmen M., and Kenneth S. Rogoff. 2008. "Banking Crises: An Equal Opportunity Menace." NBER Working Paper 14587, National Bureau of Economic Research, Cambridge, MA.

———. 2009. *This Time Is Different: Eight Centuries of Financial Folly*. Princeton: Princeton University Press.

———. 2013. "Financial and Sovereign Debt Crises: Some Lessons Learned and Those Forgotten." IMF Working Paper 13/266. International Monetary Fund, Washington, DC.

Reinhart, Carmen M., Kenneth S. Rogoff, and Miguel A. Savastano. 2003. "Debt Intolerance." NBER Working Paper 9908. National Bureau of Economic Research, Cambridge, MA.

Reinhart, Carmen M., and M. Belen Sbrancia. 2011. "The Liquidation of Government Debt." NBER Working Paper 16893. National Bureau of Economic Research, Cambridge, MA.

Reuters. 2011. "ECB Debates Ending Italy Bond Buys If Reforms Don't Come." *Reuters Business News*, November 5, 2011.

———. 2015a. "German Bank Exposure to Greece around 24 Billion Euros: Banks." *Reuters*, January 5, 2015.

———. 2015b. "Timeline: Greek Debt Crisis." *Reuters*, June 23, 2015. http://www.abc .net.au/news/2015-06-23/greek-debt-crisis-timeline/6564930.

Riley, James C. 1980. *International Government Finance and the Amsterdam Capital Market, 1748–1815*. Cambridge: Cambridge University Press.

Ritschl, Albrecht. 2012. "Germany, Greece and the Marshall Plan." *The Economist*, June 15, 2012.

Robinson, Duncan, Stefan Wagstyl, and Richard Milne. 2015. "Brussels Backs IMF over Greek Debt Relief." *Financial Times*, August 13, 2015.

Robinson, James A. 1998. "Debt Repudiation and Risk Premia: The North-Weingast Thesis Revisited." Unpublished manuscript, Harvard University, Cambridge, MA.

Robinson, William I. 2004. "Global Crisis and Latin America." *Bulletin of Latin American Research* 23, no. 2: 135–153.

Rocholl, Jörg, and Axel Stahmer. 2016. "Where Did the Greek Bailout Money Go?" ESMT White Paper 16/02, European School of Management and Technology, Berlin.

Rock, David. 2002. "Racking Argentina." *New Left Review* 17: 55–86.

Roddick, Jackie. 1988. *The Dance of the Millions: Latin America and the Debt Crisis*. London: Latin America Bureau.

Rodrik, Dani. 1997. *Has Globalization Gone Too Far?* Washington, D.C.: Peterson Institute for International Economics.

Rodrik, Dani, and Arvind Subramanian. 2009. "Why Did Financial Globalization Disappoint?" *IMF Staff Papers* 56, no. 1: 112–138.

Rogers, Chris. 2012. *The IMF and European Economies: Crisis and Conditionality*. Basingstoke: Palgrave.

Rogoff, Kenneth S. 1999. "International Institutions for Reducing Global Financial Instability." *Journal of Economic Perspectives* 13, 4: 21–42.

Rommerskirchen, Charlotte. 2015. "Debt and Punishment: Market Discipline in the Eurozone." *New Political Economy* 20, no. 5: 752–782.

Roodman, David. 2006. "Creditor Initiatives in the 1980s and 1990s." In *Sovereign Debt at the Crossroads: Challenges and Proposals for Solving the Third World Debt Crisis*, edited by Chris Jochnick, and Fraser A. Preston, 13–34. Oxford: Oxford University Press.

Rose, Andrew K. 2005. "One Reason Countries Pay Their Debts: Renegotiation and International Trade." *Journal of Development Economics* 77, no. 1: 189–206.

Rose-Ackerman, Susan, Diane A. Desierto, and Natalia Volosin. 2010. "Hyper-Presidentialism: Separation of Powers Without Checks and Balances in Argentina and the Philippines." Yale Law & Economics Research Paper 418, Yale University, New Haven, CT.

Roth, Karl Heinz. 2013. *Greece: What Is to Be Done?* Alresford, UK: Zer0 Books.

Roubini, Nouriel. 2005. "The Successful End of the Argentine Debt Restructuring Saga." *Econo-monitor*. http://www.economonitor.com/nouriel/2005/03/02/the-successful-end-of-the-argentine-debt-restructuring-saga.

———. 2012. "Greece's Private Creditors Are the Lucky Ones." *Financial Times*, March 7, 2012.

Ruggie, John R. 1982. "International Regimes, Transactions, and Change: Embedded Liberalism in the Postwar Economic Order." *International Organization* 36, no. 2: 379–415.

Sachs, Jeffrey D. 1986. "Managing the LDC Debt Crisis." *Brookings Papers on Economic Activity* 1986, no. 2: 397–440.

Sachs, Jeffrey D., and Harry Huizinga. 1987. "US Commercial Banks and the Developing Country Debt Crisis." *Brookings Papers on Economic Activity* 1987, no. 2: 555–606.

Saiegh, Sebastian M. 2005. "Do Countries Have a 'Democratic Advantage'? Political Institutions, Multilateral Agencies, and Sovereign Borrowing." *Comparative Political Studies* 38, no. 4: 366–387.

Salmon, Christian. 2015. "'We Underestimated Their Power': Greek Government Insider Lifts the Lid on Five Months of 'Humiliation' and 'Blackmail.'" *Mediapart*, July 8, 2015. http://www.mediapart.fr/journal/international/080715/we-underestimated-their-power-greek-government-insider-lifts-lid-five-months-humiliation-and-blackm.

Sandleris, Guido. 2008. "Sovereign Defaults: Information, Investment and Credit." *Journal of International Economics* 76, no. 2: 267–275.

———. 2014. "Sovereign Defaults, Credit to the Private Sector and Domestic Credit Market Institutions." *Journal of Money, Credit and Banking* 46, no. 2–3: 321–345.

Santillán Salgado, Roberto J. 2011. "Banking Concentration in the European Union during the Last Fifteen Years." *Panoeconomicus* 2011, no. 2: 245–266.

Santiso, Javier. 2003. *The Political Economy of Emerging Markets: Actors, Institutions, and Financial Crises in Latin America.* New York: Palgrave.

Sartori, Giovanni. 1970. "Concept Misformation in Comparative Politics." *The American Political Science Review* 64, no. 4: 1033–1053.

Sassen, Saskia. 1996. *Losing Control? Sovereignty in the Age of Globalization.* New York: Columbia University Press.

Schadler, Susan. 2013. "Unsustainable Debt and the Political Economy of Lending: Constraining the IMF's Role in Sovereign Debt Crises." CIGI Paper 2013/19: Center for International Governance Innovation, Waterloo, ON.

———. 2016. "Living with Rules: The IMF's Exceptional Access Framework and the 2010 Stand-By Arrangement with Greece." IEO Background Paper 16-02/08. Independent Evaluation Office of the International Monetary Fund, Washington, DC.

Schamis, Hector E. 2002a. "Argentina: Crisis and Democratic Consolidation." *Journal of Democracy* 13, no. 2: 81–94.

———. 2002b. *Re-forming the State: The Politics of Privatization in Latin America and Europe*. Ann Arbor: University of Michigan Press.

Schultz, Kenneth A., and Barry R. Weingast. 2003. "The Democratic Advantage: Institutional Foundations of Financial Power in International Competition." *International Organization* 57, no. 1: 3–42.

Schumacher, Julian, Christoph Trebesch, and Henrik Enderlein. 2014. "Sovereign Defaults in Court." Available from the Social Science Research Network: http://ssrn.com/abstract=2189997.

Schumpeter, Joseph A. 1918 [1953]. "The Crisis of the Tax State." In *International Economic Papers*, No. 4, edited by Alan T. Peacock, 29–68. London: Macmillan.

Schuster, Federico L. 2008. "Argentina—The Left, Parties and Movements: Strategies and Prospects." In *The New Latin American Left: Utopia Reborn*, edited by Patrick Barrett, Daniel Chavez, and César Rodríguez-Garavito, 158–185. London: Pluto Press and Amsterdam: Transnational Institute.

Schwarzer, Daniela. 2015. "Building the Euro Area's Debt Crisis Management Capacity with the IMF." *Review of International Political Economy* 22, no. 3: 599–625.

Scott, Hal S. 2006. "Sovereign Debt Default: Cry for the United States, Not Argentina." Critical Legal Issues Working Paper 140, Washington Legal Foundation, Washington, DC.

Setser, Brad, and Ann Gelpern. 2006. "Pathways through Financial Crisis: Argentina." *Global Governance* 12, no. 4: 465–487.

Shapiro, Robert J., and Nam D. Pham. 2006. "Discredited—The Impact of Argentina's Sovereign Debt Default and Debt Restructuring on U.S. Taxpayers and Investors." Report prepared for the American Task Force for Argentina. http://www.sonecon.com/docs/studies/argentina_1006.pdf.

Shovlin, John. 2006. *The Political Economy of Virtue: Luxury, Patriotism, and the Origins of the French Revolution*. Ithaca, NY: Cornell University Press.

Silva Herzog, Jesus. 1991. "Problems of Policy-Making at the Outset of the Debt Crisis." In *International Money and Debt: Challenges for the World Economy*, edited by Rudi Dornbusch, and Steve Marcus, 51–60. San Francisco, CA: ICS Press.

Sitrin, Marina. 2012. *Everyday Revolutions: Horizontalism and Autonomy in Argentina*. London: Zed Books.

Sitrin, Marina, and Dario Azzellini. 2014. *They Can't Represent Us: Reinventing Democracy from Greece to Occupy*. London: Verso.

Skiles, Marilyn E. 1988. "Latin American International Loan Defaults in the 1930s: Lessons for the 1980s?" Working paper, Federal Reserve Bank of New York, New York.

Smith, Helena. 2011. "Greek Leader's Referendum Bombshell Shocks Ministers at Home and Abroad." *The Guardian*, November 1, 2011.

———. 2014. "How Greece Pulled Back from the Brink of Plunging Europe into Chaos." *The Guardian*, May 22, 2014.

———. 2015. "Greek Minister Moves to Allay Fears of Bank Run." *The Guardian*, January 9, 2015.

Soederberg, Susanne. 2005. "The Transnational Debt Architecture and Emerging Markets: The Politics of Paradoxes and Punishment." *Third World Quarterly* 26, no. 6: 927–949.

Solanas, Fernando E. 2004. *El Saqueo de la Argentina* (Argentina's Economic Collapse). Documentary film about the Argentine crisis. https://www.youtube.com/watch?v=0Cz S6eHqtnQ.

Spiegel, Peter. 2014. "How the Euro Was Saved." *Financial Times*, May 11, 2014.

———. 2015. "How Jeroen Dijsselbloem Did the Deal to Extend the Greece Bailout." *Financial Times*, March 1, 2015.

Spiegel, Peter, and Stefan Wagstyl. 2015. "Greece's Alexis Tsipras Faces Syriza Rebellion over 'Humiliation.'" *Financial Times*, July 14, 2015.

Stallings, Barbara. 1987. *Banker to the Third World: US Portfolio Investment in Latin America, 1900–1986*. Berkeley: University of California Press.

———. 2013. "La dinámica de las negociaciones." Paper presented at CEPAL conference: La crisis de la deuda: 30 años despues. UN Economic Commission for Latin America and the Caribbean, Mexico City, February, 18-19, 2013.

Stangos, Angelos. 2014. "The Costs of Protests." *Kathimerini*, May 9, 2014.

Stasavage, David. 2002. "Credible Commitment in Early Modern Europe: North and Weingast Revisited." *The Journal of Law, Economics and Organization* 18, no. 1: 155–186.

———. 2007a. "Partisan Politics and Public Debt: The Importance of the 'Whig Supremacy' for Britain's Financial Revolution." *European Review of Economic History* 11, no. 1: 123–153.

———. 2007b. "Cities, Constitutions, and Sovereign Borrowing in Europe, 1274–1785." *International Organization* 61, no. 3: 489–525.

———. 2011. *States of Credit: Size, Power, and the Development of European Polities*. Princeton, NJ: Princeton University Press.

Steinkamp, Sven, and Frank Westermann. 2017. "Euro Crisis Monitor" database. Osnabrück: Institute of Empirical Economic Research. http://www.eurocrisismonitor.com.

Sterling, Toby. 2015. "Greek 'No' Risks Place In Eurozone – Dijsselbloem." *Reuters*, July 2, 2015.

Stiglitz, Joseph E. 2002. *Globalization and its Discontents*. New York: W. W. Norton.

Stinga, Laurentiu. 2009. "Still Elected Dictators? A Study of Executive Accountability in Multi-Party Democracies." Paper presented at ECPR Joint Session Workshops, Rennes, April 11.

Strange, Susan. 1986. *Casino Capitalism*. Oxford: Blackwell Publishers.

———. 1988. *States and Markets*. Oxford: Blackwell Publishers.

———. 1991. "Big Business and the State." *Millennium: Journal of International Studies* 20, no. 2: 245–250.

———. 1994. "Wake up Krasner! The World Has Changed." *Review of International Political Economy* 1, no. 2: 209–219.

———. 1996. *The Retreat of the State: The Diffusion of Power in the World Economy*. Cambridge: Cambridge University Press.

———. 1998. *Mad Money: When Markets Outgrow Governments*. Manchester: University of Michigan Press.

Streeck, Wolfgang. 2011. "The Crises of Democratic Capitalism." *New Left Review* 71: 5–29.

———. 2013. "The Politics of Public Debt: Neoliberalism, Capitalist Development, and the Restructuring of the State." MPIfG Discussion Paper 13/7, Max Planck Institute for the Study of Societies, Cologne.

———. 2014. *Buying Time: The Delayed Crisis of Democratic Capitalism*. London: Verso.

———. 2015. *The Rise of the European Consolidation State*. MPIfG Discussion Paper 15/1, Max Planck Institute for the Study of Societies, Cologne.

———. 2016. *How Will Capitalism End? Essays on a Failing System*. London: Verso.

Strong, Norman. 2002. "How to Default." *Left Business Observer* 99. http://www.leftbusinessobserver.com/HowToDefault.html.

Strupczewski, Jan. 2015. "Counting the Cost for Greece and Europe." *Reuters*, July 17, 2015.

Stuckler, David, and Sanjay Basu. 2014. *The Body Economic: Why Austerity Kills*. New York: Basic Books.

Sturzenegger, Federico, and Jeromin Zettelmeyer. 2006. *Debt Defaults and Lessons from a Decade of Crises*. Cambridge, MA: MIT Press.

Sussman, Nathan, and Yishav Yafeh. 2000. "Institutions, Reforms, and Country Risk: Lessons from Japanese Government Debt in the Meiji Era." *Journal of Economic History* 60, no. 2: 442–467.

Suter, Christian. 1989. "Long Waves in the International Financial System: Debt–Default Cycles of Sovereign Borrowers." *Review (Fernand Braudel Center)* 12, no. 1: 1–49.

Suter, Christian, and Hanspeter Stamm. 1992. "Coping with Global Debt Crises Debt Settlements, 1820 to 1986." *Comparative Studies in Society and History* 34, no. 4: 645–678.

Teichman, Judith A. 2001. *The Politics of Freeing Markets in Latin America: Chile, Argentina and Mexico*. Chapel Hill: University of North Carolina Press.

Tello, Carlos. 1984. *La nacionalización de la banca en Mexico*. Mexico, DF: Siglo XXI.

Teubal, Miguel. 2004. "Rise and Collapse of Neoliberalism in Argentina: The Role of Economic Groups." *Journal of Developing Societies* 20, no. 3–4: 173–188.

Thacker, Strom C. 1999. "The High Politics of IMF Lending." *World Politics* 52, 1: 38–75.

Thomas Jr., Landon. 2012. "Buying Back Greek Debt Rewarded Hedge Funds." *New York Times*, December 23, 2012.

———. 2013a. "In Greece, the Banking Chief Draws Scrutiny." *New York Times*, October 16, 2013.

———. 2013b. "Greek Plan May Reward Some Bank Executives." *New York Times*, June 25, 2013.

Thompson, Christopher. 2015. "Greek Bank Shares Hit as Deposits Flee." *Financial Times*, January 27, 2015.

Thompson, Helen. 2015. "Germany and the Euro-Zone Crisis: The European Reformation of the German Banking Crisis and the Future of the Euro." *New Political Economy* 20, no. 6: 851–870.

Tilly, Charles. 1982. "Warmaking and Statemaking as Organized Crime." CRSO Working Paper 256, Center for Research on Social Organization, University of Michigan, Ann Arbor, MI.

Tomz, Michael. 2002. "Democratic Default: Domestic Audiences and Compliance with International Agreements." Paper presented at the 2002 Annual Meeting of the American Political Science Association, Boston, August 29–September 1.

———. 2007. *Reputation and International Cooperation: Sovereign Debt across Three Centuries*. Princeton: Princeton University Press.

Tomz, Michael, and Mark L. J. Wright. 2007. "Do Countries Default in "Bad Times"?" *Journal of the European Economic Association* 5, no. 2–3: 352–360.

———. 2008. "Sovereign Theft: Theory and Evidence about Sovereign Default and Expropriation." Paper presented at the Conference on Populism and Natural Resources. Kennedy School of Government, Harvard University, Cambridge, MA, November, 1–2, 2007.

Tooze, Adam. 2017. "Reading Varoufakis: Frustrated Strategist of Greek Financial Deterrence." *Adam Tooze's blog*. https://www.adamtooze.com/2017/07/01/reading-varoufakis -frustrated-strategist-greek-financial-deterrence/.

Toussaint, Eric. 2017. "Thomas Piketty and Public Debt." *Committee for the Abolition of Illegitimate Debt (CADTM) blog*, April 21, 2017. http://www.cadtm.org/Thomas -Piketty-and-public-debt.

Tracy, James D. 1985. *A Financial Revolution in the Habsburg Netherlands: Renten and Renteniers in the County of Holland, 1515–1565*. Berkeley: University of California Press.

Truth Committee on Public Debt. 2015. *Preliminary Report*. Athens: Hellenic Parliament. http://cadtm.org/IMG/pdf/Report.pdf (last accessed September 7, 2015).

Turner, Frederick C., and Marita Carballo. 2005. "Argentina: Economic Disaster and the Rejection of the Political Class." *Comparative Sociology* 4, no. 1–2: 175–206.

Tussie, Diana. 1988. "The Coordination of the Latin American Debtors: Is There a Logic Behind the Story?" In *Managing World Debt*, edited by Stephany Griffith-Jones, 282–307. New York: St. Martin's.

———. 2013. "El fracaso del consenso de Cartagena." Paper presented at CEPAL conference: La crisis de la deuda: 30 años despues. UN Economic Commission on Latin America and the Caribbean, Mexico City, February, 18–19, 2013.

Uhde, André, and Ulrich Heimeshoff. 2009. "Consolidation in Banking and Financial Stability in Europe: Empirical Evidence." IWQW Discussion Paper 02/2009, Institut für Wirtschaftspolitik und Quantitative Wirtschaftsforschung (IWQW), Friedrich-Alexander-Universität Erlangen, Nürnberg.

Underhill, Geoffrey R. D., and Xiaoke Zhang. 2008. "Setting the Rules: Private Power, Political Underpinnings, and Legitimacy in Global Monetary and Financial Governance." *International Affairs* 84, no. 3: 535–554.

UNICEF. 1989. *Children in Jeopardy: The Challenge of Freeing Poor Nations from the Shackles of Debt*. New York: UNICEF.

Van Wijnbergen, Sweder. 1991. "Mexico and the Brady Plan." *Economic Policy* 6, no. 12: 13–56.

———. 2013. Interview with the author. Amsterdam School of Economics, University of Amsterdam, January.

Varoufakis, Yanis. 2013. "Johnny (Paulson) Got His Gun (and Is Aiming at Some Grim, Greek Pickings)." *Yanis Varoufakis' blog*, October 7, 2013. http://yanisvaroufakis.eu /2013/10/07/johnny-paulson-got-his-gun-and-is-aiming-at-some-grim-greek-pickings/.

———. 2014. "Burst Greek Bubbles, Spooked Fund Managers: A Cause for Restrained Celebration." *Yanis Varoufakis' blog*, December 7, 2014. http://yanisvaroufakis.eu /2014/12/07/burst-greek-bubbles-spooked-fund-managers-a-cause-for-restrained -celebration/.

———. 2016. "Greek Debt Denial: A Modest Debt Restructuring Proposal and Why It Was Ignored." *Too Little, Too Late: The Quest to Resolve Sovereign Debt Crises*, edited by Martin Guzman, José Antonio Ocampo, and Joseph E. Stiglitz, 84–101. New York: Columbia University Press.

———. 2017. *Adults in the Room: My Battle with Europe's Deep Establishment*. London: Bodley Head.

Verdun, Amy. 2000. "Money Power: Shaping the Global Financial System." In *Strange Power: Shaping the Parameters of International Relations and International Political Economy*, edited by Thomas C. Lawton, James N. Rosenau, and Amy Verdun, 77–90. Farnham: Ashgate.

Vradis, Antonis, and Dimitris Dalakoglou. 2011. *Revolt and Crisis in Greece: Between a Present Yet to Pass and a Future Still to Come*. Oakland, CA: AK Press.

Vreeland, James Raymond. 2001. "The Effect of IMF Programs on Labor." *World Development* 30, no. 1: 121–139.

———. 2003. *The IMF and Economic Development*. Cambridge: Cambridge University Press.

Wade, Robert H., and Frank Veneroso. 1998. "The Asian Crisis: The High Debt Model Versus the Wall Street-Treasury-IMF Complex." *New Left Review* I/228 (March–April): 3–22.

Wagstyl, Stefan, and Duncan Robinson. 2015. "Memo Reveals Extent of Controls on Greece." *Financial Times*, August 12, 2015.

Waldenström, Daniel. 2011. "How Important Are the Political Costs of Domestic Default?: Evidence from World War II Bond Markets." In *Sovereign Debt: From Safety to Default*, edited by Robert W. Kolb, 287–294. New York: Wiley.

Wall Street Journal. 2013. "IMF Document Excerpts: Disagreements Revealed." *Wall Street Journal*, October 7, 2013.

Walton, John, and Charles Ragin. 1989. "Global and National Sources of Political Protest: Third World Responses to the Debt Crisis." *American Sociological Review* 55, no. 6: 876–890.

Waltzenbach, Gunter P. E. 2000. "The Doubtful Handshake: From International to Comparative Political Economy?" In *Strange Power: Shaping the Parameters of International Relations and International Political Economy*, edited by Thomas C. Lawton, James N. Rosenau, and Amy Verdun, 369–389. Farnham: Ashgate.

Watkins, Susan. 2014. "The Political State of the Union." *New Left Review* 90 (November–December): 5–25.

Weeks, Natalie, and Christos Ziotis. 2012. "Greek bank deposits fell 2% in November after October plunge." *Bloomberg*, January 10, 2012.

Weisbrot, Mark, and Alan B. Cibils. 2002. "Argentina's Crisis: The Costs and Consequences of Default for the International Financial Institutions." CEPR Policy Brief, Center for Economic and Policy Research, Washington, DC.

Williamson, John. 2002. "Is Brazil Next?" International Economics Policy Brief PB 02/7. Institute for International Economics, Washington, DC.

Winecoff, William Kindred. 2015. "Structural Power and the Global Financial Crisis: A Network Analytical Approach." *Business and Politics* 17, no. 3: 495–525.

Winkler, Max. 1933. *Foreign Bonds: An Autopsy – A Study of Defaults and Repudiations of Government Obligations*. Philadelphia: Roland Swain Company.

Wolf, Martin. 2010. "The Challenge of Halting the Financial Doomsday Machine." *Financial Times*, April 20, 2010.

———. 2012. "A Fragile Europe Must Change Fast." *Financial Times*, May 22, 2012.

Woll, Cornelia. 2014. *The Power of Inaction: Bank Bailouts in Comparison*. Ithaca, NY: Cornell University Press.

Wood, Robert E. 1984. "The Debt Crisis and North-South Relations." *Third World Quarterly* 6, no. 3: 703–716.

World Bank. 1983. *Focus on Poverty*. Washington, D.C.: World Bank.

———. 2017. International Debt Statistics. https://data.worldbank.org/data-catalog/international-debt-statistics.

Wright, Mark L. J. 2010. "Restructuring Sovereign Debts with Private Sector Creditors: Theory and Practice." Paper prepared for the World Bank Economic Policy and Debt Department in Cooperation with the African Development Bank conference, Tunis, March 29–30, 2010.

Wucker, Michele. 2003. "Searching for Argentina's Silver Lining." *World Policy Journal* 19, no. 3: 49–58.

Wynne, William H. 1951. *State Insolvency and Foreign Bondholders: Selected Case Histories of Governmental Foreign Bond Defaults and Debt Readjustments*, Vol. 2. London: Oxford University Press.

Wyplosz, Charles, and Silvia Sgherri. 2016. "The IMF's Role in Greece in the Context of the 2010 Stand-By Arrangement." IEO Background Paper 16-02/11. Independent Evaluation Office of the International Monetary Fund, Washington, DC.

Xafa, Miranda. 2014. "Sovereign Debt Crisis Management: Lessons from the 2012 Greek Debt Restructuring." CIGI Paper 33.Center for International Governance Innovation, Waterloo, ON.

Zettelmeyer, Jeromin. Christoph Trebesch, and G. Mitu Gulati. 2013. "The Greek Debt Restructuring: An Autopsy." Working Paper 2013/13-8, Peterson Institute for International Economics, Washington, DC.

Zibechi, Raúl. 2003. *Genealogía de la revuelta: Argentina, la sociedad en movimiento*. Buenos Aires: Herramienta.

Zingales, Luigi. 2012. "How Political Clout Made Banks Too Big to Fail." *Bloomberg*, May 30, 2012.

# INDEX